Anthropologies of Entanglements

thinking|media

series editors:
bernd herzogenrath
patricia pisters

Anthropologies of Entanglements

Media and Modes of Existence

Edited by
Christiane Voss, Lorenz Engell, and Tim Othold

BLOOMSBURY ACADEMIC
NEW YORK • LONDON • OXFORD • NEW DELHI • SYDNEY

BLOOMSBURY ACADEMIC
Bloomsbury Publishing Inc
1385 Broadway, New York, NY 10018, USA
50 Bedford Square, London, WC1B 3DP, UK
29 Earlsfort Terrace, Dublin 2, Ireland

BLOOMSBURY, BLOOMSBURY ACADEMIC and the Diana logo are trademarks of Bloomsbury Publishing Plc

First published in the United States of America 2023
Paperback edition published in 2025

Volume Editors' Part of the Work © Christiane Voss, Lorenz Engell, and Tim Othold, 2023

Each chapter © of Contributors, 2023

For legal purposes the Acknowledgments on p. vii constitute an extension of this copyright page.

Cover design: Daniel Benneworth-Gray
Cover image © Paolo Sanfilippo

All rights reserved. No part of this publication may be reproduced or transmitted in any form or by any means, electronic or mechanical, including photocopying, recording, or any information storage or retrieval system, without prior permission in writing from the publishers.

Bloomsbury Publishing Inc does not have any control over, or responsibility for, any third-party websites referred to or in this book. All internet addresses given in this book were correct at the time of going to press. The author and publisher regret any inconvenience caused if addresses have changed or sites have ceased to exist, but can accept no responsibility for any such changes.

A catalog record of this book is available from the Library of Congress

ISBN: HB: 978-1-5013-7514-9
PB: 978-1-5013-7511-8
ePDF: 978-1-5013-7512-5
ePub: 978-1-5013-7513-2

Series: Thinking Media

Typeset by Newgen KnowledgeWorks Pvt. Ltd., Chennai, India

To find out more about our authors and books visit www.bloomsbury.com and sign up for our newsletters.

Contents

Acknowledgments — vii

Anthropologies of Entanglements: An Introduction — 1
    Christiane Voss, Lorenz Engell, and Tim Othold

Part 1 Milieus

1. Existing in Motion: Foundations for a Philosophical Media Anthropology — 15
Christiane Voss

2. Tangled Efforts and Middle-Voiced Verbs — 31
Jane Bennett

3. The Experience-Image and Collaborative Filmmaking: From Visual Anthropology to Media-Anthropological Practices — 53
Julia Bee

4. A Life in the Interstices: Micropolitics and Aesthetics in Everyday Life — 81
Christoph Carsten

Part 2 Practice and Process

5. Prosthesis for Feeling: Intensifying Potentiality through Media — 97
Mark B. N. Hansen

6. Chemæra — 131
Jason Pine

7. In Control of Algorithms: Video Analytics and Human–Machine Relations at the Train Station — 151
Gabriele Schabacher

8	On the Anthropology of the *mode double click* *Lorenz Engell*	169
9	Neutral Time *Philip Gries*	185

Part 3 Bodies in Media

10	Unfolding Bodies: Art and Ontology of the American Northwest Coast *Bernhard Siegert*	197
11	Corporeal Literacy: Alphabetic Bodies and the Logic of the Cut *Maaike Bleeker*	225
12	Torn, Crushed, Shredded: The Reconstruction of Wounded Bodies in the First World War *Johanna Seifert*	245
13	Material Dialectics of the Hard Body *Ivo Ritzer*	259
14	She Is Inseminating: On the Secret of Life in Claire Denis's Science Fiction Film *High Life* (2018) *Astrid Deuber-Mankowsky*	281

Contributors	301
Index	307

Acknowledgments

We would like to express our gratitude to Bloomsbury (and especially to Katie Gallof and Stephanie Grace-Petinos) as well as the series editors Bernd Herzogenrath and Patricia Pisters for giving us the opportunity to publish this book and all the support along the way. Many thanks also go to all the wonderful contributors to this volume—we have very much cherished working and discussing with you.

Special thanks go to Daniel Hendrickson, for all his work on this volume; to the coordination of the IKKM in Weimar, particularly Kristina Hellmann, for long years of cooperation and support; to Christiane Lewe, for her exceptional and tireless work behind the scenes; and to the State of Thuringia, for generously funding much of the work leading to this volume.

Anthropologies of Entanglements: An Introduction

Christiane Voss, Lorenz Engell, and Tim Othold

Entanglements

This volume is a collection of contributions coming together in a new perspective on the relations between humans and media. It aims to rethink the mediatic shaping and reshaping of human knowledge, practice, bodies, and ultimately modes of existence. For this pursuit, the volume assembles approaches from fields such as media theory, philosophy, anthropology, history, and film and theater studies that together form an intertwined network of collaborative thinking about the complex entanglements of humans and media.

The volume has its roots in an international conference held at the Bauhaus-University Weimar in 2019. Central to the discussions were three closely connected issues. First, there are many urgent questions that arise from the fact that "our" existence is bound up with and increasingly depends on technical media. It is not obvious how to locate and reflect on human action, experience, or existence in a world pervaded by media and information technologies: from smart devices and everyday communication to ubiquitous sensors and big data, from sharing images and impressions to intelligent prosthetics, from smart cities to surveillance technologies and predictive algorithms. How can we acknowledge on a conceptual level that human modes of existence are fundamentally entangled with processes of mediatization and re-mediatization? How can categories such as "nature," "technology," or "human" and "more-than-human" be distinguished in the face of a seamless interpenetration of our everyday lives by all kinds of media technology?

Second, many academic perspectives that focus on these kinds of relations between humans and media, especially in media studies and related fields, tend to deal with anthropological questions only in an indirect manner, if at all. Since the rise of deconstruction an anti-anthropocentric impulse informs several important theoretical frameworks, such as actor-network theory, object-oriented ontology, media philosophy, as well as, in a certain sense, approaches from the digital humanities or gender and queer theory.

Nonetheless, almost all these and similar approaches, including media theory and technodeterminism, still draw on anthropological presumptions of some kind. How can an approach that aims at the relational entanglements of humans and media relate to these other frameworks and their arguments?

Third, especially in case of the media philosophical considerations that underpin this volume, an interest in the analysis of unstable, diverse modes of existence, human and otherwise, is in part animated by the recent discourse of the Anthropocene. This discourse already emphasizes the heterogeneity of relations between human and nonhuman entities (formerly known as "Nature") and their epistemic, ontological, and anthropological dimensions. What might explorations of specific existential entanglements contribute to the broader, interdisciplinary discussion about humans and media?

These three issues (along with several more) call for an approach that can consider the practical, material dimensions of human–media entanglements as well as their theoretical implications: an approach that is non-anthropocentric while still engaging in important questions about human existence. At the Bauhaus-University Weimar these issues motivated the development of a perspective that is, in this sense, *media-anthropological* and that lead to the interdisciplinary dialogue that constitutes the present volume.

While the different chapters explore a range of subjects and engage with this field of research in their own way, they thus all circle a central interest in media-anthropological (or, more precisely: anthropomedial) entanglements. They share the realization that, given the pervasive influence of media processes and technologies and in light of the (notion of the) Anthropocene, it no longer makes sense to begin anthropological reflections with a traditional concept of a given, stable "human," contrasted against "nature," "technology," or even "the divine." Rather, human existences seem to unfold through constantly shifting relations with different environments, experiences, bodies, concepts, and so on. Being human then is an incessant process of entanglements, up to a point where we have to concede that these entanglements take precedence over their entangled elements. The *relations* between human existences, experiences and media, nature, or technology—the hyphen in "media-anthropological," one might say—exist prior to their distinction and differentiation. The relations precede the relata. With this in mind, media-anthropological analyses choose to examine situations in which elements and agents are always already entangled. They start from phenomena or from theories of entanglement instead of with fixed and more or less substantialist ideas of "the human." This interdisciplinary approach is in part in line with schools of thought from cultural studies, affect theory, aesthetics, or new materialism. Similar to them, it shifts away from traditional philosophical and anthropological attempts of defining a supposedly uniform human nature and toward a reflection and questions about how and where human–media entanglements take place. The aim is to take serious contemporary transformations in the relations between humans and media, as well as their ontological and epistemic implications.

Media

The diagnosis that human actions, communications, experiences, and so on are being transformed by media technology and that this transformation affects human modes of existence on many levels is of course not particularly new. Its media-anthropological consequences and implications, however, have to be explored much further than they have been to date. The extent, scope, and depth of the insight into this transformation depend not least on what is understood under the term "media." While empirical media and communication studies usually understand media to mean mass media, German media studies tend to employ a much broader concept of media. First, media refers to the material instances and institutions of mediation, such as devices, hardware, wires, cables, a newspaper, and so on, as well as companies (e.g., TV and radio stations, social media companies, etc.). Second, media also refers to functions and operations, such as the transmission, processing, and storing of data, signals, information, or even states. Third, media refers to mediality, meaning that which enables and informs relations in the first place, the third party that makes possible any connection—material, practical, logical, theoretical—between two other elements and thus shapes their interplay. A broad understanding of media, which is also advocated here, considers these different dimensions to be closely linked and interdependent. Nonetheless, the differences in how different schools of thought understand media must be taken into account for any project of media-anthropology.

Since the 1930s countless empirical studies have dealt with the influence of mass media on attitudes, values, and on the behavior of people and cultures. These studies usually belonged to the fields of sociology, psychology, and, somewhat more recently, communication studies or cultural studies. Without trying to level the differences in theories and methods that exist between these empirical analyses of the utilization of media, one common trend was to interpret the impact of media (in the sense of institution) on human beings according to a more or less one-directional, causal model of "sender to receiver." Accordingly, media institutions, broadcasters, or individual producers were assigned the active role of sender, whereas their audience was seen as passive receivers. The media formats, such as broadcasts, radio shows, movies, and so on, then simply occupied the intermediary room between sender and receiver and established a programmable, causal connection between the two.

While this model of the relations between humans and media has since been heavily criticized and the mentioned disciplines today employ much more complex and nuanced theories about the effects of media, a certain uncritical understanding of "media" in the sense of "mass media" remains prevalent even in contemporary research. Many studies from the last two decades start with an implicit notion of what counts as "media," of their functions and their possible effects on human behavior. Similarly, they tend to have an implicit notion of what "human" means. Even if human beings and actions are discussed in the context of large-scale historical and cultural changes, medical developments, or questions of post- and transhumanism, there often seem to be presumptions about what and how "humans" are. Both media and humans are thus taken as categories that may not necessarily be stable and unchanging, but that can be reliably identified and addressed. Their effects on one another can be examined and compared along behavioral, intercultural, or class- and gender-specific lines. Empirical research in this vein is frequently informed by specific economic and political goals, seeking to model the causal dynamics between humans and media in order to make use of them. Meanwhile, various kinds of actions, knowledge, subjectivities, and so on can be clearly ascribed to either humans or media. Questions of how experiences, behavior, and knowledge extend through and beyond individual bodies or actors, of how they encompass a multitude of operations and materialities are usually not the main focus.

In contrast to the early empirical studies on media stood more cybernetic readings of the technological permeation of the everyday that focused on the dynamic feedback processes between media technologies and biocultural bodies and practices. Norbert Wiener (1948) in his early writings still declares "the human being" to be the "terminal of all technical transformations"; nonetheless it can be said that cybernetic approaches at least put machines and human brains or mental processes on an equal footing as systems for processing and regulating information. These more system-related approaches have the advantage of drawing attention to the symmetries between so-called senders, transmitters, and receivers, whose positions start to become interchangeable in cybernetic models. But even with feedback loops in mind, one may still remain trapped in a primarily causal model, based on a preexisting division between allegedly independent elements such as stimulus, medium, and response.

The fact is that media are never merely neutral processors and transmitters of information, signals, or meanings. They are a condition of change and highly problematic in their own right. This insight has been of central importance to German media studies since Friedrich Kittler. In his view, media not only have an impact on what they process and transmit, leading to sometimes unpredictable results. They are moreover difficult to pin down and examine, as they tend to disappear into transparency. This idiosyncrasy of media and mediality undermines any attempt at putting in place a linear causality between different elements and clearly delineating their logical relationship. Media instead enable and condition not only types of relationality, such as expressions and transmissions, but also spatial relations (e.g., contiguity), temporal relations (e.g., sequentialization), forms of (re-)location, and many more. The point of Kittler's famous dictum that "media determine our situation, which deserves a description" (Kittler 1985: 3) is the fact that those supposed tools, which sovereign human actors were presumed to be in control of, had always already achieved the potential of being independent of any human intentions.

Kittler therefore considers media as agencies of creation that impose the general historical conditions for thinking and being as such. By the end of the twentieth century, he claimed, the symbolic construction of meaning would have lost its place to the logic of signal transmission. The once dominant symbolic code of human self-conception would have been superimposed and suppressed by the purely algorithmic code of information technology, that is, the medium of the computer. Kittler underlines that media can no longer be ascribed the status of a mere tool, beholden to anthropocentric intentions. Instead it is the other way around: The materiality and functionality of media take on a transcendental role. Media thus take up positions as the actual subjects of history.

Two decades before Kittler, Canadian pioneer of media theory Marshall McLuhan conceived of media as extensions of human senses and mental states. In contrast to Kittler's decoupling of algorithmic media and the domains of meaning and sensuality, McLuhan argues for a continual and historical evolution of media. As extensions of the human mind and corporeality, media technologies, including algorithmic ones, for him do not subvert the anthropocentric image of man. For McLuhan, media technology rather enhances the otherwise limited biological capabilities of human beings. It can compensate for deficits as well as extend human facilities. If Kittler can be said to argue for a technological a priori, McLuhan could be interpreted as affirming an anthropological and possibly even anthropocentric a priori.

Both authors can be interpreted in different ways, and their work is still the topic of media theoretical debate. In any case, whether one looks at the digital transformation of human bodies, subjectivities, and collectives with Kittler or with McLuhan—or coming from a third position—questions about the direction, malleability, and even conception of human existence remain prominent. In order to fully engage with these questions a theoretical approach is needed that allows for a philosophical and critical analysis of the complex relations between human and media, as they unfold in concrete environments and contexts, without presupposing either one as fixed, preexisting, or sovereign.

Examinations of media-anthropological entanglements, as this volume understands them, accept that media and forms of mediality have always been foundational for our everyday life, our habits of communication, perception, imagination, and action. This is true—perhaps especially so—even if the media in question have managed to escape our notice *as media* and have instead transformed into a kind of "black box." As media philosopher Sybille Krämer (2020) has pointed out, there is a fundamental separation between the inner workings of media technology (the "apparative") and its usage (the "operative"). Media practices and habits have effects on our world that do not necessarily depend on our knowledge about their material constructions, mathematical logic, and so on. In other words: In many cases people might not fully grasp or even care to reflect on the details of the media they are entangled with, yet these media do impact their experience, their knowledge, their subjectivity. These entanglements and their biological, cognitive, affective, and technical relations are distributed over various bodies that continually affect each other in various ways.

Acknowledging this not merely with respect to concrete examples but also on a conceptual level is especially relevant at a time where informational media technology is starting to become as invisible as it is ubiquitous. The more immersive our interactions with media become and the more embedded human beings are in interfaces, networks, and the logics of computation, the less media and technology can be considered as something separate from our habits and our habitats.[1]

Habitats

In recent years and in light of the increasingly pervasive, immersive dimensions of media technology, several perspectives have aimed to conceptualize the complex relations between humans and media in new ways. Instead of considering them as distinct entities, cast against a backdrop of further allegedly stable divisions between active and passive, technology and nature, and the like, they aim to highlight the symmetries between human and nonhuman actors, the potentials and activities inherent to matter and media, their unconscious dimensions, or the environmental or elemental qualities of computational media.[2] These perspectives have the advantage of employing much broader and more nuanced, even if sometimes implicit, notions of media and of human agency and cognition.

One worthwhile way of framing media-anthropological entanglements, that is intimately related to these new perspectives, concerns the concepts of habits, habitats, and *habitus*. A connection between *habitus* and technicity, along with subjectivity and collectivity, can be found in most situations that inform or establish modes of existence. Everyday activities such as, for example, messaging and looking up information of some kind are not mere random activities, but media-based habits. They emerge in recurring contact with a technological environment. Habitats, understood as media technical environments that shape our behavior and perception, are not, however, deterministic. As Jakob von Uexküll (1909) already realized in his investigation of biological modes of existence in relation to their environment, inhabitants and their actions also shape their respective habitat. Environments and the individuals embedded in them both inform each other. Furthermore, their interplay cannot be reduced to a simple behavioristic interaction. Especially in more complex media technical environments, habits and habitualized relations might also include forms of affect (e.g., suspense or a redirection of attention) as well as imaginative and cognitive dimensions. The anthropo-generative potential of this interplay is not identical to the purely physical conditions that, say, natural environments impose on their inhabitants.

Habitats, in this sense, can occur in many heterogenous forms, not just as natural environments but also as architecture, workplaces, traffic situations, institutions, military facilities, cultural and social settings, technical systems, and the like. Even frames of discourse, fictional worlds, and digital interfaces can be examined with regard to their situating effects, as habitats. A video game and its surrounding discourse may thus be examined as a media technological habitat that brings forth and interacts with a mode of existence called "gamer." Similarly, cinema configures itself as a habitat in an affective interplay with moviegoers as well as actors, cameras, production companies, and so on. In the context of digital media, social media, and mobile devices, many more new modes of existence emerge in a back and forth with their environments, such as "digital natives," "users," or "influencers." They are not static forms, but processes, a habitus that connects bodies, practices, and media technologies. Their actuality and potentiality cannot be abstracted from their concrete situations and operations. This observation leads the texts of the present volume to focus on instances of mediation, modulation—on processes of *becoming* instead of forms of *being*.

Anthropomediality

Trying to examine the entanglements of humans and media as *entanglements*, exploring them as complex processes of becoming, without arresting them in static concepts and premature distinctions, inevitably entails certain challenges. With a focus on the relationality of humans and media, it no longer makes sense to start a media-anthropological description with a notion of independent entities. There are no "humans" or "media" that, only after having come into existence, come into contact with one another and then end up being transformed by that contact. Instead, the existential relations between different elements precede (any possibility of) their differentiation—entities such as moviegoers, actors, cinemas, and so on only emerge in their collective entanglement. Furthermore, these relations can take place in a variety of different habitats, necessitating different methods, abstractions, and sometimes even speculations. Media-anthropological research is thus faced with a plurality of possible subjects and subjectivities whose existence is inherently unstable and who relate to each other in ways that are yet to be determined. Insights gained with respect to one case are not necessarily transferrable to other cases.

This awareness of the instability and plurality of existence resonates with similar philosophical observations. Gilbert Simondon (1958), for example, writes how "technical objects" might come into existence only gradually. Guattari and Deleuze (1980) emphasize the machinic nature of life as something that has to be sustained and reproduced, while already Spinoza (1677) described "attributes" mediating between different "modes." Etienne Souriau (1943) and along with him Bruno Latour and Isabel Stengers (2009) embrace an "existential pluralism" in which the capacity for change and evolution is no longer reserved just for biological entities, but extended to works of art, among other things. This way of thinking in terms of relations and entanglements goes hand in hand with a concept of technology and media as something that is not a mere instrument, but has to be considered as generative, creative, and full of latent potential. Humans and media in this sense do not simply coexist, they might be said to coevolve.

In order to discuss the plurality of the diverse modes of existence encountered in the course of media-anthropological research, Christiane Voss (2010) has coined the term "anthropomediality."[3] It aims to highlight the irreducible mediality of human existence as well as the immanent polymorphism of their entanglements, manifesting in concrete situations, operations, and constellations. Still, even with this goal, the concept of "anthropomediality"—same as media-anthropology—cannot avoid a linguistic difficulty. As a *term*, it seems to function as a synthesis of two concepts, "anthropos" and "media," that therefore can apparently still be separated from each other, at least analytically. But if that is the case, does this demarcation between human and nonhuman factors not repeat an implicit anthropocentric bias, a preexisting notion of "human" that a media-anthropological perspective purportedly aims to overcome? It is important in this context to draw a distinction between a methodological and a substantive anthropocentrism. The latter repeats problematic assumptions and arguments about humans and humanity, that should instead be critically examined. The former, however, seems unavoidable to a certain degree, but can take its own inescapable perspectivism into account and make explicit the assumptions and implications of anthropological questions. In this respect, a media-anthropological perspective can learn from the important theoretical interventions in the fields of sociology and ethnography, for example, queer-theoretical approaches.

Yet, the challenges of terms like anthropomediality and media-anthropology ultimately go beyond linguistic and methodological considerations. If actors, bodies, and materialities of all kinds are to be addressed in equal terms, would not an ecological, ontological, or perhaps even cosmological designation be more apt? Why not relinquish the "anthropos" altogether and proceed instead with a concept of, for example, "mediatic existences"? In other words: Why media-*anthropology* after all? An important and significant theoretical impulse of many contemporary perspectives dealing with the complex entanglements of (media) technology and human action and cognition—for example, science and technology studies, actor-network theory, new materialism, or object-oriented ontology—is to attribute formerly exclusively "human" qualities to things and matter: subjectivity, agency, creativity, and the like. With Latour's "parliament of things" in mind, these schools of thought can be said to aim at a more democratic understanding of existence. If the contributions in this volume now nonetheless argue for a concept of anthropomediality and adopt a media-anthropological approach, it is because they are intent on not only discussing hybrid modes of existence, but to also deal with questions of human self-understanding and political critique that inevitably accompany them. Questions of freedom, justice, and human rights, which have driven philosophical anthropologies for a long time, are of no less importance today. And while normative approaches in the humanistic tradition have historically no doubt proved to be more than problematic, it seems equally unwise to completely refrain from discussing these aspects of human existence. More productive, it seems to us, is to engage with the dynamic entanglements of human agency, cognition, and thought, to argue for a more democratic understanding of existence, while still keeping sight of the very concrete political and existential questions of our time.

Notes

1. As Hui and Broeckmann (2015: 16) write: "Digital technology, which was once the figure instead of the ground, slowly becomes the ground of governance, communication, and scientific research methods."
2. Although the list is certainly nonexhaustive, some noteworthy examples include Latour (2013), Bennett (2010), Hansen (2006), Thrift (2004), Hayles (2017), Parikka (2015), and Peters (2015).
3. See also Othold and Voss (2015).

References

Bennett, Jane (2010), *Vibrant Matter. A Political Ecology of Things*, Durham, NC: Duke University Press.
Deleuze, Gilles, and Félix Guattari (1980), *Mille Plateaux*, Paris: Minuit.
Hansen, Mark B. N. (2006), *Bodies in Code. Interfaces with Digital Media*, New York: Routledge.
Hayles, N. Katherine (2017), *Unthought: The Power of the Cognitive Nonconscious*, Chicago: University of Chicago Press.
Hui, Yuk, and Andreas Broeckmann (2015), "Introduction," in Yuk Hui and Andreas Broeckmann (eds.), *30 Years after Les Immatériaux: Art, Science, and Theory*, 9–24, Lüneburg: meson press.
Kittler, Friedrich (1985), *Grammophon Film Typewriter*, Berlin: Brinkmann und Bose.
Krämer, Sybille (2020), "Cultural History of Digitisation" [lecture], Humboldt Institute for Internet and Society, 13.02.2020. https://www.hiig.de/en/events/sybille-kraemer-cultural-history-of-digitisation/ (accessed July 18, 2022).
Latour, Bruno (2013), *An Inquiry into Modes of Existence: An Anthropology of the Moderns*, Cambridge, MA: Harvard University Press.
Latour, Bruno, and Isabelle Stengers (2009), *Présentation du texte,* in Etienne Souriau: Les différents modes d'existence, suivie de: Du mode d'existence de l'oeuvre à faire*, Paris: Presses universitaires de France.
Othold, Tim, and Christiane Voss (2015), "From Media Anthropology to Anthropomediality," *Anthropological Notebooks* 21 (3), Slovene Anthropological Society. 75–82.
Parikka, Jussi (2015), *A Geology of Media*, Minneapolis: University of Minnesota Press.
Peters, John Durham (2015), *The Marvelous Clouds: Toward a Philosophy of Elemental Media*, Chicago, IL: University of Chicago Press.

Simondon, Gilbert (1958), *Du mode d'existence des objets techniques*, Paris: Aubier.
Souriau, Etienne (1943), *Les différents modes d'existence*, Paris: Presses universitaires de France.
Spinoza, Baruch de ([1677] 1999), *Ethica ordine geometrico demonstrata*, Hamburg: Meiner.
Thrift, Nigel (2004), "Movement-Space: The Changing Domain of Thinking Resulting from the Development of New Kinds of Spatial Awareness," *Economy and Society* 33 (4): 582–604.
Uexkuell, Jakob von (1909), *Umwelt und Innenwelt der Tiere*, Berlin: Julius Springer.
Voss, Christiane (2010), "Auf dem Weg zu einer Medienphilosophie anthropomedialer Relationen," *Zeitschrift für Medien- und Kulturforschung* 1 (2): 169–84.
Wiener, Norbert (1948), *Cybernetics, or: Control and Communication in the Animal and the Machine*, Cambridge, MA: MIT Press.

Part One

Milieus

1

Existing in Motion: Foundations for a Philosophical Media Anthropology

Christiane Voss

Media Anthropology

Why is a media-anthropological approach toward questions of self-understanding, a critical reflection of life and its boundaries, important today? To put it bluntly: Many traditional anthropological perspectives, with their tendency toward anthropocentrism, neglect the basic medialities of (human) modes of existence, including technological ones. Such accounts therefore cannot do justice, phenomenologically and philosophically, to the multiple forms of entanglements of human and more-than-human factors that occur in the media-technological environments of contemporary everyday life. Moreover, the problematic fiction of a sovereign human subject, characterized as instrumentally subjugating the world for its own benefit, still underlies many traditional anthropologies as well as dominant intuitions of language and even critical notions such as that of the so-called Anthropocene. In light of the multiple extensions and dependencies of human existence on a global scale and also given the political and ecological consequences of such a hegemonial view of the world, it has long become obvious that this fiction of a sovereign human subject can no longer be sustained. Grappling with such issues, among others, necessitates rethinking human existence and action on a more fundamental level.

The proposal to be argued for below is situated at the intersection of philosophical anthropology, aesthetics, and media philosophy. This media-anthropological approach stems from a discomfort with the epistemic discrepancy between our everyday experiences of all sorts of entanglements and the usual theoretical reflections and descriptions of them. The manifold interconnections of our bodies, modes of articulation, and practices of orientation, for instance, with digital technologies and devices, emerge and are functional in ways that conventional descriptions of them fail to analyze or even capture. The tradition of the Enlightenment still rules our self-understanding to this day, even though human modes of being-in-the-world have undergone profound changes since then; changes and transformations that have to do with a variety of factors: political-economic shifts in global power blocks, ecological crises (climate catastrophe, migration), discursive challenges (postcolonialism, critical race theory, queer theory), scientific innovations (AI research, synthetic biology, genetics), and media technological developments (digitalization, nanotechnology). Such developments are themselves bound up with and communicated by all sorts of media, such as social media, blogs, tweets, GIFs, memes, broadcasts, magazines, and television series. These media agents no longer function simply as neutral tools for a human mind. Rather they have become "infra-existential" parts of habits and attitudes and thus of our everyday lives and actions. Advances in medicine as well as in computation or military technology have direct biopolitical effects on bodies, life plans, and lifestyles (for instance, on family planning, self-engineering and self-optimizing, networking, in drone warfare, etc.). Such transformations lead to an epistemic uncertainty, perforating any stable self-understandings of collectives and individuals, or better: of collectivized and individualized instances such as social groups, persons, and so on. The terms collectivization and individuation seem appropriate here in view of the fact that social and subjective modes of existence are emerging processes instead of static essences.

The wide-ranging (technological) transformations of modes of existence equally affect practical questions, for instance, those of expanding basic rights to non-human entities (AI, animals, biofacts), and the possibilities of limiting biogenetic as well as agrarian, military, and reproductive technologies. The category of "human" has become especially precarious in light of invasive medical technologies and prosthetics, as it can no longer be clearly stated where human life begins and ends, what counts as part of the human body, or where the latter might extend to. Entanglements of technology and biological bodies can be found at all levels of existence. Self-tracking data, selfies, photos, postings of pictures and short messages, narratives, as well as entries in institutional registries and many other administrative framings are in this sense not just neutral forms of objectification and media. They are also decisive normative framings of and for self-articulation and modes of subjectification. Even processes of dying are deeply connected with media and realized in dialogue with diagnostic, palliative, and bureaucratic systems. Throughout all stages of life and death, habits and bodies are literally attached to measuring devices, statistics, machines, (digital) images and sounds, bureaucracies, and infrastructures. One cannot remove any such entanglement without losing sight of the modes of existence in question. In light of this situation, trying to determine a stable essence of human existence, which could be abstracted without loss from its embeddedness in technological and global relationships, seems to be hopelessly naive.

Media anthropology takes on the task of intervening in the reflections of human existence, the effects of media, and the like by trying to render their notions precarious and push them beyond their limits. While media anthropology still carries the expression of "anthropos" in its name, it rejects the classical genealogy and anthropocentric meaning of the term. Instead, it employs it as a denominator for a spectrum of diversified actors and modes of existence that emerge from manifold relational scenarios.[1] In order to sharpen the contours of this philosophically oriented media-anthropological approach, it has to be distinguished from comparable and especially from empirical perspectives. Empirical media anthropologies use methods from communications theory, economics, or psychology to focus, for instance, on how social groups engage with mass media. Other empirical approaches employ methods from the fields of cultural studies and ethnology to carry out their studies, for instance, on literary, film, or other kinds of media-based self-representations of social groups and ethnicities in intercultural comparison. Although many of them are important in many ways, for instance, in the critique of powerful classifications of class, race, and gender, the majority of these approaches do not fundamentally question their own use of the terms "anthropos" or "human." They tend to employ these and similar terms in the generic singular, as if their meanings could be taken for granted.

While a philosophical media anthropology shares the interest in empirical and historical media formations and transformations of human modes of existence, it deviates from conventional views. Compared to traditional philosophical anthropologies (Helmuth Plessner or Arnold Gehlen's, for instance), it puts its emphasis on questions of *how* existence-forming processes can be described in their operational dimensions. Its analysis starts from the explication of particular experiences, whereby it must always negotiate anew exactly what might be considered the subjects and objects of these experiences.

Instead of considering modes of existence from an external point of view, a media-anthropological starting point is contemporary with what it articulates. Hence it has to be aware of its own blind spots, which are inevitable due to its own entanglement with its subject matter. Media anthropology neither wants to make prophecies, as many transhumanist and posthumanist theories do, nor can it offer a complete theory of the currently ascertainable, digital transformations that occur in all areas of life. What it can do instead are two things: (1) it can point out the terminological, epistemic, and conceptual challenges of anthropological reflections of "our" time and (2) it shifts their focus in a speculative and creative way, by producing representative analyses of processes of "doing existence" in diverse media settings.[2]

At the center of the approach outlined here is the neologistic notion of "anthropomediality." It encompasses all forms of relational modes of existence in which human and more-than-human factors are distinct, but constitutively entangled. The goal is to exercise new ways of thinking philosophically about anthropological questions, which are informed by media studies and media theory. This does not mean skipping over the critique of "old" philosophical anthropologies, which must be seen in a critical light, such as for being too subject-centered and for their ideological motivation in the tendency to universalize arbitrary and particular characterizations of "the human." Such forms of legitimate critique have long been formulated in the context of "deconstruction" (Jacques Derrida, Roland Bathes, Julia Kristeva et al.) and "discourse analysis" (Michel Foucault, Judith Butler et al.), and they continue to reverberate to this day. What is up for debate though, is how, against the backdrop of an intellectual horizon of anthropocentrism that cannot simply be discarded at will, one might nonetheless think differently about "doing existence" in a more integrative and inclusive way. The expression "doing existence" is inspired by Judith Butler's "doing gender" (Butler 1990), which describes active–passive processes, constituting social realities by means of repetition and variation of behavioral and linguistic stereotypes. While the sociocultural construction of gender, in Butler's sense, focuses on a distinctive and more or less sustainable concretization of existence (in terms of being male/female), the main interest of the present investigation is on the incoherent and constantly changing spectrum of possible constructions of existence in the plural, spread across different media settings or milieus. Existence, in this sense, is not merely given and stable, but is being performed through specific operations that in their turn are fungible within and as media.

Martin Heidegger's concept of "being-in-the-world," which itself was introduced in the course of his critique of anthropology, could serve as a further resonating concept here. But to become productive in this context, it would need to be cleared of the problematic implications of Heidegger's writings and be reframed in a new light. Without taking on the ontic-ontological difference or the fixation on the subject present in Heidegger's thought, not to mention its anti-Semitic, sexist, and racist implications, the concept's emphasis on the fundamental relational temporality of human modes of existence might be fruitful for media-anthropological concerns as well. Another philosophical concept, which was originally introduced as a critique of positivist anthropologies of the natural sciences, stems from Helmut Plessner: "excentricity" or "excentric positionality." This concept underscores the openness and inconclusiveness of human existence, while still clinging to a strongly individualized understanding of subjectivity. Negative anthropologies such as Plessner's and others, however (such as historical anthropology), share the problem of holding on to the notion of an anthropological difference and the superiority of the human species, which can no longer be presumed or justified. Although they insist on the impossibility of a conclusive and complete determinability of human existence, they still demarcate the human species qua negativity from other living beings and things.

In coining the concept of anthropomediality, media anthropology, as it is understood here, tries to work without such problematic presumptions. It shifts its focus away from metaphysical "what" questions (as in: "What is the human being?") to operational questions of "how" and "where" observable modes of "doing existence" can be found and described. Such a shift to modes and doings of existence may seem to be intending to revive existential philosophy. After all, existentialists like Sartre did assert that (relational) existence precedes all essence; "the human being" is thought to be an empty placeholder and nothing in and by itself, unless it becomes what an individual deliberately makes of themselves. But as can be easily seen, this implies an even stronger, intentional subject-centrism and anthropocentrism, since the individual subject is seen as the only master of its own destiny. Seen in the light of postcolonial critique, this implies just another universalization of the historical hegemony of a white and patriarchal individualism. A more radical turn away from anthropocentrism is necessary. The suggestion here is to bracket off the overburdened notion of "the human" and to replace it with the notion of "anthropomedial relations and entanglements." In this way the fundamental relationality and plurality of excentric doings of existence in different mediaspheres take center stage. Examinations of situated doings of existence can be pushed forward without having to assume a ready-made, static notion of "the human." What is of importance instead is to concentrate on *how* human and more-than-human elements, materialities, and practices interact and exist in their various milieus.[3] This focus on the unstable how and motion of existence is, ultimately, less in keeping with traditional anthropological questions and more in line with a media-philosophical school of thought.

Philosophy from the Margin: Media Philosophy

The material, operational, and above all relational turn in media anthropology is situated in the wider conceptual framework of recent media philosophy. Since the 1990s, particularly in Germany, media philosophy has emerged from the combination of media theory and the philosophical strands of discourse analysis and deconstruction. Comparable to tendencies also found in philosophical aesthetics (Kant, Hegel, Adorno), it generally tries to think beyond the axiom of the excluded third. Media philosophy does not only undermine basic dualistic polarizations of subject-object, nature-culture, human-animal, and the like. More than that it puts an emphasis on the immanent materiality and operationality of the intermediary zones of becoming. Departing from the conceptual limitations of binary thinking, it no longer considers coherence and the absence of contradiction to be the most or possibly only important parameters of philosophical reflection.[4]

Media philosophy naturally varies in style and direction according to the theoretical background of the researchers and their respective subject matter. But one typical media-philosophical procedure is to scrutinize whether and how philosophical texts and concepts can help to analyze (new) media phenomena and historical upheavals of media technologies. However, taking philosophical concepts into account in this sense does not simply mean applying them to new subjects. This method has an effect on the conceptual side as well, as it changes in light of media-materialistic intuitions. One way of doing this is to try to reconstruct classical topoi such as "spirit," "subject," and "consciousness" *in terms of* "materialities," "media," and "media operationalities." Subjectivity can then, for example, be regarded as something constituted by cinematographic techniques of point-of-view shots, or via editing; sense and meaning can be brought about by the configurations of material in an installation of art; and so on.

The term "media," as media philosophy understands it, comprises three components: (1) everything that lies in between, that is, the intermediate; (2) the material bodies and procedures of mediation; (3) the encompassing milieu. These three components of the intermediate, the materiality, and the milieu are irrevocably linked with each other. A media milieu—from the library and the archive through mass media, entertainment industries, and fashion to digital platforms and social media—emerges in its specificity only from the movements and causalities of the relevant materialities included, such as biological and technological bodies, operational practices and instances, as well as their intermedial affects and relations with their surroundings. The idea here is comparable to the biological milieu of Jakob von Uexküll, who emphasized the mutually permeating relationship of environment and living creatures. In the case of a technological milieu, for instance, a cinematographic media setting, such heterogeneous entities as biological bodies, perceptions, furniture, architecture, technology of projection, and screening of edited audiovisual film all belong to the realm of *materialities*, which affect each other (*mediality*), thus constituting the cinema, as a specific aesthetic *milieu*. Hence, cinema as a milieu functions in two ways at once: it emerges first and foremost from the bespoken relationalities which in their turn only materialize and individuate within the assemblage that is cinema. The three components—intermediary, materiality, milieu—can alternate their places and functions in relation to one another depending on the perspective and the situation. So each of the components might be considered the origin of the overall event. Such a relational and dynamic conception of the always already multicomponent media dispenses with the fiction of a singular origin of any mode of existence. The question of how a milieu and its corresponding modes of existence bring about each other then becomes a matter of "contingent emergence" instead of a linear and causal history. Perhaps it becomes more evident now why media anthropology avoids a reified conception of "mass media" (such as radio, newspapers, etc.), as it is used in the context of communication theory. In a media-philosophical or media-anthropological reading, the expression "media" designates a situated and circular dynamism of materialities, which stand in various relations to each other (such as electrical, chemical, affective, causal, etc.), from which emerge perceptible phenomena (milieus, users, etc.).

Since media philosophy itself functions as a mediator between philosophy and media studies, it runs into tensions resulting from the mutual unfamiliarity of these disciplines. The bulk of traditional accounts of philosophy still continues to work away without explicitly considering media. If philosophy *does* consider media, it tends to ascribe a special position to the medium of language. For philosophical anthropologies as well as for strands of the philosophy of language the linguistic medium is often even (mis)declared to be the transcendental medium of humanogenesis per se. Media philosophy and media anthropology argue against this reductionist thesis, by pointing out the reality-constituting agency of nonlanguage-based media—such as sounds, images, affects, numbers, codes, and so on. Nonlinguistic media are still not sufficiently taken into account in the humanities.

On the other side, it can be observed that this legitimate critique can sometimes also take on a disproportionately anti-philosophical tone. The demand to revise the language-fixated, abstract, and generalizing procedures of traditional philosophy in light of the materialistic and historical turns of media studies leads some media scholars, in line with Friedrich Kittler, to a position that dismisses philosophy altogether. But even in cases where some analyses of media studies overshoot their mark, they almost always open up new perspectives. This encourages dealing with phenomena that were previously neglected by philosophy as being irrelevant or minor. Supposedly banal things are elevated in this way by media philosophy and declared worthy of philosophical treatment. This widening of the perspective ensures creativity, even if this means that media philosophy gets the reputation of being mere "occasional philosophy," to use a polemic term from the German philosopher Günther Anders.

The sympathy for minor matters, however, does in fact shift themes, functions, and objects from the margins to the center of reflection. This is how media philosophy acquires new thematic fields and perspectives. A media-philosophical approach to movies, for instance, might deviate from the majority of current film philosophies in not aiming its analysis squarely at the psychological and semantic impact of a film's plot. Instead, it might focus on the physical objects of film equipment, the role of light and camera movements, or editing, while employing object-oriented concepts to look for the interplay and dramaturgical agency of these elements. Such an approach is no longer character-oriented. It ends up with a new conception of film— one that can get along *without* any fixations on individual characters and anthropocentric interpretations of their psychological motives.

To sum up: Media philosophy can be characterized by the fact that it does not place theories and objects in a hierarchical subject–object relationship, using media analyses as mere illustrations of already existing, independent theories. Furthermore, a media-philosophical analysis of the entanglements of media operations, materialities, and their motions and figurations can range on a scale from micro to macro. This means that memes, bots, social networks, and even fictional modes of existence such as mythical figures, avatars, or film stars may equally become subjects of media-anthropological interest. All such medial figurations are to be reflected anew under the label of anthropomedial constructs or anthropomedialities, since they consist of nothing but the entanglements of biological and technological functions, bodies, and operations. The orientation toward the operational dimensions of medializing relations allows us to analyze organic, technical, chemical, logical, and other functions or processes at one and the same materialistic, ontological level without having to impose a hierarchy between them. Thus, media philosophy can be taken to pursue a flat ontology, one that is immanently accessible. Its findings deal with situated phenomena, whose representative status is chronically unclear and to be negotiated repeatedly. It uses methods of analysis, such as thick description or aesthetic analysis of a milieu, which mirror the situated and performative operativity of what is conveyed by them.

Anthropomediality or a Humane Exit from Anthropocentrism

As for the operationalization of the approach of anthropomedial relations, one can benefit from the proximity of media philosophy and aesthetics in treating its own subjects with decidedly *aesthetic* methods of analysis. Appropriate analytical methods can be borrowed from the fields of, for example, film, literature, or theater analysis, which all include hermeneutic, deconstructive, and/or performative methods as well as analytically detailed descriptions of the relevant material (whereby the latter resembles the method of thick description from the social sciences). Such methods can be applied to media-anthropological scenes of interest, which are not necessarily aesthetic milieus in a strict sense. Alongside the aesthetic milieus of cinema, theater, art, museum, concert, literature, and the like, anthropomedial milieus and practices might include networked forms of cooperation and work, digital surveillance of public spaces, scenarios of self-tracking, and many others that can be examined in their (de-)stabilizing existence-forming effects. Memes, bots, social networks, and even fictional modes of existence such as mythical figures, avatars, or film stars may equally be reflected as anthropomedialities, consisting of nothing but the entanglements of biological and technological functions, bodies, and operations.

As far as the application of any method always shapes the respective findings, the application of an aesthetic method especially involves a special twist: it brings in the aestheticizing, half-distanced perspective of an interested observer. In contrast to other ways of dealing with questions of existence, aesthetic approaches always introduce a position of subjectivity. This might take shape, for example, as the position of an author or as an instance of subjective experience. In taking into account such subjective points of view and experiences, a media-anthropological endeavor, as pursued here, cannot satisfy the objectivist demands of science. This can, however, be considered a case of the glass being half full. If, for instance, immersive media practices are in question (as can be found in games, literature, architecture, or movies), an aesthetic treatment of them has to figure out in detail how their affective involvements and illusions are construed, by what means and techniques the effects, say, of modal relocation from a realistic to a fictitious realm, are brought about, and how their configurations of media elements bring about cognition and perception. In making explicit the constitutive operations at hand, aesthetic methods of analysis do not have to fall back on implicit assumptions about the nature of cognition and perception that were made independently of the experiences in question. Aesthetic analysis is not forced to proceed with an abstract or potentially wrong universal notion of "anthropos," "perception," or "cognition." Hence, media-anthropological descriptions resonate with what they bring to light in terms of style, connotation, and their own sound. Thus they produce and at the same time lay open the operational qualities of the modes of existences at hand. The special modes of (doing) existence, being made explicit, co-emerge within the performativity of detailed or thick descriptions of a milieu-based mode of existence.

But how can such a media anthropology deal with its own blind spots? At this point it may be useful to introduce a distinction between a strong and a weak anthropocentrism. A weak, heuristic anthropocentrism is inescapable as soon as we examine forms of "human" modes of existence. A strong, substantive one, however, implies a claim about a superior position and a distinctive determination of the human existence (taken as genus). It is the latter anthropocentrism that can and is to be avoided. Instead of starting the analysis with a postulated human nature in mind, the existence-forming dynamics of and within any milieu can be foregrounded in their operative dimensions. The media anthropology of anthropomediality, in this sense, differs from strongly anthropocentric theories, as it focuses on the relationalities of media-and-humans (with hyphens) right from the start.

The following scenario may demonstrate what it means to engage in a (fundamentally relational) thinking of anthropomediality. It stems from Max Bense's essay "The Self, the Automobile and Technology" ([1970] 2018). He writes:

> A self is not something that one *has*, but that one *is*. However one *has* an automobile and *is* not it, and hence the automobile *has* a self but is not one, and a self *has* an automobile but *is not* itself a car. This is a text about the difference between *having* and *being*, and this difference between having and being is also the difference between the car that drives and the self that drives it, but since that which drives can be both the car and the self, *that which drives* sublates the difference between self and car, and with this, the text about having and being, or car and self, becomes a text about driving, in which the car becomes the self, and the self the car. … In that the thinking being becomes accustomed to the driving being, self and car melding increasingly into an almost surreal automaton—however with each also remaining separate and always continuing to signify independent entities to us, namely a driving being and a thinking being—it is almost as if a new kind of existence had occured: the consciousness-like machine, the self-like automobile, a perfect human-machine team, an existential partnership

between disturbances and fears, between mechanical actions and human reactions, between signals and impulses, noises and decisions.

In this quotation it becomes quite clear how the initially clearly distinguishable positions of self and automobile, of the supposed acting subject on the one hand (the driver) and the supposedly passive object on the other (the car), start to slip into entanglement when attention is shifted to the *process* of driving. From the perspective of driving, which is, after all, a time-based relation, body and machine, technology as well as engineering knowledge and transportation merge fluidly and no longer represent delimitable entities. From an anthropocentrically trained point of view, everything about this scene would converge toward a highlighted human actor, who uses the car as an external instrument and controllable means for his movement. In Bense's account, something else happens. It is not a sovereign subject (the driver) who demonstrates his power over a device (the car.) Rather, it is an anthropotechnical amalgamation of subject and object that acts as a whole and is brought about as a mode of existence. According to Bense, it is the habit gained through practice that accomplishes this transformation. In his description, a processual event is actualized in which biological, knowledge-forming, pragmatic, and technical components form a networked collective in the sense of Bruno Latour's "symmetrical anthropology" (Latour 1999). The sociologist of technology Werner Rammert has something similar in mind when he speaks of a "distributed intelligence" in recent intelligent transport systems (Rammert 2016). For him as well, sociotechnical constellations are the smallest units of action, rather than human actors alone. While Bense's short media-anthropological scene is taken from the realm of mobility and transport, there are other contexts and milieus that also entail and produce complex assemblages of heterogeneous actors, operations, bodies, perceptions, discourses, and techniques. Media-anthropological descriptions of them take up the task of making comprehensible the potential interchangeability of subject, object, and predicate positions at the level of "doing (a mode of) existence." Places and institutions are not purely abstract entities, but also relational scenarios, in which different modes of existence can be identified and reflected in terms of aesthetic analysis (such as subjectification effects). How something or somebody exists differs in a milieu-specific way. Whether something appears in the milieu of a stage show, a lecture, a text, or a hologram marks and makes a difference.

While conventional (media) anthropologies take as a given both the viewpoint of their analysis as well as their notion of "human being," the theory of anthropomedial relations turns the tables around. It grants primacy to the relations over the relata. The claim of the primacy of relations might sound paradoxical, even wrong, since we intuitively assume that relata must be there first—a person and their mobile phone, a self, and a car—and only then can we look at their relationship(s). Although we are used to speaking in this way, this is just a habit of thought and prejudice. How one can overcome such a bias is demonstrated by Bense's description of the mode of existence of driving. Both the self *as a driver* and the car as something that is being driven only emerge out of their entanglement.

This primacy of relationality can also be demonstrated by referring to another media-anthropological scenario of contemporary life. Let us take a look, for example, at the usage of smartphones. The habits of reaching for the cell phone, regularly checking for messages, the longing expectation of lifesigns from other people and the world, carrying the phone with you in almost all situations in life, as well as conversing about its malfunctions with other phone owners—all are observable on such a scale that it has become almost an understatement to say that smartphones are an extension of ourselves. The latent (irrational) fear of being without one's phone is called nomophobia. Symptoms of this fear, as listed, for example, in studies about smart phone and internet addiction,[5] include repeatedly checking the phone's functions, having poor concentration and difficulties in dealing with quiet moments such as waiting times, a tendency toward shorter, more superficial communication with others and greater social isolation as a result, and so on. These symptoms, however, tend to describe the addictive behavior as if it took place outside of the device, belonging to the human body alone. This is not the complete picture.

The cell phone, with its various ways of capturing and processing data, phoning, taking pictures, helping the user locate it and thus themselves, playing games, educating oneself, and the like, is already a multifunctional infrastructure of our everyday actions and perceptions. It is not just a device, like a stand mixer, which can be handled without further effects on subject formation. The normal and even addictive patterns of behavior are incorporated into the technological design of the phone and its screens and are part of both hardware and software alike. Terms like "addictive design" and the habit-forming potential of media use are well known to technology and social media companies and have started to inform interfaces that are intended to address the neurochemistry of their users directly, bypassing their conscious decisions. The most important buttons, for example, are positioned with the location of the user's thumbs in mind, in order to facilitate and habitualize seemingly immediate bodily contact. In a similar vein, a function like autoplay is built into various video and streaming platforms, causing previews or the next episode to start playing on their own. The user's attention here is not only an economic resource to be captured. This function also serves to reinforce an amalgamation of body and cell phone, physically, psychically, affectively, and cognitively. On an existential level, the performance of attentively and/or addictively operating the phone, of watching the screen, and so on leads to the emergence of a relational entity of chemical and electronic signals and switches, of impulses and signs, of codes and interfaces, akin to Bense's example. The relations of overlapping and heterogeneous materials and operations bring forth the modes of existence of a cell phone user or social media addict. Viewed in light of the operative dimensions of the technological and biological bodies in question, their actions, habits, experiences, and so on, the possible hierarchies of subject and object, active and passive again become fluid. The relations do precede their relata.

Anthropomedialities exist in a myriad of everyday phenomena, some of which are even known under familiar terms. In the 1970s, for example, the figuration of the so-called couch potato could be considered such an anthropomedial mode of existence. It is characterized by spending a lot of time lying around on the sofa or in an armchair with junk food and beer, watching television, and working very little or not at all. The couch potato could only emerge from a constellation of living room, fast food industry, delivery service, television, and remote control, consolidating all of this into itself. Similarly, the internet of the 1990s led to "surfing the net" as a mode of existence and experience, which only emerged with the massive introduction of computers into private homes. This going from website to website and link to link happens on a computer, which has to be equipped with the relevant technological components, an internet connection, electricity, a screen, and so on. Again the respective mode of existence is based on a constellation of a variety of interlocking factors such as possession of hardware and software, familiarity with their operations, the possibility of forming habits in and with complex infrastructures. Their relation only unfolds over the course of the process of "surfing." It is easy to continue in this vein. It takes the operation of "liking" something in the context of social media to bring about the mode of existence of the follower; it takes the performance of assembly-line work to create the assembly-line worker; it takes going to the movies and cognitive-affective engagement with a film to breed the mode of existence of the moviegoer or the cineaste. The latter again are anthropomedial constellations of imaginations, bodily sensations, of gazes and associations guided by film-technological means, discourse, and a mix of organic, technological, and further factors. Such existence-forming and anthropomedial relations can of course also be observed outside of media settings in a narrow sense. For instance, riding a bicycle brings into relation the components of a bicycle, such as pedals, wheels, mechanical brakes, seat, handlebars, and the like with bodily behaviors and traffic in such a way that the mode of existence of a *bicycle rider* comes into being.

All these only cursory examples await a more detailed and research-based scenic description, one that is able to properly articulate the entanglements of human and nonhuman factors in each case. For reasons of space this cannot be done here. But one thing is perhaps clear: a perspective oriented toward anthropomediality gives rise to other possibilities of describing and interpreting situated performances of existence, which do not require adding new verses to the old song of the sovereign human subject. The fact that there is heuristic interest in questions of subjective qualities of everyday existence (weak anthropocentrism) does not necessitate sticking with a strong, substantive anthropocentrism. Instead, existential partnerships between disruptions and anxieties, between mechanical and organic actions, between signals and impulses, between noises and decisions, between codes and affects of milieu-specific performances of existence can be identified as the smallest interpretive units of media-anthropological reflection.

The complex multiplicity of anthropomedial relations entails that its detailed descriptions and scenic analyses bear considerable weight in its analytical work. If this is to be considered a disadvantage at all, it is an acceptable price to pay, when otherwise the relational, processual character of hybrid modes of existence cannot be appropriately portrayed, or it cannot be shown what it means to be operatively entangled with a myriad of (nonhuman) factors. This is not the only reason that aesthetic analysis is the methodology of choice to gain the necessary distance to the phenomena being examined. It is grounded in its subject matter, since it is able to express the poetic reality of modes of existence, always already bound to their milieu. This poetic aspect of anthropomedial realities does not consist in simply invoking a romanticized harmony of everything being connected with everything else. Rather, the poetic aspect can be seen where descriptions of modes of existence that arise from a nexus of intermediaries, medialities, and milieus (e.g., users, spectators, service providers, etc.), themselves take recourse to the operational logics of transfer, amalgamation, replacement, and deferral, which correspond to those of metaphors and metonymies. Those metaphors shed light on the emergence of new forms of entanglement and hence new modes of existence such as, for instance, the shift from "Web 1.0" to "Web 2.0," in which users, supported by interactive applications, can create, edit, and distribute content themselves, thus constituting their own networks. But the poetic logic of an entanglement of activity and passivity, of technicity, affect, and habitus, is perhaps not solely a characteristic of living in the age of computers. Perhaps it only finds its operative model there, which can be mirrored backward into the history of the genesis of anthropomediality.

Notes

Translation: Daniel Hendrickson
1. A philosophically oriented media anthropology has been an important area of research at the Bauhaus-University Weimar for several years, first at the Media Anthropology Centre of Excellence (KOMA, 2014–19) and currently at the DFG-funded postgraduate program Media Anthropology (GRAMA, 2020–ongoing).
2. The "our" here refers to an unspecified formation of human modes of existences and is thus not necessarily reduced to societies of the Global North, even if I, as the author of this text, am biographically located in Germany.
3. The resulting insight that there is no central, synthetic subject, surveying all the different modes and doings of existence from above, holding together and making coherent their collapsing boundaries, is not specific to the anthropomedial approach. A similar loss of such a conceptual instance has been amply demonstrated, for example, in the field of psychoanalysis, already since Freud ("the ego is not master in its own house").
4. Since the 2010s, both in Germany and internationally, an increasing number of professorships for aesthetics also include "media philosophy" in their title.
5. See, for example, the self-diagnostic *Smartphone Addiction Scale* (Kwon et al. 2013), the *Mobile Phone Dependence Questionnaire* (Chóliz 2012), as well as the earlier *Internet Addiction Test* (Young 1998).

References

Bense, Max ([1970] 2018), "The Self, the Automobile and Technology," *Interface Critique Journal* 1: 112–17, DOI: 10.11588/ic.2018.0.44745.

Butler, Judith (1990), *Gender Trouble. Feminism and the Subversion of Identity*, New York: Routledge.

Chóliz, M. (2012), "Mobile-Phone Addiction in Adolescence: The Test of Mobile Phone Dependence (TMD)," *Progress in Health Sciences* 2 (1): 33–44.

Kwon, Min, Joon-Yeop Lee, Wang-Youn Won, Jae-Woo Park, Jung-Ah Min, Changtae Hahn, Xinyu Gu, Ji-Hye Choi, and Dai-Jin Kim (2013), "Development and Validation of a Smartphone Addiction Scale (SAS)," *PloS one* 8 (2): e56936, DOI: 10.1371/journal.pone.0056936.

Latour, Bruno (1999), *Pandora's Hope: Essays on the Reality of Science Studies*, Boston, MA: Harvard University Press.

Rammert, Werner (2016), *Technik—Handeln—Wissen. Zu einer pragmatistischen Technik- und Sozialtheorie*, Heidelberg: Springer Nature.

Young, Kimberly S. (1998), "Internet Addiction: The Emergence of a New Clinical Disorder," *CyberPsychology & Behavior* 1 (3): 237–44.

2

Tangled Efforts and Middle-Voiced Verbs

Jane Bennett

Essay

"Essay," is both noun and verb, thing and act: a written composition of moderate length on a particular subject, and the generic activity of trying, attempting, endeavoring.[1] What follows is an essay that endeavors to write up, in human words, the more-than-human character of essaying. It is an attempt to remember the extent to which writing is itself a more-than-human effort. It is an essay about the multispecied nature of essaying, and about how to use words to bespeak that nature.

An essay is a venture, a pitch whose impact rebounds back upon the pitcher. Zeus's thunderbolt, thrown as if from a pure outside and without consequence for him, is not an essay. An essay is a venture amid other ventures: it enjoins a potentially dangerous throng, it engages a contagious swarm, it takes (on) a pulse, it tangles with a tangle. I notice that the four figures of grouping just invoked are not perfect synonyms: "throng" marks the denseness of a pack of entities (bodies), whereas "pulse" and "swarm" draw attention toward the activity-style—the rhythm or buzz—of forces (energies) less distinguishable from one another. What about the "tangle" of *Anthropologies of Entanglements*? Tangle too is both thing and movement-style: it appears in the sixteenth century as a general term for seaweed (ensnared with shells and other things), but its earliest usage, in the fourteenth century, is as a verb denoting the effort involved in engaging affairs from which it is difficult to get free.[2] To tangle is to be caught and to move, to essay.

Must essaying involve an agential entity behind the action? As Nietzsche famously noted, the "grammatical functions of language" insistently separate out a substantial "something that makes it happen" from "what happens," thus insinuating that the former is cause of the latter defined as effect (Nietzsche 2016: 139). It is thus not at all easy for modern language-users to keep the recursive process in the conceptual and perceptual foreground, or to remember that even apparently singular actors are porous, transitioning shapes pulsing with a long history of mimetic relays and still vulnerable to new ones. I compose the English words of my essay, but these sentences are also aftereffects-with-a-twist of the myriad proposals and impressions that have (to use Whitehead's term) "ingressed" into me.[3] Many of these ingressions have, for reasons of duration or familiarity, taken on the cozy feeling of being my own personal intentions. Many, but not all—for there persists a sense of presences less integrated.

Henry Thoreau, in a weird journal entry describing his tangle with atmospheric and vegetal forces, highlights those presences. I shall first consider the way Thoreau writes up—elaborates, elongates, decorates—one of his walks during the summer of 1851. I then turn to walks taken in 2020 by the lines of some decorative doodles. That lines, too, go walking is Paul Klee's insight: he tells his Bauhaus art students in the 1920s that "an active line, moving freely, goes for a stroll on its own, without destination."[4] Can doodles and doodling, like encounters with Thoreau's nature-writing, enhance receptivity to the throng-pulse-swarm-tangle of efforts in which essays are caught up? Human essays (even the most whimsical) are imbued with gravity, geological tremors, atmospheric pressures, or other heavenly influences; with the endeavors of a gut microbiome and a collective unconscious or public mood; with the propensities of a horde of techno-affordances ranging from fire to eyeglasses, antibiotics, and vaccines. But how to bespeak such a trans-specied vibrancy within an official grammar of (active) subjects and (acted-upon) objects? The last part of this essay thus turns to middle-voiced verbs, which are formally unmarked but still operative in English. These process-forward verbs, in neither an active nor passive voice, denote action-amid, and they join Thoreau and doodles in the pushback against the singularity of the subject and anthropocentrism.

Walking with Ether and Rye

Walking is a balancing act, reliant upon and in tension with gravity. (Kathy Ferguson (2017: 709) calls it a "forward-leaning process in which we almost-but-not-quite fall down.") Walking is good for your health, and, as an old peripatetic tradition attests, its pace is somehow also good for philosophizing: "Let us walk along the Ilissus river as we talk," says Socrates to Phaedrus as he adds his voice to "the shrill summery music of the cicada-choir" (Plato 1972: 23, 25). Thoreau loved to walk, or, to be more precise, he favored the unhurried, undirected tempo of sauntering, which, he says, "is beautifully derived 'from idle people who roved about the country, in the Middle Ages, and asked charity, under pretense of going *a la Sainte Terre*,' to the Holy Land" (Thoreau 2007: 216). Thoreau's walks, like Klee's line's strolls, are not linear,[5] and yet they create vectors and exhibit an onwardness or endeavoring quality shared by the written essay. One thing (step, segment, hesitation, word) leads to another.

On July 23, 1851, Thoreau sauntered outside; he then went inside to make a journal entry that is both a faithful phenomenological description and a fanciful elaboration—or, rather, that exposes how the two genres implicate each other. Attending carefully to his companions—the weather and the grasses—he reports on the variegated landscape of his mood. Trying to "walk so gently as to hear the finest sounds," Thoreau notices that he is already amid a swirl of nonhuman efforts: he is "pressed down" upon by the atmosphere ("15 pounds to a square inch" of barometric pressure), a weight that he also describes, in a fabulous oxymoron, as "stupendous piles of light ethereal influence" (Thoreau [1851] 1993: 126). In days with more comfortable weather, that pressure would have gone unnoticed as a mere background condition, but on that hot and heavy day, the ether announces itself as an active force, as a stupendous influence capable of altering the relative strengths of Thoreau's faculties.[6] For example, his capacity for thought (along with the sounds of its words) is "drowned" by the whirr of those mighty yet ethereal influences.[7]

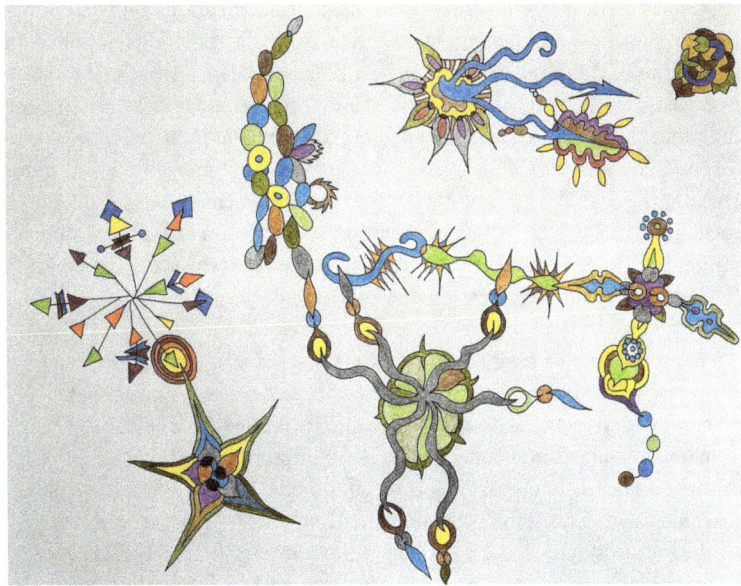

Figure 2.1 One Thing Leads to Another.

Figure 2.2 Stupendous Piles of Influence.

(David Hinton (2016: 46), writing in the context of Daoist poetry, notes that "thought is always *about* something outside itself, creating the illusion that we are somehow fundamentally separate from the Cosmos (emphasis in the original)."[8]) But outside on July 23 in Massachusetts, it was just too hot, heavy, and noisy to think, and, as a result, Thoreau inhabits himself not as individual but as one of many, many, so many ambient influences.

As Thoreau's thoughts recede, he participates more fully in other somatic powers. What come to the fore, as the journal notes, is his inner, meteorological-vegetal faculty of reception/absorption: a capacity to "store up influences" (like the ether does) and to "nod like the ryeheads in the breeze."[9]

Here is the journal entry:

> You must walk so gently as to hear the finest sounds, the faculties being in repose. Your mind must not perspire. True, out of doors my thought is commonly drowned as it were & and shrunken, pressed down by stupendous piles of light ethereal influence—for the pressure of the atmosphere is still 15 pounds to a square inch—I can do little more than preserve the equilibrium & resist the pressure of the atmosphere— I can only nod like the ryeheads in the breeze. I expand more surely in my chamber, as far as expression goes, as if that pressure were taken off; but here out-doors is the place to store up influences. (Thoreau [1851] 1993: 126)

Thoreau reports his (subjective) moods and also the (objective) press of atmosphere and rye. A living pile of influences enjoins his sensitive flesh as his cognitive pressure drops and his posture and rhythm subside into that of nodding ryegrass. Sun and wind infuse atmosphere; breeze moves rye; rye respirates water vapor into already humid air; man in-hales air and nods before going inside to ex-press. Each of these acts is more an inducing or inflecting than the production of an effect, for each enjoins tendencies already within the materials of the bodies involved. The flesh of man and the cellulose of ryegrass are, for example, porous and sensitive to wind, heat, and moisture; they are configured such that they can stand upright; and they are sufficiently rooted to engage in the movement-style of the sway, bob, and nod.[10] What is at work at the scene that Thoreau writes up in his chamber, then, is a kind of agency—a model of endeavor—consisting in a cascade of inducements between givers and receivers continuously exchanging roles. The efforts that compose the nod, for example, are multiple and multispecied, such that it is quite impossible to identify any single or original impetus. Did the nod come from Thoreau? From the mimetic circuit of ryegrass and man? From the downward pressure of the atmosphere upon jointed neck and head? From the exhalations of men and grasses imparted to the ether? It's hard to say. (Nod becomes shrug.)

After Thoreau goes back inside, his think-power returns: "I expand more surely in my chamber, as far as expression goes." (He is able now to express what Hans Ulrich Gumbrecht (2004: XV) calls the "presence effects" of things.) Thoreau is able now to write up recent happenings as a poetic scene of atmospheric infusion, cognitive-suspension, and vegetal nod-activation. In his chamber, ether, grass, and the motion of nodding recompose as meaning-filled squiggles on the page. In a lecture delivered three months earlier, he had called this "speaking a word for Nature," that is to say, translating for bodies and forces whose voices are not, in the first instance, linguistic.[11] Via the leanings of pencil, ink, paper, and the cooler and less glaring ambiance of his chamber, via Thoreau's memories, ideas, and what Merleau-Ponty (2014: 112–14) will call the motor intentionality of fingers and forearms, the vaguely felt admixture of outside influences becomes journal entry. Text hums along with, while adding to, an ongoing tune: Thoreau's literary output, Klee might say, is a riff on a (self-)expressive, creative cosmos.

Strolling Lines → Doodles

In a lecture called "Creative Confession," Paul Klee (2013) says that the graphic line is "charged with energy of various kinds." From whence comes

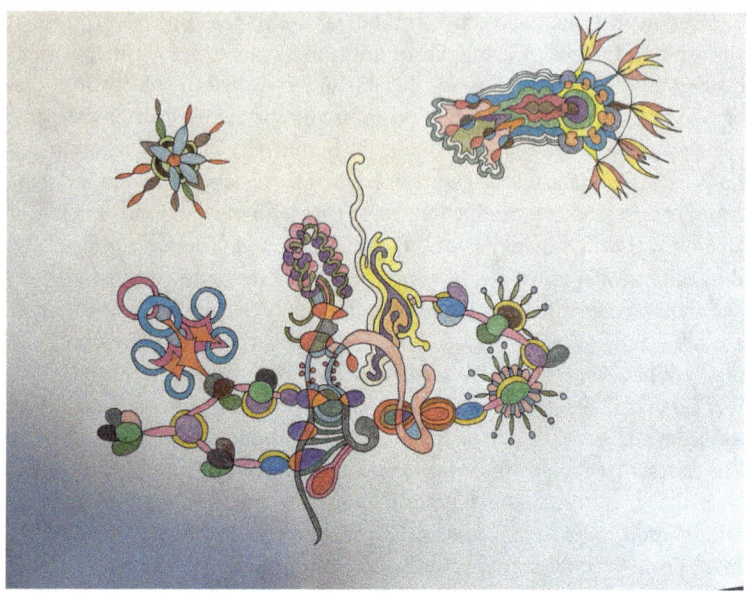

Figure 2.3 Creative Cosmos.

this "energy"? Klee at first responds through an anthropocentric lens, identifying as motive force the artist's "ideas" (and moving arm): An "energy-charge" is transferred from artist to page as he pulls "a blunt crayon across the paper." Later in his talk, he repeats the point: "A certain fire, an impulse to create, is kindled, is transmitted through the hand, leaps to the canvas, and in the form of a spark leaps back to its starting place, completing the circle—back to the eye and further (back to the source of the movement, the will, the idea)."

But what, one might ask, *prompted* the ideas that fire the arm that leaps to the canvas? Was there not also an energetic prod from abroad, from beyond the human's body? In *Difference and Repetition*, Deleuze presents a model of "thinking" designed to counteract the (post-Kantian) tendency to elide nonhuman vitality in favor of the conceptual constructions of the human mind. According to Deleuze, concepts "lack the claws ... of a strangeness or an enmity which alone would awaken thought from its natural stupor .... Something in the world forces us to think. This something is an object not of recognition, but of a fundamental *encounter*" (Deleuze 1994: 139, emphasis in the original).[12] Paraphrasing Deleuze, then, one could respond to the question "What moves Klee's line?" by saying, "Something in the world forces us to draw."

Klee himself approaches this claim when he says, later in the lecture, that the artist "goes through the motions of a hound following a scent." Here the energetic prompt is the ingression of a scent from elsewhere, which im-presses without doing so overtly or visibly. (After all, says Klee (2013), "the visible world is merely an isolated case in relation to the universe and … there are many more other, latent realities.") Klee again acknowledges the essays of a lively, more-than-human cosmos when he says that "in the universe, … movement is the basic datum," and that it is an "idle question" to ask for the first cause of movement, since motion is the default nature of things: "On this earth, repose is caused by an accidental obstruction in the movement of matter. It is an error to regard such a stoppage as primary" (ibid.). The artistic "impulse to create" is itself one manifestation of the perpetually mobile, self-starting matter of the cosmos. "Each work of art is an example … of the cosmic."[13] A graphic line is in this sense no different from the flight path of a falling star. "It goes out for a walk, so to speak, aimlessly for the sake of the walk."

As an inveterate doodler, I am familiar with the feel of strolling lines, as they slide down arm, fingers, pencil, and out the graphite tip, joining and diverging from trajectories already taken by predecessors on the page. Lines saunter, curve, loop, zig-zag, double back to the east, north, south, west. They lay down paths of different speeds and shapes: languid or intense, fractal or fringed, tight or billowy. Doodles are rarely born out of doors, more often emerging in a chamber where a meeting or phone conversation or Zoom lecture is the official site of attention. Doodles don't need a lot of space: they make landfall on margin of text, corner of napkin, upside down is fine, though, as Klee notes, they do like to roam. They might resemble the "customary path of a child" with its "lines of drift" with different loops, knots, speeds, movements, gestures" (Deleuze and Guattari 1986: 311–12).[14] You feel their strolling shapes as something other than, or in excess of, the expression of prior intentions. Even more than the less "absent-minded"[15] works called drawings or paintings, doodles *surprise* she who holds the pencil.[16] "Lo, a shape!" I say to myself (quoting Walt Whitman 2002b: 224) as they emerge on the page. Doodles do not have the same prideful feel as, say, the diagram I put on the blackboard to visualize the logic of an argument or the chart I draw to operationalize a plan.

More faithful to the phenomenology of doodling, then, is to speak of an efficacy that is ontologically multiple, variegated, and distributed across a broad field. David Maclagan, in a fine study of doodling called *Line Let Loose*, approaches this when he invokes the agency of "the drawing process itself," whose kinetic energy (the "to-and-fro of the pencil") is such that a doodler watches her hand "as if it belonged to someone else" (Maclagan 2014: 84–7). Deleuze and Guattari (1986: 367) might say that the doodle follows the rules

Figure 2.4 Out for a Walk.

of "protogeometry," which concerns itself not with the established shapes of cone, parallelogram, sphere, and the like, but with forms that are essentially "anexact," vague, vagabond, or nomadic.

For the surrealists, the unplanned quality of doodles suggests that they express an obscure region of the human psyche called the unconscious—what

Figure 2.5 Lo, a Shape #1.

Jung (2011: 73) calls the "unfathomable dark recesses of the conscious mind" with its "wealth of subliminal perceptions" (ibid.: 68). For Max Morise, doodles are "spontaneous images" prompted by "imperceptible undulations of the flux of thought" (in Toub 2014: 473). Surrealist games of automatic drawing, such as the game of the exquisite corpse, aim to unearth the secrets of this psychic strata and render more perceptible thought's undulations (ibid.: 479). There is no doubt that the figure of an inner unconscious realm has much explanatory and therapeutic power. But it does not capture well the doodler's sense of the presencing of a flux that *exceeds* intra- and inter-psychic relations, which overflows the frame of human thought/mind and operates (in what Thoreau calls) "out-doors." The anthropocentrism of surrealism—which involves switching so much of agency into the human unconscious—makes it difficult for them to detect (and decorate) ahuman prompts from ether, flora, breezes, sounds, fauna—as such. Whitehead comes closer to acknowledging these when he speaks of a "visceral" form of "prehension," wherein the influx of "actual entities" is "felt" even though it does not register as a sense-perception but rather as an "affective tone" operating with "the vagueness of the low hum of insects in an August woodland" (Whitehead 1978: 176).

Had Maclagan's study of doodles attended more closely to these ethereal but still material-physical influences—perhaps with the help of Deleuze's figure of a "virtual" realm that is real despite not being fully actual—he might have spared himself the either/or question that organizes his book: Is doodling automatic or intentional? Such a bad, either/or question is a precipitate of a binary grammar of active subjects and relatively passive objects; it also insinuates that artistry is itself an exclusively human power. But if, instead, bodies and forces of many different sorts are presumed capable of the effort of *impress operations*, then other questions concerning doodling can come to the fore. Instead of focusing on which of the human faculties produce and direct doodling, how about these questions: How does doodling unravel an anthropocentric model of action, of what it is to essay? How do doodles bear witness to outside forces that have seeped in, and to a distributive, conjoint quality of action? A messy swarm of outdoor elements activates a drawing process, which leans into the momentum of the strolling line, which taps the shoulder of the human doodler, who lends her arm to the pencil, which gives the nod to emergent shapes (with vice versas all around).

Writing Up

I turn now to the productive paradox of *writing* up that which includes the ahuman and alinguistic. What are the characteristics of a rhetorical style that is least distorting of these? What grammar, syntax, tropes, and tricks are most pertinent?

Thoreau's writing, which hovers between the genres of botanical close description, political theorizing, myth-making, and poetry, is very good at

Tangled Efforts and Middle-Voiced Verbs 41

Figure 2.6 Lo, a Shape #2.

acknowledging the contributions made by forces whose first language is not human. Thoreau writes up his encounters in ways that mark how not-quite-human vitalities prompt written texts, and continue to inform and deform them each time they are read. Thoreau ([1851] 1993: 188), moving as "the scribe of … the corn and the grass and the atmosphere writing," insinuates into the reader an uncanny sense that, at this very moment, one is amid a bevy of active forces, some human and many not.

A poetics that nods to the contributions of ahuman endeavoring might dramatize the fact that metaphors *remain infused and fueled* by the physical forces more obviously at work when one is out in the sun on a really hot day. It "does not depict those [forces] in some metaphoric way; ... it *enacts* them" (Hinton 2016: 90). Every essay, every endeavor, is (at least) coauthored: "The two of us wrote *Anti-Oedipus* together. Since each of us was several, there was already quite a crowd" (Deleuze and Guattari 1986: 3). Such writing could show, for example, how the throat-and-chest feeling of breathing and the texture of wind on your face still vibrate inside the word "inspiration," or how hearing the phrase "on the one hand ... on the other hand" induces a subtle rocking to-and-fro of your body (Schneider et al. 2013: 319–20). Such a rhetoric might also push the "metaphorical" to the point where it becomes uncertain whether a sentence speaks in a descriptive or an aspirational voice, and also uncertain whether the speaker is positioned above the scene like a bird or a god[17] or positioned as a body floating in a processual sea.

Such a rhetoric would, as Michel Foucault dreams, "bring an oeuvre, a book, a sentence, an idea to life," showing not only how sentences *ex-press* the human-societal forces, but are *pressed on* by a vitality proper to ahuman influences. Such mimetic sentences would "light fires, watch the grass grow, listen to the wind, and catch the sea foam in the breeze and scatter it."[18] Sentences brought *to life* make a point of exhibiting how (what Thoreau calls) "natural influences" still linger in language even after the heyday of Romanticism and even within the Anthropocene. Walt Whitman (2002a: ll. 189–90) too sought such a poetics, one "done with reviews and criticisms of life" and instead is "animating now to life itself." To "animate" to life is to toss-and-be-tossed into an ongoing creative process. It is neither to *take* a decisive action (as in "to act more animatedly") nor to endure as a patient of an outside force (as when Frankenstein's monster is animated by electricity).

Such a rhetoric might also speak with a tongue that is ramified or many-branched, like a huge old tree or a neural network. Or perhaps with a voice that is rhizomatic in the sense of being all branches and no trunk, and which leans toward the molecular (energetic and manifold) and away from the molar (morphological and unified).[19] Such a rhetoric would be roomy enough to accommodate a heterogeneous swirl of agents, some human, some not. It would acknowledge that while some situations call for acts based upon the shorthand of subject-and-object,[20] there is also a need to find work-arounds to that grammar in order to expose the overlapping waves of effort, some mine, some yours, and some apersonal. Which brings us, finally, to the middle voice.

Middle-Voiced Verbs

What middle-voiced verbs do is name action coming from within an ongoing process, where the action engages and affects the actors. The subject of the predicate neither directs the activity (the active voice) nor is merely acted upon (the passive voice): It participates in a lively process while being processed. In the middle voice, there is not posited an "agent ... *anterior* to the process" (emphasis in the original) but, rather, the "subject is immediately contemporary with the [act], being effected and affected by it" and "remains enveloped in the released action." In the middle voice, the alteration effected is not something "delivered by the simple initiative of the subject" (Barthes 1972: 143, 151). The middle voice is a grammatical form appropriate to, prompted by, and traversed by stupendous, ethereal influences. Middle-voiced verbs are marked formally in classical Greek and Sanskrit but not in English. The middle voice distinguishes a mode of action whose prompts come from *multiple sources* and whose efficacy is the function not of a discrete agent or agency but of a *complex, recursive process*. "I was out."

According to linguist Emile Benveniste, the dominance of two voices (active and passive) was a relatively late development of the Indo-European verb form. It was transformation of an older linguistic order in which the key difference was between (1) activities in which an actor stands *outside* the activity and thus not changed by it ("external diathesis") and (2) activities in which an actor is *inside* and *amid*, and thus also subject to being altered by the process ("internal diathesis"). Internal diathesis would only later be presented as *midway* between active and conditioned verbal forms. Benveniste makes the case that the "middle" of middle-voiced verbs is thus *not* a mean between an active and a passive voice. It indicates instead an effectivity *amid* a (complex, heterogeneous) atmospheric process. Any acting I "effects while being affected, in the middle" (Benveniste 1971: 149–50, see also White 2010: 255–62).

It is difficult to understand how the middle voice works if you speak "a language like English, which has almost entirely eradicated it" (Parkinson 2011: 277). The awkwardness of attempts to do so reminds us of the power of grammar to circumscribe what can be felt of life.[21] Let me emphasize, however, that this circumscription is not *complete*: linguistic forms that nod to a distributive kind of agency persist. They can be amplified through practices of writing up. Take, for example, Whitman's "I sing the body electric," whose (radically plural[22]) I is enmeshed in a process with flesh, electricity, and sound. Or consider Whitman's phrase "It sails me, I daub with bare feet," where the I is suspended between the status of the passively windblown and the volitional toe-tapper:

> I hear the train'd soprano. (what work with hers is this?)
> The orchestra whirls me wider than Uranus flies,
> It wrenches such ardors from me I did not know I possess'd them
> It sails me, I dab with bare feet. (Whitman 2002c: 52)

Or take these more everyday examples of middle-voiced phrases: "It sounds good,"[23] "I be going now," or "We died out there."[24] All are responses to happenings in which the speaker remains entangled, in the lived protraction of the present. The act named is less an intervention by a discrete self into a background environment than a movement within and by virtue of a heterogeneous, creative-destructive atmosphere.

All this suggests that a rhetoric for composite or compositional or composted (?) agency is sprinkled liberally with process-oriented verbs—to induce, to animate to, to inflect, to partake, to sing, to sound, to die. Such verbs mark activities with multiple loci of impetus, and they position partakers as already caught up in an ongoing flow that precedes them and to which they may add impetus, drag, swerve. Such verbs position human participants as always already involved in a creative flow before it is possible to feel themselves being so. Before they "take" action. We are middle-voiced partakers even more than actors *or* recipients.

In Media Res

Writing cannot be wholly faithful to influences that filter into syntax: every rhetoric, every poetics, will be more or less in sync with the stupendous, ether-like influences that signal without words.[25] But writing can give the nod or toe-tap toward them. Indeed, the translation of ongoing processes into words, while "an operation that undoubtedly consists in subjugating, overcoding, metricizing," also provides "a milieu of propagation, extension, refraction, renewal, and impulse" (Deleuze and Guattari 1986: 486). Figured as a generative milieu whose efflux is irreducible to its inflows, Thoreau's journal entries, like Klee's lines and my doodles, are "media."

But they are media conceived not as objects distinct from the realms of life and essaying but, rather, as "always already intermingled facets of a broader dynamic configuration." In their reconceptualization of "media" and "the human" as "intertwined entities or anthropomedialities," Tim Othold and Christiane Voss (2015: 75) highlight how "technology and per extension media are inherent to life and human experience from their very beginning" (ibid.: 79). Othold and Voss propose "anthropomediality" as a heuristic that persistently calls (conceptual and sensuous) attention to *relationality* rather

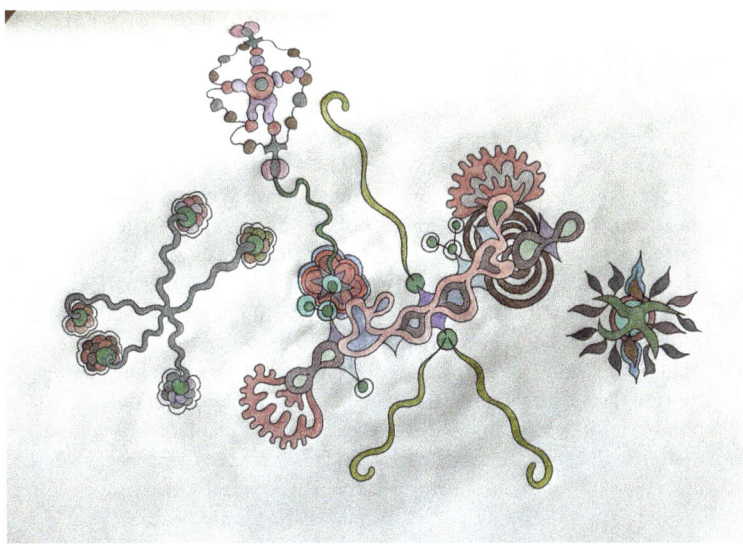

Figure 2.7 Anthropomediality.

than relata. Middle-voiced verbs might thus be taken up as a linguistic tactic on behalf of an anthropomedial scholarship, and doodling engaged as one of its visual accompaniments. Finally, the figure of "ethereal influences" might be explored further in the effort to include atmospheric or virtual forces within a media-centric mode of analysis.

Notes

1. Generic in the sense of all-purpose but also non-purposive or open-ended.
2. Today tangle may invoke an image of *thread*, itself both entity and successive process (as anyone who has on Monday used a needle-and-thread and on Tuesday followed the thread of an online conversation knows).
3. "My" essay enjoins the tryings and try-outs of all those writers I've met, heard, or read; the rhythmic efforts of the cicadas in the garden during earlier drafts; the pulse of Red Garland's piano music playing during revisions; the inclinations of the typing posture and the tendencies encouraged by the configuration of the keyboard; the unsettling trajectory of climate change and of my background anxiety about continuing to participate in a political economy of waste, extraction, and exploitation as well as inspiration from the many and various efforts of others to live

otherwise. (I try to imitate laudable forays toward ecological justice and health, and not get "swamped" in critique, which can unwittingly intensify the pulse of its target.)

4. *"Eine aktive Linie, die sich frei ergeht, ein Spaziergang um seiner selbst willen, ohne Ziel"* (Klee 1964: 105). As Andrew Hewish (2015: 8) notes, "Klee's words enact one of the major tropes of Modernity—the individualistic and free employment of movement through space. What characterises the flaneur from an ordinary walker is the emphasis on experience of the journey; but what allows Klee's statement to resonate powerfully, and dissonantly, is that the nature of the experience is not centred in the artist's experience, but rather in the line that does the strolling. It is the line, not the (displaced) artist, that goes for a stroll."

5. "'Linearity' is more often than not suggestive … of a straight line, that shortest distance between two points … So part of the power of Klee's phrase ['an active line, moving freely, goes for a stroll on its own, without destination'] is the conjuring of that which is constantly suppressed—the unstraight line of the stroll. This tension between ideally held historic line and suppressed possibility, or in psychoanalytic terms, the disavowed, is part of the engine of the power of circulation of Klee's phrase" (Hewish 2015: 6).

6. Tim Ingold (2010: 122) too marks the exchanges between persons and weather: "as we walk, we do not so much traverse the exterior surface of the world as negotiate a way through a zone of admixture and interchange" with the earth and with "the volatile medium of air …. The experience of weather lies at the root of our moods and motivations."

7. Thoreau notes elsewhere (in *The Maine Woods* and *Walden*) that these sounds include the buzz of millions of insects and the hum of telegraph wires. For a fascinating discussion of the hearing of vibratory atmospheres, see Ganchrow (2021: 82): "Human abilities to hear large sections of air appear when weather barometers link-up with telegraphy. The earliest recognized atmospheric fluctuations at global scale originate in intense volcanic and meteorite explosions around the turn of the 19th century. Until that point, human perceptions of atmosphere oscillations were clearly divided between sounds the ear registers (as far as the wind blows and thunder rumbles) and changes in weather patterns (inaudible yet tangible oscillations of mercury columns and barometer read-outs). Those distinctions were nullified with the 1883 eruption of Krakatoa in Indonesia when the bottom end of sound dropped open into an abyss of ultra-slow atmospheric oscillations. Sounds from the massive volcanic explosions were audible to the naked ear in more than 50 widely-spaced geographic locations covering an area equivalent to approximately one thirteenth of the globe."

8. Hinton (2016: 62–3) repeats the point later: "In the Western mimetic model, language is experienced as a transcendental realm of arbitrary (alphabetic)

signs that refer to reality. This referential relationship fundamentally separates us from reality, distancing it as a kind of elsewhere, and its rigid category of nouns ossifies things into static and lifeless entities. By contrast, classical Chinese was understood as part of the existence-tissue's movements. In Chinese with its empty grammar, Absence appears as the space surrounding ideograms, and ideograms emerge from that empty source exactly like Presence's ten thousand things—a fact emphasized in the pictographic nature of ideograms … This sense was no doubt often lost in day-to-day utilitarian uses of the language by artist-intellectuals in their highly textual bureaucratic and intellectual lives. That routine use of language would have created a rupture in the existence-tissue much like Western languages do …, hence the need for the spiritual practices of ancient China."

9. One could say that, in the nod, Thoreau enters something akin to what Deleuze and Guattari (1986: 479, 488) call "smooth" (rather than "striated") space: if "in the striated forms organize a matter, in the smooth materials signal forces and serve as symptoms for them." In smooth space, "space and that which occupies space tend to become identified, to have the same power."

10. "Grasses, whether annual or perennial, are mostly herbaceous (not woody), monocotyledon plants with jointed stems and sheathed leaves. They are usually upright, cylindrical, with alternating leaves, anchored to the soil by roots. Grasses have leaves (blades that narrow into a sheath), a stem (culm), a collar region (where leaves attach to the stem), roots, tillers, and during the reproductive stage an inflorescence or seedhead develops" (Forage Information System 2022).

11. "I wish to speak a word for Nature, for absolute freedom and wildness, as contrasted with a freedom and culture merely civil,—to regard man as an inhabitant, or a part and parcel of nature, rather than a member of society. I wish to make an extreme statement, if so I may make an emphatic one" (Thoreau 2007: 205). This essay, "Walking," began as a lecture to the Concord Lyceum on April 23, 1851.

12. What forces us to think, Deleuze (1994: 139) continues, includes *entities* ("Socrates, a temple, or a demon") but also that which, like Thoreau's "ethereal influences," are too delicate or too anexact to be marked explicitly by either cognition or sense-perception.

13. Klee speaks of the "wretched light of the intellect." Deleuze (1994: 137), although speaking specifically of Kantian-style "critique," makes a similar point about the limits of critical intelligence: "Critique has … a tribunal," but it does not have "the power of a new politics which would overturn the image of thought." In "On Modern Art," Klee (2012) says that "juices flow upward [from the earth] to the artist, passing through him, through his eye …. Moved and compelled by the power of those streaming juices, he conducts what he is looking at into the [art]work."

14. For a fine discussion of Deleuze and Guattari's uptake of Klee's theory of lines, which also explores its implications for geopolitical borders, see de Bruyn (2014).
15. "Doodles are the scribbled drawings or markings that are spontaneously produced absent-mindedly, when one's mind is preoccupied with something else rather than concerned solely with the process of drawing itself.... For the purposes of this study, doodles are understood as a subjective phenomenon involving the subconscious" (Watson 2008: 35–6).
16. "The drawn line in its initiation is always new, and therefore to be discovered during its production. The more intriguing part of Klee's thought, perhaps, is the question of how it is that subject might 'discover' something that has been produced (determined being perhaps too strong a term) by its own hand" (Hewish 2015: 11).
17. Donna Haraway (1988: 581) speaks of "the God trick of seeing everything from no where."
18. "I can't help but dream about a kind of criticism that would try not to judge but to bring an oeuvre, a book, a sentence, an idea to life; it would light fires, watch the grass grow, listen to the wind, and catch the sea foam in the breeze and scatter it. It would multiply not judgements but signs of existence; it would summon them, drag them from their sleep. Perhaps it would invent them sometimes—all the better. All the better. Criticism that hands down sentences sends me to sleep; I'd like a criticism of scintillating leaps of the imagination. It would not be sovereign or dressed in red. It would bear the lightening of possible storms" (Foucault 1997: 323).
19. "In Bergson there is a distinction between numerical or extended multiplicities and qualitative or durational multiplicities. We are doing approximately the same thing when we distinguish between arborescent multiplicities and rhizomatic multiplicities. Between macro- and micromultiplicities. On the one hand, multiplicities that are extensive, divisible, and molar; unifiable, total-izable, organizable; conscious or preconscious—and on the other hand, libidinal, unconscious, molecular, intensive multiplicities composed of particles that do not divide without changing in nature, and distances that do not vary without entering another multiplicity and that constantly construct and dismantle themselves in the course of their communications, as they cross over into each other at, beyond, or before a certain threshold. The elements of this second kind of multiplicity are particles; their relations are distances; their movements are Brownian; their quantities are intensities, differences in intensity" (Deleuze and Guattari 1986: 54).
20. For a discussion, see chapter VI, "Introduction to Metaphysics" in Bergson (1946). My thanks to Bill Connolly for this reference.
21. Scott (1990: 18–19) also notes how "the dominance of the active and passive voices [in modern European languages] makes inevitable the priority of the

spectator-subject for philosophical thought, whereas the middle voice yields a different way of thinking."
22. "I am large, I contain multitudes," is one of the most famous lines from Whitman's "Song of Myself."
23. Languages such as classical Greek, Sanskrit, or modern Hungarian do register "middle marking ... in verbs that might more usually be considered passive. Constructions such as the German ... 'es hort sich gut an' [it sounds good] use middle forms ... to de-emphasize the agent" (Barry 2008: 116). Barry uses "It sounds good" as an example of a sentence that is "agentless but not devoid of agency" in the context of a discussion of the rhetoric of Samuel Beckett.
24. I am grateful to Christiane Voss for this last example, which marks how the creative process includes destruction.
25. What is more, each writer will contaminate the influences she targets for expression with other influences embedded in her perceptual, ideological, social-positional, and body-capacity styles. And at least some dimensions of our "subject-position" must remain unmarked, unconscious, vague to their bearer. The attempt to unearth these, and to confess to their influence, is a valuable element within (postcolonial, anti-racist, anti-patriarchal, neuro-diversifying) strategies of resistance. For an excellent discussion of the politics and philosophy of neurodiversity, see Manning (2016). The point I am trying to make, with the help of Manning and others, is a non-anthropocentric extension of the claim (characteristic of the linguistic turn) that the writer is not to be understood as only directing language but as also affected by the force of the writing.

References

Barry, Elizabeth (2008), "One's Own Company: Agency, Identity and the Middle Voice in the Work of Samuel Beckett," *Journal of Modern Literature* 31 (2): 115–32.
Barthes, Roland (1972), "To Write: An Intransitive Verb?," in Richard Macksey and Eugenio Donato (eds.), *The Structuralist Controversy*, 134–44, Baltimore, MD: Johns Hopkins University Press.
Benveniste, Émile (1971), "Active and Middle Voice in the Verb," in *Problems in General Linguistics*, trans. Mary Elizabeth Meek, 145–52, Miami, FL: University of Miami Press.
Bergson, Henri (1946), *Creative Mind: An Introduction to Metaphysics*, New York: Citadel Press.
de Bruyn, Eric C. H. (2014), "Beyond the Line, or a Political Geometry of Contemporary Art," *Grey Room* 57 (Fall): 24–49.
Deleuze, Gilles (1994), *Difference and Repetition*, New York: Columbia University Press.

Deleuze, Gilles, and Félix Guattari (1986), *A Thousand Plateaus*, Minneapolis: University of Minnesota Press.

Ferguson, Kathy E. (2017), "Anarchist Women and the Politics of Walking," *Political Research Quarterly* 70 (4): 708–19.

Forage Information System (2022), "Summarize the Distinctive Physical Characteristics of Grasses," *National Forage and Grasslands Curriculum*, Oregon State University. Available online: https://forages.oregonstate.edu/nfgc/eo/onlineforagecurriculum/instructormaterials/availabletopics/grasses/characteristics (accessed June 27, 2022).

Foucault, Michel (1997), "Ethics: Subjectivity and Truth," in Paul Rabinow (ed.), Michel Foucault, *The Essential Works of Foucault, 1954–1984*, vol. 1, New York: New Press.

Ganchrow, Raviv (2021), "Earth-Bound Sound: Oscillations of Hearing, Ocean, and Air," *Theory & Event* 24 (1): 67–116.

Gumbrecht, Hans Ulrich (2004), *Production of Presence: What Meaning Cannot Convey*, Stanford, CA: Stanford University Press.

Haraway, Donna (1988), "Situated Knowledges: The Science Question in Feminism and the Privilege of Partial Perspective," *Feminist Studies* 14 (3): 575–99.

Hewish, Andrew (2015), "A Line from Klee," *Journal of Visual Art Practice* 14 (1): 3–15.

Hinton, David (2016), *Existence: A Story*, Boulder, CO: Shambhala.

Ingold, Tim (2010), "Footprints through the Weather-World: Walking, Breathing, Knowing," *Journal of the Royal Anthropological Institute* 16: 121–39.

Jung, Carl (2011), "Unconscious, Dreams, the Suprapersonal," in Carl Jung, *Dreams*, Princeton, NJ: Princeton University Press.

Klee, Paul (1964), *The Thinking Eye*, London: Lund Humphris.

Klee, Paul (2012), "On Modern Art," in John Sallis (ed.), *Paul Klee. Philosophical Vision: From Nature to Art*, 9–14, Chestnut Hill, MA: McMullen Museum of Art, Boston College.

Klee, Paul (2013), *Creative Confession*, London: Tate Enterprises.

Maclagan, David (2014), *Line Let Loose: Scribbling, Doodling, and Automatic Writing*, London: Reaktion Books.

Manning, Erin (2016), *The Minor Gesture*, Durham, NC: Duke University Press.

Merleau-Ponty, Maurice (2014), *Phenomenology of Perception*, New York: Routledge.

Nietzsche, Friedrich (2016), *Writings from the Late Notebooks*, Rudiger Bittner (ed.) and Kate Sturge (trans.), Cambridge: Cambridge University Press.

Othold, Tim, and Christiane Voss (2015), "From Media Anthropology to Anthropomediality," *Anthropological Notebooks* 21 (3): 75–82.

Parkinson, Gavin (2011), "(Blind Summit) Art Writing, Narrative, Middle Voice," *Art History* 34 (2): 268–87.

Plato (1972), *Phaedrus*, R. Hackforth (trans.), Cambridge: Cambridge University Press.

Schneider, Iris K., Anita Eerland, Fren kvan Harreveld, Mark Rotteveel, Joop van der Pligt, Nathan van der Stoep, Rolf A. Zwaan (2013), "One Way and the Other: The Bidirectional Relationship between Ambivalence and Body Movement," *Psychological Science* 24 (3): 319–25.

Scott, Charles (1990), *The Question of Ethics*, Bloomington: Indiana University Press.

Thoreau, Henry David ([1851] 1993), "July 23, 1851," in H. Daniel Peck (ed.), *A Year in Thoreau's Journal: 1851*, New York: Penguin.

Thoreau, Henry David (2007), "Walking," in J. Moldenhauer (ed.), *The Writings of Henry David Thoreau: Excursions*, Princeton, NJ: Princeton University Press.

Toub, Jim (2014), "In and Out of the Margins: The Doodle in Art and Popular Culture," *SECAC Review* 16 (4): 472–84.

Watson, Benjamin (2008), "Oodles of Doodles? Doodling Behavior and Its Implications for Understanding Paleoarts," *Rock Art Research* 25: 35–60.

White, Hayden (2010), *The Fiction of Narrative*, Baltimore, MD: Johns Hopkins University Press.

Whitehead, Alfred North (1978), *Process and Reality*, New York: Free Press.

Whitman, Walt (2002a), "By Blue Ontario's Shore," in Michael Moon (ed.), *Leaves of Grass and Other Writings*, New York: W.W. Norton.

Whitman, Walt (2002b), "Europe, the 72nd and 73rd Years of These States," in Michael Moon (ed.), *Leaves of Grass and Other Writings*, New York: W.W. Norton.

Whitman, Walt (2002c), "Song of Myself," in Michael Moon (ed.), *Leaves of Grass and Other Writings*, New York: W.W. Norton.

3

The Experience-Image and Collaborative Filmmaking: From Visual Anthropology to Media-Anthropological Practices

Julia Bee

Introduction

In order to develop a notion of media anthropology, I would like to revisit three scenes from the history of visual anthropology; sensory ethnography, cinéma vérité, and collaborative cinema. They are rooted in documentary traditions hailing from anthropological backgrounds and developed critical and reflexive ways of doing audiovisual research. Media anthropology focuses on the entanglement of humans and media (Voss 2019: 34). The notion of anthropomediality offers a conceptual frame for situational analyses of these assemblages in which neither humans nor media exist apart from each other. Viewed through the lenses of media anthropology, I describe three relationships between humans and media: first, the exploration of environments through experience in sensory ethnography; second, subjectivation and "fabulation" (Deleuze) in cinéma vérité; and third, the pragmatics of collaborative cinema and "shared anthropology" (Rouch 2003: 44). Finally, for each anthropomedia constellation there is also a relation between knowing and being, in which knowledge and modes of existence cannot be considered separately (Barad 2007; Simondon 2009: 13). That means anthropomediality itself is facilitated by forms and practices of media as an audiovisual form of knowledge. That includes the anthropological works of Véréna Paravel and Lucien Castaing-Taylor, the theatrical forms of film in cinéma vérité by Jean Rouch and Pierre Perrault, and in shared forms of knowledge production in collaborative-produced films by Vídeo nas Aldeias and Instituto Catitu with anthropological and Indigenous documentary filmmakers from Brazil.

I want to trace a movement in which visual anthropology does not only represent knowledge of anthropology (Heider 1976: 2), as it was long seen in the history of visual anthropology or ethnographic filmmaking, but creates modes of existence or ways of being in the world (Latour 2013; Souriau 2015). Film thus can become a milieu for "individuations" (Simondon 2009, 2020).

With this I also aim to draw a line from experience in sensory ethnography to practices and performance in collaborative filmmaking. Instead of viewing ethnographic film only as a form of representation of groups, places, cultural practices, or ecologies, I view it as media-anthropological practice in three cases: as a practice of experience, as a practice of performance, and as a practice of collaboration.

Sensory Ethnography

In the past fifteen years, the Sensory Ethnography Lab (SEL), a visual anthropology research lab based in Harvard, has in its productions broken with ocular centrism and thus with the link between seeing and knowing (Bee 2017) by working with multiple sensuous dimensions in filmmaking. Here, experimental research methods focus on sensuous perception. Film is used as a methodology in anthropological research and no longer has an inferior role in the research setting (Grimshaw and Ravetz 2005; Schneider and Wright 2013). In the films of the SEL, sensory qualities in particular become relevant, breaking the nexus of "seeing and knowing" (Foucault 1995; in reference to colonialism Kaplan 1997). Sensory ethnography is about an extension of the sensory experience of film's visuality to other qualities (Pink 2013). That is, through a sensory multiplicity, they shift the centering of vision to one of hearing, the sense of movement, haptics, and, most importantly, the interconnection of all sensory levels (Elsaesser and Hagener 2015). This is expressed in the intertwined representation of ship, sea, and machine through hypermobile camera perspectives in Véréna Paravel and Lucien Castaing-Taylor's *Leviathan* (2012) (see Figures 3.1–3.4).

Leviathan is about industrial fishing off the coast of New Bedford, Massachusetts. Through mobile GoPro cameras, perspectives of fish, fishermen, machinery, and cranes are staged. Thus, uncommented on by a narrator, the film creates an intertwined ecology of human and nonhuman actors. Through the strong emphasis on movement, haptics, and acoustics, machine, sea, human labor, and dying fish are closely intertwined on a sensual level (Bee and Egert 2018). The ancient story of man and the sea is no longer told with man at the center. Rather, he is situated in an ecology of machines, sea, wind, weather, extremely hard work, and in the midst of mass fish mortality as well as a chain of actions that transforms fish from a living being into a commodity: lifting them out of the sea, cutting them up, then processing and freezing them on site. Man is no longer either the center of the narrative here or the center of agency. Man is part of this ecology of power, the power of capitalism and labor, the power of tides and weather. Close-ups of textures underline the materiality and the force of the aesthetic milieu of the ship. Textures like the smooth orange-colored rubber of rain

Figures 3.1–3.4 *Leviathan* (2012), dir. Lucien Castaing-Taylor and Véréna Paravel, New York: Cinema Guild.

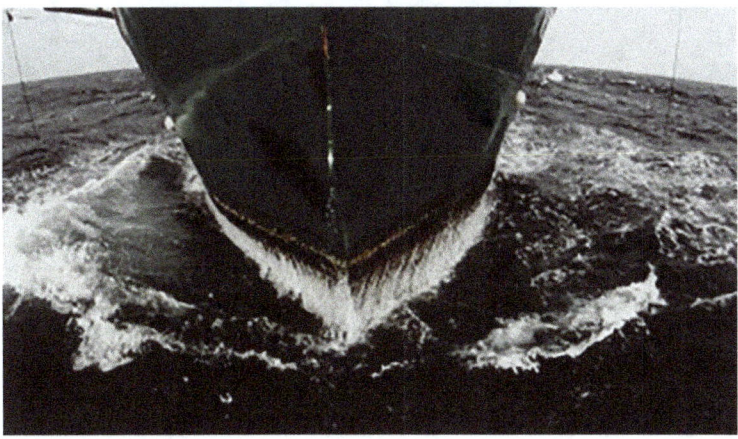

Figure 3.2

Figure 3.3

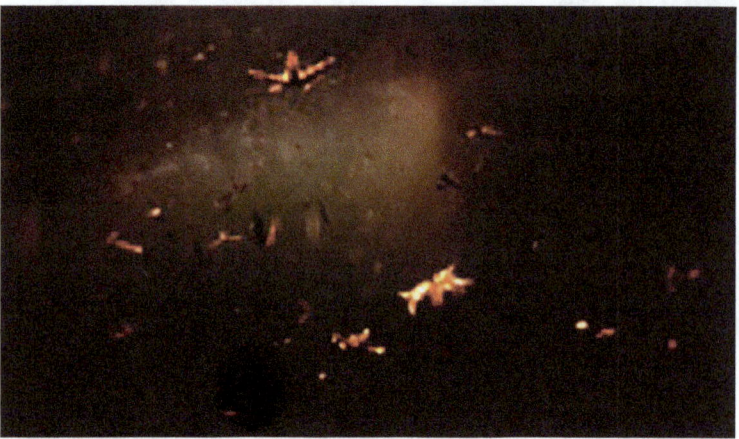

Figure 3.4

coats, the coarseness of the deck of the ship or water drops on the camera lens create zones of encounter between the experience of things and their agency.

Constant forces act on each other—this is made clear by the soundscape composed by Ernst Karel, in which human voices are also decentered, their conversations forming only one level of meaning among many acoustic levels, for example, the effervescent rushing and monotonous humming of the machines (Thain and Kara 2014). The ecology of sea, work, and machines forms a scene where the human being we encounter is situated. The human in the film *Leviathan* does not master the sea, s/he is a situational scenic figure that emerges from and then disappears again into the sea. The human is here a human *of* the milieu and not just *in* the milieu. *Leviathan* and the research apparatus connected with it makes visible a human connected to an environment, a human of the environment. The film also inscribes itself into this environment. Through GoPro cameras and wiggly close-ups of things, fish, and water, *Leviathan* experiments with immanent perspectives, what Macarena Gómez-Barris calls a "fish-eye episteme" (Gómez-Barris 2017: 91–109; see also Thain 2015). Instead of the bird's eye view of the distant gaze, it is an embedded, immanent perspective affirming participation in the environment (Thain 2015). The cinematic figure of the human, the cinematic research, and the milieu form a coherence: human and film alike work their way through the milieu.

In another work by Véréna Paravel and Lucien Castaing-Taylor titled *Ah humanity!* multiple forms of media are combined as a technique of visual research. In *Ah humanity!*—the title refers to Bartley's last words in Herman Melville's *Bartleby, the Scrivener* (1853/2020) as ascribed to him by the narrator—the two anthropologists focus on the mediality of knowledge production. The work combines optical and acoustic media to create a geology of knowledge (following the expression geologies of moral by Deleuze and Guattari (1987: 39–73)). Like *Leviathan*, the audiovisual installation creates a multimedia format of knowledge production highlighting sound and kinesthesia in vision. Instead of GoPros, like in *Leviathan*, vision is reflected by using smart phones combined with telescope lenses, reflecting the status of witnessing by using alienating perspectives. The combination of documentary, scientific, and fictional media points to fiction in reality, that creates the constant background noise of any documentary film and is seen as not only an interference but also a milieu in which the human exists. What is worked with in *Leviathan* is the myth of the sea, the narrative element of man and sea, of Moby Dick (also not coincidently written by Melville), of the colonial fascination with unknown land and so-called white spots. The title also refers to the Biblical-Talmudical mythical monster, Leviathan, whose features resemble those of the monsters—mostly dragons—marking unknown spots in medieval maps. Both pieces acknowledge the different forms of media with which the human is closely entangled—be it narrations, imagery, mobile phones, myth, or concrete media assemblages and dispositifs. Moreover, the media itself becomes an agentive force, namely the method of investigating the mediated existence of humans: a media-anthropological method of research into the entanglement of human and forms of media.

Figures 3.5–3.9 *Ah Humanity!* (2015), dir. Lucien Castaing-Taylor, Véréna Paravel, and Ernst Karel, Cambridge, MA: Sensory Ethnography Lab (SEL).

Figure 3.6

Ah humanity! is situated in Fukushima after the atomic meltdown caused by the earthquake and tsunami in the Tōhoku region in 2011. Through sound elements of disaster movies from Japan, recordings from memorial sites for the atomic bombings of Hiroshima and Nagasaki as well as geo-acoustic

Figure 3.7

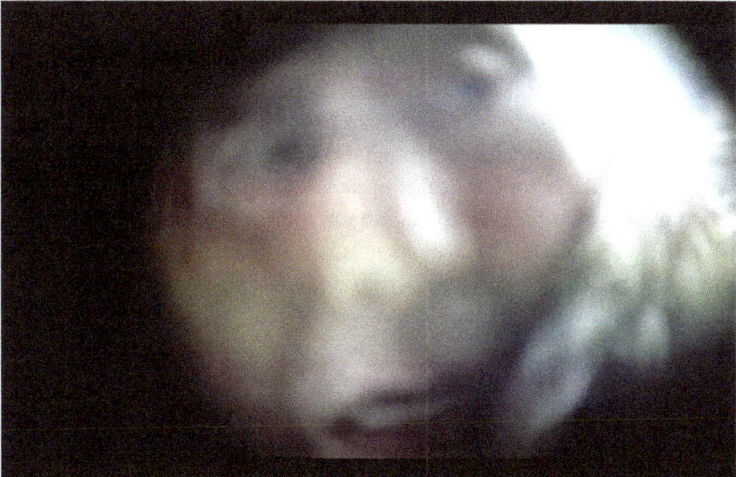

Figure 3.8

signals and images from a cell phone camera, the sound is haunting and addresses multiple levels of reality, past and present. It combines layers of trauma with the sound of earth movements. The film only uses images of the region taken after the catastrophe. The catastrophe has taken place already—in a double sense. The acoustic elements were created in the

Figure 3.9

cultural and traumatic aftershocks caused by the atomic bombs. The past catastrophe, which still lingers in the collective memory, overshadows the perception of the more current catastrophes. Here, the fictionalization of the catastrophe becomes a perceptual form of the current. Fictionalization thus brings with it a form of reality of its own. The different sound elements are combined with cell phone images from today's Fukushima. The imagery is taken by mobile phone cameras enlarged with telescopes. Thus, all the views framed by the circular aperture seem strangely distant since they also have an extreme zoom. The media of the documentary thus come into view, their particular materiality of being at the same time near and far. The temporal layers of the geological, the traumatic, and the current dimension embodied by the assembled forms of media are also near and far at once. The media assemblage thus articulates a mélange of temporal layers in its form that do not leave out the earth's interior: Part of the soundtrack is the geo-acoustic sound of the tsunami that originally caused the reactor meltdown at Fukushima, recorded with geophones by the ENS Geo lab in Paris. This geomedial assemblage (Cubitt 2017; Parikka 2015) characterizes the relationship between humans and their environment "in catastrophic times," as Isabelle Stengers (2015) puts it. Enclosed in this story of failed technological invincibility, with all its "fragility" (Nowak 2020) and volatility, is the fact that we are in the middle of a climate catastrophe and of a new mass extinction of animal and plant species. The film, through its media-technological layering of human and environmental trauma, thus examines catastrophes as complex, global, and nonlinear events. This attempt of understanding human impact in terms of scale, captured in the term Anthropocene, here becomes an artistic articulation oscillating between proximity and distance, between small human and large geological movements that are visually embodied in a visual-acoustic montage of urban movements and geo-acoustic recordings. This is similar to *Leviathan*, whose imagery is highly concrete and at the same time abstract, far and near, direct and metaphoric, embodied and symbolic, natural and artificial. Nature and culture come together here also on the level of sound (Thain and Kara 2014). The acoustic carpet interweaves human voices, engine room, and sea without making one the backdrop of the other. In *Ah humanity!* the earth is likewise not a background or stable, silent, passive underground. Just as the sea in *Leviathan* is "given a voice," Karel's acoustic installation also evokes the earth's liveliness via the geo-acoustic signals. One can read it as a reflection on the Anthropocene (Nowak 2020) and the role of the human being as a cause of catastrophe. What appears here is a human of catastrophe, a form of the "human of the film" (Engell 2015: 67, translation J. B.): The human appears as entangled with her catastrophic milieu. *Ah humanity!* situates the human of this toxic catastrophe in a larger catastrophe of an anthropogenic climate catastrophe and the mass extinction of species. Although humans— some human ways of living and extracting from the earth—are responsible for climate change, they appear not as a monolithic being. This paradox is reflected in *Leviathan* as well: *because* the human is cause of catastrophes her conditions are represented as a complex milieu and as entangled with other beings. The entanglement is not a way to muddy the sources of responsibility but an attempt to describe the multispecies entanglements (for multispecies thinking, see Haraway (2016)) including that of humans and media.

Both film and installation shed light on the entanglement of knowing and being that is produced. The media of research do not remain external to the scene but intervene in these geo-ontological events. The film interacts with a technical milieu and connects itself to it.

The technical and toxic milieu of nuclear contamination makes visible how closely interwoven and how inseparable human modes of being are from their environment, always on the verge of becoming ahuman—as the title *Ah humanity!* suggests. It is in this sense that *Ah humanity!* is a media-anthropological work. For the film does not merely represent or document, but speculates and philosophizes, explores, and even *participates*. *Leviathan* and *Ah humanity!* are not forms of representing existing knowledge, instead they generate and operationalize knowledge in a media-specific way, while reflecting their own mediality and use of media (Murphie 2014).

Knowledge and Being

Both films are apparatuses of knowledge production, not despite of but because of their deployment of fictional elements. In Karen Barad's sense, apparatuses are performative practices of measurement (Barad 2007: 141–6). Barad, writing from the perspective of quantum physics, describes the entanglement of apparatus and reality in generating knowledge in which the apparatus of measurement inscribes itself. Following the wave particle dualism debate by Bohr and Heisenberg, Barad sticks with Bohr in that the impact of apparatuses of measurement is not epistemological but has ontological consequences. Reality does not just withdraw its true nature from practices of measurement; these practices create different realities depending on the performance of the apparatus of measurement (ibid.: 115–18). Something very similar to this can be seen in documentary filmmaking (Sarris in Perez 1998: 46), in which there are different ways of approaching reality, and different techniques and styles produce different realities. Ethnographic film also generates specific entanglements of "knowing and being" (Barad 2007: 185).

As ethnographic filmmaker David MacDougall (1998: 246) writes, ethnographic films and texts not only create versions of the same but different realities. To me it is important that the knowledge a documentary film creates is, under certain circumstances, not just a different form of representation but a different form of knowledge *production*, comparable to interviews or other empirical methods. Also, as Barad (2007: 83) suggests, the nature of reality is not independent of apparatuses of measurement. In their respective works, Lucien Castaing-Taylor and Véréna Paravel not only record the various technical-social and ecological milieus to underline a media-anthropological argument of men and milieu mutually informing each other, but have apparatuses inscribe themselves in the scene and create a different technical milieu. They performatively combine practices and experiences, doing and perception and thereby create not only knowledge or a theory of, but also experiences of media anthropology.

Collaborative Filmmaking and Shared Anthropology

The second approach in ethnographic filmmaking that I want to consider in terms of media anthropology is cinéma vérité. I will take a detour to link the third movement of visual anthropology addressed here to the second one and make its influences visible.

All filmmaking is collaborative, but "collaborative filmmaking" in a more narrow sense addresses a specific practice of participatory filmmaking (White 2003). Collaborative filmmaking refers to participatory strategies in documentary filmmaking that enable people formerly filmed by documentary filmmakers or anthropologists to become agents in the filming of their lives—and they often become filmmakers, too (Seibel 2019). This can address power structures in representation—but cannot definitively solve all of them. It can, however, make media practices more accessible to change and transformation and is often discussed as a technique of empowerment (White 2003: 66; Zoettl 2012: 210–11).

Recent projects like *Les Sauteurs* (dir. Moritz Siebert, Estephan Wagner, Abou Bakar Sidibé 2016) document forced migration and life at the borders of "Fortress Europe" by providing cameras to those illegalized and pushed back, living in camps. In *Les Sauteurs*, filmmaker Abou Sidibé, who now lives in Berlin, documented his migration together with two filmmakers from Germany and Denmark. Another approach is that of ethnographic filmmaker David MacDougall, who educates children in India in film workshops to document their own lives (see, for instance, *Eleven in Delwara* 2014).

Historically and conceptually important shifts emerged during the 1960s (Crocker 2003; Waugh, Brendan, and Winton 2010). For example, the Canadian program Challenge for Change was rooted in movements of the new left that wanted to empower and educate people in their dealings with media technologies to participate in the creation of images of themselves. The aim was to provide citizens with knowledge about mass media and enable them to tell their own stories, to produce imagery and narrations of themselves (Druick 2010: 345). One can describe it as an early form of citizen science, except that it aims at empowerment and not so much at knowledge production. These approaches are rooted in the idea of creating a film with amateurs, of filming together. Bonnie Sherr Klein, for example, did work with a poor francophone community in *VTR St-Jacques* (1969). This was part of a larger initiative by the Canadian National Film Board, in which filmmakers and citizens collaborated on film projects.[1]

Facilitating participation in image production for those formerly filmed and framed by imagery also creates other forms of reception and identification and therefore empowerment. Working together on a film is a way of creating a collective, because people have to decide what is important to the community, what should be filmed, and how. So aesthetic and political forms of representation merge into the reflection of one's own social environment.

Many approaches of collaborative filmmaking go back to the work of "shared anthropology" emerging in the 1950s and 1960s (Seibel 2019). The concept famously stems from filmmaker Jean Rouch (2003: 44). Rouch worked a lot with young workers on the Ivory Coast in the 1950s and 1960s. He did not hand the camera over but tried to create spaces for those former objectivized to subjectivize themselves. He mostly did this by creating space to speak up or to work with reenactments of people's lives like in *Moi, un noir* (1958) (Hohenberger 1988: 285–327).

Rouch understood film experiments to be decolonial interventions. The notion of reality therefore became more complex and ambivalent by using film as an intervention. Reality and fiction blurred. This was because people were enabled to become someone else, partly amateur actors, playing their own lives. Today this is known as ethnofiction. Rouch intervened in reality instead of reproducing it as it is or was. And that was an important step in the decolonization of ethnographic filmmaking, although Rouch still was accused of not being entirely free of a colonial mindset (Sembène 1997). But, along with others, he triggered a movement of filmmaking that no longer sought to manifest reality as it is, but to change it through filmmaking.

Cinéma vérité emerged at the beginning of the 1960. In this movement documentary film was no longer seen only as a medium to get across information. Forms of voice-over to explain imagery were no longer deployed. New techniques emerged and were experimented with, not least because of technological developments like synch sound and light-weight cameras.

The production process itself gained in importance in relation to film as a product. This is where new conditions of documentary filmmaking not only create images of humans, but also change the conditions under which the human is seen as well as produced by film. This development was famously described by Gilles Deleuze (1989: 147) as a shift in the cinematic time of documentary filmmaking, which led to new forms of documentation. I suggest to understand this as a media-anthropological movement as well. Film here operates as an anthropomedia technology.

Fabulation

Gilles Deleuze refers to Rouch's practices as catching the protagonists "making legends" (Deleuze 1989: 151). Legends in this case are cultural artifacts or self-images that emerge because filmmakers seek out places and groups to tell a story and for film this story becomes the starting point for reflexive procedures of reenactment. What is of interest is no longer the profilmic, but the reality *of* the film, the intra-filmic reality: the reality of cinema instead of the cinema of reality as Deleuze (1989: 151) writes. This includes spontaneous actions in some scenes, deliberately staged provocations of the directors in others. For instance, Rouch, in *La pyramide humaine* (1961), asks Black and white youths from a high school graduating class in Abidjan to make friends in front of the camera. In *Moi, un noir* (1958) they give themselves new identities, modeled after famous film characters. In *Chronicle of a Summer* (1961) they dramatize their relationships: Rouch and his co-filmmaker Morin deliberately put their friends, workers, and intellectuals into new relationships. Everyday life and fiction are intentionally blurred. For Deleuze, there are no events or characters preceding the shooting, only the characters *of* the film. Film generates spaces for fictionalization or play, to refer to oneself as someone else instead of the reality that was very much influenced by the truth of the colonizer (Deleuze 1989: 150; 1990: 125–6).

The film literally becomes a "mediator" as Deleuze's term *intercesseurs* (1989: 222; 1990: 121–34) has been translated. What Deleuze describes as mediators can be seen as modes of existence, which are mutually related to their environment—in this case a film milieu. Similarly, Faye Ginsburg (1995) wrote of films by Indigenous collectives[2] as a mediation of social and cultural processes. I will come back to this later. Intercessors/mediators are persons or narrations, who or which help an author express what he wants while conversely the protagonists express their story through the author (Deleuze 1990: 125). In Pierre Perrault's, Marcel Carrière's and Michel Brault's *Pour la suite du monde* (1963), these are the forgotten whaling techniques that were still practiced in the 1920s. In the 1960s, Perrault wanted to make a film about the community on Isle-aux-Coudres in the St. Lawrence River in Canada. On the occasion of the filming, the practice of beluga whaling is reconstructed. Here, the francophone islanders "use" the author Perrault for their cultural self-discovery, while Perrault uses the minoritarian French to film his story (Deleuze 1990: 125–6). In doing so, he makes his contribution to the emancipation of Franco-Canadian culture—both become mutual intercessors. Even today, the film remains an important reference point of cultural identity for French Canadians. Central to the film is speaking Québécois, a political act when Québec was not yet officially francophone. The history of whaling is reconstructed and an excess of oral history of how to reconstruct history emerges. Most importantly, the storytelling of a fictionalized origin practice generates ever-new versions. So, too, a whaling that allows the whale to live (but, terribly, in an aquarium!). Ultimately, the film captures this negotiation and discourse, the dispute over the correct reconstruction—the practice of recounting the past itself becomes its *sujet*. The negotiation becomes its content and its form, the milieu for new individuations to emerge, thus causing new modes of existence. The film itself becomes a catalyst for this negotiation, in which many voices are heard and generations begin to communicate with each other again (Scheppler 2006). The film of cinéma vérité or cinéma vécu (Deleuze 1989: 150) is here a practical or pragmatic form of media anthropology, a film about modes of existence that are created in and for the film.

From the Cinema of Practices to a "Cinema of Ways of Existence" (Deleuze 1989: 127)

Originally, Bergson used fabulation to refer to culture as the ossification of life, acquiring a momentum of its own and disconnecting from élan vital. Deleuze's affirmative treatment of the term understands culture—Bergson refers primarily to religion in *The Two Sources of Morality and Religion* (1935)—as itself a source of fabulation. Cinéma vérité and direct cinema valorize this speaking for itself. By the end of the 1950s, people could speak in films with synchronized sound. With the documentary film of the 1960s, speaking as free indirect speech began, first in the films of Pier Paolo Pasolini, who employed the direct tone of interviews (Deleuze 1989: 148). In the 1960s, Rouch's films responded to the problem of speech. This problem is at the same time an ethical one, that of the documentary giving voice to people perceived to be without adequate media representation; a technical one, that of the possibility of synchronous sound; and a philosophical one, that of existentialism, structuralism, and discourse. This complex refers to direct speech in documentary: with synchronous sound recording and the styles of cinéma vérité and direct cinema, spoken language can take root in film and a *"cinema of the speech act"* (Deleuze 1989: 222) emerges. This speech is performative in its consequences of forming a collective in and through filmmaking (Deleuze 1989: 221).

Deleuze discusses this in a later chapter in reference to anticolonial filmmaking in the Americas and Africa. Because colonialism erased references to one's own culture—languages were banned, structures destroyed—any reference to self in the Third Cinema films discussed by Deleuze is necessarily a fabulation, a documentation that creates a milieu.[3] It becomes a documentation of the future, so to speak. In collective practices and speech acts, the fabulative practices continue as group-forming: a so-called people emerges in films by Ousmane Sembène (*Ceddo* 1977) or Glauber Rocha (*Black God, White Devil*, 1964; *Entranced Earth*, 1967; *Antonio das mortes*, 1969). Unlike the masses in Eisenstein's cinema, who were able to perceive themselves as revolutionary subjects in the film, here the film is more than a representation of the oppressed classes; it is a mediator of the group, a direct tool for political formation (Deleuze 1990).

The crucial point here is that instead of representing, film intervenes and forces us to act differently. "I is another," Deleuze (1989: 133) writes about the rupture of the documentary in the modern procedures of the camera provocateur, quoting Rimbaud. Film thus becomes a vehicle of becoming other, it provokes dramatizations of everyday life, of relationships and subjectivity. Film thus participates directly in these processes, it does not show them from the outside. In this way, theory is not depicted but embodied. Following the Canadian cinéma vécu as by Perrault, one might say: it is lived. Here, we find another form of what can be termed an experience-image in the aftermath of Deleuze.

Indigenous Collaborative Filmmaking

Practices of cinema vérité that were the basis for more playful and spontaneous filming of everyday life were taken up in the collaborative and activist films of groups in Brazil in the 1980s (Aufderheide 2008; Graham 2014a, b). Indigenous film has been used as "cultural activism" (Graham 2014a: 90) to self-archive culture in a processual way (Lacerda 2018), connect with other groups (ibid.: 6), and organize politically. From the mid-1990s, for example, the NGO Vídeo nas Aldeias (*Video in the Villages*) has directly applied techniques from cinéma vérité to train film enthusiasts (Aufderheide 2008; Lacerda 2018; Vídeo nas Aldeias 2014).[4] Mari Corrêa, filmmaker of Vídeo nas Aldeias and Instituto Catitu, participated in the documentary film workshops *Ateliers Varan*, founded with the support of Jean Rouch in Paris, and brought these techniques to Vídeo nas Aldeias (Graham 2014a: 90). In particular, spontaneous everyday actions and playful performance with and for the camera are in the foreground. In *Bicicletas de nhanderú* (dir. Patrícia Ferreira, Ariel Duarte Ortega 2011), for example, two children spontaneously perform a version of Michael Jackson's *Beat It*, while before and after this they instruct the cameraperson on how to film trees, or where ghosts live (Graham 2014b: 88).

Film has been used in the Americas since the mid-1990s to create a panindigenous transcultural communication, as Freya Schiwy (2009) argues, for self-presentation and thus self-determination of one's own image, for example, in *From the Ikpeng Children to the World* (dir. Natuyu Yuwipo Txicão, Karané Txicão, and Kumaré Txicão 2001), a video letter from the point of view of children.

Film in these instances becomes an important part of cultural communication, with the Brazilian public and with the international public, which is to be informed about land theft and unpunished or underinvestigated killings of activists (see Vincent Carelli's, Tatiana Almeida's, and Ernesto de Carvalho's Film *Martírio*, 2016), as a counter-film to stereotypes and a means of engaging with film culture (Graham 2014b: 88). But, most importantly, film also creates a record of cultural practices. It becomes a way to create a living heritage that does not "pre-exist[s] filming" (Lacerda 2018: 7). Video and film are integrated into other cultural practices and creatively appropriated, as Turner (2002) argues (see also Ginsburg 1995). Cinematic forms of communication can be used to contact other Indigenous groups or present oneself (Graham 2014b: 87).

From a media-anthropological perspective, a knowledge different from the knowledge of anthropology also emerges. This includes, for example, testimonials of the climate catastrophe, told by those impacted by deforestation and agroindustry as well as by illegal logging as the documentaries produced among others by Instituto Catitu show (*Heat*, 2019, Mari Corrêa; *Where Did the Swallows Go*, 2016, Mari Corrêa; *Ka'a Zar, Ukyze Wà* (Forest Owners in Danger), 2019, Flay Guajajara, Edivan dos Santos Guajajara, and Erisvan Bone Guajajara). Forms of collaborative filmmaking did not just adapt the ethnographic perspective and self-applied it, they changed it entirely combining "cultural production with ethnographic representation" (Bessiner 2009: 103). The audience has changed in equal measure, and this is no accident. It is not the presentation of the other marked as foreign to the North American or European audience that is foregrounded, but other Indigenous groups: "indigenous media creates networks through which indigenous communities exchange information and thus create the possibility of developing alternative forms of political and economic organization" (Schiwy 2009: 57).

Film also becomes the occasion for negotiating what is "one's culture," what is worth filming, visible or invisible, and who has the right to film; collective reception thus becomes a feedback loop. The anthropologist Terence Turner calls this "self-dramatization" in his work on Brazil referring to Faye Ginsburg's (1995) work on Indigenous mediation of culture through filmmaking:

> The act of video-making itself, when done to by an indigenous person or member of a local community, begins to "mediate" a variety of social and political relationships within the indigenous community .... In the process, cultural forms, together with the capacity and motivation of social actors to produce them, are reinforced, rearticulated, and transformed in various ways through the use of new techniques of

representation and new social forms of utilizing and circulating them. (Turner 2002: 78)

This self-dramatization speaks to the performative or even operational nature of films that take up the experimental character of cinéma vérité with its reenactments and collective storytelling. Within complex knowledge practices, film also plays an altered role. It is performative not only in relation to viewers' experiences, that is, creating sensation, but also in the very making, especially in involving the community (White 2003).

Films like *A gente luta mas come fruta*/We Struggle But We Eat Fruit (Wewito Piyãko, Isaac Pinhanta 2006) also show concrete cultivation practices of forest and soil and form an archive of socio-ecological knowledge. *We Struggle But We Eat Fruit* presents plants and animals as well as practices of filmmaking itself together, on one "flat" plane (Latour 2005: 171–2) (Figures 3.10–3.13).

Through the film it becomes clear how much work is involved in the supposedly wild forest (a typical colonial image) and what role film can play in the preservation of a cultural ecology. Local knowledge, such as how seedlings are conserved, or how water turtles are raised, is shown in *We Struggle But We Eat Fruit* as an educational practice for the coming generation

Figures 3.10–3.13 *A gente luta mas come fruta*/We Struggle But We Eat Fruit (2006), dir. Wewito Piyako and Isaac Pinhanta, Olinda, Pernambuco: Vídeo nas Aldeias.

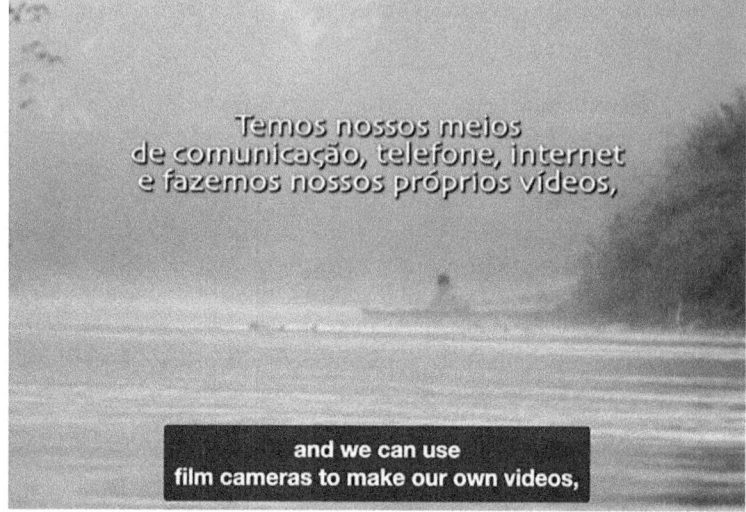

Figure 3.11

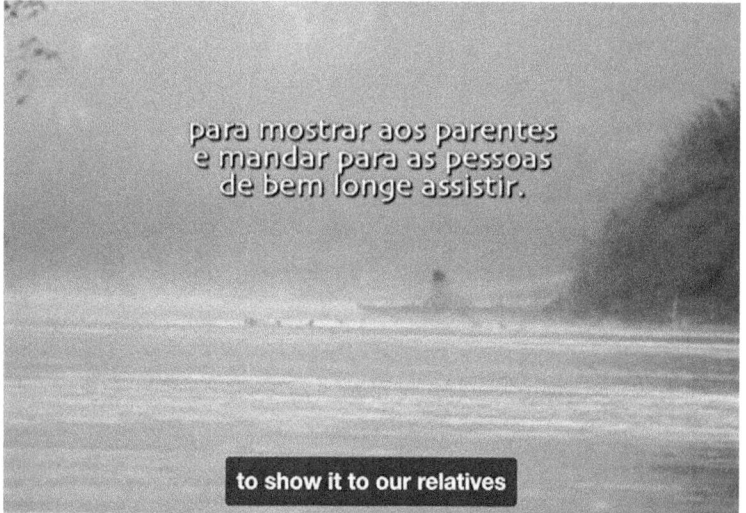

Figure 3.12

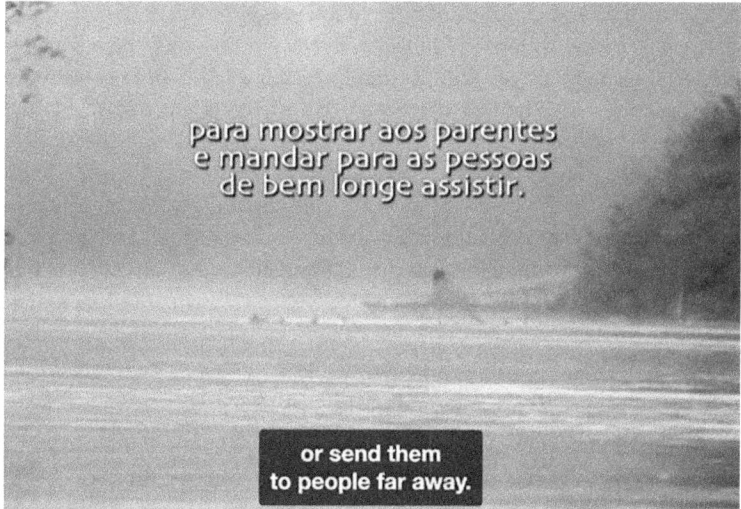

Figure 3.13

and other local groups. Here, a different knowledge is generated by gathering knowledge together with the filmmakers for the film and thus archiving it audiovisually. By becoming itself part of "inter-indigenous alliances" (Schiwy 2009: 103) as well as epistemic counter knowledge that subverts forms and "flows of knowledge" (Schiwy 2009: 59), film thus essentially shapes cultural, collective, and individual self-relations as well as relationships with other groups with whom to associate and share knowledge as Freya Schiwy describes it in relation to Andean filmmaking (Schiwy 2009: 72).

The archive created by film is in transition because it also includes the struggle to form that archive and the feedback loop to those involved. From a media-anthropological perspective focusing on the relation of media and human modes of existence, film is part of several cultural practices and techniques. Film practices take part in creating human–media relationships.

This becomes clear in the Instituto Catitu production *My first contact/ Pïrinop* (Mari Corrêa and Karané Ikpeng 2005), in which the past is reenacted from different points of view to complement the recordings of the anthropologists who resettled the group of the Ikpeng in 1964. This technique of reenactment, which cinéma vérité also used, is deployed to creatively challenge anthropology's archive and its method of knowledge production. Here, film acts as a catalyst for processes that show the performative nature of culture and how deeply it is entangled with techniques and practices of memory, appropriation of cultural techniques, and bricolage. For example, different versions of the first contact are replayed one after the other in a theatrical manner, but the film does not present any of them as being more true than the rest. The film accompanies how the group documents the negotiation processes involved. The turning back to one's roots becomes a new becoming for the group. Questions like "Where to?," "How?," "With whom?," "What maps are there?" aim not only at finding the origin, but also at departure and the negotiation of a future place of belonging. And this place can be found by working through the past and archival material. Film here becomes a mediator for collective processes seen through Deleuze's notion of fabulation as a political tool (1990). Film can transform *and* strengthen culture at the very same time (Lacerda 2018).

In *Pĩrinop, We Struggle But We Eat Fruit*, and other films, the situation of shooting the film is itself shown and thus the materiality and media are explicit subjects of negotiation. They refer to the joint work, discuss its usefulness, criticize how something was recorded. Just as in *Pour la suite du monde*, it is about filming as an occasion and as an aesthetic and sociocultural practice. While in the case of the fishermen in Canada it was whaling, here it is other cultural techniques that reinforce and intensify their performance in the media of film. Here film is more than a form of documentary representation. It becomes a practice of anthropomediality.

Deleuze extends the notion of fabulation to decolonial cinematographies of the Third cinema. Filmmaking here establishes a minor language, a new consciousness of a "people ... [that] are missing" (Deleuze 1989: 220) and have to be constituted by media like film. In *Cinema 2: The Time-Image*, the concept of fabulation has the task of de-essentializing both thinking and a people.

In the destructive relations of colonialism, which is the context of the films Deleuze refers to with his notion of fabulation, world relations became fragile. Inside and outside became equally political, and so it is not surprising that the speech act, free indirect speech, finally replaces the inwardness of thinking in the cinema books. Since cinema changed after the Second World War and after the Shoah, the sensorimotor bond also breaks. The film of the time-image responds to this with a direct image of time as well as a direct thinking: film can no longer show the world, it must itself provide the "link" (Deleuze 1989: 172) to the world anew: It becomes a media-anthropologic technique. Deleuze suggests this in relation to neorealism, but also to cinéma vérité. If we follow that line of thought in relation to collaborative and/or Indigenous film practices, the films of *Vídeo nas Aldeias* and *Instituto Catitu* contain this bond to the world directly, they establish multiple links by making cinema a practice of "cultural activism" (Graham 2014a) or "activist documentary" (Waugh, Brendan, and Winton 2010). The cinema has passed into a practice, a "cinema of modes of existence." Film creates bonds to the world, through the world of practices (Deleuze 1989: 280).

Although the film projects I introduced here hail from different contexts, they all shift the focus from the product to processes of production (Bessire 2009: 101; White 2003: 64–6; Zoettl 2012) and shed light on the media that is part of what the film documents. They all show or performatively enact the entanglement of humans with media *by* using media technologies. Film here figures both as an apparatus of knowledge production as well as a tool for community building (Crocker 2003: 132). Both operations intersect. They produce a different form of knowledge, no longer a representation of anthropology. That is one reason why collaborative films can be discussed in relation to knowledge practices without subsuming them under the somewhat problematic label of "ethnographic films." The specific materiality of film refers to a form of situatedness (Haraway 1988), it demonstrates that knowledge has different forms with a crucial impact on the production and distribution of knowledge.

This knowledge is situated reflecting the specific social contexts in which knowledge is produced and by whom. Even more, to echo Karen Barad, it is an entanglement of knowing and being, in which film is first entangled with reality, and second provokes collective processes. The becoming of knowledge, the becoming of a film, and the becoming of a group are mutually entangled processes in collaborative filmmaking.

Film becomes a medium that no longer creates knowledge through its detachment from, but precisely through its embeddedness in media-cultural practices in collaborative filmmaking. Film can be described as "thinking [filming] through the milieu," to use a term by Isabelle Stengers (2005: 187).

From Visual Anthropology to Media Anthropologies

The pragmatic turn in the consideration of visual anthropology, primarily theoretically traced and developed here by Deleuze's two books on cinema, shifts the perspective from representation to that of an anthropomedial relation between human and films. Media anthropology, as I understand it following Voss, perceives entanglements of humans and media to be modes of existence. Visual anthropology also can be seen as participating in this very process of performing the entanglements of humans and media. In all three approaches of visual anthropology that I discussed here—sensory film, cinéma vérité, collaborative filmmaking—questions of representation are expanded into questions of media-anthropological practices: they become an intervention in and/or a milieu for modes of existence, which are entangled with forms of media. All three approaches are also closely related to the knowledge practices of visual anthropology.[5] With the films of Lucien Castaing-Taylor and Véréna Paravel, specific apparatuses of knowledge production emerge that closely intertwine man and milieu and also inscribe the practice of filmmaking in them. With the action-oriented forms of cinéma vérité, fabulations emerge that facilitate cinematic living conditions or milieus. In collaborative filmmaking, in turn, forms of knowledge emerge from collective projects. All three formats intertwine human, milieu, and film into media-anthropological modes of existence—like the human of the (milieu of the) catastrophe in *Ah humanity!* and film collectives in *Pour la suite du monde* and Vídeo nas Aldeias/Instituto Catitu. These forms of filmmaking create shared forms of knowledge production as an embodied, practical media anthropology.

Notes

1. Influences of the cinemas of the 1960s are found today in *Wapikoni mobile*. Here, mobile traveling video workshops offer support to communities to make documentaries or video essays about their lives and to facilitate professionalization in First Nation filmmaking, see Bee (2021).
2. Barclay (2003a, 2003b) extends the notion of Third cinema (see footnote 3) to an Indigenous Fourth Cinema, one that controls the conditions under which it is produced by Indigenous filmmakers instead of just narrating Indigenous stories by non-Indigenous directors. "Fourth" here does not point to a hierarchy but differentiates this kind of cinema from First (Hollywood), Second (auteur) and Third (decolonial) cinema (see on differences between Third and Indigenous cinema also Schiwy (2009: 55, 73–84, 163–4)).
3. Third cinema refers to the decolonial cinematic practices that were established in the 1960s in former colonies. See Solanas and Getino (1997) programmatic text on this subject.
4. VNA was founded in 1987.
5. Although collaborative and Indigenous filmmaking are interventions into the politics of representation of ethnographic filmmaking, they are not to be understood as self-proclaimed ethnographies about oneself. This is related to a different understanding of ethnography in a sense of post-anthropological modes of knowledge production that change the ways of knowing themselves.

References

Ah Humanity! (2015), [Film] Dir. Lucien Castaing-Taylor, Véréna Paravel, and Ernst Karel, Cambridge, MA: Sensory Ethnography Lab (SEL).

Antonio das Mortes (1969), [Film] Dir. Glauber Rocha, Rio de Janeiro: Mapa Filmes.

Aufderheide, P. (2008), "You See the World of the Other and You Look at Your Own: The Evolution of the Video in the Villages Project," *Journal of Film and Video* 60 (2): 26–34.

Barad, K. (2007), *Meeting the Universe Halfway: Quantum Physics and the Entanglement of Matter and Meaning*, Durham, NC: Duke University Press.

Barclay, B. (2003a), "An Open Letter to John Barnett from Barry Barclay," *Onfilm* 20: 11–14.

Barclay, B. (2003b), "Celebrating Fourth Cinema," *Illusions* 3: 7–11.

Bee, J. (2017), "Erfahrungsbilder und Fabulationen. Im Archiv der Visuellen Anthropologie," in Lena Stölz and Vrääth Öhner (eds.), *Sichtbar-Machen. Politiken des Dokumentarischen*, 93–110, Berlin: Vorwerk 8.

Bee, J., and G. Egert (2018), "Waves of Experience: Atmosphere and Leviathan," in Susanne Schmitt and Sara Asu Schroer (eds.), *Exploring Atmospheres Ethnographically*, 102–14, London: Routledge.

Bee, J. (2021), "Prekäre Dokumentarismen—mediale Trans/Individuationen. Von Challenge for Change bis Wapikoni Mobile," in Astrid Deuber-Mankowsky and Philipp Hanke (eds.), *Queere Ästhetiken als Dokumentation des Prekären*, 249–75, Berlin/Vienna: Turia und Kant.

Bergson, H. (1935), *The Two Sources of Morality and Religion*, London: Macmillan & Co.

Bessire, L. (2009), "From the Ground, Looking Up: Report on the Vídeo nas Aldeias Tour," *American Anthropologist* 111 (1): 101–3.

Bicicletas de Nhanderú (2011), [Film] Dir. Patricia Ferreira and Ariel Duarte Ortega, Olinda, Pernambuco: Vídeo nas Aldeias.

Black God, White Devil (1964), [Film] Dir. Glauber Rocha, Rio de Janeiro: Copacabana Filmes.

Ceddo (1977), [Film] Dir. Ousmane Sembène, Dakar, Senegal: Filmi Doomi Reew.

Chronicle of a Summer (1961), [Film] Dir. Edgar Morin and Jean Rouch, France: Argos Films.

Cubitt, S. (2017), "Three Geomedia," *Ctrl-Z 2017*. Available online: http://www.ctrl-z.net.au/articles/issue-7/cubitt-three-geomedia/ (accessed June 27, 2022).

Crocker, S. (2003), "The Fogo Process. Participatory Communication in a Globalizing World," in S. A. White (ed.), *Participatory Video. Images That Transform and Empower*, 122–41, New Delhi: Sage.

Deleuze, G. (1989), *Cinema 2: The Time-Image*, Minneapolis: University of Minnesota Press.

Deleuze, G. (1990), "Mediators," in *Negotiations*, 121–34, New York: Columbia University Press.

Deleuze, G., and F. Guattari (1987), *A Thousand Plateaus. Capitalism and Schizophrenia 2*, Minneapolis: University of Minnesota Press.

Druick, Z. (2010), "Meeting at the Poverty Line: Government Policy, Social Work, and Media Activism in the Challenge for Change Project," in T. Waugh, M. B. Baker, and E. Winton (eds.), *Challenge for Change: Activist Documentary at the National Film Board of Canada*, 337–53, Montréal: McGill-Queen's University Press.

Eleven in Delwara (2014), [Film] Dir. Mumta Prajapet, Shaied Mohammed, Puja Prajapet, Monish Prajapet, Mayank Ved, Kundan Talwar, Kiran Khartik, Khalid Hussein, and David MacDougall, Berkeley, CA: Berkeley Media.

Elsaesser, Thomas and Malte Hagener (2015), *Film Theory: An Introduction through the Senses*, 2nd ed. New York: Routledge.

Engell, L. (2015), "Der Film zwischen Ontografie und Anthropogenese," in Voss, Christiane / Engell, Lorenz (eds.), *Mediale Anthropologie*, 63–82, Munich: Fink.

Entranced Earth (1967), [Film] Dir. Glauber Rocha, Rio de Janeiro: Difilm.

Foucault, M. (1995), *Discipline and Punish: The Birth of the Prison*, New York: Vintage Books.

From Ikpeng Children to the World (2001), [Film] Dir. Kumaré Txicão, Karané Txicão, and Natuyu Yuwipo Txicão, Olinda, Pernambuco: Vídeo nas Aldeias.

A gente luta mas come fruta (We Struggle But We Eat Fruit) (2006), [Film] Dir. Wewito Piyãko and Isaac Pinhanta, Olinda, Pernambuco: Vídeo nas Aldeias.

Ginsburg, F. (1995), "Mediating Culture. Indigenous Media, Ethnographic Film, and the Production of Identity," in L. Devereaux and R. Hillman (eds.), *Fields of Vision: Essays in Film Studies, Visual Anthropology, and Photography*, 256–91, Berkeley: University of California Press.

Gómez-Barris, M. (2017), *The Extractive Zone: Social Ecologies and Decolonial Perspectives*, Durham, NC: Duke University Press.

Graham, Z. (2014a), "'Since You Are Filming I Will Tell the Truth': A Reflection on the Cultural Activism and Collaborative Filmmaking of Vídeo nas Aldeias," *Visual Anthropology Review* 30 (1): 89–91.

Graham, Z. (2014b), "Three Decades of Amazonian Filmmaking," *Anthropology Now* 6 (1): 89–91.

Grimshaw, A., and A. Ravetz (eds.) (2005), *Visualizing Anthropology. Experimenting with Image-Based Ethnography*, Portland: New Media Intellect Books.

Haraway, D. (2016), *Staying with the Trouble. Making Kin in the Chthulucene*. Durham, NC: Duke University Press.

Haraway, D. (1988), "Situated Knowledges: The Science Question in Feminism and the Privilege of Partial Perspective," *Feminist Studies*, 14: 575–99.

Heat (2019), [Film] Dir. Mari Corrêa, São Paulo: Instituto Catitu and Rede de Cooperação Amazônica (RCA).

Heider, K. (1976), *Ethnographic Film*, Austin: University of Texas Press.

Hohenberger, E. (1988), *Die Wirklichkeit des Films. Dokumentarfilm. Ethnographischer Film. Jean Rouch*, Hildesheim: Georg Olms Verlag.

Kaplan, A. E. (1997), *Looking for the Other: Feminism, Film, and the Imperial Gaze*, New York: Routledge.
Ka'a Zar, Ukyze Wà (Forest Owners in Danger) (2019), [Film] Dir. Flay Guajajara, Edivan dos Santos Guajajara, and Erisvan Bone Guajajara, Brazil: Mídia Índia.
Lacerda, R. (2018), *The Collaborative Indigenous Cinema of Video nas Aldeias and the Intangible Cultural Heritage*, Memoriamedia Review, 3: 1–12.
Latour, B. (2005), *Reassembling the Social, an Introduction to Actor-Network-Theory*, Oxford: Oxford University Press.
Latour, B. (2013), *An Inquiry into Modes of Existence: An Anthropology of the Moderns*, Cambridge, MA: Harvard University Press.
Leviathan (2012), [Film] Dir. Lucien Castaing-Taylor and Véréna Paravel, New York: Cinema Guild.
Les Sauteurs (Those Who Jump) (2016), [Film] Dir. Moritz Siebert, Estephan Wagner, and Abou Bakar Sidibé, Denmark: Final Cut for Real.
MacDougall, D. (1998), *Transcultural Cinema*, Princeton, NJ: Princeton University Press.
Martírio (2016), [Film] Dir. Vincent Carelli, Tatiana Almeida, and Ernesto de Carvalho, Olinda, Pernambuco: Vídeo nas Aldeias.
Melville, H. ([1853] 2020), *Bartleby, the Scrivener: A Story of Wall Street*, Berlin: Insel Verlag.
Moi, un noir (1958), [Film] Dir. Jean Rouch, Paris: Films de la Pléiade.
Murphie, A. (2014), "Making Sense: The Transformation of Documentary by Digital and Networked Media," *Studies in Documentary Film* 8 (3): 188–204.
My First Contact/Pïrinop (2005), [Film] Dir. Mari Corrêa and Karané Ikpeng, São Paulo: Instituto Catitu.
Nowak, A. (2020), "Ah Humanity!," in *Exhibition Catalogue Ah Humanity!* Kunsthaus Hamburg. Available online: https://kunsthaushamburg.de/wp-content/uploads/2020/04/Besucherblatt_Ah-humanity-komprimiert.pdf (accessed June 27, 2022).
Parikka, J. (2015), *A Geology of Media*, Minneapolis: University of Minnesota Press.
Perez, G. (1998), *The Material Ghost. Films and Their Medium*, Baltimore, MD: Johns Hopkins University Press.
Pink, S. (2013), *Doing Visual Ethnography. Images, Media, and Representation in Research*, London: Sage.
Pour la suite du monde (1963), [Film] Dir. Michel Brault and Pierre Perrault, Montreal, Canada: National Film Board of Canada (NFB).
Rouch, J. (2003), *Ciné-Ethnography*, ed. Steven Feld, Minneapolis: University of Minnesota Press.
Scheppler, G. (2006), "Pour la suite du monde," in J. White (ed.), *The Cinema of Canada*, 43–50. London: Wallflower Press.
Schiwy, F. (2009), *Indianizing Film: Decolonization, the Andes, and the Question of Technology*, New Brunswick: Rutgers University Press.

Schneider, A., and Wright Christopher (2013), *Anthropology and Arts Practice*, London: Bloomsbury.
Seibel, S. (2019), "Die Kamera übergeben. Montage und kollaboratives Filmemachen in Les Sauteurs," in M. Doll (ed.), *Cutting Egde. Positionen zur Filmmontage*, 157–85, Berlin: Bertz & Fischer.
Sembène, O. (1997), "'Tu nous regarde comme des insectes', Du schaust uns an, als wären wir Insekten. Eine historische Gegenüberstellung zwischen Jean Rouch und Ousmane Sembène" (1965), in M. H. Gutberlet and P. Metzler (eds.), *Afrikanisches Kino*, 29–32, Bad Honnef, Germany: Horlemann.
Simondon, G. (2020), *Individuation in Light of Notions of Form and Information*, Minneapolis: University of Minnesota Press.
Simondon, G. (2009), "The Position of the Problem of Ontogenesis," *Parrhesia* 7: 9–16.
Solanas, F., and O. Getino (1997), "Towards a Third Cinema. Notes and Experiences for the Development of a Cinema of Liberation in the Third World," in M. T. Martin (ed.), *New Latin American Cinema. Volume One: Theories, Practices, and Transcontinental Articulations*, 33–58, Detroit, MI: Wayne State University Press.
Souriau, È. (2015), *The Different Modes of Existence*, Minneapolis: University of Minnesota Press.
Stengers, I. (2015), *In Catastrophic Times: Resisting the Coming Barbarism*, London: Open Humanities Press.
Stengers, I. (2005), "Introductory Notes on an Ecology of Practices," *Cultural Studies Review* 11 (1): 183–96.
Thain, A. (2015), "A Bird's-Eye View of *Leviathan*," *Visual Anthropology Review* 31 (1): 41–8.
Thain, A., and S. Kara (2014), "Sonic Ethnographies: Leviathan and New Materialisms in Documentary," in Holly Rogers (ed.), *Music and Sound in Documentary Film*, 186–9, New York: Routledge.
Turner, T. (2002), "Representation, Politics, and Cultural Imagination in Indigenous Video: General Points and Kayapo Examples," in F. D. Ginsburg, L. Abu-Lughod, and B. Larkin (eds.), *Media Worlds: Anthropology on New Terrain*, 75–89, Berkeley: University of California Press.
Vídeo nas Aldeias (2014), *Vídeo nas Aldeias 25 Anos*. Available online: http://videonasaldeias.org.br/loja/livros/ (accessed June 27, 2022).
Voss, C. (2019), "Anthropomediale Perspektiven," in Philipp Stoellger (ed.), *Figurationen des Menschen. Studien zur Medienanthropologie*, 33–51. Königshausen: Würzburg.
VTR St-Jacques (1969), [Film] Dir. Bonnie Sherr Klein, Montreal, Canada: National Film Board of Canada (NFB).
Waugh, T., M. Baker Brendan, and E. Winton (2010), *Challenge for Change. Activist Documentary at the National Film Board*, Montréal: McGill University Press.
Where Did the Swallows Go (2016), [Film] Dir. Mari Corrêa, Brazil: Instituto Catitu and Instituto Socioambiental.

White, S. A. (2003), "Participatory Video. A Process That Transforms the Self and the Other," in S. A. White (ed.), *Participatory Video. Images That Transform and Empower*, 63–102, London: Sage.

Zoettl, P. A. (2012), "Images of Culture: Participatory Video, Identity and Empowerment," *International Journal of Cultural Studies* 16 (2): 209–24.

4

A Life in the Interstices: Micropolitics and Aesthetics in Everyday Life

Christoph Carsten

In this essay, I am trying to develop a new perspective on what everyday life is, on what it does, and especially on how it becomes what it is. I want to develop a notion of the everyday that no longer conceives it as a banal sphere of dull routine, habit, and repetition where nothing ever happens. Everyday experience, here, is not conceived as something that only happens in the consciousness of a human subject but as a spectrum, which—even though it might tend toward the repetition of the same in some cases—is at the same time full of potential and traversed by untimely forces that lead to constant change, however slightly this might be. Anthropological questions are thus central to the project, but in a way that at the same time challenges conventional conceptions of anthropology, as will become clear in the further course. By foregrounding the relationality of everyday practices, I want to make the everyday understandable as a specific quality of experience that is always more than human. With this in mind, the concept of affect plays a key role because it is all about the relations that hold us, that we live, and that we ultimately are, day by day.

With this relational and processual perspective, I want to point to the fact that there is an other-worldly potential immanent in every event of the everyday. All of this could be considered a political, or at least proto-political, question. It is true that the everyday unfolds within certain power relations that materialize in particular normative subjectivities. However, as I will argue in the further course of this essay, the apparatuses of power can never fully control the excess of experience from which the everyday emerges. There is always something more, a life stirring underneath what at first glance seems solid and stable. This is why it is important how we live this dimension of the *what else*, how we care for our becoming-with-the-world, and which practices we engage in during the process. What I call micropolitics here is not necessarily small, it is not a question of scale. It is about qualitative transformations in the different ways of living our relations, about new associations, affinities, and affects. This is a politics of entanglement directly investing in the anthropomedial relations that make us in continuous variation.[1] It happens in the interstices of everyday life.

The Everyday Escapes

The line of thought I would like to engage in here starts from Maurice Blanchot's essay "Everyday Speech." The main thesis of Blanchot's text is that the everyday escapes. He goes on to ask: "Why does it escape?" (Blanchot 1987: 18). Living the everyday, I must abandon myself to something that is beyond my control, that is not only beyond and beneath language, but also beyond conscious perception, quantifiability, the law, the subject/object divide. The everyday is not private or personal, it does not refer to the life of an individual (Blanchot 1987: 18–19). Nor is it public, in the sense of being fully determined by the structures of society at a given moment. Even though I intuitively seem to know what is meant by the notion of everyday life and have an even stronger feeling for it. A quantitative enumeration does not seem able to capture everyday life in its emergent complexity. There is always something more, stirring in the background, hardly ever consciously perceived, and for which I lack the words. That means: something always resists the attempt to be put into a final and stable concept of everyday life, establishing resistance itself as a key factor at the heart of what the everyday might be or could possibly do. No matter how many elements I want to add to the list, the everyday keeps running through my fingers like sand. It is like the futile attempt to get hold of the stream of experience by grabbing it with my hands.

Blanchot's "Everyday Speech" presents itself as a review of Henri Lefebvre's works on everyday life. But far from simply tracing Lefebvre's train of thought to verify or criticize the consistency of his argument, Blanchot builds on Lefebvre's work to develop his own concept of the everyday. Whereas Lefebvre is especially interested in how capitalist modernity affects the everyday as a totality of social practices (Lefebvre 1991), Blanchot primarily works from an exploration of language to give his concept of the everyday a closer contour. In my own reading of Blanchot I want to encounter his text in an affirmative way, but at the same time give it another twist, this time in a process-philosophical direction.

My uneasiness here results from the fact that Blanchot's language-centered framework inevitably leads him toward a notion of the everyday that circles around the foundational law of the signifier. Even though Blanchot insists that the everyday keeps escaping the violent grip of the generalizing concept and emphasizes the singularity of everyday life, he can only apprehend it negatively. Aporia and indifference are the only remaining ways to get anywhere close to *what else* might be there—and consequently are the only thinkable forms of resistance left. However, for an activist philosophy, an approach that begins with the all-too-human primacy of the law and promotes a certain form of passivity as the political tactics of choice must remain unsatisfactory in its rather depotentializing nature. An escape is never really passive, it is a creative and joyful act of collectively inventing more livable modes of existence (which in no way exclude laziness, being angry, the refusal to participate, hesitation, or staying in bed all day). A process-philosophical account does not take language, laws, or norms as foundational in any sense. Instead, it focuses on the relational field of experience, where experience is still in the making and from which all juridical or language-based laws first emerge. Even though the latter may well condense into structures or systems at times, there still is an eventful multitude of micropolitical activity and minor practices, always preceding those apparatuses of capture, without being in any sense undifferentiated. "*A structure is defined by what escapes it,*" says Brian Massumi (Massumi 1992: 57, emphasis in the original). Neither the subject, nor the law, nor language are the ultimate concepts here, but rather *event*, *relation*, and *process* (cf. Massumi's discussion of Agamben in Massumi 2015: 44–9; and fundamentally Whitehead 1978).

Blanchot defines the everyday as "what we are first of all, and most often: at work, at leisure, awake, asleep, in the street, in private existence. The everyday, then, is ourselves, ordinarily" (1987: 12). However, for Blanchot, the everyday exceeds the consciousness of an autonomous subject at any moment. It is not a mode of life-living that could be occupied by a single subject, choosing it as if from the outside. It does not fit into conventional categories, as they are promoted so neatly and pedantically by the informational language model. And yet, Blanchot says, we ourselves *are* the everyday most of the time, it is not outside of us (although it is not *in* us neither). We intuitively feel what it means to live in the mode of the everyday. The everyday is a *quality of experience*, coloring our journeys through life most of the time. As a quality of experience, it cannot but be felt. As a felt quality of experience, everyday life is a *mode of existence*. The everyday is a differential of experience-in-the-making, of feelings in continual co-composition, prior to any notion of a conscious subject, and yet a relational field full of nascent subjectivities.

That the everyday is beyond the subject does not, however, mean that Blanchot, at this point, was interested in bringing society into the field against the individual. He clarifies that the everyday is also "no longer the average, statistically established existence of a given society at a given moment" (Blanchot 1987: 13). Even though I am dwelling in "everydayness" most of the time, the everyday not only surpasses me as an individual subject but also the status quo of a society at a given moment. This makes it an untimely force, as Nietzsche might say. Blanchot claims: "Man (the individual of today, of our modern societies) is at the same time engulfed within and deprived of the everyday" (1987: 13). The strangeness of the everyday results from its paradoxical nature of being at once far from unusual (it is just "us" everyday), but at the same time an "oblique existence" (Blanchot 1987: 12) that escapes the confinement in the body of a conscious human subject or in the status quo of a given society (it is always more-than "us," or "us" becoming otherwise).

The everyday is neither subject nor object. This is the main point of Blanchot's essay. Life-living the everyday is anonymous, insofar as it is neither the individual subject living it nor the other as its dialectical counterpart. "In the everyday we have no name, little personal reality, scarcely a face, just as we have no social determination to sustain or enclose us" (Blanchot 1987: 17). At the same time, however, the everyday cannot be reduced to the instrumental use of technical objects. The everyday is the in-betweenness of the not-yet, emerging from an experiential zone where subject and object have not yet come into existence. This is the point where Blanchot meets William James. In his *Essays in Radical Empiricism* James develops the concept of "pure experience." For James, in pure experience there is no separation between subject and object, observer and observed, inside and outside. James writes:

> *Experience, I believe, has no such inner duplicity; and the separation of it into consciousness and content comes, not by way of subtraction, but by way of addition*—the addition, to a given concrete piece of it, of other sets of experiences. (1912: 9, emphasis in the original)

Pure experience, for James, is "the immediate flux of life which furnishes the material to our later reflection with its conceptual categories" (James 1912: 93). "Pure," in this sense, does not refer to some essential substance or an experience purified of all disruptive factors, but to a simple "*that* which is not yet any definite *what*, tho' ready to be all sorts of whats" (James 1912: 93, emphasis in the original). It is a stream of experience, constantly changing, so that "no points, either of distinction or of identity, can be caught" (James 1912: 94). Just as in everyday life pure experience escapes its separation into the categories of subject and object. "It is only virtually or potentially either object or subject as yet. For the time being, it is plain, unqualified actuality, or existence, a simple *that*" (James 1912: 23, emphasis in the original). In pure experience, such distinctions exist only potentially and can always only be made retrospectively. Only after conventional categorizations are applied ("added") to pure experience, does it become an identifiable "what." This makes James such a fruitful thinker for the project of media-anthropology, which also starts from the idea that relation precedes its relata (cf. endnote 1).

For Blanchot, it is above all language that attempts to subject the not-yet-determined sphere of everyday life (the experiential flux of life) to the rule of generic difference. It is exactly in its resistance to be fully captured by the regime of signification and its refusal to be represented that the everyday gains its political potential. Although incapable of lying, the everyday moves through the great, cold universes of general ideas as a trickster. There is no truth to the everyday, for truth, understood as a general set of propositions adequately representing reality, for Blanchot, is solely generated through the creation of generic differences in the act of signification. In contrast, for him, the everyday is *singular*. Singularity, however, cannot be addressed by language (at least not in the usual sense of language as communication). Therefore, Blanchot is skeptical of any notion of totality, which in his language-centered account inevitably leads back to the tyranny of the signifier. In this respect, Blanchot clearly departs from Lefebvre's claim to "opening the everyday to history, or even, of reducing its privileged sector: private life" (Blanchot 1987: 12). Similar to Heidegger, Blanchot seems to associate the public sphere with the rule of generality, collective uniformity, and common sense. Blanchot refers to the French Revolution as a historical formation where everyday life tended toward the public and the political in the most radical way, but in the same breath also turned into a place for repression and terror. He thus defends the ontological and epistemological instability of the everyday against any kind of collective action that goes along with an assembly under the notion of the "universal." He writes: "Hegel showed that each time the universal is affirmed in its brutal abstract exigency, every particular will, every separate thought falls under suspicion" (Blanchot 1987: 12). Where Lefebvre might have referred to the festival (*la fête*) as a public form of collective resistance within everyday life, Blanchot points to the authority of the state and the law of the signifier, which make for apparatuses of capture that do not allow us to think collectivity in any other way than as a forced conformity toward universal ideals.

However, as we have seen, the everyday does not bow down to the state law. To the contrary, it "breaks down structures and undoes forms, even while ceaselessly regathering itself behind the form whose ruin it has insensibly brought about" (Blanchot 1987: 17). As an "oblique existence" and a "fleeting presence" (1987: 12) it is always threatening hegemonic powers. It resists any kind of dialectical sublation and falls out of both the juridical and linguistic frameworks of the law. As a singular mode of existence, it reveals that any law claiming to represent universal ideas can in the end be traced back to the particular will of the one governing. Here, we can see why it finds itself under current attack. Precisely *because* it does not fully submit to the hegemonic generalizations of the state law, the latter tries even harder to subject it to its own logic and to force it into the representational clarity of easy-to-manage generic difference. Refrain: *A Structure is defined by what escapes it.* This is what makes everyday life irreversibly "suspect." "The suspect: any and everyone, guilty of not being able to be guilty" (Blanchot 1987: 13).

A suspect is someone who attracts the attention of the law because she does not seem to stick to the rules. A suspect becomes suspect only under the stern eye of the judge. So, then, *what else* might this suspicious mode of existence that we call everyday life be, namely in the very moments it escapes the judge's gaze? Blanchot's answer: an "indeterminate manner of being: everyday indifference" (Blanchot 1987: 13), "insignificance" (18), a simple "nothing happens" (15). This is the point where Blanchot's deployment of the suspect as the conceptual persona motivating his approach to everyday life becomes problematic. Blanchot's overall conceptual framework is organized around the law of the signifier. The everyday use of language as well as the language of the sciences claim to represent the outside world, which, for Blanchot, is nothing more than an illusion. For him, language brings us into existence, but at the same time distances us from the "real world." Since we become subjects only by entering the world of language, the world of singularity that lies beyond it must remain closed to us forever. It is only through poetry that we may get a feeling for the singular reality beyond the symbolic order—if only negatively. For Blanchot, this is the closest we can get to the ineffable, the singularity of life.

So even though Blanchot is keen on defending everyday life in its singularity against any fixation on the all-consuming generalizations of language, he nevertheless starts from the law of the signifier. For him, anything that does not submit to this law's rule must fall into epistemological unintelligibility. Nothing positive can be said about it. What remains is the silence of the abyss designating the everyday. Difference comes into the world only by the act of differentiation, understood as the selection of specific characteristics, which then allows us to distinguish one thing from another. *A* is *A* because it is not *B*. Consequently, everything that falls out of this classificatory framework must inevitably be conceived as "indifferent." Even though we can say that indifference does escape the law of generic difference established by language to a certain degree, it still remains tied to it and will never be able to shake off its shackles entirely. This is because it gains its status of being indifferent only in contrast to the classificatory gesture of language. It is only indifferent because it is not differentiated (it is *A* because it is not *B*). Blanchot, here, must inevitably remain attached to the logic that he actually wants to defend the everyday against.

The mode of political action corresponding to Blanchot's indifference is actually not an action at all. It is passivity. This is not supposed to be a question of banning passivity in its entirety from a potential repertoire of techniques for political activism. Since Melville's *Bartleby*, at the latest, we know that passivity can be most effective in its potential to disrupt solidified structures, just by the act of not participating (and here we can see that even passivity is never really "passive"). The problem arises when passivity becomes the only remaining form of resistance, as is the case in Blanchot. If that happens, passivity changes affiliation and moves toward generality, losing all its creativity, as creativity can always only exert its force as an ever-new improvisation with the potentials and constraints of a singular situation. This is where passivity becomes "really" passive: Nothing happens.

Nothing happens is what finally happens in Blanchot, too. As we have seen, there is a conflict between language as communication—or "everyday speech" as the title of Blanchot's essay goes—and the singularity of everyday life. The desire "to seek an always more immediate knowledge of the everyday" (Blanchot 1987: 14) fails whenever it employs communication, understood as a means for the transmission of information, to capture the fleeting everydayness. This is because, for Blanchot, the everyday itself is nothing more than a "movement of universal transmission" (Blanchot 1987: 14) and cannot be represented in the form of fixed and stable entities, waiting to be put into words and images. For him, mass media falsely suggest that we have an immediate access to what is going on in the world. However, what the flickering television pictures actually produce is nothing more than an "insistent prolixity that says and shows nothing" (Blanchot 1987: 14). Here, the "average man" is satisfied with being exposed to the "distant and sufficient noise" (Blanchot 1987: 14) of the TV or the radio, which "he" hardly listens to, but which nevertheless provide "him" with a feeling of mastery, facing the everyday spectacle in passing. "We are no longer burdened by events, as soon as we behold their image with an interested, then simply curious, then empty but fascinated look" (Blanchot 1987: 14). "Man," as characterized here, lives an irresponsible, depoliticized life, gripped by a movement of continuous solidification. Blanchot's conclusion at this point is: Nothing happens; this is the everyday (Blanchot 1987: 15).

Nothing happens. Or: "The everyday is without event" (Blanchot 1987: 18). This is the inevitable consequence of choosing the supremacy of the law, with language's generic difference as its favored technology of power, as one's starting point. It is thus only logical that, for Blanchot, it is in boredom that we encounter the nothingness of the everyday in the most intense way possible. Boredom is the privileged mode where what usually remains unperceived—the everyday—becomes manifest. In boredom the everyday's incapability to (fully) actualize actualizes. Boredom happens to us as if out of nowhere. It puts us into a mode where the rhythms that otherwise carry us through life seem to be interrupted. We find ourselves in a spacetime of torturing slowness, looking into the abyss of everyday nothingness, "incapable of deciding if there is a lack of the everyday, or if one has too much of it" (Blanchot 1987: 16). However, it shows us that the everyday is an "inapparent and nonetheless unhidden part of existence" (Blanchot 1987: 16). Only when I no longer move through it without paying attention does the everyday rise to consciousness—except that, in the strict sense of the word, it is not the everyday anymore, for its major trait to usually remain unperceived is being lost. Thus, as a mode of existence, the everyday, for Blanchot, is above all two things: "insignificant because always before what signifies it" (Blanchot 1987: 16) and "silent, but with a silence that has already dissipated as soon as we keep still in order to hear it" (Blanchot 1987: 16–17).

The question is: Is this silence really that silent? Is this nothingness really everything that could possibly be said about boredom? Is there really nothing happening but the nothing-happening? Imagine a situation in which you are really bored. Maybe you are sitting on the sofa in your living room, your gaze wandering around the things that populate the shelves. Somehow their affordances don't seem to appeal to you today. You just don't know what to do. There! A fly attracts your eye, as it crawls across the window pane. Your eyes begin to follow its movements. After a while, the fly's buzzing begins to weave into the tick-tock of the clock you hadn't noticed until just now. There's a car passing by outside, adding another timbre to this little everyday symphony. Suddenly you find yourself in the midst of an emergent polyphonic sound-event, full of microperceptual activity and certainly neither undifferentiated nor nothing. Maybe you start snapping your fingers or begin to hum a little melody—whatever you finally come up with, there will already have been incipient action before you actually started it. The rhythms of the everyday don't fall silent just because the rhythm of my personal daily routine is interrupted.

To consider the everyday as indifferent is to employ the Hegelian concept of difference Deleuze so strongly rejects in *Difference and Repetition* (1994). Deleuze criticizes the subordination of difference to identity, opposition, analogy, and resemblance and aims at developing a thinking outside the realm of representation. He especially attacks Hegel's concept of difference as contradiction, where difference is a secondary quality that emerges out of the comparison of already constituted entities. Instead, Deleuze says, "an entire multiplicity rumbles underneath the 'sameness' of the Idea" (Deleuze 1994: 274). Novelty, then, always emerges out of this interplay of differences, it is dragged into existence by the force of relation.

Thinking from the Middle

The everyday escapes. That much we know. But what if it also escaped Blanchot's approach to it? What if it didn't submit to its seemingly inextricable ties with the law? What if the everyday didn't care about the reign of the signifier at all, moving beneath and beyond it instead, affirming its own processual autonomy?

To get to a different perspective on the everyday I would like to start with the notion of the event instead of the subject. To start there is to start in the middle, as Deleuze and Guattari put it (1987), in the immediate middling of experience-in-the-making. The world is not passive matter, waiting to be formed by the hands of a human subject. Nor is it the case that there would be preexisting structures (like language, technology, ideology, or capital), inaugurated to bridge the supposed gap between experience and the world "out there" by means of representation. Notions like the former often posit stable and unchanging factors as determinants of the world's becoming. The problem is that what gets lost this way is movement itself, which can now only be conceived of as changes between fixed positions within a preexisting cultural matrix (Massumi 2002: 1–5). To begin in the middle, however, means to recognize that the "fundamental concepts are activity and process," as Whitehead says (1968: 140). There is always already a more-than-human worldly activity going on, a continually varying ecology of experience, in which we participate, constantly changing our capacities to act and to be acted upon. Thus, a process-philosophical account would have to be highly skeptical of any notion of preexisting structures, systems, or orders that are supposed to exist outside of and prior to process and the relational field of the event. This does not mean that there were no conditioning factors or tendencies, immanently modulating the unfolding of the event, but they do always have to come back through the middle. The potentials, tendencies, and conditioning factors of the past push toward the future and actualize in the immediacy of the event. Even higher cognitive functions like juridical structures or the law do not exist prior to this relational field of potential, they always come back through the quasi-chaotic excess of experience-in-the-making, where they have to be reactivated as formative factors of experience (Massumi 2011: 11).

Given this primacy of relation it has to be clarified at this point that this does not refer to a notion of relationality that understands it as external relations between preexisting terms. So, if Blanchot claims that the everyday is "prior to all relation" (Blanchot 1987: 15), we will have to answer, "yes, but only if we understood relation as an extrinsic form of connection between already constituted terms, which are then subsequently related to each other."

Within such a framework, change can only be thought of as the realization of external configurations already given in an a priori structural matrix (cf. Massumi 2002: 70). However, in the in-betweenness of everyday experience nothing is constituted yet. It is a mode of existence that emerges from the middle of what I would like to call *immanent relation*. Immanent relation cuts across the individual points to create a "zone of indeterminacy," as Deleuze and Guattari put it (1987: 293).

This gives the event a certain *indeterminacy*, but without making it in any way indifferent, as in Blanchot. Massumi writes: "There is an inaugural moment of indecision between the already-going-on-around and the taking-in-to-new-effect, before the culmination of this occurrence has sorted out just what occasion it will have been" (2011: 2). In the immediate unfolding of the event, the drops of experience that compose it are interrelated in such a way that does not actually allow them to be viewed as separate entities. Even more: The individual and distinguishable elements first emerge from this relational field as its "products, effects, coderivatives" (Massumi 2002: 71), coming into being *just this way* only once, that is, in just *this* event. In immanent relation, "*the relations between things, conjunctive as well as disjunctive, are just as much matters of direct particular experience, neither more so nor less so, than the things themselves*" (James 1912: 2, emphasis in the original), as the mantra of James's radical empiricism goes. In this eventful zone of indeterminacy different elements of experience, each with its own tendencies, potentials, and affective capacities, come together to form an immanent relational field full of resonances, interferences, and vibrations—the situation is charged with intensity. Something is stirring, but we cannot know yet which potentials will actualize, and what the subjective form of the coming event will have been in the end. It is only after the event has run its course that we would know what it will have turned out to be. Then we would be able to take a distance from the event and determine its individual elements, which would then be available for conscious reflection as objects of the past. But however indeterminate the event might have been during its unfolding, we do know all the time that something *will* finally be happening, that there will be a collective individuation (Simondon 2005), which does not leave the experiential elements involved in the event unchanged. Thus, Brian Massumi speaks of the event's indeterminacy as being determined-to-be-determined (2015: 32).

Micropolitics of Affect

It is exactly in this indeterminate phase of the everyday event, where its potentiality has not yet fully actualized, that the everyday escapes. Not because it is indifferent nothingness, but because it is overfull, an excess of potential that can never be fully actualized. Something will always remain unperceived, overlooked, or declared insignificant, but will nevertheless have been a formative force in the event's coming into being. As I said at the beginning: The everyday keeps running through my hands like sand. And yet, I can feel the everyday grains of sand as they glide through my fingers. I experience the everyday as a *quality of feeling*, even though in most cases it only registers nonconsciously. In the following, I would like to introduce the concept of *affect* to further explore how the everyday is a quality of feeling, emerging from the ecology of experience that makes up the everyday as a mode of existence with its own *affective tonality*.

The body is the human's primary technique to feel itself into the world. As a technique of existence—that is, a technique enabling us to speculatively pragmatically relate to the potentials, tendencies, and cofactors of the becoming event (Massumi 2011: 26–7)—it is always already more-than-human. The body is our point of participation in a complex worlding, full of activity, which is not separated from "us," but closely related to our own becoming. The body is a technique to selectively channel those nonhuman and more-than-human elements of experience and transduce them into its own coming activity (e.g., via sense perception). Always in movement and itself radically open, the body is an eventful bodying rather than a closed container (Manning 2012: 10). It is affectively becoming-with-the-world, a body-world in continual variation. Each creature is life-living its own body-world, and it is never clear from the start what this body can do. This is because as a bodying the body is continuously affected by the ongoing worldly activity surrounding it, and in this way always transforming its affective capacities.

Thus, the basic definition of affect, as it comes from Spinoza, is a body's capacity to affect and to be affected (Spinoza 1985). Massumi, who takes up this thought and develops it further, defines affects as felt intensities circulating in the in-betweenness of multiple bodyings, accompanying bodily transitions. Affects describe the way a body prehends the intensities of a becoming event, into which it finds itself immediately drawn. The body becomes part of the affective movement of the event and is changed in the course of it. Affect would thus be a concept of the threshold: it describes the felt quality of an experienced transition. All of this does not necessarily happen on a conscious level (in fact, most of the time it does not). Affect is the immediate feeling of our participation in the excess of the virtual, which is, however, too overfull to be registered at a cognitive level in all its experiential richness or to be directed toward predefined goals. Massumi, therefore, insists on the pre-subjective and pre-cognitive nature of affect: the relational field of collective individuation ontogenetically precedes any subjectivity. The bodies perceive the intensification of the field in a direct way, but without the affective fullness of the event rising to consciousness. Our perception of the affect always comes a little too late. Insofar as affect cannot be separated from the event, it is never just something personal. There is a certain autonomy about it, which escapes any capture in language or the conscious perception of a subject. Although there is a good chance that affect will finally actualize in a clearly definable emotion, this emotion is never able to capture affect in its full potentiality. Instead, emotion can be understood as the personalized content of affect, as a conventional fixing of the affective quality of an experience, such as anger, sadness, happiness, and the like (cf. Massumi 2002: 23–45).

Affects constitute a certain dimension of every event in the everyday. Despite their autonomy, there is no chance of escaping them. Whether it is a chance encounter on the street, the haptics of the pen between our fingers, a little melody from around the corner, or the warmth of the evening sun on our faces as we set off home after work—we are always affected in some, perhaps minimal way by those encounters, and the movements of our bodies are given a direction that is not solely subjected to our free will. All of this is about the qualitative-relational dimension of our everyday mode of existence, about the increase or decrease of the affective capacities of the becoming body-worlds we inhabit in our daily lives. It makes a difference how our bodies relate to the world and there is always a potential to live our relations differently. Affects are forces of change. How can this not be political—or at least proto-political, in the sense that affects are at work everywhere that the political is just emerging?

A micropolitics of everyday life is about affirming the force of life-living, always shifting the relational field of the everyday, carrying with it the potential for ever new experiential modes of existence. This is all the more important as "we have so many reasons not to believe in the human world" as Deleuze and Guattari say (1994: 75). However, we cannot but move with the rhythms of *this* world, since there is no other one, which does not mean accepting it as a given. To the contrary: The task is to most intensely compose with the forces and potentials immanent to this world, to modulate the conditions of its eventful emergence from within, in the direction of other-worldly encounters. Media-anthropology teaches us to be attentive to the messy entanglements everyday life is made of and to affirm the transformational powers of the ordinary—sometimes dissonant, sometimes even scary, but always carrying the potential of letting the unknown emerge from the all too familiar.

Note

1. The project of media anthropology as it has been advanced within German media studies over the last years turns against deterministic conceptualizations of technology on the one hand and the communicational model of media as simple tools on the other. Instead, media anthropology thinks the relationship between media and the constitution of the human as an immanent relation. Christiane Voss has coined the term of *anthropomediality* to account for this. Anthropomediality refers to the modes of existence that emerge from the entanglement of man and medium without being reducible to either side. These anthropomedial relations no longer conceive man and medium as autonomous entities, but as subsequent products of a primordial relatedness. Depending on the ways these relationships are organized, different modes of existence may emerge. These modes of existence, however, are not to be understood as static, but as dynamic expressions of existence, which are re-actualized in continual variations: they are processual (cf. Engell and Siegert 2013; Bennke et al. 2018; Voss 2011; Voss, Krtilova, and Engell 2019).

References

Bennke, Johannes, Johanna Seifert, Martin Siegler, and Christina Terberl (eds.) (2018), *Das Mitsein der Medien. Prekäre Koexistenzen von Menschen, Maschinen und Algorithmen*, Munich: Wilhelm Fink.

Blanchot, Maurice (1987), "Everyday Speech," *Yale French Studies* 73, Everyday Life: 12–20.

Deleuze, Gilles (1994), *Difference and Repetition*, trans. Paul Patton, London: Continuum.

Deleuze, Gilles, and Félix Guattari (1987), *A Thousand Plateaus. Capitalism and Schizophrenia 2*, trans. and foreword by Brian Massumi, Minneapolis: University of Minnesota Press.

Deleuze, Gilles, and Félix Guattari (1994), *What Is Philosophy?*, trans. Hugh Tomlinson and Graham Burchell, New York: Columbia University Press.

Engell, Lorenz, and Bernhard Siegert (2013), "Editorial," *Zeitschrift für Medien- und Kulturforschung* 1: 5–10.

James, William (1912), *Essays in Radical Empiricism*, New York: Longman Green.

Lefebvre, Henri (1991), *Critique of Everyday Life. Volume One. Introduction*, trans. John Moore, London: Verso.

Manning, Erin (2012), *Always More Than One. Individuation's Dance*, Durham, NC: Duke University Press.

Massumi, Brian (1992), *A User's Guide to Capitalism and Schizophrenia. Deviations from Deleuze and Guattari*, Cambridge, MA: MIT Press.

Massumi, Brian (2002), *Parables for the Virtual: Movement, Affect, Sensation*, Durham, NC: Duke University Press.
Massumi, Brian (2011), *Semblance and Event. Activist Philosophy and the Occurrent Arts*, Cambridge, MA: MIT Press.
Massumi, Brian (2015), *Ontopower: Wars, Powers, and the State of Perception*, Durham, NC: Duke University Press.
Simondon, Gilbert (2005), *L'individuation a la lumiere des notions de forme et d'information*, Grenoble: Editions Jerome Millon.
Spinoza, Baruch (1985), *The Collected Works of Spinoza. Vol. 1*, ed. and trans. Edwin Curley, Princeton, NJ: Princeton University Press.
Voss, Christiane (2011), "Auf dem Weg zu einer Medienphilosophie anthropomedialer Relationen," in Kirsten Maar, Fiona McGovern, and Gertrud Koch (eds.), *Imaginäre Medialität—Immaterielle Medien*, 73–88, Munich: Wilhelm Fink.
Voss, Christiane, Lorenz Engell, and Katerina Krtilova (2019), *Medienanthropologische Szenen. Die conditio humana im Zeitalter der Medien*, Munich: Wilhelm Fink.
Whitehead, Alfred North (1968), *Modes of Thought*, New York: Free Press.
Whitehead, Alfred North (1978), *Process and Reality. An Essay in Cosmology*, New York: Free Press.

Part Two

Practice and Process

5

Prosthesis for Feeling: Intensifying Potentiality through Media

Mark B. N. Hansen

The Paradox of the Human

My aim in this chapter is to sketch out a theory of media as "prosthesis for feeling" where "prosthesis" supplements not just the human body or human cognition but the continuous process of the world itself. My theoretical resource for this sketch will be the process philosophy of Alfred North Whitehead. Whitehead's philosophy offers a broad and open account of what we might well call "cosmic causality," an account that takes full measure of the role contingency and novelty play in process and one that seeks to encompass every perspective *on* the universe as a perspective *of* the universe, without privileging any in particular. In accord with this aim, Whitehead views causality first and foremost as an metaphysical operation, not an epistemological one, and one that is always, to some minimal degree at least, indeterminate and inclusive of contingency and potentiality. Because his aim is to address cosmological process *from the perspective of the universe itself*—or, more exactly, *from the perspective of the concrete situations or events* constituting the universe from atomic moment to atomic moment—Whitehead's philosophy provides a fertile ground to conceptualize the contemporary melding of media into an ever increasing share of worldly experience.

An argument about the primacy of feeling lies at the heart of Whitehead's philosophy. Feeling (or, in Whitehead's technical vocabulary, "prehension") is the basic operation of process: it is through feeling that the past can be inherited in a new present. Feeling also accounts for what makes the new present distinct from the past, for feeling feels not just the actuality of the past (what Whitehead calls the settled world) but the unrealized potentiality that informed that actuality and that remains available to inform new actualities. In technical terms, feeling feels the past *both physically and conceptually* (meaning in its potentiality), and thus performs the important task of *evaluating* the past, of deciding on its relevance for new actualities.[1] In this way, Whitehead's account challenges our default conception of experience. Although we have been acculturated to think of feeling in correlation with a feeler, with an agent of feeling, and thus with living beings of a certain complexity, Whitehead's conception extends feeling to encompass *everything that contributes to cosmological process*. For Whitehead, atoms or rocks feel the past in a manner that is "formally" identical to the manner in which humans do so: in all of these cases, the new present inherits the past *through one and the same operation*. Given this commonality of feeling, what distinguishes the rock from the human as distinct types of entity is the balance between physical and conceptual inheritance informing them. From atomic moment to atomic moment, the rock inherits the past almost exclusively in a physical mode, with minimal or no role played by potentiality; if the rock changes, it does so because external objects act on it, not because it evaluates its own past. By contrast, the human inherits the past with extensive freedom: because of its capacities to entertain potentiality, the human can evaluate the past in ways that engage its indeterminateness, its full potentiality.

The human is, accordingly, both *like everything else* in being the issue of cosmological process and *unique* in its capacities for grasping—and, as we shall see, manipulating—how process operates. By combining a *generic* account of the mechanics of process with a *graduated* account of its complexity, Whitehead's philosophy offers a nuanced vision of human being that, despite being formulated nearly a century ago, seems designed to meet the concrete challenges of today's globally interconnected world. On this score, Whitehead's conception of human being offers an important alternative to the many recent theoretical developments in the humanities— the speculative realisms, new materialisms, actor network theories, and so on—that have sought to decenter, if not simply to dissolve, the cognitive and epistemological agency of the human. What differentiates Whitehead's vision—how he understands the unique role of the human—is also what makes it particularly powerful in the face of contemporary phenomena such as climate change or global financial flows. Humans are the pinnacle of cosmological process, but are also very much a product of that process: in no way does their "privilege" entail their exemption from universal process. What distinguishes humans, accordingly, is how their specific form of becoming arises from, and makes a crucial contribution to, the complexification of process itself. Or, more precisely still, how their ongoing becoming as highly complex "enduring objects," what Whitehead calls "societies" of actualities (and of subsocieties of actualities) united in their continuous processual reiteration, comes to exert some control over their future development, and specifically, over the ongoing genesis of the very actualities of which they are composed.

Superjects and Societies

To grasp the specificity of Whitehead's nuanced understanding of the human, let us focus on his distinction between subject and superject, which, taken together, compose process.[2] Whitehead deploys the term "subject" to describe the "concrescence" of new actual entities, the process through which the universe continuously renews itself, in ways that are both reproductive and novel. Actual entities (or actual occasions) "prehend" (i.e., *feel*) the entirety of the settled world, including its potentiality, and "decide" its relevance in virtue of their specific "subjective aim."[3] And once their prehension of the world is complete, their subjective phase terminates (or "perishes"[4]); they become "objectified" and are added to the settled world. To describe this process, Whitehead speaks of the multiplicity becoming one and then rejoining the world as an addition to its multiplicity: what he calls "creativity"—the "principle of novelty"—is "that ultimate principle by which the many, which are the universe disjunctively, become the one actual occasion, which is the universe conjunctively." Or, more simply still: "The many become one, and are increased by one" (Whitehead 1978: 21). This operation is generic and characterizes all levels of process. For Whitehead, accordingly, the human is part of a graduated scale of enduring entities *all of which share a common metaphysical origin*: the atomic actual entities composing enduring entities are the "really real things" that are the only reasons in his account. In this sense, actual entities take the place of foundations in traditional metaphysics: if they are "foundational" in any sense, they are foundational only of themselves: they carry with them—and indeed generate—their own reasons.

One key challenge Whitehead's generic metaphysics faces is how to account for the "direction" of process, the fact that process tends toward increased complexity and intensity. How, we must ask, can actual entities, the really real things that are the only reasons in our universe, themselves wield the power to direct the universe toward increased value and importance? This question has, to a great extent, been sidelined by Whitehead's introduction of a metaphysical God in *Process and Reality*; Whitehead's God conceptually prehends all potentiality and for this reason not only accounts for "eternality" of eternal objects but also provides an origin for the "subjective aim" informing all concrescing actual entities. Recent readers like George Allan and Jude Jones have questioned the need for this metaphysical God and have argued that Whitehead's philosophy is more powerful without it.[5] For these readers, process itself provides the vehicle for its own direction and itself originates the subjective aims animating the ongoing concrescences that constitute it. As Allan explains, every new actuality prehends (feels) its past (including the conceptual potentiality adherent to it) not in the mode of physical necessity, but in the mode of potentiality: on such an account, and this is the key point, *even the physical component of past process* is inherited *as potentiality,* which is to say, not deterministically but on the basis of an evaluation of its relevance for future process. Any such evaluation is "performed" through the contingent confluence of superjects, not by a preexisting subject. Accordingly, it is through such evaluation that new actualities are "bootstrapped" into becoming, and indeed, into becoming *subjects.*[6]

This priority of superject over subject, together with the blurring of the boundary distinguishing them, calls for a broader revision of Whitehead's philosophy than I can engage in here. What I do want to explore is how this priority arises in Whitehead's post-*Process and Reality* work, and specifically how it goes hand in hand with the increasing centrality Whitehead lends enduring entities or "societies"—of which humans are the highest "species"— as vehicles for shaping the happening of process. If actual entities are the really real things, they must be the ultimate source for the novelty of process. However, because they "perish" upon completion, and are thus not temporally extended, enduring entities, they cannot *by themselves* account for the ongoing development of complexity and value in the universe. As "aggregates" of actual entities linked together *serially* through a common pattern imposed by their environment and by their own contribution to it, societies provide a temporal framework for *atomic* actual entities to obtain and experience continuity. It is by means of this temporal framework that the ontological power of actual entities, the creativity of process, can be designed and modulated; by shaping process in a continuous framework, that is, across temporal duration, societies provide a further source for creativity, for a creativity relative to particular (and especially to higher order) experiential orderings of process. In line with the priority of the superject, this temporal framework cannot be entirely passive, as Whitehead for the most part maintains it is in *Process and Reality*. Rather, it must contribute to process in an active and positive way—such contribution being its very purpose in Whitehead's scheme. For if societies are themselves generated by the activity of a host of actual entities feeling their immediately past actual entities *in aggregation* and in relation to a common environmental factor, once constituted, they operate as quasi-autonomous, higher-order vehicles of continuous process. Indeed, as enduring temporal processes, not only do societies *host* the happening of the atomic, "perpetually perishing" actualities that compose them, but they both solicit and influence this happening, thereby exerting a direct impact on the really real things that lie at the core of process. In so doing, moreover, societies do not simply influence actualities piecemeal, but configure aggregations that draw maximally on the concrete potentiality informing them: societies modulate their intensity as a factor of their societal aim.

It is as societies in this sense that Whitehead's philosophy helps us reconceptualize human beings in the wake of the challenges of our contemporary world. As the most complex entities in the universe, humans are enduring societies composed of myriad subsocieties of actualities, all of which share a common pattern that informs their separation from and ongoing relation to the environment. From the process philosophical perspective, nothing more is involved in identity or subjectivity: like other higher-order entities, humans are the products of process incrementally advancing from atomic moment to atomic moment, and when we conceive of them, which is to say, of ourselves—as we almost invariably do—as substantial entities, as persisting identities or subjects, we are abstracting from the concreteness of (human) experience, from its concrete mode of existence as continuously reiterated and renewed, environmentally and societally constrained products of process. On this account, what makes humans unique—and what informs their privilege as designers of process *par excellence*—is simply their status as enduring societal entities of a certain complexity, or put another way, their emergence from and ongoing participation in process once it reaches the necessary threshold of complexity. If humans are uniquely able to intervene in the happening of process, it is because they, more so than any other entity, engage process in its potentiality, and thus with a significant degree of conceptual freedom. It is this unique capacity to intervene in process, to submit process to the force of its own potentiality, that constitutes whatever privilege humans have and that constitutes it as a concrete privilege associated with process itself, not with their abstract status as substantial entities. Humans, in sum, are part of an achievement of cosmological feeling, and while it is certainly the case that they participate in complex forms of feeling, they never do so as exclusive subject, as sovereign feeler, of these complex feelings. Rather, humans continuously become humans as *part of* larger feelings that encompass the entirety of the relevant potentiality of the past and that exceed what is accessible to them as narrowly cognitive agents.

It is in his final philosophical text, *Modes of Thought* (1938), that Whitehead confronts the apparent paradox of the human as a privileged form of process. Following *Process and Reality* (1929), which culminates the dissolution of the bifurcation of nature begun in *The Concept of Nature* (1920), the human emerges as Whitehead's central theme. Accordingly, in *Modes of Thought*, humans are conceptualized as vehicles for appreciating and enhancing the importance and value of the universe and all things that compose it. What accounts for this privilege is their capacity to entertain unrealized potentials and unrealized ideals as the source for future becoming, a point Whitehead makes explicit in distinguishing humans from so-called higher animals, animals of greater intensity and complexity:

> There is, however, every gradation of transition between animals and men. In animals, we can see emotional feeling, dominantly derived from bodily functions, and yet tinged with purposes, hopes, and expression derived from conceptual functioning. In mankind, the dominant dependence on bodily functioning seems still there. *And yet the life of a human being receives its worth, its importance, from the way in which unrealized ideals shape its purposes and tinge its actions.* The distinction between men and animals is in one sense only a difference in degree. But the extent of the degree makes all the difference. The Rubicon has been crossed. (Whitehead 1938: 27, emphasis added)

Whitehead's language here—*a difference in degree that makes a difference*—perfectly captures the nuance of his conception of the human. Humans *are not* different in kind from anything else in the universe: like all other enduring entities, they are composed of aggregates of actualities; and yet, just as all other enduring entities are unique in their particular manners of feeling, humans *are* different from everything else, unique, in their capacity to feel the past through unrealized potentiality, in line with ideals that do not match what is actual.

Technical Media Are Proposition Machines

By according humans this capacity to experience process through its open potentiality, and thus with a significant margin of freedom, Whitehead installs them in the role of designers of process. My aim here is to explore how media—in particular, computational and algorithmic media—enhance this capacity for designing process. Because they vastly expand the domain of unrealized potentiality informing the feeling forward of the past, media literally extend the scope of process itself, enfolding "more" potentiality, "more" intensity, into its happening. Elsewhere, I have argued that algorithms are "proposition machines," taking "propositions" in the sense Whitehead understands them, namely as "lures for feeling" that propose divergent, counterfactual trajectories for unrealized past potentiality to bear on the future.[7] Here, I want to "theorize" this operationality of media as a "prosthesis for feeling": by expanding the potentiality that informs feeling, computational and algorithmic media intensify the ways in which the past can be felt forward. Conceptualizing this operationality of media will require us to explore how humans and media operations cooperate in larger societies where media have the specific function of expanding the domain of potentiality available to feel the past beyond what humans can intuit or experience directly. Operating in a "real togetherness," human–media aggregates introduce and engage a dimension of potentiality which, though not directly accessible to human perception and conscious experience, can nonetheless be felt.

Whitehead does not have much to say about technology, and much of what he does say about it, primarily in *Science and the Modern World* (1925), concerns its contribution to the accomplishments of science in (Western) world history. However, when in *Process and Reality* he characterizes "suspended judgments" as "weapons essential to scientific progress," Whitehead introduces the key idea that scientific experimentation operates as a machine for generating propositions. Suspended judgments constitute a "third case" of judgment, alongside affirmative and negative intuitive judgments, which, Whitehead notes, "is in fact the more usual one." In suspended judgments, the subjective form is disjoined from the "eternal objects exemplified in the objectified nexus"; neither compatible nor incompatible with the objectified nexus, the suspended judgment effectively reserves judgment and thereby opens wide the ways in which potentiality can be brought into play. "The suspended judgment," Whitehead writes,

> thus consists of the integration of the imaginative feeling with the indicative feeling, in the case where the imagined predicate fails to find identification with the objectifying predicate, or with any part of it; but does find compatible contrast with it. It is the feeling of the contrast between what the logical subjects evidently *are*, and what the same subjects in addition *may be*. (Whitehead 1978: 274, emphasis is in the original)

The suspended judgment, in other words, marshals the *potential* divergence opened by propositions—between what logical subjects *are* and what they *may be*—as an element informing feeling. The suspended judgment, accordingly, is an extreme case in which imaginative feeling *contrasts* with indicative feeling but nonetheless "leaves its mark on the emotional pattern" of the integral feeling.

Unlike "negative intuitive judgments," which mark the "triumph of consciousness" because they generate "conscious feeling of what might be, and is not," suspended judgments open feeling to unrealized potentiality *that can only be felt nonconsciously, outside the abstraction of consciousness*. This feeling of unrealized potentiality informs the operation of inference, thus making suspended judgments crucial for science:

> Our whole progress in scientific theory, and even in subtlety of direct observation, depends on the use of suspended judgments. ... a suspended judgment is not a judgment of probability. It is a judgment of compatibility. The judgment tells us what *may* be additional information respecting the formal constitutions of the logical subjects, information which is *neither included nor excluded by our direct perception*. (Whitehead 1978: 274–5)

As machines for producing propositions that multiply and intensify the unrealized potentiality-informing process, "what may be additional information" relevant for its ongoing concrescence, computational and algorithmic media expand and generalize the role of suspended judgments as vehicles for the unconscious feeling of potentiality not tied to objectifications that would make them true or false. When contemporary algorithmic and machine learning systems entertain myriad possibilities for how the past can produce the future, they are effectively entertaining suspended judgments in just the sense Whitehead lends the term: judgments that are *in themselves* neither true nor false, but that *may* furnish additional information relevant to future process.

Whitehead seeks to explore the role suspended judgments play in science understood as a phenomenotechnical operation.[8] In this deployment, suspended judgments constitute a mechanism for discovering novelty, as it were, through feeling; that is precisely why Whitehead considers them to be "weapons essential to scientific progress." By contrast, their deployment within today's ubiquitous algorithmic systems imposes an instrumental abstraction that forecloses their central role as vehicles for introducing unanchored (i.e., imaginatively expanded) potentiality into process. Following this abstraction, suspended judgments are stripped of their connection to the breadth of process—what Whitehead, in *Modes of Thought*, repeatedly refers to as the "vague totality" informing experience—and transformed into positivities that can be assigned probabilities.

Although his thought belongs to a world in which computation proper had not yet been introduced, with his distinction between "compatibility" and "probability," Whitehead manages to pinpoint the key factor for developing a nonalgorithmic understanding of algorithms.[9] Whereas probability characterizes the suspended judgment in isolation from the unanchored potentiality it carries, and thus as an element of a closed system or abstraction, compatibility preserves the embeddedness of process in potential, designating the vehicle through which such unanchored potentiality can inform process in its concrete openness. The "conventional" use of algorithms in our advanced capitalist society is to preserve a social order, rather than to innovate or create; by shutting down or delimiting the open potentiality of process, algorithms generate a stable order that provides a basis for making predictions, and, in particular, for "discovering" correlations within high-dimensional spaces. This use is propositional, to be sure, but the propositions at issue propose only a narrow subset of potentiality, potentiality rendered as predetermined possibility. By contrast, what is at issue in compatibility, and in the open, creative deployment of algorithms, is the broad conformation of feeling to the past in its "entirety," which is to say, with its full dose of potentiality. Rather than performing an instrumental abstraction that reduces the past to what matters for a dimensionless decision in the present, deploying algorithms to expand compatibility—to encompass more potentiality in process— requires an engagement of algorithms as instruments in a different, well-nigh Bachelardian sense: as instruments of process, algorithms operate within and as a function of the broader operation of feeling.

A nonalgorithmic account of algorithms counters any tendency to conceptualize algorithms as autonomous "actants" operating independently from the humans who design them. In line with Whitehead's conception of compatibility, such an account incorporates algorithms into larger societies for technical feeling in which humans and algorithms combine to intensify the potentiality informing feeling. In such societies, the feeling of the vague totality is paramount, meaning that humans and algorithms cooperate in the genesis of feelings that exceed both of their respective operational domains, and for that reason, *cannot be considered to be the feelings of either one alone*. Rather, the feeling at issue here is a feeling *of the situation itself*, in which algorithmically generated propositions, operating as "suspended judgments," introduce "additional information" according to their compatibility with the larger society in which they are included.

It is precisely with this in mind that I propose to conceptualize media as "prosthesis for feeling" itself. Because they can introduce unanchored, techno-imaginatively generated potentiality into feeling, algorithms and other computational media expand the scope of feeling itself: they quite literally broaden the terrain on which feeling operates. Technical media, then, do not supplement the perceptual and cognitive operations of human beings conceived and operating as individuated substances, as the standard prosthetic account contends. Instead, because they enlarge the scope of feeling itself, technical media *intensify the very "medium" of togetherness*: they expand the potentiality of the past through which humans (continually) re-become human, thereby bringing a greater share of "humanness" into process. In this sense, "humanness" correlates directly to the level of potentiality involved in process, and it would be more accurate to qualify *process itself* as human, since it is process itself, once it has reached a certain threshold of complexity, that generates the very "humanness" humans have been mistakenly held to possess. In sum, humans are "agents" in media's operation as "prosthesis for feeling": they actively contribute to actualizing the margin of potentiality media introduce. But humans are in no way its "subject," since they are themselves continuously regenerated through and as part of the very feeling that media intensifies.

Anthropomedial Entanglement

Combined with Whitehead's nuanced conception of the human as "a difference in degree that makes a difference," this conception of media as prosthesis for feeling, together with the just mentioned notion of "humanness," yields something of a prescription for what an "anthropomedial entanglement" is and can be. This version of human–media entanglement explains why media, and, in particular, technical and computational media, hold a special place among all the environmental "actants" that have recently been called into action in the theoretical humanities. Because they operate as "possibility intensifiers," as vehicles for expanding the conceptual potentiality of process, technical media are distinct from other "actants," like seatbelts or the electricity grid, that channel physical force.[10] When she characterizes computers as the quintessentially "cognitive" technology and humans as the quintessentially "cognitive" species, underscoring the affinity binding them, Katherine Hayles makes a similar point (Hayles 2017: 34).[11] Yet where her explanation engages humans and computers as already individuated and hence separate entities, that is, as always already differentiated from one another (and everything else), my Whitehead-inspired account situates and addresses entanglement at a more fundamental level where, as Voss, Engell, and Othold's description for this volume puts it, "bodies, experience, and media" are "immanently entangled and mutually constituting, *prior to any possible distinction between them.*"[12]

The Whiteheadian prescription for anthropomedial entanglement provides a definite answer for how such "immanent entanglement and mutual constitution" can occur as "real togetherness" "prior to any distinction" separating media-generated and bodily-generated operations: as the basic unit of process, feeling is, in every instance, the "real togetherness" of all that goes into it, the confluence of all elements of the past, including its unrealized potentiality, that inform new actualities. Because this level of feeling encompasses process in its vague totality, entangled feeling happens "prior" to the separations that epistemology, at least in its traditional form, assumes and institutes. Accordingly, when humans experience feeling *directly*, as the content of consciousness, they do so—and can only do so— as separately individuated perceiving and cognizing entities, as subjects abstracted from the very process informing their operation. Debaise captures this perfectly when he qualifies subjectivity, and above all *human* subjectivity, as "retrospective": feeling itself is and must always already be "in some way" subjective; the subject is simply the "retrac[ing of] the steps of its development" (Debaise 2017: 55–6).

The primacy Whitehead accords feeling fundamentally reorients how we can think about anthropomedial entanglement. As the basic unit and site of process, feeling is an operation in which distinct elements—human, technical, and myriad others—coalesce into "real togetherness." And, even though they merge into unity, each of these elements introduces something specific; each remains ineradicably and utterly concrete. Not only do different combinations of elements yield different gradations of process, but each element also carries its own "subjectivity" with it and brings this "subjectivity" to the mix. Here we encounter the principal challenge facing Whiteheadian process philosophy: how can we affirm the certain "sameness" that allows for elements to merge together with one another, and at the same time insist on the functional "differentiation" of these very elements within the aggregate as a whole? How can we think process as the togetherness of the distinct, and not a fusion that renders everything indistinct?

Though Whitehead doesn't pose this question as such, his philosophy never ceases addressing it. Just as Wilfrid Sellars distinguishes between the reasons for knowing and the knowing of reasons (Sellars 1963: 169), and just as Gilbert Simondon distinguishes between the individuation of the real and the individuation of the knowledge of the individuation of the real (Simondon 2020: 20–1), so too does Whitehead construct his philosophy around the distinction between two orders: the order of reasons and the order of experience. And even though he begins *Process and Reality* by laying out the "Categoreal Scheme" of his metaphysics, Whitehead makes it clear that this scheme can only come to be known through experience, that experiential entities—humans above all—must discover it, as it were, *within* experience. "The elucidation of immediate experience," he writes at the outset of *Process and Reality*, "is the sole justification for any thought" (Whitehead 1978: 4). This emphasis Whitehead lends to experience informs the priority of the notion of "adventure" across his entire philosophical career: "rationalism," he observes at the outset of his metaphysical master work, "never shakes off its status as experimental adventure" (9). On Whitehead's account, accordingly, the privilege of experience cannot but entail some irreducible operation of phenomenology: given that it is always from some particular phenomenological perspective that process can be known, humans know process *because we are products of process*. As Whitehead recognizes whenever he addresses the relative privilege of consciousness, our own experience is most proximate for us, even if it is not, properly speaking, "our" own experience.

What this means is that we come to know process *through criticizing the abstraction that is our own conscious experience*. What we thereby come to know is our embeddedness in the vague totality that, for Whitehead, simply *is* fully concrete experience, even though it can never be "experienced" as a totality. At the level of this embeddedness, every actuality is a perspective *of* the universe itself, the universe contracted through one of its occasions. Every actuality is the universe as a whole, as it is felt from a particular perspective. And every particular perspective *is* the universe itself contracted through a given actuality, and not the universe viewed from the perspective of an actuality, a mere perspective *on* it.

So long as it operates autonomously, consciousness can only give us a perspective *on* the universe, a perspective that remains separated from the process informing it. When, however, we criticize the abstraction at the heart of its purported autonomy, consciousness can be seen to be one perspective *of* the universe among others. Indeed, like every perspective, consciousness is a concrete contraction of process, what we might think of as a "good abstraction." Yet this perspective of "reformed" consciousness differs from all other perspectives because it—or rather the coalescence of feelings that materialize it from atomic moment to atomic moment—aims to express the universe without reducing or denying its complexity. If this perspective of "reformed" consciousness constitutes what Whitehead would call a "good abstraction," that is because it entertains a significant degree of potentiality, or perhaps more precisely, because it submits itself to the vague totality in which potentiality inheres.

The contraction of the universe into consciousness—or into any other perspective—does not furnish a merely inert manifestation of the underlying operations, the really real things, informing it, however. Insofar as it is the accomplishment of superjectal power, every new actuality is shaped, as it were, in advance, by the enduring societal entity to whose endurance it contributes. This is why, as I suggested above, the priority of the superject goes hand in hand with the increasing centrality of societies in Whitehead's philosophy after *Process and Reality*. What Whitehead comes to see ever more clearly is that actualities do not prehend or feel the settled world ex nihilo, as a neutral or flat repository of potentials. Rather, every new prehension, every new feeling, arises on the basis of a concrete world shaped by the products of process, and most proximately, by those concrete enduring objects to which they themselves contribute. Because these enduring objects or societies attain their unity through some common form shared among the actualities informing them, they cannot but exert an influence on any and all subsequent actualities that prolong their endurance.

For Didier Debaise, this societal shaping of superjectal power occurs through the constraint it imposes on process. From moment to moment, the concrete operation of process constrains the world that informs it:

> it is the world *and its existents* that solicit what is relevant and what is possible with regard to the state of the world in which they find themselves. It is as if the universe, in its creative advance, never ceases to create new constraints, *which are the existents themselves*, canalizing how they inherit what is possible, in a new way. (Debaise 2017: 66, emphasis added)

The shaping power of worldly constraint reaches its pinnacle with the appearance of humans: the very capacity that makes humans human on Whitehead's account—the capacity to entertain possibility—also makes humans maximally capable of shaping and designing process. We must remember, however, that this shaping power is not and cannot be exercised directly by humans as autonomous, individuated entities: though consciousness is its vehicle, it is not a power of consciousness operating on the world, but one that arises in the wake of the "self-critique" of consciousness, of the recognition that consciousness is an abstraction from the vague totality of concrete process. The shaping power at issue here is a power of process itself, specifically of process involving higher-order feelings that experience significant contrast and intensity; humans are those enduring entities most capable of having such feelings, and accordingly hold a relative privilege to guide or direct—from a place or perspective *within* experience—the ongoing happening of process. Humans constrain and thus shape process in a manner different only in degree and not in kind from all other enduring entities in the universe, but, again, it is "the extent of the degree" that makes all the difference. Accordingly, humans influence process, and can only influence process, indirectly, as societies constraining, and thereby shaping, the genesis of future actualities.

What Whitehead calls "propositions" are the main vehicles for humans to shape process: propositions allow the exercise of worldly constraint with maximum openness. In contrast to their narrowly logical function,

Whitehead views propositions as "lures for feeling," proposals for how the past can be felt into a new present. Propositions are how the pure potentiality of eternal objects (pure conceptual prehensions) enters the world of experience;[13] accordingly, they are the "datum" of what Whitehead calls "impure prehensions," that is, prehensions (or feelings) that combine pure conceptual prehension with physical prehension, that ground potentiality in past physical actuality. For my purposes here, we might say simply that propositions express the *real* potentiality of the settled world at any given atomic moment, the potentiality of *this* world to give rise to new, divergent but equally concrete, worlds.

If humans are the enduring entities (most) capable of wielding the constrained freedom introduced by propositions, it is *not* to the consciousness of humans that propositional potentiality is revealed. As we noted above, propositions are not just statements of potential possibilities—alternate possibilities for new worlds—awaiting conscious selection or decision. On the contrary, propositions are emergent actions, or direct though unconscious contributors to actions, actions of feeling: propositional potentiality *is felt* into actuality at the more primordial level where feeling just is the happening of the "really real things." This primacy of unconscious action over conscious selection stands at the very heart of Whitehead's own account of how propositions "realize" potentiality:

> A proposition is the potentiality of the objectification of certain presupposed actual entities via certain qualities and relations, the objectification being for some unspecified subject for which the presupposition has meaning in direct experience. The judgement is the conscious affirmation by a particular subject—for which the presupposition holds—that this potentiality is, or is not, realized for it. It must be noticed that "realized" does not mean "realized in direct conscious experience," but does mean "realized as being contributory to the datum out of which that judging subject originates." (Whitehead 1978: 196–7)

Propositions intensify feeling by supersaturating it with potentiality, and humans are the feeling entities—or perhaps we better say, those entities within larger societies of feeling—that can best harness and deploy this intensity. Propositions *directly* express some concrete possibilities of the vague totality of process, thereby making available a higher degree of potentiality to inform new actualities. In this way, propositions literally lure feeling into action.

It is precisely to situate their operation at the level of feeling that Whitehead—against the tide of what would become "analytic" philosophy—insists that propositions are felt *unconsciously*. He writes in *Process and Reality*:

> The interest in logic has obscured the main function of propositions in the nature of things. They are not primarily for belief, but for feeling at the physical level of unconsciousness. They constitute a source for the origination of feeling which is not tied down to mere datum. A proposition is "realized" by a member of its locus, when it is admitted into feeling. (Whitehead 1978: 186)

Propositions are proposals for how the physical datum—the past datum that is the settled world—can be felt or prehended *as potentiality*, rather than as fully determined and determinate fact. Accordingly, propositions are, as it were, immediately felt: entertained by an incipient feeling as the concrete potentiality that both lures it into feeling and that it feels.

Propositions multiply and intensify the potentiality informing new process. And humans are those societal entities most able to deploy the expanded margin of freedom propositions thereby introduce. The larger societies constituted through their entanglement or real togetherness furnish a particularly efficacious "medium" for potentiality—what in *Feed-Forward* I have called worldly sensibility—to inform process, to contribute to the genesis of the "really real things." The enduring entities produced by propositionally lured, human-felt feelings, what we might call "societies for possibility intensification," feel the past into the future with the maximum possible intensity. When she likens algorithms to propositions in Whitehead's sense, Louise Amoore perfectly grasps how contemporary computational media technologies like machine learning and algorithmic systems extend the potentiality-intensifying power of propositions (Amoore 2021). Following her lead, we can in turn perfectly grasp how these media operations come to inform process by intensifying how potentiality is felt into the future. In contrast to the imagination, whose operation they in some sense displace, if not indeed replace, media operations multiply possibilities by an order of magnitude, and in so doing, directly increase the share of conceptual potentiality-informing process.

We can now grasp more concretely why I propose to conceptualize media operations as "prostheses for feeling." Rather than supplementing some separable or separately operating, distinctly human capacity, media directly affect how the past can be felt forward into the future: by proposing original ways of realizing real potentiality, technical media intensify the very operations through which superjects inform process. Machine learning and algorithmic operations should be conceptualized as superjectal intensifiers in just this sense: by increasing the information available to the larger societal entities of which they are part, they modify the ongoing operation of these societal entities in ways that, while requiring human capacities to evaluate and appreciate potentiality, can in no way be attributed to humans as already individuated, somehow autonomous cognitive and perceptual agents. Here we again encounter the crucial question that has shaped my discussion thus far: how can the human be *both* a continuously becoming product of process no different in essence than all other such products *and at the same time* unique in, and in some sense privileged on account of, its capacities for grasping and designing how process operates moving forward?

Feeling before Thought, or against Assemblage

To explore this apparent conundrum further and in more concrete terms, let us turn to Katherine Hayles's analysis of what she calls "cognitive assemblages," her preferred term for what this volume conceptualizes as anthropomedial entanglement. Hayles's notion proffers a starting point for us to consider how humans and technologies co-function in the generation of experience. Although I shall ultimately demur from Hayles's bias in favor of cognition and insert "feeling" in its place, Hayles's thematization of a certain sharing between humans and technologies, a sharing at the level of nonconscious operations, will help us appreciate how societies for technical feeling include human bodily feeling as one of their parts while also simultaneously allowing one of their products—human perceptual consciousness—to serve as its (partial) subject.

Hayles introduces her concept by differentiating it from Latour's and Deleuze and Guattari's respective notions of assemblage. The crucial point of difference concerns the role played by "cognition" in Hayles's vision: whereas Latour's and Deleuze and Guattari's notions level distinctions in defiance of any divide separating material and living processes, Hayles insists on the necessity to differentiate and privilege cognition within assemblages:

> The term I use to describe these complex interactions between human and nonhuman cognizers and their ability to enlist material forces is "cognitive assemblage." While Latour and Deleuze and Guattari also invoke "assemblage," a *cognitive* assemblage has distinctive properties not present in how they use the term. In particular, a cognitive assemblage emphasizes the flow of information through a system, and the choices and decisions that create, modify, and interpret the flow. While a cognitive assemblage may include material agents and forces

(and almost always does so), it is the cognizers within the assemblage that enlist these affordances and direct their powers to act in complex situations. (Hayles 2017: 115–16, emphasis in the original)

By differentiating cognitive from material operations, Hayles aims to address the conundrum of the human in a way that can do justice to its status as the quintessential cognitive being while simultaneously acknowledging the importance of other nonhuman cognitive "actors."[14] Not only does she thereby position the human as the most important, if not exclusive, cosmological actor capable of designing the future (e.g., by taking steps now to mitigate future harms of climate change), but she is also able to diagnose the Achilles' heel of materialisms that seek to dispense with human privilege in favor of a purely flat ontology. For Hayles, and I concur wholeheartedly, these positions yield a glaring "performative contradiction" insofar as they remain unable to account for their own source, the very human actors that formulate and cognize them; "only beings with higher consciousness can read and understand these arguments," she astutely observes, "yet few if any new materialists acknowledge the functions that cognition enables for living and nonliving entities" (Hayles 2017: 66).

Unlike "networks," which are composed of clean edges and nodes, assemblages enfold heterogeneous materialities: they "allow for contiguity in a fleshly sense, touching, incorporating, repelling, mutating," and they include "information transactions across convoluted and involuted surfaces" (ibid.: 118). For this reason, assemblages are able to integrate diverse cognitive (and material) operations, and in particular, to host the confluence of two distinct categories of cognition: "cognitive nonconscious" cognition and "technical nonconscious" cognition. For Hayles, a generic mode of cognition thus sutures operations across the biotic–abiotic divide, linking cognitive operations of embodied beings (above all, humans) with those of technical processes. Hayles defines this generic mode of cognition in terms of the operation of interpretation: cognition, she writes, is "a process of interpreting information in contexts that connect it with meaning" (ibid.: 118). By shifting the focus from consciousness to the myriad nonconscious operations informing and supporting it, this generic mode of cognition opens cognition well beyond the bounds of *human* thought: it "foregrounds interpretation, choice, and decision and highlights the special properties that cognition bestows, expanding the traditional view of cognition as human thought to processes occurring at multiple levels and sites within biological life forms and technical systems. Cognitive assemblage emphasizes cognition as *the common element* among parts and as the functionality by which parts connect" (Hayles 2017: 32).

By defining cognition generically and positioning it as a "common element" capable of functionally unifying disparate operationalities, Hayles fundamentally resituates the locus at which humans and technologies are coupled. Technologies do not, first and foremost, provide prosthetic supplements for human consciousness and thought. Or rather, if they do so, it is only derivatively and as the result of a different, far more fundamental analogy:

> Although technical cognition is often compared with the operations of consciousness …, the processes performed by human nonconscious cognition form a much closer analogue. Like human nonconscious cognition, technical cognition processes information faster than consciousness, discerns patterns and draws inferences, and, for state-aware systems, processes inputs from subsystems that give information on the system's condition and functioning. (Hayles 2017: 11)

Reminiscent of the extended mind thesis proposed by philosophers David Chalmers and Andy Clark (Chalmers and Clark 1998), Hayles's account does not, however, simply aim to scaffold thought by extending the material infrastructure for human cognitive operations into the environment. Rather, by displacing the focus from consciousness to nonconscious cognition, Hayles proposes to rethink what it is that gets extended: on her account, computational technologies do not supplement *thought* so much as they supplement—or indeed, *substitute for*—the infrastructural operations that, in humans (and other higher order animals), inform and condition the genesis of thought.

The parallels between the nonconscious cognition informing the cognitive lives of humans and the nonconscious cognition performed by computational technologies "are not accidental," according to Hayles, but manifest a massive expansion in the "exteriorization" of cognition that, following the thesis she shares with Bernard Stiegler, has conditioned the evolution of the human since its origin. The analogy between these two distinct forms of noncognitive cognition results from "the exteriorization of cognitive *abilities*, once resident only in biological organisms, into the world, where they are rapidly transforming the ways in which human cultures interact with broader planetary ecologies. Indeed, biological and technical cognitions are now so deeply entwined that it is more accurate to say they interpenetrate one another" (Hayles 2017: 11). Although the exteriorization at issue here does not originate with the advent of computation—indeed, on the "technogenesis" thesis Hayles, following Stiegler, derives from Andre Leroi-Gourhan, it characterizes "human" cognition from the outset—Hayles is certainly correct in her assessment of the massive escalation of cognitive interpenetration in contemporary technoculture.

But what exactly does it mean to assert that "biological and technical cognitions" interpenetrate one another? For Hayles, it means that biological and technical cognitions enact *functionally* similar processes, despite their manifest differences:

> My comparison between nonconscious cognition in biological life forms and computational media is not meant to suggest, then, that the processes they enact are identical or even largely similar ... Rather, they perform similar functions within complex human and technical systems. Although functionalism has sometimes been used to imply that the actual physical processes do not matter, ... the framework advanced here makes context crucial to nonconscious cognition ... Notwithstanding their profound differences in contexts, nonconscious cognitions in biological organisms and in technical systems share certain structural and functional similarities, specifically in building up layers of interactions from low-level choices, and consequently very simple cognitions, to higher cognitions and interpretations. (Hayles 2017: 13)

There is a difference, however, between Hayles's claim concerning the *fact* of cognitive interpenetration and more specific assertion she advances here concerning its *how* and *why*. Indeed, the *functional* similarity introduced in this passage concerns a similarity of form and history, rather than an actual cofunctioning or functional cooperation: it only tells us that two distinct kinds of nonconscious cognition, taken separately, "share certain structural and functional similarities," but says nothing about how those similarities coordinate or combine in the service of concrete cognitive operations.

Hayles offers no mechanism whatsoever to account for the ways in which technical cognitive operations either replace or cooperate with the nonconscious cognitive operations informing cognition in higher-order biological, and in particular, human beings. The cognitive interpenetration she postulates is, accordingly, a purely de facto one involving the confluence of structurally similar, but materially distinct operations of *already fully individuated cognizers*. With this, we find the answer to the question posed above: on Hayles's account, biological and technical forms of nonconscious cognition interpenetrate one another *as separate processes*; they do not intermingle in a "real togetherness" of feeling. We must accordingly distinguish Hayles's "cognitive assemblage" from the notion of "anthropomedial entanglement" that, taking up Voss, Engell, and Othold's invitation, I am seeking to theorize here: whereas Hayles can only *assemble* distinct components of larger cognitive systems piecemeal—as structurally/functionally similar but operationally distinct and (quasi-) autonomous elements—proper entanglement entails their fusion within one larger and unified operation or unit of process, into a "real togetherness."

Put another way, nonconscious cognition in complex biological beings *necessarily* operates as part of larger cognitive—or I might rather say, sensitive—systems that, at least in the case of the human, involve consciousness together with other modes of presentification (although, as we have seen, only as abstractions from the larger, vague totality of process). To the extent they involve—or better, are generated by, through, and as—entanglements at the level of feeling, such larger sensitive systems (or societies) cannot themselves be abstracted from the elements entangled within them; nor can these elements be separated from the given larger systems (societies) in which they are entangled. This "real togetherness" of elements within larger systems finds a powerful advocate in the neuroscientific research on which Hayles draws and which increasingly underscores the cross-scale inter-imbrication of processes: for scientists like Damasio and Dehaene, "core consciousness" (Damasio's term) is an evolutionary achievement that forms the basis for higher-order consciousness. While such a minimal form of consciousness may well predominate in less complex organisms, it can never be separated and treated piecemeal from the larger cognitive ecology to which it belongs.

This particular holism that characterizes biological entities does not, however, carry over into the technical domain. Although they may involve escalating layers of interactions, as Hayles underscores, technical systems lack an abiding *internal* force of cohesion or consistency, a source of constraint on the operation of their elements, that would bind them into a "real togetherness." On the contrary, as contemporary examples like machine learning and algorithmic programs make all too clear, whatever global coherence informs the co-development of individual technical elements is either imposed *externally* by their designers or, in cases where coherence is discovered through operation, extrapolated from and generated iteratively on the basis of individual operations, occurring piecemeal, independently from one another.

Though intended to buttress the analogy linking biological and technical (nonconscious) cognition, Hayles's invocation of evolution only underscores their fundamental difference. Whereas cognition in biological beings results from the complexification of evolutionary processes, meaning that its operation rests on—indeed, is the concrete fruit of—the entire history of its evolution, technical cognition can be considered an evolutionary accomplishment only figuratively. The "stronger evolutionary potential" Hayles attributes to computational media is not actually evolutionary at all. Rather, it is a capacity to "simulate any other system" (Hayles 2017: 33). Accordingly, when Hayles attributes an evolutionary logic to computers, what is at issue is something quite different from evolution in the biological sense. This becomes altogether patent when Hayles justifies the elective affinity linking humans and computers:

> The analogy [of human cognitive capacities] with the cognitive capacities of computational media suggests that a similar trajectory of worldwide influence is now taking place within technical milieus. Fueled by the relentless innovations of global capital, computational media are spreading into every other technology because of the strong evolutionary advantages bestowed by their cognitive capabilities … Consequently, technologies that do not include computational components are becoming increasingly rare. Computational media, then, are not just another technology. They are the quintessentially cognitive technology, and for this reason they have special relationships with the quintessentially cognitive species, Homo sapiens. (Hayles 2017: 34)

If Hayles is right to ascribe something like a "survival of the fittest" principle to technological change, her ascription disguises a semantic slippage from evolution to adaptation—from evolution in its proper, deep historical sense to "evolution" in a figurative sense, as the "dynamics of competition, cooperation, and simulation" between fully actual "media forms" (Hayles 2017: 33). The two conceptions of "evolution" at issue here do not designate two subspecies of one and the same process, however. Rather, in the figurative use Hayles puts it to, "evolution" characterizes the narrow, predominately presentist logic by which media forms compete with one another and thereby develop into ever more powerful variants. The key point here is that, unlike evolution as a biological process, which always involves the vague totality of process yielding new actuality, technical "evolution" arises from competition among extant technical possibilities at specific historical moments.[15] In some irreducible sense then, technical "evolution" is both self-contained and instrumental: because it occurs against the backdrop of predominately presentist environments, technical "evolution" is cut off from the broader history of evolutionary process.[16] While technical "evolution" is always imbricated within the broader operation and history of process, this latter impacts it only externally, by posing constraints and challenges that require adaptation, and not internally through constraint on potentiality, as a processual, historical, and properly evolutionary logic by which potentiality yields new actuality.[17] Accordingly, what Hayles calls "technical cognition" constitutes a logic of adaptation, not one of evolution proper.

By exploiting what we have now seen to be a merely superficial analogy between biological evolution and technical adaptation, Hayles is able to present them as two subspecies of evolution proper. In so doing, she secures the possibility to conceptualize technical cognition not simply as functionally analogous to—but as substitutable for—nonconscious biological cognition. Indeed, when she says that technical cognition exteriorizes cognitive abilities once resident only in biological organisms, Hayles is effectively claiming that we can divorce these abilities from their evolutionary heritage and context, and predicate them of a starkly distinct kind of entity, one which is artificial, the product of engineering or technical invention, and not naturally or biologically evolved.

The reality, however, is that Hayles does not—and I would add, *cannot*—furnish any coherent argument for how technological cognitive abilities, the fruit of a presentist competition among local technical possibilities, can replace evolutionarily derived nonconscious cognition, the domain of "biological cognition" that, following recent neurobiological research, undergirds and informs higher-order modes of cognition. Simply put, technical cognition does not operate by substituting for nonconscious biological cognition. Whatever superficial resemblance it may have to nonconscious cognition notwithstanding, technical cognition arises from operations that are *different* from—indeed, often *radically* different from—the operations underlying human biological cognition. This very difference is precisely what informs media's potentiality to enlarge the domain of experience. Because computational media vastly outstrip human perception and imagination in their sheer capacity to enumerate possibilities for future process, they are, quite literally, *machines for producing suspended judgments*—proposals or lures for feeling concerning how the past can be felt forward with maximal potentiality. That these suspended judgments only become actual when they are "received" by feeling reminds us that, in themselves, they are simply enumerations of many divergent possibilities awaiting the opportunity to be felt.

There is, accordingly, no "technical cognition" that is independent of "biological cognition." Rather, forms of cognition involving technical elements result from the process through which technical amplifications of potentiality are felt together with biological ones. What appears as "technical cognition" is the fruit of this real togetherness: though distinct in their social orders, biological and technical feelings coalesce in the concrete feelings of enduring societal entities. With Hayles, we can call the achievement of this coalescence "technical cognition," but only if we acknowledge that such a mode of cognition is nothing more nor less than an abstraction from the underlying coalescence that generates it in the first place.

Intensifying Technical Feeling

It is important that, on Hayles's account as on mine, humans remain centrally involved in operations of anthropomedial entanglement. Humans, Hayles insists, are a special kind of "cognizer" among cognizers: their distinctive cognitive abilities have allowed them to "achieve planetary dominance within their ecological niche" (Hayles 2017: 33–4). Accordingly, despite any implication that humans somehow fuse with computational media within cognitive assemblages, on her account they retain both a centrality and a specificity of function. This *persistence of the human* directly informs Hayles's suggestion that computational media operate in one of two modes: either, like High Frequency Trading, as surrogates for human agents; or, like self-driving cars, as supplements to the limited bandwidth of human attention.[18] To the extent that both modes underscore the centrality of the human as that in virtue of which technologies are deployed, Hayles's focus appears to be directed toward conceptualizing cognitive technologies as supports for some of the natural, evolutionarily acquired nonconscious cognitive infrastructures of human cognition. In other words, despite all her efforts to counter human exceptionalism, on Hayles's account humans remain the "subjects," the "privileged agents," of cognitive assemblages in an altogether traditional sense. Human subjects are the ethical agents within assemblages; they are alone among the components of such assemblages in having the capacity to make decisions for the whole. Cognitive technologies simply expand the scope of action on which decisions can be made.

On my account, the human likewise remains privileged, though in a fundamentally different way. The qualified privilege I want to retain is in no way a property of human beings; rather, it is a privilege associated with and derived from *the level of process* that ontogenetically gives rise to, and experientially includes, humans. It is a privilege correlated with and derived from what I have above called "humanness," that is, a sufficiently complex level of process that engages a substantial, if not indeed maximal, degree of worldly sensibility or potentiality. As we have seen above, what distinguishes human beings from animals (and, scaling down, from all other entities in the universe) is a *difference in degree that makes a difference*. This difference is not a difference of essence or kind (to recall Bergson's distinction, with which Whitehead was quite familiar): it is not a difference that, because *it is possessed by* certain kinds of beings, makes a difference. Rather, it is a difference *of process* that arises when a certain threshold of complexity is reached: a difference emerging from and within process itself at the point when it—or rather, the entities materializing it—attains a certain capacity to embrace conceptual potentiality as creative source for feeling the future. Not being a substance, set off against all else and enjoying some absolute and "magical" agential autonomy, the human is not privileged *in and for itself*.

Indeed, the human is not anything "in and for itself." It is, rather, a vehicle of process once it has reached a certain level of complexity, a vehicle of what I am calling "humanness." The privilege that human beings enjoy following Whitehead's nuanced conceptualization thus stems from a capacity *that cannot be separated from the vague whole of process* with which it is ineradicably bound up and from which it attains its force. Again, for Whitehead, it is always the really real things—the actualities that are (or can be) felt together from atomic moment to atomic moment—that furnish the reasons for why experience is what it is: these really real things are the elements of process that converge into "real togetherness," again and again, as Whitehead puts it, "until the crack of doom."

Human beings are particularly complex "societies" of such actualities—societies enfolding a maximal quantity of "objective" elements, of past feelings or superjects, in their incremental iterations. The *power* or *force* of the "agency" they obtain *as societies* derives from and remains dependent on the actualities—that is, the superjects—that continuously come together in an ongoing process of composing the world anew from atomic moment to atomic moment. Like all other enduring entities, humans exert constraint on future process, on the "really real things" to come, but they do so in the most open and capacious way possible. Through such constraint, humans exemplify the capacity of enduring entities to shape process, to guide and direct the ongoing yet atomic concrescing of the really real things that are the *only reasons*. Only because they are societies created through the processual organizing of the togetherness of actualities in certain complex patterns do humans become—and *continuously* become—human: whatever privilege humans enjoy stems from the degree of complexity of this societal organization which, far from qualifying a pre- or separately existing self or interiority, and far from being a product of such separate agents, operates to channel the objective domain or the outside—past objective actualities or superjects—into a continuous collusion of micro-subjectivities yielding enduring macroscale consistency over time.

By conceptualizing technical media as "prosthesis for feeling," I aim to explore how technical processes can expand the scope of action—and beneath it, the scope of feeling—in ways that cut against the agential separateness informing Hayles's understanding. On my account, computational media technologies intensify the process—that is, the coming together of concrete actualities, the really real things—that yield human-level complexity. But in so doing, they do not—and *cannot*—simply stand over against human societies as separate objects to which humans are or would be experientially coupled. They are emphatically not prostheses for the human. Rather, technical media operations coalesce with human societies to compose yet larger societies, societies that integrate technical and biological (human) operations in a single higher-order togetherness. Contemporary machine learning and algorithmic media directly amplify the force of potentiality informing the ongoing becoming of the very societies—the enduring human societies—that design and create them. They intensify process by informing feeling *directly*, which is to say, by "participating" in the basic operation that—uniformly though differentially—generates *all* entities in the universe, actualities and societies alike. In so doing, they fuse with human societies to conjure societies of a new type into being. These new societies—"societies for technical feeling" (or "societies for possibility intensification")—integrate the superjectal power informing human societies *and* the amplified superjectal potentiality introduced by media, commingling them as data to be felt in one indivisible operation of "real togetherness."

In one sense, what media introduce is simply an intensification of human-level process—of superjects continuously bootstrapping themselves into becoming through the power of open potentiality. But the point I want to emphasize is that the humans implicated in such process are not its subject, a subject that would be the *recipient* of intensified potentiality. Rather, humans are only one component, one subsociety, among others within a larger receptive society that, with "graduated" input from all of its interlocked subsocieties of actualities, shapes the becoming of process. It is this larger society as a whole, as a "real togetherness" of actualities and subsocieties of actualities, including human ones, that feels the potentiality of the past into the future. Accordingly, when machine learning technologies and algorithmic media propagate proposals for how the past can be felt into the future, the resulting *propositions* (or "*lures for feeing*") are not addressed to the cognitive capacities of separate, already individuated human subjects, nor are they received by such subjects as conceptual contents. Rather, like all propositions, they are felt unconsciously by the larger society for technical feeling that is their subject, and they shape process not by offering alternative *cognitive* possibilities for human subjects to select—a multiple-choice array of possible worlds—but directly by intensifying and thereby influencing how past potentiality is felt into the future. If humans are critical to this latter operation, it is because they—or rather, the complex feeling composing human-level process—can feel the presentationally immediate data generated by the algorithmic enumeration of possibility *as potentiality* relevant to the future.

If human beings hold a privileged role within societies for technical feeling, it is precisely because they are their most complex subsociety and, as such, are capable of recognizing the larger societies in which they participate *as abstractions* from the vague totality of process. And if humans thereby become capable of *designing* process, which necessarily involves some reckoning with the vague totality of what could be, it is because they can assess the operation of larger societies for technical feeling *as if* they were its subject. However, it is important to recognize that such retrospective evaluation[19]—what I have, in a more narrow usage, called "feed forward" (Hansen 2015)—occurs through the medium of the body, which is to say, through the medium of the world, concentrated into "that portion of nature with which each moment of human experience intimately cooperates," that is, the body (Whitehead 1938: 115). As such, the retrospective composition of consciousness occurs as a feeling of a feeling—as the bodily feeling of a larger societal feeling that includes bodily feeling among its subsocieties. Feeling, not cognition, provides the common currency of process. Feeling, not cognition, is its generic operation.

Toward a Nonalgorithmic Theory of Algorithms

It is precisely here—at the point where feeling takes precedence over cognition—that Hayles's account of nonconscious cognition can prove helpful. Notwithstanding her bias in favor of higher-order cognitive operations, which ultimately stands behind her ratification of a quite traditional account of humans as privileged ethical agents,[20] Hayles's account helps elucidate how propositions can be felt unconsciously—how they are felt, and *must be* felt, *before they can be cognized*. By exposing the functional correlation binding technical and biological nonconscious cognition, Hayles gives a concrete picture of how "technically intensified" potentiality can be directly felt. As technical components of feeling—literally, "machines for generating propositions"— algorithms and machine learning operations increase the potentiality that can be felt; and to the extent that this increased potentiality is felt *bodily*, these technical operations directly inform, that is, inform by complexifying, the nonconscious infrastructure of feeling. Any conscious feeling that may ultimately arise from such technical intensification of nonconscious feeling is (like all conscious experience on Whitehead's account) an abstraction from process. Conscious feeling neither *coincides with* nor *represents* the nonconscious bodily feeling that is its source; rather, consciousness is always an *indirect* experience of—a derivative causal emanation from—bodily feeling. It thus stands at a remove from whatever data (i.e., feeling) feeds forward into it.[21]

Whitehead's philosophy of feeling furnishes a broader framework within which to appreciate the important contribution that Hayles's account of nonconscious cognition makes to our understanding of contemporary technical life. Three aspects of Whitehead's program in particular serve to exemplify the primacy of nonconscious feeling in today's highly mediated forms of process.

First, nonconscious feeling creates an infrastructure that allows for the imbrication of technical with biological (and human) feeling, but—and this is the crucial point—this imbrication does not and cannot take the form of a substitution, whether partial or wholesale, of technical for biological processes. Far from replacing them, technical elements of feeling blend together with biological elements, creating what we might call "technically intensified" feelings.

Second, every feeling is a concrete "togetherness of the distinct," a "real togetherness" in which disparate elements compose together without losing their specificity or distinction. In stark contrast to assemblages that are made up of previously differentiated cognitive operations, operations involving *substantially* or *functionally* distinct entities (e.g., of humans co-functioning with computers), anthropomedial feelings are produced by the very societies ("societies for technical feeling") that they simultaneously serve to constitute. As compositions of past feelings unified by *new* acts of feeling, anthropomedial feelings are *entanglements*, not assemblages: their togetherness arises together, as it were, with the distinct specificities of their components. Or, more simply put, their togetherness is, in every instance, utterly concrete: every technical feeling, every anthropomedial entanglement, *is* a togetherness of the distinct, not a fusion that renders everything indistinct.

Third, the relation of the technical to the biological remains asymmetrical to the extent that human (and other higher-order) operations possess greater capacities for—and thus assume more of the burden of—feeling. For this reason, technical intensifications of feeling are effectively *mediated* by living (human) feelers. To the extent that human feeling predominates in societies for possibility intensification, whatever contribution such societies make to informing contemporary process is filtered through the operation of feeling capable of receiving the force of their intensification of potentiality. In short, the creativity introduced by today's societies for technical feeling is necessarily filtered through *human* feeling. As intensifiers of feeling, technical media operate, in short, by fusing together with the bodily feeling of causal efficacy that they intensify. Indeed, they operate precisely *by intensifying* this very bodily feeling.

Perhaps alone among worldly entities, humans thus enjoy a double status: they are at once the perpetually reiterated achievement of ever new actualities collaborating to maintain a given societal organization *and* they are the *retrospective* subjects, or more precisely, the retrospective *partial* subjects, of the larger process informing their incremental becoming and of which they are only a part, though a predominate one. Although I can't develop it here, this is where what I might now call the *weak* phenomenology of process enters the picture[22]: humans learn about, and thereby come to assume, their own qualified privilege only by experiencing their proximate modes of becoming—sense perception, consciousness, and the like—as abstractions from the vague totality of process. What humans thus come to experience is precisely their double status, the fact that their phenomenal feeling of the world does not and cannot coincide with the nonphenomenal feeling that literally feels it into becoming. Although the apprehension of this noncoincidence may well be experienced by human consciousness as a disempowerment, as a fatal blow to human autonomy, the broader realization that it positions humans to experiment counterfactually with the potentiality informing process marks a crucial achievement: the capacity for certain products of process—certain societies of actualities—to retrospectively become the (partial) subject of process. Rather than an achievement of particular, fully individuated entities, this capacity for subjecthood qualifies process itself, and should be understood, first and foremost, as a claim about humanness, as the designation for process once it has crossed a certain threshold of complexity.

The Whitehead of *Modes of Thought* understands this capacity in terms of value and importance: because they grasp that their own becoming is part of a larger process, humans are proxies for "humanness" and are able to serve as (partial) subjects for all (or at least potentially all) entities in the universe. Humans, that is, are those enduring processual entities capable of appreciating the value and importance of everything in nature. If it is on account of this capacity that humans obtain their qualified privilege, we can see that this privilege is not one of essence, not one that elevates them above other entities. Rather, as Whitehead clearly expresses when he understands the human to be the result of a difference in degree that makes a difference, it is a radically pragmatic privilege: humans are those entities most capable of feeling on the basis of potentiality. They are those entities most capable of experiencing process in the fullness of its vague totality. And, insofar as contemporary machine learning and algorithmic technologies operate *precisely* to expand and intensify the potentiality informing process, they are, as it were, *processually imbricated* with humans. Societies for technical feeling are *the products* of this imbrication: they combine technical operations and human sensitivity in a real togetherness of feeling that can be modulated retrospectively, by humans acting as (partial) subjects, with the aim of designing prospectively for particular desired futures.

Conceptualized as active "agents" or "designers" of process, societies for technical feeling thus open hitherto untapped potentialities for algorithms to enhance experience in ways hardly imaginable in our contemporary capitalist technoculture. They furnish a powerful "weapon" for overcoming the onto-epistemological cleavage separating humans from everything else, and thus for "upholding the value intensity" of the universe. Conceptualizing our contemporary situation through this potentiality, we can exercise the "difference in degree" that makes all the difference, the *human* difference, by asking these crucial counterfactual questions: What might our world become if algorithms functioned to intensify rather than to instrumentalize the broad potentiality of process? What might we become capable of realizing if, instead of capturing process in the service of narrow and short-term, "predatory" abstractions, algorithms were deployed to engage process in and through its fullest potentiality?

Notes

I want to thank Tim Othold and David Rambo for their incisive comments on this chapter.

1. Allan's key argument hinges on the capacity for actual entities to arise solely on the basis of the resources of their inheritance of the past. Because a new concrescing actual entity engages its past—which is to say, the physical inheritance of its past, *as potentiality*—it arises through the operation of evaluating and "transmuting" the past, not simply by reproducing it. This operation is itself the source for the subjective aim that, on Whitehead's account, can only be explained by God's conceptual prehension of all eternal objects. Allan writes: "A conceptual feeling has a subjective form provided by the concrescing subject, its manner of prehending that feeling, one that involves a valuation of what was felt physically. The nascent actual entity not only registers the possibility but also judges it. It thereby 'endows the transcendent creativity with the character of adversion, or of aversion' (276). Because these adversive and aversive judgments are applied to physical feelings from which the now-evaluated conceptual feelings were derived, *how those physical feelings are henceforth felt is as possibilities worthy of actualization.* They are felt as relevant or irrelevant, significantly so or trivially, to an outcome. 'Creative purpose' thus emerges in the actual entity's initial prehendings. How it acquires subjectivity is through becoming 'a determinate of its own concrescence.' It determines 'its own ideal of itself' by means of the 'eternal principles of valuation' described in the categoreal obligations, in the generic conditions of Creativity which it has 'autonomously modified' by giving them an existential application, thereby transforming a generic aim into a subjective aim" (Allan 2020: 65).

2. "It is fundamental to the metaphysical doctrine of the philosophy of organism, that the notion of an actual entity as the unchanging subject of change is completely abandoned. An actual entity is at once the subject experiencing and the superject of its experiences. It is subject-superject, and neither half of this description can for a moment be lost sight of. The term 'subject' will be mostly employed when the actual entity is considered in respect to its own real internal constitution. But "subject" is always to be construed as an abbreviation of 'subject-superject'" (Whitehead 1978: 29).
3. In his account of how new actualities feel or prehend the *entirety* of the past, settled universe, Whitehead distinguishes between positive and negative prehension. Positive prehensions, or feelings proper, are the feelings of past actualities that are relevant to the new actuality. Negative prehensions, by contrast, involve the dismissal of feelings of past actualities that are not relevant to the new actuality. For Whitehead, importantly, such negative prehensions or dismissals of past actualities nonetheless constitute a relation that itself is relevant to the actuality at issue. For further discussion, see Hansen (2015: 10, 13, 100).
4. Whitehead borrows the term "perpetual perishing" from John Locke, though not without a critical emendation: "The ancient doctrine that no one crosses the same river 'twice' is extended. No thinker thinks twice; and, to put the matter more generally, no subject experiences twice. This is what Locke ought to have meant by his doctrine of time as 'perpetual perishing'" (Whitehead 1978: 29). Or again: "Locke's notion of passage of time is that something is 'perpetually perishing.' If he had grasped the notion that the actual entity 'perishes' in the passage of time, so that no actual entity changes, he would have arrived at the point of view of the philosophy of organism" (147).
5. See Jones (1998) and Allan (2020). Allan argues that Whitehead's God is inconsistent with Whitehead's metaphysical scheme and that Whitehead adapted his conception of how eternal objects function in order to accord with God's manner of eternality.
6. See Allan (2020: chapter 3).
7. For Whitehead, propositions operate at a level prior to judgments and beliefs. "A proposition," Whitehead states, "is an element in the objective lure *proposed for* feeling, and when admitted into feeling it constitutes *what is felt*" (Whitehead 1978: 187). Propositions are what judgments and beliefs qualify. As such, propositions need not be either true or false in themselves. Indeed, as Whitehead puts it in one of his more quotable statements, "in the real world it is more important that a proposition be interesting than that it be true" (259).
8. A phenomenotechnical operation is an instrumental, scientific experiment involving the inseparable co-participation of both human and material elements. I borrow the concept from philosopher Gaston Bachelard who develops it in reference to the challenges posed by quantum physics. For

more on the concept of phenomenotechnics, and its role in conceptualizing digital culture, see Hansen (2020).
9. For more on what a nonalgorithmic theory of algorithms is or might be, see Hansen forthcoming.
10. These examples reference discussions by Latour (1992) and Bennett (2010), respectively.
11. I cite the relevant passage below. See also Hayles (2017: chapter 6).
12. David Rambo has pointed out to me the need to qualify the use of distinction here. Strictly speaking, on Whitehead's account, it is inconsistent to posit a stage of process that is not utterly concrete, and thus distinct from all else, "distinct in itself," as it were. For Whitehead, various social orders must be *both* mutually together *and* distinct from one another. Indeed, on his account, it is precisely their distinction, their singular concreteness, that contributes to their mutual togetherness; such togetherness of the distinct is the source for the complexity that informs the superject's intensity. So, to be strictly correct, we would need to qualify Voss, Engell, and Othold's statement to reflect this situation: "bodies, experience, and media" can only compose together in the way both they and I propose because they are distinct processes, and hence distinct perspectives of a common becoming. However, because this distinction only comes into being through the actual process of composition, it is "distinct" from distinction at the higher level of already individuated experiential entities. Alternatively put, this distinction among individual entities is an epistemological one that arises on the basis of a prior metaphysical togetherness.
13. In *Process and Reality*, Whitehead draws a categorical distinction between two modes of potentiality: "pure" and "real" potentiality. Pure potentiality is the generic potentiality of the universe and characterizes the mode of potentiality of eternal objects (sense qualities, mathematical relations, etc.). Real potentiality characterizes the concrete potentiality of process at any given atomic moment, and thus makes potentiality subject to the constraint of the settled world. Propositions are one mode in which the potentiality of eternal objects is constrained by the physical past of process; they combine conceptual potentiality with physical fact and are thus "impure" in Whitehead's terminology. Following John Dewey's lead, I have questioned the coherence of Whitehead's notion of "pure potentiality," along with the *purity* he ascribes to eternal objects that are, on his account, its vehicles. See Hansen (2015: 171–4, 240–1).
14. In her effort to replace the human–nonhuman distinction with that between cognizer–noncognizer, Hayles differentiates between "agents" and "actors": "For their part, noncognizers may possess agential powers that dwarf anything humans can produce: think of the awesome powers of an avalanche, tsunami, tornado, blizzard, sandstorm, hurricane. ... since material processes are the underlying forces that nourish and give rise to

life, they deserve recognition and respect in their own right, as foundational to everything else that exists. What they cannot do, acting by themselves, is make choices and perform interpretations. A tornado cannot choose to plow through a field rather than devastate a town. Material processes, of course, respond to contexts and, in responding, change them. But because they lack the capacity for choice, they perform as agents, not as actors embedded in cognitive assemblages with moral and ethical implications" (Hayles 2017: 31).

15. French philosopher of technology, Bertrand Gille (a key source for Bernard Stiegler), characterizes technical evolution as a "loose determinism" and conceives of it as an (to some extent) open process whereby the development of technical forms is open to a range of uses: for Gille, the possibilities presented by a technical system are "quasi-obligatory paths" (Gille, *History of Technics*, cited in Stiegler 1998: 34–5). I thank David Rambo for pointing me to this heritage.
16. For Hayles, it is capitalism—and not the intrinsic "evolution" of technics—that is most responsible for this instrumental reduction of technology. More could be said about this distinction—it lies at the heart of Simondon's theory of concretization—but would be outside the scope of the current discussion.
17. Whitehead's debt to Darwinian evolutionary theory has become more clear with the recent publication of the first volume of his Harvard Lectures (Whitehead 2020).
18. "Cognitive technologies show a clear trajectory toward greater agency and autonomy. In some instances, they are performing actions outside the realm of human possibility, as when high-frequency trading algorithms conduct trades in five milliseconds or less, something no human could do. In other cases, the intent is to lessen the load on the most limited resource, human attention—for example, with self-driving cars. Perhaps the most controversial examples of technical autonomy are autonomous drones and robots with lethal capacity, now in development. In part because these technologies unsettle many traditional assumptions, they have been sites for intense debate, within both the military and civilian communities. They can therefore serve as test cases for the implications of distributed agency and, more broadly, for the ways in which cognitive assemblages interact with complex human systems to create new kinds of possibilities, challenges, and dangers" (Hayles 2017: 45–6).
19. Debaise elucidates the rationale for subjectivity's retrospective orientation. Commenting on Whitehead's arguments that the philosophy of organism "conceives the thought as a constituent operation in the creation of the occasional thinker" and that "the thinker is the final end whereby there is thought," Debaise writes: "This subject that is in full possession of itself and, hence, of its feelings (or, in Whitehead's example, of its thoughts), and that seems to be below its alterations and to act as a support for them, should not

be considered as a primary reality but, quite the opposite, to be retrospective. The subject is the outcome of a "chain of experiences" from which it becomes fully itself and acquires its own completeness. The subject appears at the moment that its feelings crystallize into a unified experience, a complex of feelings becomes a singular experience. Most of the time, a thought does not need to be tied to a subject, but if, retrospectively, we try to retrace the steps of its development, we can add a subject to it, when it is actually derivative" (Debaise 2017: 55).
20. Consider, for example, the following passage from *Unthought*: "The human designer has a special role to play not easily assigned to technical systems, for she, much more than the technical cognitive systems in which she is enmeshed, is able to envision and evaluate ethical and moral consequences in the context of human sociality and world horizons that are the distinctive contributions of human conscious and nonconscious cognitions. Consequently, we need a framework in which human cognition is recognized for its uniquely valuable potential, without insisting that human cognition is the whole of cognition or that it is unaffected by the technical cognizers that interpenetrate it" (Hayles 2017: 136).
21. The noncoincidence of consciousness with its causal source is one of the major arguments I develop in *Feed-Forward*. In my treatment, it serves to distinguish Whitehead's speculative philosophy, including its phenomenological dimension, from orthodox, that is, Husserlian, phenomenology, which is quite literally animated by the dream of such coincidence.
22. By characterizing Whiteheadian phenomenology as "weak," I recur to and in some sense further specify the account I developed in *Feed-Forward*. Where my emphasis there—on the post facto human evaluation of data fed forward into consciousness—did not require me to interrogate and reconceptualize the composition of consciousness itself, here that is precisely what is at issue. Humans must learn through a "phenomenology of experience" that their cognitive and perceptual grasp of the world is a necessarily partial abstraction from a larger vague totality of process, and that the source of this "self-critical" phenomenology is process itself, not the capacities of human subjects or minds.

References

Allan, G. (2020), *Whitehead's Radically Temporalist Metaphysics: Recovering the Seriousness of Time*, Lanham, MD: Lexington Books.

Amoore, L. (2020), *Cloud Ethics: Algorithms and the Attributes of Ourselves and Others*, Durham, NC: Duke University Press.

Bennett, J. (2010), *Vibrant Matter: A Political Ecology of Things*, Durham, NC: Duke University Press.

Chalmers, D., and Clark, A. (1998), "The Extended Mind," *Analysis* 58 (1): 7–19.
Debaise, D. (2017), *Nature as Event: The Lure of the Possible*, trans. M. Halewood, Durham, NC: Duke University Press.
Hansen, M. (2015), *Feed-Forward: On the Future of Twenty-First Century Media*, Chicago: University of Chicago Press.
Hansen, M. (2020), "The Critique of Data, or towards a Phenomenotechnics of Algorithmic Culture," in E. Hörl, N. Pinkrah, and L. Warnsholdt (eds.), *Critique and the Digital*, Zurich: Diaphanes.
Hansen, M. (forthcoming), "Incompressibility of the Sensible."
Hayles, N. K. (2017), *Unthought: The Power of the Cognitive Nonconscious*, Chicago: University of Chicago Press.
Jones, J. (1998), *Intensity: An Essay in Whiteheadian Ontology*, Nashville, TN: Vanderbilt University Press.
Latour, B. (1992), "Where Are the Missing Masses? The Sociology of a Few Mundane Artifacts," in W. E. Bijker and J. Law (eds.), *Shaping Technology/Building Society: Studies in Sociotechnical Change*, 225–58. Cambridge, MA: MIT Press.
Sellars, W. ([1963] 2017), "Empiricism and the Philosophy of Mind," in *Science, Perception and Reality*, 129–94, Atascadero, CA: Ridgeview.
Simondon, G. (2020), *Individuation in the Light of the Notions of Form and Information*, trans. T. Atkins, Minneapolis: University of Minnesota Press.
Stiegler, B. (1998), *Technics and Time 1: The Fault of Epimetheus*, trans. R. Beardsworth, Stanford, CA: Stanford University Press.
Whitehead, A. N. (1920), *The Concept of Nature*, Ithaca, NY: Cornell University Press.
Whitehead, A. N. (1925), *Science and the Modern World*, New York: Macmillan.
Whitehead, A. N. (1938), *Modes of Thought*, New York: Free Press.
Whitehead, A. N. (1978), *Process and Reality*, ed. D. R. Griffin and D. W. Sherburne, New York: Free Press.
Whitehead, A. N. (2020), *Whitehead at Harvard, 1924–25*, ed. B. Henning and J. Petek, Edinburgh: Edinburgh University Press.

6

Chemæra

Jason Pine

During hunting season Camille goes with her boyfriend over the border to Illinois to get his meat cured and that's when she'll buy suet for her feeders. The cardinals and the blue jays and the mourning doves come every day, even in winter. Her cats watch them from the bedroom window. When she's not up at the Trattoria waiting tables or soaking in the bath, Camille lays on the bed watching too.

But behind the scene of frenzied feeding is another scene she can't help but notice. Meth Mountain. She hated that people called it by that name. The side of the steep wooded hill has colors and shapes that don't belong to it. When there isn't a lot of snow, you can see them. Orange-capped Gatorade bottles, empty aluminum blister packs, white plastic jugs with emerald green labels ... *Lowes. Never Stop Improving.*

Meth Mountain is in a county people used to call the meth capital of the world. Hundreds of small-scale labs were busted here year after year for over a decade. People cook meth often to feed their desire to be amped, to work longer and harder at their blue-collar jobs, and to tinker at home, which includes meth cooking. Making meth and taking meth makes a living wage, until consumption catches up with production.

Eastern Missouri is what Kim Fortun (2012) might describe as "late industrial"—an ongoing deindustrialization characterized by dilapidated infrastructure, ecological injury, joblessness, and the nevertheless persistent desire for toxic goods that fuels industrial production (Fortun 2012).[1] Camille lives in a region home to the very first and latest Walmarts. It's also the Old Lead Belt, fifteen minutes downstream and downwind from the last American primary lead smelter, which closed just a few years ago.

It's irresistible to try to connect the high incidence of lead poisoning and its neurochemical expression in attention deficit disorder with the fact that so many residents of this region pursue amphetamines, a remedy that pharmaceutical companies aggressively market.[2] The lead smelter, just one part of a giant Missouri operation, provided a livelihood for people while

 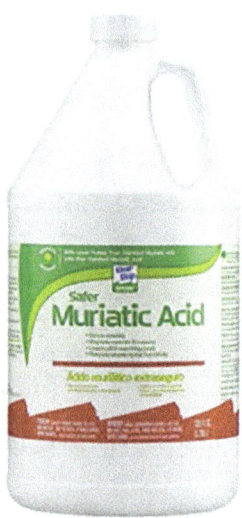

Figure 6.1 Product advertisements.

contaminating their air, soil, and water. Remedy morphs into poison morphs into remedy.

Although the causal link between lead poising and amphetamine-seeking in Eastern Missouri is impossible to prove, the underlying supposition that a body, its labors, and an ecology are ontogenetically entangled is made plain by Meth Mountain, an industrial chemical landscape inhabited by chemically particular beings. Meth cooks are late industrial alchemists who assist postnature in exceeding itself so that it may sustain a postlife arrangement of human species, chemical species, and late industrial ecologies.[3] Biological and industrial consumer existents intermingle on uncertain ground, producing a chimerical de/composition.

*

One of the times I followed the gravel road that winds up Meth Mountain, I found what looked like an abandoned trailer. It was cold outside and no one was in sight, but an outdoor light was on, throwing a glow over the strange leavings in the dirt. They were remnants not of the one-pot Shake-n-Bake method (muriatic acid, instant cold packs, lithium strips from batteries, pseudoephedrine), but of the Red and Black (red phosphorous, iodine, and lye). This was the preferred method of longtime cook Ray, who I talked to in the county jail.

Red and Black is more precise. It's harder to make, and when I got good at it I felt good that I could do something. They told me, *it's gonna take you a year to learn how to do it.* It took me eight weeks. I'm talking about eight weeks of cookin' *every day all day*—until I got it *right*. I mean I wanted to be perfect. I wanted people to always talk about it. I had the best shit that there was on the street.

Ray says he was more addicted to cooking it than using it. This isn't only because he, like many cooks, did not wear a gas mask or a wet rag to filter the airborne meth dust that is suspended in the air before settling on all the furniture, floors, and walls, from which it can desorb for years.[4] The high is also the thrill of exercising mastery over matter and anticipating success despite the risk of a bust or combustion. Many cooks say the anxious energy makes them better at what they do. Self-modulated fear turns intense risk into value. Through a hyperactivated sensorium, meth cooks are entrained to their new workaday ordinary—chemically, affectively, bodily: the wide-ranging and perduring "normalization of disequilibration."[5] This is the description Randy Martin (2012) uses to indicate that the 2008 financial crisis is more (or less) than a series of causes and events. Riding precarity like a high,[6] meth cooks fully realize what Papadopoulos et al. call embodied capitalism, the reorganization of a body's "intrinsic structure and of its connections to other human bodies, machines, animals, and things" in order to maintain the productivity of labor (Papadopoulos, Stephenson, and Tsianos 2008: 225).

*

I treated people right. I'm not the normal run-of-the-mill cook that would take advantage of people. If I seen you gettin' out there I'd cut you off, OK? I don't wanna take bread and food off your table and your kids don't eat. OK? I was running around back then with a hat on that had a gold cross. It was my ministry. That's gonna sound crazy, but that's how I looked at it. I'd help you pay your bills if you were behind. I would only do it *one time*, get you out of the hot. It was my ministry. I thought I could run around and do all this stuff because God didn't want me to get caught. And the Bible says I can take the worst of the worst, the evil of evil and turn it around and make it into good, so why can't I do it this way?

Ray also describes his work as a "maintenance program." He likens it to God's work. He administered a pharmakon, a remedy that at the wrong dose or in the wrong circumstances can become a poison.[7] This is how, at the same time, Ray can declare, "There's no ifs, ands, or buts about it. Meth is sorcery."

Figure 6.2 Book jacket, Meth = Sorcery by Steve Box (2000).

*

Ray is referring to a book popular in evangelical faith-based treatment programs in prisons and churches in the Ozarks. In the years following the book's publication in 2000, its author, Steve Box, spoke at "freedom from meth" rallies to which cooks, users, and others affected by meth were invited:

> Now, understand methamphetamine has to be transformed with some kind of metal—it revolves around this.
> Methamphetamine is what Satan has been working on for hundreds and hundreds of years developing a substance that would transform the human person into a likeness of him. A substance that when taken, magically transforms that person's values, morals and character into an exact opposite of the Creator. This has been withheld until now when the return of Jesus Christ is closer than ever before.
> Understand that there is a vast satanic kingdom in the spiritual realm … where anything that can destroy humans is developed and perfected and is constantly being worked on. [Meth] has been developed so that almost anyone can cook it. It has a demonic bewitchment over it …
> How this is accomplished is through the bewitchment … and the sorcery and alchemy that underlies the brew itself. It's the stirring and bubbling and smoking … how ingredients are placed in then taken out. (Box 2000: 28)

In his book, Box compiles the many references to sorcery found in the Bible. He argues that they all literally point to methamphetamine as sorcery's materialization. Himself a former cook, Box emphasizes how methamphetamine captures all thought, energy, and desire. You live for meth and without it you can't live. However, he proclaims, citing Exod. 22:18: "Thou shalt not suffer a witch to live" (Box 2000: 30).

To suffer a witch to live—in their book *Capitalist Sorcery* (2011)—Philippe Pignarre and Isabelle Stengers conjure the same realm of associations to critique capitalism. They use the term "sorcery" to identify forms of destruction that are pitched as necessary sacrifices, as "the price to pay for the triumph of a liberating rationality" (Pignarre and Stengers 2011: 41). Echoing Horkheimer and Adorno (2002), they argue that Enlightenment thinking defined itself as the liberation from magical thinking. However, they write that Enlightened thought conjures its own magical allure at the same time. Through techniques of industry, science, and medicine, it disenchants the world but, more significantly, it *enhances* global capitalist hegemony with sorcerous power (Latour 1993; Taussig 1987).

Meth, the pharmakon, opens a "streaming metamorphicity" (Taussig 2006: 140), blurring Ray's techniques (his meth cooking and ministrations) with his enchanted parishioners' enhanced techniques of everyday living with the routine techniques of capitalism. Meth = capitalist sorcery.

The routine techniques of capitalism, Pignarre and Stengers write, recast any politics that would undermine capitalism as "infernal alternatives" (Pignarre and Stengers 2011: 40). And so we may chant, *without the invisible hand of the market, we would have no life-enhancing technologies*. The spell erases the political terrain that has made life-enhancing technologies like meth feel necessary. This is what Pignarre and Stengers call sorcery, alerting us to our vulnerability before a cunning system of capture where "the slightest point of agreement with it … is lethal" (ibid.: 55). Ray does more than agree. He takes capitalist logic to its infernal extreme, enhancing the spell rather than breaking it.

*

Unlike the Shake-n-Bake method, the Red and Black requires bulky equipment, which is harder to conceal, but cooks devise ways to camouflage their work. Ray once hid a methlab in a hole he cut in the bedframe of his

Figure 6.3 Police-confiscated imitation tree stump, Missouri.

Figure 6.4 Police-confiscated imitation tree stump, Missouri.

room in an extended stay hotel, retooling a sleep technology as a laboratory of wakefulness. And on Meth Mountain, meth labs *are* the woods:

> We found a ton of these slices of tree out in the woods, they were parts made out of a mold, made of just rubber.

> And then we found this finished stump. The bark is imitation, but the lid is actually wood—he'll just take a slice of tree to put on top. Would you notice that out in the woods? This guy had a whole room dedicated to this shit where he was makin' this stuff. There were like four or five of 'em. I mean, you think this guy could design this shit for theme parks and movies.

The designs that narcotics agents found on Meth Mountain were, in fact, part of a scenography, a recomposition of late industrial ruins for staging another mode of existence.[8] A meth cook is a demiurge, a late-industrial alchemist, who hastens the work of postnature, where human and chemical species take up shared non/living arrangements on uncertain ground.[9] A faltering struggle for a life otherwise (Povinelli 2012).

*

This faltering struggle began long ago in the early decades of American industrialization.[10] In fact, the metamorphic relation of enchantment to enhancement figures large Frank Baum's "immortal American fantasy" (Littlefield 1969: 50) of 1900, *The Wizard of Oz*, which allegorizes features of the Populist resistance to the excesses of industrialization. The story of the Tin Woodman is particularly resonant.

*

A young man, the son of a Woodwoman who died, became himself a Woodman and took care of his widowed father, chopping wood until the day his father died. Then when he was all on his own, the Woodman decided he did not want to grow lonely, so he sought a mate. He then found love in a tree stump.

The tree stump told the Woodman it would marry him if he built a house fit for them both to live in. Inspired, the Woodman got to work. But the tree stump worked as a chopping block in the house of a wealthy woman who did not want to let it go. And so the wealthy woman went to the Witch of the East and offered him two boxes of Sudafed to prevent the marriage.

Enthralled by the gifts, the Witch enchanted the Woodman's axe. And as the Woodman chopped wood for the new home that he planned to share with his mate, his axe swung not at the wood, but at his own leg.

At first the Woodman despaired. What good is a Woodman with only one leg? But then he had the idea to ask the Tinsmith to fashion a replacement for him. The Tinsmith indeed built him a new leg, and thus remade, the Woodman set out again at making his house.

The Witch of the East was irked, so he enchanted the axe again and caused the Woodman to chop off his other leg. But the Woodman again took himself to the Tinsmith and had him make a tin leg to replace what he had cut off.

The Witch, now enraged, made the axe chop off each of the Woodman's arms. The Woodman, however, found that the Tinsmith could replace those too.

Unrelenting, the Witch cut off the Woodman's head, and now the Woodman was sure he was done in. Fortunately, however, the Tinsmith just happened to pass by and he stopped to make the Woodman a head of tin to replace what he had lost.

Believing he was now free, the Woodman set back to work on his house with renewed vigor. But the Witch would not be beat. Once again, he *enhanced* the axe so that it split the Woodman's body in half. But the Woodman found a solution for that too. He went to the Tinsmith and the Tinsmith made him a body.

But now the Tin Woodman had no heart and he no longer loved the tree stump.

Figure 6.5 Tim Haley as The Tin Woodman in *The Wizard of Oz* (Metro Goldwyn-Mayer Studios).

But his body shone in the sun and of that he was proud. And if his axe slipped again, it would not harm him, and that made him bold.

The only danger was rain, for if the Tinman's iron joints rusted, he would be paralyzed. He therefore carried with him at all times an oilcan. Just a few drops meant mobility—it meant life.

*

Frank Baum's tale describes workaday bondage (for both the Tin Woodman and the Munchkin) and the doomed attempt to free oneself by enhancing capitalist-enchanted labor. "Eastern" capital (as in the East Coast of the United States) enchanted the independent laborer to work harder and faster until he became less-than-human.

The Wizard of Oz has been celebrated more in its film version from 1939. The book was condemned by fundamentalist Christians because it suggests that human virtues are "individually developed rather than God-given" and because it depicts "good" witches (who ruled the North and South) (Culver 1988: 97).[11]

In the movie Dorothy *dreams* of Oz, but in the book Oz is "a fantastic world that is *just as real as* and *contiguous with* Kansas" (ibid.: 99, emphasis added).

In the book, Kansas is not a black-and-white pastoral opposed to the glittering Emerald City of modern capitalism. Instead, Kansas is gray and barren. "Nature on the plains reduces everything to the same gray indifference" (ibid.: 100).

Baum was editor of the *Saturday Pioneer* and documented the financial and natural disasters that inspired agrarian resistance to the corporate organization of farming, the speculative finance of the Northeast, and a shrunken money supply caused by the demonetization of silver. The resistance crystallized in the Populist belief that agrarian life was morally superior to unregulated industrial production.[12] By using direct labor, the family farm produces commodities that satisfy direct needs (ibid.: 101).

Baum was writing in the aftermath of Populism's failure. In his Emerald City, the color green (which everyone sees through the lenses they're required to wear) is an evanescent quality that trumps the potential material value of all objects. In the Emerald City, people pursue value in the abstract, which is only manifest in the moment before objects are put to use (ibid.: 103).

Baum didn't disavow the sparkle of industrial capitalism. He believed that industrial-consumerist desire was one expression of a fundamental lack that made humans who they are: never-complete desiring machines. In 1900 he also published *The Art of Decorating Dry Goods Windows*, where he elaborated techniques for shop window advertising.

The Tin Woodman resembles a manikin. If his story is read as a sketch for shop window advertising, it shows that manikins are only lifelike if they manifest completion while dramatizing lack, inciting in consumers the desire for an evanescent object that promises to complete them yet defers satiation (ibid.: 110).[13]

Figure 6.6 Top: Still from *The Wizard of Oz* (1936, Metro Goldwyn-Mayer Studios). Bottom: farmhouse in Chamois, Missouri.

Figure 6.7 Still from *The Wizard of Oz* (1936), Metro-Goldwyn-Mayer Studios.

Figure 6.8 "The Vanishing Lady," from L. Frank Baum, *The Show Window*. Yale Collection of American Literature, Beinecke Rare Book and Manuscript Library, Yale University.

Figure 6.9 Buddy Ebsen's makeup test. Metro Goldwyn-Mayer Studios.
Source: The official Tumblr of the Academy of Motion Picture Arts and Sciences.

*

In the film version of *The Wizard of Oz*, Buddy Ebsen originally played the Tin Woodman, but the aluminum powder in his makeup sent him to the hospital for two weeks. He was replaced by Jack Haley and the aluminum powder with aluminum paste to prevent inhalation. Haley also suffered poisoning, but he stuck with the role (Fricke and Shirshekan 2009).

*

Like the Tin Woodman, many Missouri meth cooks pursue an obsolete, and now toxic, American dream—to make a little life—and in so doing they transmute life.

*

In the movie, Dorothy only dreams of Oz. In the book, however, Oz is a fantastic world that is contiguous with and just as real as Kansas. Likewise, Meth Mountain is real and fantastic and it's a place somewhere here, in town. It's where everyday consumer products dance on the threshold between life and nonlife, promising to hasten the work of postnature and bring alchemical completion: immortality and gold.[14]

But while in Oz the sorcery of industrial products can be dispelled by invoking the commodity fetish concept (an enlightened discourse), the sorcery on Meth Mountain calls attention to an insistent chimærical chemical figure, one that arose from an ecology composed of an industrial chemical apparatus, the tweaked forces of social labor, and a body's neurobiological architecture.[15] This *chemæra* responds to the conditions of its making by taking them on. It is precariously real, hovering in the murk of deep ontological plasticity. And it cannot simply be dispelled.

*

Work in anthropology, sociology, geography, queer studies, social studies of science, and critical neuroscience have contributed to understandings of a contemporary figure that consolidates scientific practices, political economic interests, and discourses on personhood and health. These include the "neurochemical self" (Rose 2003), "pharmaceutical self" (Dumit 2002, 2012; Jenkins 2011a, b), "pharmaceutical person" (Martin 2006), and "psychotropic self" (Schlosser and Hoffer 2012). Other figures consolidate onto-epistemic productions of toxicity and human and nonhuman life, such as "toxic threat" (Chen 2012), "hot spot" (Krupar 2013), and "chemical infrastructure" (Murphy 2013). This essay considers a figure emerging from a chemical refrain that draws neurochemical, pharmaceutical, *and* industrial chemical content into a yet indeterminate arrangement, an ecological de/composition: the *chemæra*, its suspended expression (Choy and Zee 2015).[16] Figures, Haraway (2008: 4) writes, are "material-semiotic nodes or knots in which diverse bodies and meanings coshape one another." The chemæra is an idiom that gives expression to the elusive qualities (McLean 2011) of the ontological murk that it is. And these might be qualities of who will be us (Povinelli 2017).

A chimera is commonly figured as a hybrid embodiment of two or more creatures, from its early mythological to its contemporary genetic expression. Haraway's (1991) chimera, the cyborg, is indeterminately extensive, looped

Figure 6.10 Chæmera by Jason Pine, from the exhibit *Altered Being*, curated by Nick Shapiro, Chemical Heritage Foundation Museum, Philadelphia, September 18–19, 2015.

into wider technoscientific apparatuses and troubling borders to a then unprecedented degree. The chemæra emphasizes the leaky and diffuse chemical composition of a late industrial, late liberal chimera. Quite unlike any other chimera, it alters and pulls up "the ground behind it" and casts "new terrains ahead" (Casid 2011: 63).

*

Camille paid a young pregnant woman and her boyfriend 15 bucks to pick up the trash on Meth Mountain so she didn't have to look at it. They needed the cash. But the trash keeps reappearing. Years ago, the natural spring down the road was laid waste by a new McDonalds, even though the historical society Camille had co-founded tried to block it. Now she can't wait until the developers come in so she can sell her house and move. Maybe they'll put in a Home Depot or a Lowes.

*

Ray was sensing his time was up, his time with Jason. Put me on ten years' probation, you know, make me do ten thousand hours, I don't care. I'm done. I'm done with that life.

Then Ray remembered that idea he had the other day—maybe it would convince Jason. There were a couple of times when I got clean that I thought

I could be a drug counselor. I have no problem being able to tell somebody how to live their own life. Now for myself, to put it in my own practice, that's the hard part. When it comes to other people the situation is always pretty clear. And that's a skill, being able to read the signs, but really, they're right there in front of you if you pay attention.

He was getting nothing. It was true, he wasn't convincing, Ray knew it. Sure, for me, it's a skill I used mostly to keep cooking and avoid trouble, but there's no reason I can't take what I learned and apply it to doing good.

Ray was getting that sinking feeling again. Whenever he hoped for something, there it was. And both feelings just goaded each other on. I've always said it, I could write a book—or a movie. I know someone who'll write the music … Well, when you're done maybe I can get a copy of your book?

Notes

1. "Toxic" applies to both human bodies and the ecologies of which they are a part. Other writers, like Metzl and Kirkland (2010), emphasize that concepts and practices of "health" construct social physiologies.
2. In 2014 the US Department of Justice alleged that Shire Pharmaceuticals made claims about Adderall XR (mixed amphetamine salts) without clinical data to back them up, including that the drug would improve academic performance, reduce unemployment, prevent criminal behavior, and normalize children by reducing their symptoms to the levels of non-ADHD-affected children. Shire settled the case with a sum of $56.5 million but did not admit to any wrongdoing (DOJ 2014).
3. The following words were ascribed to the medieval alchemist Roger Bacon (1597: 14–15): "For the forerunners of this Art, who have founde it out by their philosofie do point out with their finger the direct & plain way, when they say: 'Nature, containeth nature: Nature ouercommeth nature: & Nature meeting with her nature, exceedingly reioyceth, and is changed into other natures.'"
4. Phosphine, hydrochloric acid, and iodine are also airborne before they settle, but in smaller amounts. See Weisheit (2008). Cooks using the Red and Black method often blocked their vents to prevent outsiders from smelling their work, preventing the otherwise quick dissipation of phosphine and hydrochloric acid.
5. Martin (2012: 64n5) writes that most accounts of the ongoing global financial crisis that had its peak in 2008 tend to focus on finite causes (poor regulation and insolvency) or minority protagonists (rogue financial engineers and traders), thereby failing to recognize that there has been a wide-ranging and perduring "normalization of disequilibration."

6. Sinisterly, Lea (2012) finds that parallel affects move the bureaucrats who formulate and implement social policy for the "anarchic" Indigenous.
7. Cf. Jacques Derrida (1981), "Plato's Pharmacy." For the ambiguities disavowed by modern pharmacology and science more broadly, see Stengers (2010: 28–41).
8. In his "Compositionist Manifesto," Latour (2010) writes that decomposed Progress, Reason, and Nature are the ruins of the "modernist mise-en-scène," and that a more livable project has not yet taken its place (476–7).
9. Alchemical writings often describe alchemy's Great Work as the hastening and completion of nature's processes, but contemporary late industrial alchemy works in postnature. Povinelli (2016) writes that in contemporary late liberalism a "biontological orientation and distribution of power" concerned with the relationship of life and death is giving way to a geontological orientation and distribution of power concerning the relationship of life and nonlife.
10. See Dudley (2002) for its recurrence in farming's boom and bust in the 1970s–80s, which was cast with an "aura of inevitability" and the "routine financial transactions" of borrowing and capital investment, and debt amassment took on a spirit all their own (21–42).
11. The Witch of the West may have represented the unforgiving forces of nature (e.g., cyclones and drought) and the witches of the North and South the joint forces of factory and agricultural labor movements.
12. Which they hoped could in part be mitigated by the eight-hour workday.
13. This can also be said of the Scarecrow.
14. The goal of alchemy across Chinese, Indian, and Alexandrian traditions has most often been either the production of the elixir of life or the transmutation of base metals into gold. See, for example, Bensaud-Vincent and Stengers (1996).
15. Shapiro (2015) tracks the making and working of a related figure, the "human Geiger counter." Weston (2012) argues that affective attachments and the "capital-intensive regimes of production designed to elicit them" result in a "continuous sensory engagement with industrially sourced experiences of consumption" (making impossible any arrangements other than what I suggest here is capitalism's infernal extreme).
16. Choy and Zee (2015) write that "ethnography constitutes a work of suspension" and "turns attention from the powers of the makers to the powers of their monster: the contents and discontents of modern atmosphere." For content, expression, and refrains, see Deleuze and Guattari (1987: 310–50).

References

Bacon, Roger (1597), *The Mirror of Alchimy*, London: Richard Olive.

Bensaud-Vincent, Bernadette, and Isabelle Stengers (1996), *A History of Chemistry*. Cambridge, MA: Harvard University Press.

Box, Steve (2000), *Meth=Sorcery: Know the Truth*. Pierce City, Missouri: Above All Ministries.

Casid, Jill H. (2013), "Chimerical Figurations at the Monstrous Edges of Species," in Stephanie LeMenager, Teresa Shewry, and Ken Hiltner (eds.), *Environmental Criticism for the Twenty-First Century*, 61–84, New York: Routledge.

Chen, Mel Y. (2012), *Animacies: Biopolitics, Racial Mattering, and Queer Affect*, Durham, NC: Duke University Press.

Choy, Timothy, and Zee, Jerry (2015), "Condition—Suspension," *Cultural Anthropology* 30 (2): 210–23. http://dx.doi.org/10.14506/ca30.2.04.

Culver, Stuart (1988), "What Manikins Want: The Wonderful World of Oz and the Art of Decorating Dry Goods Windows," *Representations* 21: 97–116.

Deleuze, Gilles, and Felix Guattari (1987), *A Thousand Plateaus: Capitalism and Schizophrenia*, trans. Brian Massumi, Minneapolis: University of Minnesota Press.

Derrida, Jacques (1981), "Plato's Pharmacy," in *Dissemination*, ed. Barbara Johnson, 61–171, Chicago: University of Chicago Press.

Dudley, Kathryn Marie (2002), *Debt and Dispossession: Farm Loss in America's Heartland*, Chicago: University of Chicago Press.

Dumit, Joseph (2002), "Drugs for Life," *Molecular Interventions* 2 (3): 124–7.

Dumit, Joseph (2012), *Drugs for Life: How Pharmaceutical Companies Define Our Health*, Durham, NC: Duke University Press.

Fortun, Kim (2012), "Ethnography in Late Industrialism," *Cultural Anthropology* 27 (3): 446–64.

Fricke, John, and Jonathan Shirshekan (2009), *The Wizard of Oz: An Illustrated Companion to the Timeless Movie Classic*. New York: Fall River Press.

Haraway, Donna J. (2008), *When Species Meet*, Minneapolis: University of Minnesota Press.

Haraway, Donna J. (1991), *Simians, Cyborgs, and Women: The Reinvention of Nature*, New York: Routledge.

Horkheimer, Max, Theodor W. Adorno, and Gunzelin Schmid Noeri (2002), *Dialectic of Enlightenment*, Stanford, CA: Stanford University Press.

Jenkins, Janice H. (2011a), "Introduction," in Janice H Jenkins (ed.), *The Pharmaceutical Self: The Global Shaping of Experience in Psychopharmacology*, 3–16, Santa Fe, NM: SAR Press.

Jenkins, Janice H. (2011b), "Psychopharmaceutical Self and Imaginary in the Social Field of Psychiatric Treatment," in Janice H. Jenkins (ed.), *The Pharmaceutical Self: The Global Shaping of Experience in Psychopharmacology*, 17–40, Santa Fe, NM: SAR Press.

Krupar, Shiloh R. (2013), *Hot Spotters Report: Military Fables of Toxic Waste*, Minneapolis: University of Minnesota Press.

Latour, Bruno (1993), *We Have Never Been Modern*, Cambridge, MA: Harvard University Press.
Latour, Bruno (2010), "An Attempt at a 'Compositionist Manifesto,'" *New Literary History* 41 (3): 471–90.
Lea, Tess (2012), "When Looking for Anarchy, Look to the State: Fantasies of Regulation in Forcing Disorder within the Australian Indigenous Estate," *Public Culture* 32 (2): 109–24.
Littlefield, Henry M. (1964), "The Wizard of Oz: Parable on Populism," *American Quarterly* 16 (1) (Spring, 1964): 47–58.
Martin, Emily (2006), "The Pharmaceutical Person," *BioSocieties* 1: 273–88.
Martin, Randy (2012), "A Precarious Dance, A Derivative Sociality," *TDR* 56 (4): 62–77.
McLean, Stuart (2011), "Black Goo: Forceful Encounters with Matter in Europe's Muddy Margins," *Cultural Anthropology* 26 (4): 589–619.
Metzl, Jonathan M., and Anna Kirkland (2010), *Against Health: How Health Became the New Morality*, New York: New York University Press.
Murphy, Michelle (2013), "Chemical Infrastructures of the St. Clair River," in Nathalie Jas and Soraya Boudia (eds.), *Toxicants, Health and Regulation since 1945*, 103–15, London: Pickering and Chato.
Papadopoulos, Dimitris, Niahm Stephenson, and Vassilis Tsianos (2008), *Escape Routes: Control and Subversion in the Twenty-First Century*, London: Pluto Press.
Pignarre, Philippe, and Stengers, Isabelle (2011), *Capitalist Sorcery: Breaking the Spell*, trans. Andrew Goffey, London: Palgrave.
Povinelli, Elizabeth (2012), "The Will to Be Otherwise/The Effort of Endurance," *South Atlantic Quarterly* 111 (3): 453–75.
Povinelli, Elizabeth (2016), *Geontologies: A Requiem to Late Liberalism*, Durham, NC: Duke University Press.
Povinelli, Elizabeth (2017), "Fires, Fogs, Winds," *Cultural Anthropology* 32 (4): 504–13.
Rose, Nikolas (2003), "The Neurochemical Self and Its Anomalies," in Richard V. Ericson and Aaron Doyle (eds.), *Risk and Morality*, 407–37, Toronto: University of Toronto Press.
Schlosser, Allison V., and Hoffer, Lee D. (2012), "The Psychotropic Self/Imaginary: Subjectivity and Psychopharmaceutical Use among Heroin Users with Co-occurring Mental Illness," *Culture, Medicine and Psychiatry* 36 (1): 26–50.
Shapiro, Nicholas (2015), "Attuning to the Chemosphere: Domestic Formaldehyde, Bodily Reasoning, and the Chemical Sublime," *Cultural Anthropology* 30 (3): 368–93.
Stengers, Isabelle (2010), *Cosmopolitics I*, Minneapolis: University of Minnesota Press.
Taussig, Michael (1987), *Shamanism, Colonialism and the Wild Man: A Study in Terror and Healing*, Chicago: University of Chicago Press.

Taussig, Michael (2006), "Viscerality, Faith, and Skepticism: Another Theory of Magic," in *Walter Benjamin's Grave*, 121–56, Chicago: University of Chicago Press.
U.S. Department of Justice, Office of Public Affairs (2014), "Shire Pharmaceuticals LLC to Pay $56.5 Million to Resolve False Claims Act Allegations Relating to Drug Marketing and Promotion Practices," *Justice News*, September 24. Available online: https://www.justice.gov/opa/pr/shire-pharmaceuticals-llc-pay-565-million-resolve-false-claims-act-allegations-relating-drug.
Weisheit, Ralph (2008), "Making Methamphetamine," *Southern Rural Sociology* 23 (2): 78–107.
Weston, Kath (2012), "Political Ecologies of the Precarious," *Anthropological Quarterly* 85 (2): 429–55.

7

In Control of Algorithms: Video Analytics and Human–Machine Relations at the Train Station

Gabriele Schabacher

Within the field of digital control, various types of socio-technical entanglements can be found. The following article focuses on one particular type, namely, the development and implementation of surveillance technologies in urban settings. Progress in this field is regularly attributed to countries whose data protection regulations are less strict or even nonexistent, such as Great Britain or China. However, this essay will concentrate on a more local setting, namely the German debate on "intelligent video analysis" that accompanied recent tests of pattern recognition systems in Berlin. As the article will show, this debate can illustrate in great detail how the ambition to control a complex situation creates an even more entangled constellation. The regimes of control that these tests advocate and that are attributed to the software systems used will be understood here as a "work of purification" (Latour 1993: 11), which only intensifies the proliferation of hybrids that make up the situations. An analysis of the paradoxes and inconsistencies in the execution and evaluation of these surveillance tests will show the increasing entanglement of humans and machines at several levels, the influence of which has largely been overlooked in assessing the efficacy of the systems.

My argument takes up a perspective from media and cultural theory and is unfolded in three steps. To begin with, I will briefly contextualize the relevance of the train station with respect to security issues. In the main second part, I will present a German pilot project in detail—the Berlin Südkreuz case with its two subprojects—and analyze this "surveillant assemblage" (Haggerty and Ericson 2000) by outlining the conditions of the test, the actors involved, as well as the results and hopes produced by them. On this basis, it will become clear that the implementation of facial recognition and other pattern recognition technologies cannot be seen as adding an "Unterstützungsinstrument" (supporting tool) for police work in reducing crimes (Bundespolizei 2018: 7). Rather, they interfere and intermingle with other actors so that they cannot be easily controlled, but create new sets of problems, questions, and answers, which even increase the complexity they are said to reduce.[1] In conclusion, I will highlight some aspects of my argument that provide a basis for further discussion.

Train Stations and Security Issues

To focus on train stations when talking about digital regimes of control is not necessarily obvious. Although European cities have implemented video surveillance since the 1990s, especially to monitor traffic systems, the debate on security issues after 9/11 concentrated on the airport as an international hub of global flows (Potthast 2011). Train stations, however, have only recently become part of the common imaginary of threatened places (think of the Cologne New Year's Eve 2015 or the eight-year-old boy who was killed at the Frankfurt main rail station after being pushed in front of an arriving ICE train in July 2019).[2] This is consequential, as large train stations are public urban spaces where heterogeneous groups of people and different traffic flows have intermingled intensively since the nineteenth century.[3] They thus represent places of a very dense exchange of people, goods, and messages, and are therefore subject to various procedures of regulation. We can think of the material-operational functioning of train stations as "process architectures" (Jany 2019), which seek to coordinate processes through spatial organization (through waiting rooms, counters, luggage storage, etc.). From an infrastructural perspective, such control regimes also include personal and symbolic actors that intervene in a regulating way too, for example, in the form of supervisors or signs. This is because infrastructures do not simply function per se, but are kept functioning through a variety of measures, that is, "infrastructure work" (Schabacher 2021b, 2022): order at the train station must therefore be established anew time and again.

Due to their fundamental openness, train stations are much more difficult to control than airports, with their strict segmentation (clearly separated areas, barriers, gates) and their location at considerable distance from the city centers. Although there is an international trend for train stations to become more airport-like in terms of security—such as the new train stations in Beijing (2008) or the reconstruction of the Gare Saint-Lazare in Paris (2019)—train stations in Germany continue to be accessible to everyone, even without a ticket, in order to create further zones of consumption in urban areas—the Deutsche Bahn is pursuing the concept of the "Einkaufsbahnhof" (shopping station) here.[4] In order to ensure and control traffic in such comparatively complex public urban spaces, surveillance systems are used. The surveillance technologies employed in these settings combine and enhance two different "traditions" of surveillance: on the one hand, visual surveillance in the tradition of panoptism (Foucault 1979) and CCTV (Levin, Frohne, and Weibel 2002; Lyon 2001), which nowadays includes the use of mobile monitoring devices such as bodycams. On the other hand is the tradition of "dataveillance" (Clarke 1988), meaning the tradition of bureaucratic registering and management of subjects. Intelligent video surveillance, that is, the automated algorithm-based recording and analysis of video image data (Stanley 2019; in broader perspective: Andrejevic 2020), should therefore be understood as a field that merges the (older) real-time dimension of video surveillance with the (newer) informational dimension of surveillance (mass data). Compared to historical surveillance regimes, the current situation is characterized mainly by two (technical) extensions. On the one hand, it is possible to combine different types of data—in addition to biometric data, for example, audio data, environmental data, location and tracking data, personal data, usage data—and, on the other hand, to store large amounts of data and keep them ready for potential, future (retrograde) evaluations or applications (pattern recognition, data mining). In doing so, the technology enables two things simultaneously: the recording of quantitatively extensive characteristic group patterns as well as the potential to address every concrete individual.

Testing Intelligent Video Analysis at Berlin Südkreuz

In the context of civilian use, the new technologies of intelligent video surveillance are intended to enable automated detection of dangerous situations and crimes and are therefore promoted as a valuable tool for police work. This is countered by massive data protection concerns, particularly with regard to the retrograde evaluation of video material.

In the following, I will focus on a German pilot project for intelligent video analysis that was carried out at Berlin's Südkreuz station between 2017 and 2019. Parts of the station were temporarily converted into a kind of experimental laboratory to investigate the introduction of certain measures under real conditions. Such model tests are intended to reveal any problems that might arise with regard to the technological implementation, everyday suitability, or social acceptance of these systems. Since Berlin Südkreuz was a government pilot project, there was an intense public debate in Parliament, the civil society, and the mass media.[5] Against the backdrop of stricter data protection regulations in Germany than in other countries, this can reveal problematic situations regarding the regulatory and surveillance technologies in question that would not become explicit in the nonpublic sphere or in countries with less stringent data protection directives. In the following, I would therefore like to analyze the controversy surrounding Berlin Südkreuz in more detail. To this end, I will look at the framework of the project, parliamentary requests to the federal government, statements by NGOs and other actors, media coverage, as well as the final report of the Bundespolizei (Federal Police), published in September 2018 concerning the first part of the project (Bundespolizei 2018), and show how the effort to regulate and control a complex situation such as a train station results in even more complex entanglements.

In terms of its layout, the pilot project "Sicherheitsbahnhof Berlin Südkreuz" was a collaboration between the Federal Ministry of the Interior, the Federal Police, the Federal Criminal Police Office, and Deutsche Bahn AG to explore the possibilities of intelligent video analysis in detecting criminal behavior and dangerous situations at public transport hubs. Berlin Südkreuz station, which had already been used frequently by the Deutsche Bahn to test digital innovations, lent itself to this, being Berlin's third-largest long-distance station with connections to regional and suburban rail services and modernized surveillance cameras. The pilot project consisted of two parts. While the first project, under the leadership of the German Federal Police, tested biometric facial recognition software in two phases in 2017 and 2018, the second project in 2019, which was led by the Deutsche Bahn, examined pattern recognition technologies for defined hazard situations. Although this second project, which tested software for intelligent situation and behavior analysis, was more advanced in terms of international security research, it was less controversial publicly than the first project on facial recognition. This has its reasons, from a cultural studies perspective, in the historically developed and affectively occupied relation between identity and face (Belting 2017; Weigel 2017).[6] While the first test was supposed to identify individuals on the basis of their facial data, the second test detected behaviors with regard to dangerous situations without including the face.

Facial Recognition Systems

The first project at Berlin's Südkreuz station took place in 2017 and 2018 and was designed to test different proprietary facial recognition systems. On site, three of the station's seventy-seven video cameras were selected (entrance, exit, and escalator of the west hall) (Bundespolizei 2018: annex 1). As the test was to take place under real-life conditions, the lighting conditions were not improved (ibid.: 14, 32). The signage indicated "non-detection areas" so that passers-by could avoid detection.[7] Three AI systems with comparable functionalities (Herta Security's "BioSurveillance," Idemia's "Morpho Video Investigator," and Anyvisions's "Anyvision") were tested, whose algorithms used neural networks and were capable of learning accordingly (ibid.: 14, 18). The test was carried out with the existing hardware of the station (video cameras, architecture)—a factor that often imposes limits on the implementation of digital systems—while the servers with the corresponding software and notebooks for displaying the hits were located in a separate room with appropriate access control (Bundespolizei 2018: annex 2, appendix 3). The first phase of the test (August 2017–January 2018) involved 312 participants, while the second phase (February–July 2018) involved 201. As they were all commuters, they used the station regularly. They participated voluntarily and agreed to carry a transponder when passing the station to validate the hits.[8]

If we now look in more detail at the strong efforts to control and monitor the station by the use of surveillance technologies, we realize diverse human-machine entanglements coming to the fore. The technologies used lead to an increase in complexity that cannot be compensated for by the technology itself. What had actually been introduced to objectify and clarify unmanageable situations now required extensive measures to achieve any results at all with regard to the recognition of faces. Three problems shall be briefly highlighted to illustrate this fact: the instability of the face, the representativeness of the sample, and the calculation of hit rates.

A first problem concerns the fundamental *instability of faces*. The programs tested translated the faces detected into templates according to calculable characteristic features (Bundespolizei 2018: 18–20). For identification purposes, these templates were matched with the digitally captured facial images of the participants that corresponded to biometric standards and were stored in a local reference database. A match was defined numerically as "Übereinstimmungsgrad" (degree of correspondence) (Bundespolizei 2018: 20) between the template of the detected face and the template in the reference database. Based on a predefined threshold, the system decided whether there was a match or not (ibid.). In facial recognition systems, recognizing a face is a binary decision that de facto covers a spectrum of more or less similarity. In this context, it is a well-known problem of facial recognition that differences between the faces of different people are often smaller than those between different images of the same person. This "instability of faces" (Gates 2011: 17) is caused by changing lighting conditions, age, facial expression, hairstyle, glasses, as well as beards, among other factors. Thus, the object of control—the face itself—is already much more variable, unstable, and thus complex than recognition technologies usually assume. This was one reason for changing the quality of the images in the local reference database during the first project. Instead of high-quality photographs, several lower-quality images of a person were used for matching in the second phase. However, since these images were taken from the video stream of the first phase (Bundespolizei 2018: 21), critics suspected this to be the reason for the improved performance of the systems in the second phase (CCC 2018). Each step in the complex technical construction of a biometric face image and the related identification and verification processes (Kloppenburg and van der Ploeg 2020: 60–1) thus implies new possibilities for error, deviations, and inconsistencies in relation to the reference individual, which constantly increases the artificiality of the (biometric) face image.

A second problem concerns the *representativeness of the sample*. The recruitment of volunteers worked with an incentive system: if they passed the test area regularly, they received a "recognition" of 25 euros. In addition, they could win prizes (Apple Watch, fitness watch, GoPro camera) if they passed the test area most frequently on at least thirty days (Bundespolizei 2018: annex 2, appendix 1, items 6 and 7). Despite the comparatively small group of participants, which included members of the Berlin Federal Police Headquarters, the final report of the Federal Police claimed it to be a representative sample of the users of the Berlin Südkreuz station (ibid.: 30 and annexes 3, 2). Critics, however, objected that neither had a representative selection with regard to gender, age, and skin color been made—all 312 people who had registered were simply accepted for the test (ibid.)—nor had attention been paid to possible discriminatory algorithms or effects of biometric facial recognition, especially with regard to the rate of matches and false positives for people with darker skin color (Deutscher Bundestag 2018: 7). A possible bias of facial recognition systems with regard to skin color and ethnicity was thus not taken into account in the German test, although this would have made perfect sense for the intended comparison of three proprietary systems, and the topic has been intensively discussed at the latest since the spectacular misjudgements of Amazon's "Rekognition" software (Snow 2018).[9]

But not only was the representativeness of the participants controversial, this was also the case for the sample of weeks measured. Based on the (problematic) assumption that the differences between the individual weekdays occur repeatedly in the various weeks, individual measuring days ("Messtage") were combined to measuring weeks ("Messwochen"). Only one week per month was selected for evaluation; this week had to consist of seven "überwiegend zusammenhängenden" (predominantly consecutive) weekdays (Bundespolizei 2018: 30 and 31). The wording indicates that, if necessary, seven individual days per month also qualified as a measuring week (which is not an unusual procedure in empirical data collection). This included the possibility of removing such data that would distort desired results, that is, "dirty data" (Marx 1984; with regard to pattern recognition: Steyerl 2018). Moreover, this demonstrates that the entanglements at issue not only bring together very heterogeneous entities (hardware, software, station architecture, test subjects, programmers, personnel, lighting, costs, legal aspects, etc.), but at the same time are so dense and complicated that "Rohdaten" (raw data) (Bundespolizei 2018: 31) can only be generated through a high degree of constructive work.

A third problem is related to the *number of matches* of the tested systems. Facial recognition software works as a "binary classifier" (ibid.: 30), which means that there are always four options in terms of recognition: first, true positives (the person is in the reference database, which is why the software outputs a match); second, true negatives (the person is not in the reference database, which is why no match is reported); third, false positives (the person is not in the reference database, but a match is still output); and fourth, false negatives (the person is in the database, but the software does not report a match). The category of false positives is of particular interest with regard to questions of discrimination, as this is the group of people who are wrongly suspected. If there is a threat of terrorism, the final report argues, a high number of such false positives is justifiable in terms of a "Güterabwägung" (balancing of interests) between the state and the individual (ibid.: 37–8). However, since these false positives have to be manually checked and sorted out (ibid.: 29), the risk increases that, on the one hand, innocent people remain registered as suspects and, on the other hand, the real suspects are overlooked in the sheer volume of data generated. Added to this is the deliberate deception of systems by criminals, both through forms of camouflage and morphing of passport images (Tolosana et al. 2020), with AI systems recently being used for this purpose (Mitchum 2020).

If one looks at the results produced by the first Südkreuz test, we again find intensive effort at purifying and constructing. So when the final report claims that the first test had produced "ausgezeichnete Ergebnisse" (excellent results) (Bundespolizei 2018: 8), which, given appropriate camera positioning (angle, zoom, lighting conditions), would allow match rates of over 80 percent to be expected for facial recognition systems on the market (ibid.: annexes 3 and 19), this statement is astonishing in several respects. First, because the federal government had claimed in advance that it did not want to measure the success of the project in terms of hit rates: "A successful testing outcome is not dependent on specific detection rates. From the perspective of the Federal Ministry of the Interior, a successful trial result exists if a significant additional value for the police tasks of the Federal Police can be identified" (Deutscher Bundestag 2017: 8, my translation). Moreover, the aforementioned 80 percent was considered an "imaginary figure" (CCC 2018), as none of the tested systems achieved this average score; it was only obtained when all three systems were combined, one of which, according to the final report, only achieved a hit rate of around 31 percent (Bundespolizei 2018: 24 and 25). De facto, the average hit rate of even the best system in the first phase was no more than 68.5 percent. Accordingly, as critics calculated, based on an average number of 90,000 passengers per day, this would mean that the systems would misidentify up to 600 people per day (Deutscher Bundestag 2018: 2), leading to the sum of about 219,000 misidentifications per year. Notably, the premise that is crucial to the "success" attributed to the Südkreuz test, namely combining the work of the three systems—which in practice would mean purchasing, implementing, and maintaining multiple facial recognition systems simultaneously—is not discussed anywhere in the final report. There is only a reference to two possible modes of operation, which presuppose the existence of several systems without comment. While in everyday police work, hits would only be produced if two or more systems agree on identifying a person ("AND connective"), in certain police situations (e.g., terrorist threat) a hit would be produced as soon as one of the systems identifies a person ("OR connective") (Bundespolizei 2018: 24). Which mode would be used at which time would be up to police assessment.

However, the described constructive work in stabilizing the face, creating the sample, and producing the results should not be viewed simply as an expression of avoidable inaccuracy. Rather, it is to be understood as part of knowledge production, which in the case of the Südkreuz test makes evident the complex medial entanglement of technologies, architectures, users, weather conditions, authorities, financial frameworks, and the like. That facial recognition systems do not necessarily attract criticism can be seen in other developments concerning the station that do not primarily address security issues. For example, "gateless gatelines" use facial recognition to regulate access on a "pay-by-face" basis.[10] The idea of making traffic "smarter" in this way is reminiscent of applications in e-consumer markets, where payment by facial recognition is becoming increasingly popular (e.g., Alibaba in China). All these technologies promise connectivity and access in the simplest (i.e., most convenient) way, while at the same time feeding user data into diverse databases, constantly enriching the "data doubles" (Haggerty and Ericson 2000: 613) and further differentiating user profiles. Such forms of "smart" technology use lead to new forms of habitualizing everyday lives. Facial recognition technologies, it could be argued, are accepted here because of their functionality for consumerism, not because of their promises of safety and security. They become naturalized components of our daily lives,[11] and their status as tools of digital control recedes into the background. This habituation can be seen as the flip side of those entanglements that make testing facial recognition software in terms of police identification so difficult.

Behavioral and Situation Recognition Systems

The second project, which took place at Südkreuz station in 2019, tested software systems for automated behavioral and situation recognition from IBM, Hitachi, and Funkwerk/G2K.[12] The focus was on detecting five predefined hazard situations in the context of rail security ("lying (helpless) person," "entering defined areas," "flows or gatherings of people," "people counting," "abandoned objects") as well as two additional functionalities (tracking of individuals and objects and the "retrograde evaluation" of video material) (Bundespolizei 2019; Deutscher Bundestag 2019). Looking at the scenarios mentioned, we can easily find topoi of our cultural imaginary for dangerous situations. There is the abandoned suitcase used to hide bombs, the tracking of people belonging to such objects, the lying (injured or killed) person, and the crowd that abruptly disperses or gathers due to a disruption. At the same time, it is by no means trivial to ask what can and should be described as a pattern of danger, and how a respective test situation can be created and how results can be generated. As with the first project, the test for automated behavior and situation recognition also requires a great deal of constructive work. I would like to briefly highlight three aspects to illustrate the entanglement of the actors involved: the normalization that takes place, the temporal vector of patterns, and the importance of scenarios.

As far as the aspect of *normalization* is concerned, the epistemic status of the second Südkreuz test must be considered. Unlike facial recognition systems, which lead to comparatively high numbers of matches on the basis of biometric facial images, and which are therefore already in use to operationalize the decision about excluding or including individuals, for instance, in the context of border architectures, this is by no means true for pattern recognition of behaviors and situations. Recognition here concerns specific patterns of movement, relative differences in speed, or changes in state. The discriminating factor is not a biometric body feature (facial geometry, hand lines, gait pattern, etc.) but, among other things, the time interval. After all, not every suitcase that is left behind is suspicious, because someone may only be visiting the restroom or getting a coffee. Only after a certain time does such a suitcase become a cause for alarm. Accordingly, crowds do not gather around every person lying down. A software that identifies lying bodies will therefore in principle also be able to identify homeless people (as unwanted persons), as well as the backpacker saving on the cost of accommodation. Such a system is thus not solely concerned with recognizing certain patterns of behavior and situations, but also with normalizing them by allowing certain movements and actions (e.g., shopping), while defining and preventing others as deviant (e.g., lying on the floor). Pattern recognition technologies are combined here with other programs for disciplining and controlling people in station areas, such as benches with seat divisions that prevent people from lying down, or missing waiting rooms that allow people to stay in areas of consumption (restaurants, stores) but reduce the amount of time spent on platforms or in station halls. Thus, media technologies of situation recognition show certain presuppositions, which are not made transparent, based on the configuration of their learning parameters (what is defined as dangerous) and implemented at the level of code. They have a discriminatory bias similar to that already discussed for facial recognition systems with regard to race, gender, class, and the like.

A second aspect concerns the *temporal vector* of patterns, that is, the "conservative" orientation of patterns. In their study on the importance of patterns in the field of predictive policing, Mareile Kaufmann et al. emphasize that the use of electronic prediction programs (such as PredPol in the United States or PRECOBS in Germany)[13] reinforces the "epistemological authority" of patterns in the context of policing (Kaufmann, Egbert, and Leese 2019: 684).[14] The authors distinguish between different styles of pattern recognition, each with its own rationalities, which reveal different "politics of patterns" (ibid.: 681) and which shape and formalize different understandings of crime. They differentiate four aspects regarding the authority of patterns in the context of crime control. First, patterns are formed only where regularities exist: "Patterns can only capture offenses that follow rules" (ibid.: 684). Accordingly, an affect-driven violent crime cannot be predicted any more than a single crime without an identifiable cluster. Second, in most cases patterns extrapolate the future not from live data but from past data, so they tend to be "conservative" (ibid.: 685). Third, assumptions about crime patterns feed back into policing cultures, that is, they have a "self-reinforcing logic" (ibid.: 687), in which a mutual reinforcement of the assumed pattern and the efficiency of the police work directed at it takes place. Fourth, they change the relationship between crime and the norm in general. This is because, from the perspective of the applied programs, "(criminal) behavior must be a regularity, otherwise it is not graspable by patterns" (ibid.). And thus patterns (clusters, categories, accumulations) reinforce the impression of the normality of crime without encouraging reflection on the motives and causes of crime (ibid.: 689). Beyond their normalizing tendency, the presuppositions inscribed in pattern recognition software therefore also have a conservative and preserving orientation: what has been crime before will be crime again. Thus, the results of predictive policing have a discriminatory and stigmatizing effect.

A third aspect regarding the constructive work directed at algorithmic media technologies at Berlin Südkreuz concerns the use of *fiction*. As mentioned earlier, the chosen topoi of dangerous situations refer to a richly illustrated cultural imaginary. In this context, the situations tested are always referred to as "Szenarien" (scenarios) (Bundespolizei 2019). How is this relevant in the horizon of media technologies of situation recognition? In general, recognition algorithms working on the basis of neural networks must be trained so that they correctly identify the relevant patterns (faces, objects, etc.) after the training phase. This is done by means of so-called training data. However, such training and verification data are a "scarce resource" (Mühlhoff 2020: 1869), as every AI application in industry and research relies on such data. For this reason, interfaces are increasingly being created that can also be understood as an "infrastructure for obtaining data," since they are based on the more or less "free and implicit human participation" (ibid.).[15] While facial recognition programs can learn on the basis of existing image material, this is not possible in the case of behavior and situation recognition. Here too, however, the algorithms must be trained to learn what exactly constitutes a "dangerous" situation. For this reason, various hazard scenarios—"use cases" (Bundespolizei 2018: 40) were simulated and recorded with a group of actors at Südkreuz station, with the "Drehbuch" (script) comprising a total of 1,600 situations (Bundespolizei 2019) including so-called "Abgrenzungsszenarien" (demarcation scenarios). The intention was to distinguish the previously defined hazard situations from similar but nonsignificant constellations, that is, to avoid the so-called "Kontrabass-Fehler" (double bass error),[16] in which a musical instrument is mistakenly recognized as a person lying on the ground. Practically, this meant recording a series of situations with an appropriate number of repetitions (five to fifteen) two days a week at different times of day to test the performance of the three selected pattern recognition systems. Calibration of the systems alone, however, proved to be more complicated than expected, in part because of the highly variable lighting conditions (the station has a glass roof). Long shadows, for example, could not be distinguished from people lying on the ground—the aforementioned double bass error. The technical evaluation of the test did not take place on site, but it was subsequently carried out by the Universität der Bundeswehr München, which had also provided the sixteen "actors" (young adults of Asian origin)[17] as well as a special app for the test supervisor. With this app, the scenes were precisely logged in terms of time (especially beginning and end) in order to ensure an exact assignment of scene, script, and recording in the context of the later evaluation.[18]

As these examples of possible hazard situations at the train station show, various presuppositions and world models go into the production of training data. This is accompanied by the promise that the more accurately the world is simulated in the training data, the more precisely the systems will work. This brings us to the categories of the theatrical and performative that appear in the description of the second test: scripts, scenarios, actors. Already for RAND theorist Herman Kahn it had been true: "The scenario is an aid to imagination," that is, a possibility "to describe in more or less detail some hypothetical sequence of events" (Kahn 1962: 143). Insofar as Kahn was concerned with scenarios of thermonuclear warfare, they were in his view not a means of prediction but a way of dealing with an "unknown and unknowable future" (ibid.: 145). To refer to Kahn in the context of pattern recognition reflects his general appreciation of imagination: "Imagination has always been one of the principal means for dealing in various ways with the future, and the scenario is simply one of the many devices useful in stimulating and disciplining the imagination" (ibid.). The scenarios tested in the second Südkreuz project are, as described, "typical situations in the station" (Bundespolizei 2019) that have already been identified as dangerous in the past. To ensure their recognition, "demarcation scenarios" are designed at the same time, which share similarities with the dangerous situation but are not intended to trigger an alarm. Thus, operations of designing, staging, and imagining (fiction) are fundamentally connected with the media technologies of pattern recognition.[19] This refers not only to an imaginary dimension of supposedly objective technology, but also to the fact that the demarcation of case and non-case, of a dangerous and a normal world, does not emerge by itself, but must always be elaborately produced (through scenarios and demarcation scenarios), so that a match—as in other forms of pattern recognition—can be understood as a statistical approximation to a predefined default value.

Conclusion: Entanglements

In this article, I have focused on digital control in urban settings, especially at transport hubs such as metropolitan train stations. I have concentrated on the German debate on intelligent video analysis, since it is precisely this debate that reveals the fundamental entanglements of the entities involved. In contrast to countries such as Great Britain, the United States, or China, where surveillance technologies spread in a climate of less-pronounced data protection provisions, the German example unfolds against the background of a long-standing political and cultural debate concerning privacy issues. The German negotiations therefore show the paradoxes, problems, and inconsistencies posed by surveillance technologies and make evident how the idea of controlling certain situations and environments results in complex efforts of construction and imagination to cope with the entanglement of humans and machines that make up such situations.

We found these kinds of efforts in the test on facial recognition software at Berlin Südkreuz with respect to the object of surveillance (the face), the creation of the sample (test persons and measured weeks), as well as the results (hit rate). In contrast, taking into account the testing of economic applications of facial recognition systems (such as gateless gatelines), it can be argued that the implementation of these media techniques is less a question of security than of habitualizing "smart access" in everyday life by implementing structures that afford convenience. Here, the entanglement of human and machines is pushed forward quite openly, in order to increase their interrelations. For the test on pattern recognition concerning hazard situations, I discussed the normalizing and conservative quality of patterns and stressed the imaginative dimension going along with them, that is, the theatrical production of so-called scenarios by which the software is supposed to learn what a dangerous situation is.

Although the constructive element of this process is even more visible than in the case of labeling images for training data sets in the field of facial recognition, the belief in the autonomous recognition capacities of algorithms and neural networks is fully alive. Therefore, it is not only a question of digital control *by* machines that we should worry about, but also of people, institutions, and platforms generating uncontrollable socio-technical entanglements by declaring our convenient connection to machines to be the suitable way to achieve a smart and secure life.

Notes

1. For a discussion of the Berlin Südkreuz project with respect to the processes of human differentiation, cf. Schabacher (2021a).
2. On the relation between cultural imaginaries, disruptions, and fear, see Koch, Nanz, and Pause (2018). On rail risk management in the face of terrorist threats, cf. Luxton and Marinov (2020).
3. On the history of the train station, see Richards and MacKenzie (1986).
4. Cf. the website "Mein Einkaufsbahnhof," https://www.einkaufsbahnhof.de/ (accessed September 10, 2021).

5. Cf. for example, the parliamentary debate on the introduction of automated facial recognition, January 30, 2020, https://www.bundestag.de/dokumente/textarchiv/2020/kw05-de-gesichtserkennung-679992 (accessed February 27, 2022), the critical public discussion on the German-language news website Netzpolitik.org, cf. Netzpolitik (2022), and the documentary *Face_It! Das Gesicht im Zeitalter der Digitalismus* (2019), [Film], Dir. Gerd Conradt, Germany: Missing Films.
6. For biometric images, cf. Wichum (2017).
7. On the data protection concept, see Bundespolizei (2018), annex 2. On the criticism of this concept, cf. BlnBDI (2018: 75–7); BlnBDI (2019: 155–7).
8. Bundespolizei (2018: 21–2 and annex 2, appendix 1, item 5). On the criticism of this reference system, cf. Digitalcourage (2017). On this phase of the first project, see Chase (2017).
9. For new developments and the related ethical concerns in the field of biometric recognition and behavioral detection, cf. also the report by the Policy Department for Citizens' Rights and Constitutional Affairs, Wendehorst and Duller (2021).
10. Cubic Transportation Systems, the US firm behind London's Oyster Card, claims that "such a system could in the future ease rush hour crowds by funnelling people through virtual corridors linked to facial recognition cameras, confirming customers' identities" (Blunden 2018).
11. This naturalization of technologies through habitualizing them can also be understood as an expression of their infrastructuralization, see Schabacher (2022).
12. Even though the test has long since been completed, a final report on the second Südkreuz project is still pending. Rather, in December 2020, a joint statement by the German government and the Deutsche Bahn announced a continuation. The testing of intelligent video analysis technology is to be continued and expanded in a three-year test project at the Südkreuz station (BMI 2020; Deutsche Bahn 2020).
13. Cf. the corresponding websites of the US company PredPol, https://www.predpol.com/ (accessed September 14, 2021), and that of the Oberhausen Institut für musterbasierte Prognosetechnik (IfmPt), which developed PRECOBS, http://www.ifmpt.de/index.html (accessed September 14, 2021).
14. On predictive policing, see Perry et al. (2013) and Ferguson (2017).
15. Mühlhoff (2020: 1874–8) is thinking here of various ways in which such interfaces capture human cognitive resources in order to use them for AI applications: Gamification, reCAPTCHA, social media such as Facebook, nudging, and other incentive structures, but also human click work such as in the case of Amazon Mechanical Turk.
16. Mail response from the press officer of DB-Konzernsicherheit Holger Bajohra, May 6, 2019.

17. However, these were not professional actors, but young students who received an expense compensation in the amount of a student job (on-site interview, October 1, 2019).
18. On-site interview with the test supervisors, October 1, 2019.
19. This simulation aspect is being further developed. For situation recognition systems, for example, it is being tested to what extent the image material can be enriched with virtual persons in order to create the corresponding scenarios for the training data, cf. Hoffmann et al. (2019).

References

Andrejevic, M. (2020), *Automated Media*, New York: Taylor & Francis.

Belting, H. (2017), *Face and Mask: A Double History*, Princeton, NJ: Princeton University Press.

BlnBDI (Berliner Beauftrage für Datenschutz und Informationsfreiheit) (2018), "Datenschutz und Informationsfreiheit," Jahresbericht 2018. Available online: https://www.datenschutz-berlin.de/infothek-und-service/veroeffentli chungen/jahresberichte/ (accessed September 13, 2021).

BlnBDI (Berliner Beauftragte für Datenschutz und Informationsfreiheit) (2019), "Datenschutz und Informationsfreiheit," Jahresbericht 2019. Available online: https://www.datenschutz-berlin.de/fileadmin/user_upload/pdf/publikationen/jahresbericht/BlnBDI-Jahresbericht-2019-Web.pdf (accessed September 13, 2021).

Blunden, M. (2018), "Could Scanners Like These Solve Tube and Train Crowds? 'Pay-by-Face' System May End Need for Train Station Barriers," *Evening Standard*, November 2, 2018. Available online: https://www.standard.co.uk/tech/could-scanners-like-these-solve-tube-and-train-crowds-a3997036.html (accessed September 14, 2021).

BMI (Bundesministerium des Inneren, für Bau und Heimat) (2020), "Bundesregierung und Deutsche Bahn beschließen Maßnahmen für mehr Sicherheit an Bahnhöfen," press release, December 13, 2020. Available online: https://www.bmi.bund.de/SharedDocs/pressemitteilungen/DE/2020/12/sicherheit-bahnhoefe.html (accessed September 15, 2021).

Bundespolizei (2019), "Test intelligenter Videoanalyse-Technik," June 7, 2019. Available online: https://web.archive.org/web/20200428131610/https://www.bundespolizei.de/Web/DE/04Aktuelles/01Meldungen/2019/06/190607_videoanalyse.html (accessed September 14, 2021).

Bundespolizei (2018), "Abschlussbericht des Bundespolizeipräsidiums Potsdam zum Teilprojekt 1 'Biometrische Gesichtserkennung,'" September 18, 2018. Available online: https://www.bundespolizei.de/Web/DE/04Aktuelles/01Meldungen/2018/10/181011_abschlussbericht_gesichtserkennung_down.pdf?__blob=publicationFile&v=1 (accessed September 11, 2021).

CCC (Chaos Computer Club) (2018), "Biometrische Videoüberwachung: Der Südkreuz-Versuch war kein Erfolg," October 13, 2018. Available online: https://www.ccc.de/en/updates/2018/debakel-am-suedkreuz (accessed September 13, 2021).

Chase, J. (2017), "Facial Recognition Surveillance Test Extended at Berlin Train Station," *DW.com*, December 15, 2017. Available online: https://www.dw.com/en/facial-recognition-surveillance-test-extended-at-berlin-train-station/a-41813861 (accessed September 15, 2021).

Clarke, R. (1988), "Information Technology and Dataveillance," *Communications of the ACM* 31 (5): 498–512.

Deutsche B. (2020), "Bundesregierung und Deutsche Bahn beschließen Maßnahmen für mehr Sicherheit an Bahnhöfen," press release, December 13, 2020. Available online: https://www.deutschebahn.com/de/presse/pressestart_zentrales_uebersicht/Bundesregierung-und-Deutsche-Bahn-beschliessen-weitere-Massnahmen-fuer-mehr-Sicherheit-an-Bahnhoefen--5795990?qli=true&subjekteFilter=&Monat=2020-12-01T00:00:00&itemsPerPage=10&pageNum=0&contentId=1204030 (accessed September 15, 2021).

Deutscher B. (2017), "Drucksache 18/13350, 18 August 2018. Antwort der Bundesregierung auf die Kleine Anfrage, Drucksache 18/13229." Available online: http://dipbt.bundestag.de/dip21/btd/18/133/1813350 (accessed June 22, 2020).

Deutscher B. (2018), "Drucksache 19/6076, 28 November 2018. Antwort der Bundesregierung auf die Kleine Anfrage, Drucksache 19/5744." Available online: https://dip21.bundestag.de/dip21/btd/19/060/1906076.pdf (accessed September 13, 2020).

Deutscher B. (2019), "Drucksache 19/11771, 19 June 2019. Antwort der Bundesregierung auf die Kleine Anfrage der Abgeordneten Joana Cotar u.a., Drucksache 19/11333, Auswirkungen der biometrischen Gesichtserkennung." Available online: https://dip21.bundestag.de/dip21/btd/19/117/1911771.pdf (accessed September 14, 2021).

Deutscher B. (2020), "Kontroverse um Einführung einer automatisierten Gesichtserkennung," Deutscher Bundestag, Dokumente. Available online: https://www.bundestag.de/dokumente/textarchiv/2020/kw05-de-gesichtserkennung-679992 (accessed: February 27, 2022).

Digitalcourage (2017), "Gesichtserkennung am Südkreuz. Bundespolizei hat falsch informiert—Wir fordern Abbruch des Tests," August 21, 2017. Available online: https://digitalcourage.de/blog/2017/gesichtsscan-beenden (accessed September 13, 2021).

Ferguson, A. G. (2017), *The Rise of Big Data Policing: Surveillance, Race, and the Future of Law Enforcement*, New York: New York University Press.

Foucault, M. (1979), *Discipline and Punish: The Birth of the Prison*, London: Penguin.

Gates, K. A. (2011), *Our Biometric Future: Facial Recognition Technology and the Culture of Surveillance*, New York: New York University Press.

Haggerty, K. D., and R. V. Ericson (2000), "The Surveillant Assemblage," *British Journal of Sociology* 51 (4): 605–22.

Hoffmann, D. T., D. Tzionas, M. J. Black, and S. Tang (2019), "Learning to Train with Synthetic Humans," in G. A. Fink, S. Frintrop, and X. Jiang (eds.), *Pattern Recognition (GCPR): 41st DAGM German Conference, DAGM GCPR 2019 Dortmund, Germany, September 10–13, 2019 Proceedings*, 609–23, Cham, Switzerland: Springer.

Jany, S. (2019), *Prozessarchitekturen. Medien der Betriebsorganisation (1880–1936)*, Konstanz: Konstanz University Press.

Kahn, H. (1962), *Thinking about the Unthinkable*, New York: Horizon Press.

Kaufmann, M., S. Egbert, and M. Leese (2019), "Predictive Policing and the Politics of Patterns," *British Journal of Criminology* 59 (3): 674–92.

Kloppenburg, S., and I. van der Ploeg (2020), "Securing Identities: Biometric Technologies and the Enactment of Human Bodily Differences," *Science as Culture* 29 (1): 57–76. Available online: DOI: 10.1080/09505431.2018.1519534 (accessed September 13, 2021).

Koch, L., T. Nanz, and J. Pause (2018), "Imagined Scenarios of Disruption. A Concept," in L. Koch, T. Nanz, and J. Pause (eds.), *Disruption in the Arts: Textual, Visual, and Performative Strategies for Analyzing Societal Self-Descriptions*, 63–81, Boston, MA: De Gruyter.

Latour, B. (1993), *We Have Never Been Modern*, Cambridge, MA: Harvard University Press.

Levin, T. Y., U. Frohne, and P. Weibel (eds.) (2002), *CTRL [SPACE]: Rhetorics of Surveillance from Bentham to Big Brother*, Karlsruhe, Germany: ZKM.

Luxton, A., and M. Marin (2020), "Terrorist Threat Mitigation Strategies for the Railways," *Sustainability* 12 (8): 3408. Available online: https://doi.org/10.3390/su12083408 (accessed September 8, 2021).

Lyon, D. (2001), *Surveillance Society: Monitoring Everyday Life*, Buckingham: Open University Press.

Marx, G. T. (1984), "Notes on the Discovery, Collection and Assessment of Hidden and Dirty Data," in J. Schneider and J. Kitsuse (eds.), *Studies in the Sociology of Social Problems*, Norwood: Ablex. Available online (unpaginated): http://web.mit.edu/gtmarx/www/dirty.html (accessed September 13, 2021).

Mitchum, R. (2020), "A New Tool to Protect Yourself against Facial Recognition Software," *University of Chicago News*, August 3, 2020. Available online: https://news.uchicago.edu/story/new-tool-protect-yourself-against-facial-recognition-software (accessed September 13, 2021).

Mühlhoff, R. (2020), "Human-Aided Artificial Intelligence: Or, How to Run Large Computations in Human Brains? Toward a Media Sociology of Machine Learning," *New Media & Society* 22 (10): 1868–84.

Netzpolitik (2022), "Thema Südkreuz," available online: https://netzpolitik.org/tag/suedkreuz/ (accessed February 27, 2022).

Perry, W. L., B. McInnis, C. C. Price, S. Smith, J. S. Hollywood (2013), *Predictive Policing: The Role of Crime Forecasting in Law Enforcement Operations*, Santa Monica, CA: RAND Corporation.

Potthast, J. (2011), "Sense and Security: A Comparative View on Recent Changes of Access Control at Airports," *Science, Technology & Innovation Studies* 7 (2): 87–106.

Richards, J., and J. M. MacKenzie (1986), *The Railway Station: A Social History*, Oxford/New York: Oxford University Press.

Schabacher, G. (2021a), "Infrastrukturen und Verfahren der Humandifferenzierung. Medienkulturwissenschaftliche Perspektiven," in D. Dizdar, S. Hirschauer, J. Paulmann, and G. Schabacher (eds.), *Humandifferenzierung. Disziplinäre Perspektiven und empirische Sondierungen*, 287–313, Weilerswist: Velbrück.

Schabacher, G. (2021b), "Time and Technology. The Temporalities of Care," in A. Volmar and K. Stine (eds.), *Media Infrastructures and the Politics of Digital Time. Essays on Hardwired Temporalities*, 55–75, Amsterdam: Amsterdam University Press.

Schabacher, G. (2022), *Infrastruktur-Arbeit. Kulturtechniken und Zeitlichkeit der Erhaltung*, Berlin: Kadmos.

Snow, J. (2018), "Amazon's Face Recognition Falsely Matched 28 Members of Congress with Mugshots," *ACLU*, July 26, 2018. Available online: https://www.aclu.org/blog/privacy-technology/surveillance-technologies/amazons-face-recognition-falsely-matched-28 (accessed September 13, 2021).

Stanley, J. (2019), "The Dawn of Robot Surveillance: AI, Video Analytics, and Privacy," *American Civil Liberties Union (ACLU)* 2019. Available online: https://www.aclu.org/report/dawn-robot-surveillance (accessed September 10, 2021).

Steyerl, H. (2018), "A Sea of Data: Pattern Recognition and Corporate Animism (Forked Version)," in C. Apprich, W. H. K. Chun, F. Cramer, and H. Steyerl (eds.), *Pattern Discrimination*, 1–22, London: Meson Press.

Tolosana, R., R. Vera-Rodriguez, J. Fierrez, A. Morales, and J. Ortega-Garcia (2020), "DeepFakes and Beyond: A Survey of Face Manipulation and Fake Detection," *arXiv.org*, Cornell University, June 18, 2020. Available online: https://arxiv.org/pdf/2001.00179.pdf (accessed September 13, 2021).

Weigel, S. (ed.) (2017), *Das Gesicht. Bilder, Medien, Formate*, Göttingen: Wallstein.

Wendehorst, C., and Y. Duller (2021), *Biometric Recognition and Behavioural Detection: Assessing the Ethical Aspects of Biometric Recognition and Behavioural Detection Techniques with a Focus on Their Current and Future Use in Public Spaces*, Study Requested by the JURI and PETI committees of the European Parliament, Brussels: Policy Department for Citizens' Rights and Constitutional Affairs.

Wichum, R. (2017), *Biometrie. Zur Soziologie der Identifikation*, Paderborn: Fink.

8

On the Anthropology of the *mode double click*

Lorenz Engell

A Mouse Click Away

The world is only a mouse click away. That's what advertising teaches us. And what used to be true of the mouse click can today be said of all kinds of touch-and-touchpad or touching-screen-button relations. The mouse click and its more recent follow-ups are thus claimed to be a way of being in the world, an anthropomediatic relation. It is a way of being. In his great study on modes of existence, Bruno Latour (2013a) lists fifteen different ways of being or modes of existence. One of them is the *mode double click*. It belongs to a group of three modes of existence, which are at the same time procedures of scientific investigation itself, and hence meta-existences or meta-modes (ibid.: 33–45, 613). Nonetheless, all three, as epistemic relationships and forms of behavior, shape existence far beyond science, in everyday life for example.

Interestingly, among the three meta-modes there are two good ones (in Latour's sense) and one bad one. The bad one is the *mode double click*. We will come back to it in a moment. The good ones are the networking mode or *mode réseau* on the one hand and the préposition mode, *mode préposition* on the other. *Mode réseau* means that the scientific procedure takes place in the collective in the broadest Latourian sense (ibid.: 33–5). It includes the possible participation of all, not only all people, but also all possible instruments of knowledge and objects of knowledge. *Mode réseau* proceeds in the transdisciplinary traversal of the fields of knowledge. It also permeates the distinction of the humanities and natural sciences, and correspondingly it is methodically pluralistic. Latour is certainly thinking especially of his own inquiry here. From the point of view of media philosophy, we would of course at first be interested in the support and instrumentation of the network, such as the aesthetics, the technological materialities, and the epistemic operativeness of the networks (Engell 2011; Schabacher 2013).

Mode préposition, on the other hand, thinks and does everything under the auspices of approaching and approaches (Latour 2013a: 61–3). It is aspection. Prepositions are intermediate things, operators of the opening *of* something and at the same time *toward* something. They bring about the relative and relational location of something with regard to something. They work in and on space and time, in and on causality and modality. Once again we would think of media anthropology here and of specific anthropomediatic relations (Othold and Voss 2015; Voss 2010). The modes of operation of anthropomediality, as we have examined them in our KOMA Project during the last few years, are also prepositional; they deal with the positioning and dispositioning, the constellation, conversion, and displacement of modes of existence in their respective media habitats (Voss 2019). *Mode préposition* quite deliberately and affirmatively includes the danger of committing category errors, namely of seeing something from the position or bias of something else, to which it does not belong at all, and of addressing something as what it is not (Latour 2013a: 48–9, 237). In the sense of the claim on the mouse click quoted above: The world is only a mouse click away, the distance, the closeness, and remoteness of the world, is also a question of *mode préposition*.

Mode double click

Finally, Latour has *mode double click* emerge as an evil ghost in his inquiry over and over again, but with no specific chapter dedicated to it. *Mode double click*, Latour states, does everything the investigation does not want to and should not do, and it lurks everywhere in it:

> It is at this very moment that a sort of Evil Genius comes into play, having waited for the chains of reference to be deployed and stabilized before it intervened. In an allusion to the digital mouse, we are going to call this devil **Double Click**. (Latour 2013a: 93)

Mode double click, according to Latour, does not operate in any kind of in-betweenness or interconnected way, but denies all connection and commitment:

> Based on a real enough experiment—reference permits access—this Evil Genius is going to whisper in your ear that it would surely be preferable to benefit from free, indisputable, and immediate access to pure, *untransformed* information. (ibid., emphasis in the original)

Double Click completely denies that information needs to *pass through* any hiatus, any discontinuity, any translation whatsoever. (ibid.: 137)

Mode double click knows no minglings, intertwinings, and mixtures; no transitions and translations of the same into the other; no metaphors and no metamorphosis (ibid.: 200). *Mode double click* is the unapproachable leap from the same directly into the other, but without leap, that is, without movement, without flight and in-between.

[With *mode double click*, L. E.] we would be demanding the impossible: a displacement *without transformations of any sort*—beyond mere **displacement**. (ibid.: 93)

Mode double click is the pure and almost bodiless distinction. The Other simply switched on in *mode double click* is nothing but the new or other Same. That's why you can also switch back without loss in *mode double click*. Then you are back to the same thing again, unimpressed, and unaltered. Exactly this is the core of the moderns and their procedures in science and everyday life.

By a dangerous inversion of the two senses of the word network, Double Click has begun to propagate everywhere an accusation of irrationality about everything that needs ... a certain number of operations of transformation or displacement—operations that are, however, as we have seen, a matter of reason itself. ... By claiming to give a unique and inaccessible model—displacement without transformations, reason without networks—to all forms of veridiction, this Evil Genius would by contrast make all other distinctions between truth and falsity irrational and arbitrary. (ibid.: 94)

The moderns, according to Latour, tend toward distinguishing everything from everything else sharply and seamlessly as well as reversibly. It is a world and a life of the excluded third. The *tertium non datur* is the first of the two main features of the *mode double click*.

The second one is that the *mode double click* can only access that what is, what is already and anyway being there. Unlike the *mode tech* of bringing machines into existence and operating technology, or the *mode fic* (like fiction) of artistic imagination and of the art work under way, it is unable to produce something new. It can only choose or select from or address what exists. It never goes into the void or the open. For *mode double click*, therefore, there is not even a hiatus between possibility and reality, or desire and reality.

Everything is available for *mode double click*. Following Heidegger (1977) one could say: the world is a stock (*Bestand*) for it, the world has already been ordered and worked (*bestellt*); and this has long since applied economically as well, if one follows Günter Anders (1956).

Mode double click is of course itself a metaphor. The exclusion of the third is much older than the mouse (Aristotle). But with the actual double click of the mouse button, the *mode double click* has taken recourse to itself and crystallized compactly into an artifact, a medium. Where the mouse button and all its derivatives and spin-offs become the privileged medium of world access and human subjectivations, of collectivization, knowledge management, and the entanglement of world and human being, *mode double click* penetrates pervasively into all areas of life and thus into all other modes of existence (Latour 2013a: 200, 237).

Now in Latour, unlike in media anthropology, the medium does not occur (Latour 2013b). Latour does not tell us anything about the mouse button itself as device, as interface between human and machine, and as a form of anthropomediatic relation. We also learn nothing about how the mouse in turn drives the concept of the *mode double click* recursively in the first place. In terms of media anthropology, we must therefore investigate how *mode double click*, the stipulated embodied axiom of the excluded third, actually guides the mouse. Through the mouse click, the exclusion process returns to itself, but not so much as it is, but in another way, namely altered; not as an axiom, but as a cultural technique in the full sense of the term. As Latour (2013a: 218) himself concedes:

> But, as usual, instead of rejecting such a manifestly inadequate template, he has chosen to bring technology, too, into this Procrustean bed. Whereas the whole experience rebels against such a mutilation, he has acted as though technology, too, *transports* mere information, mere forms, *without deformation*. It is true that the engineers haven't protested; they go to great lengths to resemble the image of stubborn and somewhat dopey characters that has often been attributed to them! Double Click strikes everywhere: knowledge, yes, psyches, yes, but also, but especially, matter. If we want to measure the gulf that the Moderns are capable of digging between practice and the account of their practice, we must look not only into epistemology, psychology, or theology but also into technology (used here in the sense of reflection *on* technology) (emphasis in the original).

In the double click, the axiom of logic runs through the device and through the handling, and that means: through the hand of the body that serves it.

It takes up the gesture of the hand and comes upon it, one way or the other. Only once we have examined this we can really judge *mode double click*.

Toward a Media Anthropology of the Mouse Click

So let us add this to the picture. For reasons of space, we will leave aside the state of media archaeological research on the invention, development, and industrial history of the mouse, although it is interesting and well documented (Bardini 2000; Roch 1996). It should be noted, however, that the mouse alone cannot do very much. In order to be able to double click and instrumentalize *mode double click*, there has to be something that can be clicked. It requires the interaction between mouse and button, and, on the screen, between cursor and icon. Mouseable screens are multiple buttons, clickable computer pictures are, like the television pictures before them, switch images (Engell 2021). Mouse technology and window technology form an assembly. The mouse is an accessory to the window, in McLuhan's (1964) sense, an extension of the screen. Moreover, it only makes sense if there are a large number of buttons and windows on the screen to select from, otherwise the "Enter" key on the keyboard would be sufficient.

Mode double click does not simply access the world right away, but controls a computer via a flat surface or interface that is unbounded and protracted into space, into the room in front of it and with which it is connected in a network. Likewise, the remote control of television, the preform of the computer mouse, was an extension of the television set into the room in front of the device (Engell 2021: 179–212). But the mouse is more complex. It first comprises the relation of the multitude of overlapping or juxtaposed windows to each other, which are at the same time, secondly, switching and control elements of the computer behind the screen, and in turn can, thirdly, operatively change the existence and status of the windows in a difference of before and after.

Fourth, it comprises the causal relationship between mouse operations on the one hand and windows on the screen on the other, and fifth, and decisively, the connection with the user on this side of the screen, with his or her expansive neurological and physiological apparatus, which we are particularly interested in when we do media anthropology. Only in this complex interaction do computers, mouses, windows, other windows, and user bodies become functional at all. In short, without the mode of networking, *mode réseau*, and without that of preposition, *mode prep*, the mouse click does not work. In isolation, there is no *mode double click*.

All of this, however, does not yet constitute a full anthropomedial relation or a mode of existence (Voss 2019: 40–2). This requires the being-in-the-world (Heidegger 2010: 53–62; Voss 2019: 36). Lest we forget: the world is only a mouse click away. The mouse click requires a shaping and integration into a habitat, in reciprocal access and mutual intervention. It belongs to an episteme, a behavior, a form of experience. It requires an external effect of the complexly coupled mouse click on the world on the other side of the screen and the device. Otherwise the mouse click is not operative in the sense of an intervention into something. It has to reach behind the screen, run on the screen, and protract in front of the screen.

Behind the Screen

We therefore switch from media anthropological considerations to media ontological ones for an intermediate step. First, the computer must cooperate with other computers, for example with servers. So by means of the mouse click other computers beyond my one computer here are at least controlled and queried. Second and more complicated, however, is the intervention into the extra computer world via the mouse click. As long as it goes beyond the control of computers, it affords a world that has always assumed the format of a data record or a file. It is not facts that can be clicked, only sites of data (Kittler 1999).

They must have already been remediated twice (Bolter and Grusin 1999). On the one hand, they have been transferred from the medium of matter or *physis*, of the physical, social, biological, psychological, or aesthetic occurrences and phenomena into other media, namely into texts, diagrams, pictures, sounds, signs of all kinds, and inscriptions. After all, the clickable windows do not show the things, persons, and relations themselves, which as such, below the remediation of physis in (which can mean within as well as into) description, do not even exist. We know from Latour in particular, but also from juridical procedures, that it is the often intertwined transmissions between physis and inscription that generate facts in the first place (Latour and Woolgar 1979).

On the other hand and in a second remediation, these data sets, that is, the descriptions, sound documents, and visualizations, are then digitized, meaning subjected to calculation. Only then can a computer finally process them and only then do they become clickable. And thus the mouse click actually *does* belong in a certain way to the world of the axiom of the excluded third, without which no binary system can function and to which only the mouse click has access, even if it constantly contaminates it, as we will see in a moment, with the world and the mode of existence of translation, transmission, mixing, and coupling.

On the Screen

All of this, however, only applies to what lies behind the windows, be it the world or the device. But it does not apply to the surface dimension of the screen and its coupling with the world on *this* side of it, on our side of the screen, or the second screen, or all the more recent interfaces that operate without any screen in the strict sense. In this world, users also occur. But let's first look at the relationship between the windows on the screen surface. Latour seems to assume that in *mode double click* we switch seamlessly from one window to another; that is, that what we click excludes what we do not click. What we click is there, and what we do not click is not there, and we switch from being to non-being and back without intermediate status and without bridging.

> [With *Mode double click*] everything is seemingly still in place, and yet everything is profoundly different, since on both sides the motor that made it possible to achieve displacements is missing. The race is always already won in advance—without any need to budge. We are now going to act as though there were cost-free displacements of constants both in the world—*res extensa*—and in the mind—*res cogitans*. (Latour 2013a: 112)

If applied to the actual functioning of the computer mouse, though, nothing could be less convincing. Unselected windows and buttons are by no means nonexistent and irrelevant. They are as real and present as the selected ones, only in a different mode. The function, value, degree, and mode of the presence of a selected window is determined to a large extent by its relation to the other, dimmed windows, and their status in turn depends on their accessibility, depending on the number of clicks required to find and reach them. This relation can be described by modal terms such as the manifest and the latent or the actual and the virtual, or by the aesthetic metaphor of foreground and background (Deleuze 2013: 71–101). The latter is probably particularly promising because of the superposition of the windows on the screen.

Here, already the well-established distinction between different styles of selection, to use Niklas Luhmann's terms, could lead to differentiation within the rigid models of presence and absence, existence and nonexistence, or the Same and the Other (Luhmann 1995: 141–7). Even with traditional theoretical means, styles of selection can be distinguished. I can, for instance, make a positive decision for something very specific at the click of a mouse, against everything else. That would be an indefinite negation that unseenly deselects everything that is not the chosen one (Luhmann 1990: 21–79). Or I decide for something arbitrary, no matter what, as long as it is not this one that I do not want, as in the form of definite negation (Luhmann 1981). That then makes a considerable difference to the way of being of the chosen one. Both selection styles naturally interlock in practice.

By the way, they cannot even be clearly assigned to either a simple click or a double click. Although a simple click is always sufficient to deselect and a double click always opens up something, a simple click can also bring something up or back. A simple click can lift something into accessibility, but this pre-activation of a window antecedently requires a control by the cursor. The cursor is moved with the mouse in a continuous movement over every window or button on the screen before the mouse click. Sometimes it lifts the window or the button into latent activity already by this mere touch. Double click then finally puts the window in the position of being selected or of activation, but even that is sometimes possible with a single click.

And there is more. In general, the distinction between clicking and double clicking is a question of the speed with which the keystrokes follow each other. Whether a sequence of touches functions as a double click or as two consecutive clicks is determined by the time difference between the two. We have to realize that click and double click have to work together first of all to work at all; second, both have to be coupled with another mode, namely that of the mouse movement from the wrist; and third, in the end they are numerically clearly different, but operatively only fuzzily distinguishable from each other.

Contingency and Virtuality

What is decisive in any case, however, is that the respective other, the other window next to or behind it, the latent, the virtual, is by no means excluded and absent. It is technically impossible to jump by mouse click to something that is not displayed on the screen and not clickable. We can only jump over to something that is already displayed on the screen and therefore present. First, the deselected or not yet selected remains visible, even if it is just a tiny icon of its own continued presence at the edge of the screen. Even closed windows can remain active in the background, and continue. Second, through this coexistence, the deselected places the selected under conditions and therefore determines its way of being. The deselected is always present in the selected. It can even be more effective than the chosen one itself.

This is all the more true since everything selected is always equipped with the index of provisionality and the lack of inevitability or necessity. Instead of the actually elected, something else could always be in the former's place; so everything that appears to be is contingent. So at least we must concede that *mode double click* charges the world with contingency (Luhmann 1995: 107–8, 365–7). The world may be a stock or *Bestand* in this mode, but what it comprehends is contingent in each single case, it could also be completely different or not be at all (Heidegger 1977). We can also observe this again with one of the precursor technologies of the mouse click, namely the remote control of the television set (Engell 2021: 179–212). Here, too, the various channels accessible by remote control set conditions for each other; here, too, the deselected channel continues to run and is contained in the attention, however dimmed.

Thirdly and decisively, however, the windows and buttons can change their relative status at any time with a mouse click. They are not simply logged out, but are always on the go. There is an oscillation space between them in which they move, in which they are, and in which they *are* at last. What is present right now is what will be gone in a second and what hence is virtually absent already now, and vice versa. What is the case cannot just be the case in the world of the mouse either, and what is not the case can nevertheless become the case. That is why Gilles Deleuze (2013: 73–5) speaks of the "coalescence of the virtual and the actual." For him, the virtual and the actual are "different, but indistinguishable." (ibid.: 56, 71–2) And different, but indistinguishable, are then also the same and the other in *mode double click*.

One could therefore say that *mode double click* does not exactly mean to skip the jump, but on the contrary to constantly stay in it instead of, for example, stay with the things, namely with the windows themselves. And this is all the more true when one considers that the distinction between the—relatively few—windows that are currently open or can be opened on a screen and the vast number of windows that circulate out there and run on some other computer, which are not accessible from here and now by double click, is also exactly not possible by double click, but has to be made accessible only in tedious, time-consuming step-by-step sequences of mouse movements, simple clicks, and double clicks. Moreover, each new window has an area of other windows available like a halo, which can be opened, that is, clicked, from it. Then we are even more between the same and the other, always under way. *This* is the mobile place, where we are with mouse and window, and not a simple "there" ("*da*") and "not there" ("*nicht da*").

In Front of the Screen

But of course empirically and as bodies we are at the same time mainly here, in this room, in front of our screen, as mouse operators with our mouse. We thus return from ontological to anthropological considerations in the narrower sense. They start from the relation and the coupling between our body and the technical body as it is characteristic for everything we can look at as being a gesture, according to Vilém Flusser (2014), that is, a handling. Like all switching, this coupling also functions in the *mode double click*, taken literally and technologically, via contact, via physical touch, and therefore via the sense of touch as a specialization of the tactile (Engell 2013).

Following Michel Serres (2008) and others we can identify two different regimes in the realm of the tactile. One is the regime of the enveloping, the encompassing, the all-over, the wrapping by which an entity is generated like an organic body by the skin, not through distinction, but through coupling. It is flat like the skin and three-dimensional like the body. It is a regime of firstness in the sense of the semiotic (and that means: the relational and operative) ontology of Charles Sanders Peirce. Thus, firstness is the mode of being of what is one. The tactile in this function is the sensory operation that makes the least distinction between subject and object, but always entangles both. It is not possible to perform a touch without immediate feedback: whatever I touch touches me at the same time, and vice versa.

The relation of the keystroke or pressing the button is therefore a basic form of the anthropomediatic relation (Othold and Voss 2015). With *Understanding Media*, Marshall McLuhan (1964: 346–58) developed the first media anthropology to be flagged out as such. In doing so, he raised the idea of the tactility of the media and unfolded it using television as an example. For McLuhan (ibid.: 246–8), television is not a visual medium, but a tactile one. In McLuhan, the enveloping, comprehensive character of the tactile is reflected in ideas such as the interplay of the various sensory organs, their folding into the medium of the sense of touch, and the global village (ibid.: 274–5).

But here, in *mode double click* and in digitality, the other regime of the tactile is at play, that is, the regime of touching with the finger, of switching and triggering, selecting, pointing, and counting (Engell 2013). It is a directed or even targeted and punctiform touch that tends to turn into movement and continue into movement. The stretched-out finger or whole arm is the organ of deixis, of addressing, of efficacy, of agency, directionality, and causality (Serres 2008: 17–21). The extension of the finger and the touch with the fingertip are its basic operations, or better: its basic gestures, exactly as Vilém Flusser (2014) understood the term of gesture. For Flusser, gestures always arise from the interplay of body and device, such as photography, telephoning, and shaving. Accordingly, for the sense of the touch with the index finger, the coupled device would be the button, and button and sense of touch naturally belong together in terms of anthropomediality. Buttons here and fingers there only grow out of the relation of touch.

So the gesture here, in *mode double click*, would characteristically be the movement of the keystroke with the finger *bent* as with the mouse button. After several million years, the gesture of pointing, addressing, and effectuating is no longer performed with the finger stretched but with the finger bent. This alone is basically an anthropologically innovative and possibly disturbing fact. And the moment of touch between the finger and the button is repeatedly continued in the device: the sensors (from mouse ball to laser ray) touch the surface, the pressure on the button electromechanically brings together two contact points, flows of electric current are triggered, electromagnetic waves are released, and so on.

Indexicality

The tactile regime of the *mode double click* is, in Peirce's (1998: 258–99) sense, one of secondness. Secondness is the mode of being of what is as it is, since it functions, or is, in connection with something else. That is a relevant finding for two reasons. First of all, according to Peirce, secondness always includes firstness (ibid.: 274–5). This means that the entanglement between subject and object, which characterizes the first regime of the sense of touch, also continues in the regime of secondness. Second, however, this means that the basic onto-operational status of the anthropomediatic relation of pushing the button is that of indexicality (Engell 2013). Alfred Gell (1998) dedicated a highly instructive investigation to the anthropology of indexicality. Already the title of his book, *Art and Agency*, indicates a close relationship with the approaches of Actor-Network Theory. Gell sees in indexicality the common dimension of aesthetic or artistic practices, as we flag them out in the cultures of the West, and magical, for instance totemistic and animistic practices. In short, they have in common the indexical basic function of addressing, of pointing, and above all, of effecting.

According to Gell (ibid.: 28–51), works of art and designed objects in the first place, apart from everything else, are specific insofar as they denote their own creation, their efficacy. They describe themselves indexically—not least through signs such as the signature or traces such as handwriting—as the product of a creation. For Gell, the same applies to magical objects, which are produced and placed here by ancestors, spirits or gods, or even magicians. Second, according to Gell (ibid.: 56–258), we attribute to works of art an agency of whatever kind, be it on ourselves or on others; works of art, although by definition purposeless, do impress, do please, frighten, and disappoint, they entail reactions, judgments, or insights. It is precisely this intrinsic ability attributed to them, according to Gell (ibid.: 13, 35–7), that they also denote. This applies even more to magical objects, voodoo objects, and magic wands. They work and denote their effectiveness and their agency indexically; that is precisely where their effect and their agency lies.

This efficacy and agency has a direction and orientation, and it can be both an effect of contact magic and a working on distance, in remote control mode. The mouse button belongs, just like other switches, to the same realm of the agent object. In this sense it has never been modern (Latour 2015). It is therefore also, however small, an instrument of power. This was already the case with its predecessor, the television remote control, although the latter was clearer and rougher in this respect. Whoever operates the remote control has power over the television.[1] The shape of the remote control has also made its pointing, directional potential clearer.[2] Nevertheless, pointing and effecting is also the basic function of the mouse.

As an indexical, directional, and contact-magical instrument of the power of touch and guidance, the mouse button extends an impulse of movement that it itself has made possible and that it denotes beforehand. It expands a neurological impulse, which it itself provokes, even if only in the multiple feedback interactions with computer, window, sensors, and networking as we have seen above. Depending on the respective theoretical preconceptions, we can also read this impulse in an anthropocentric way as well, as intention, as action. In terms of media anthropology, however, the mouse click is still ahead of it. In his book on the five senses, Michel Serres (2008: 21–3) describes the shift of the proprioceptive point of gravity of our body from the center to the periphery, for example in juggling, in the trick of the conjurer, or in the erotic touch. This path from the center to the periphery extends via the switches, through the mouse button and the double click, beyond the biological body into the device and through the latter's networking even far beyond it into the world.

Upload and Double Contingency

The skipping of the jump, the deletion of the clash of the same with the other, the renunciation of transmission and translation, the separation of the superimposed may exist as an axiom in terms of pure logic, bodiless as it were, but it cannot be at work anywhere. *Tertium non datur* is not the empirical, the technological, and anthropological reality of double clicking, and perhaps it is even a deception anyway, albeit effective. Media anthropology can show that it is different. Not much remains of the demon of *mode double click* when you unfold it with the help of media anthropology. In the end this may also apply to the assumption that double click could not add anything to the world, that it did not aim at the open, and that it merely allowed selection from what already existed or offered, as in a supermarket (de Certeau 1984). This assumption is of course not unfounded in neoliberal consumer capitalism.

But once again it is not the whole picture. First, the upload of something additional to the web is also effected in *mode double click*. Even if the uploading itself does not generate the new, added possibilities, it does set them free in a way and puts them out into the—relatively—open. Second, the processes of choosing, the selection operations, are recursively coupled to each other. On the web, they intertwine and interweave and feed backward in repetition and feed forward in expectation. They even generate the most economically important good of digital economies: data—for instance, consumer data. Doing so, they generate a structure quite close to what Niklas Luhmann (1995: 107–8) assumes to be double contingency and thus the basis of communication.[3] To select something in these terms means at the same time to offer something to choose from. And third, even if one admits that in *mode double click* nothing new enters the world, this world would still be a Pascal world. In it, Pascal's sentence applies: "Qu' on ne dise pas que je n'ai rien dit de nouveau: La disposition des matières est nouvelle" (1660: 8). The world may remain constant, but its orderings may change.

Conclusion: The Stroll and the Broom

At the very end, this remains to be noted: All this is highly transient and short-lived. It is possible and probable that the mouse click will disappear again soon. It could soon be completely replaced by speech input, for instance. Then the anthropomediatic paradigm in play is no longer the touch and the switching, but the feedback between voice and ear. In any case, another tactile operation has already in part replaced the *mode double click*: the new gesture not of switching, but of swiping. It is even more blurred than a double click. It is still tactile, but exceeds the pointing and hence the point in a lateral movement and hence takes the form of a line. There is something analog about it. But at the same time, much more so than a double click, it is a negation operation: not this, maybe next. It moves less in the realm of pointing and addressing and deixis than somewhere between turning pages and dumping. Should the swiping become established as the new anthropomediality, then we may soon need a new mode of existence. The French could probably call it *mode bal*, like *la balade*, the stroll, and at the same time like *le balai*, the broom mode. But this is another story.

Notes

1. Names of early remote controls expose this, like "Mystery Control" or "Space Command" or (in Germany) "Teledirector."
2. The early "Flash Matic" device had the shape of a pistol and was used by aiming at sensors at the edges of the TV set.
3. As Tim Othold has remarked, Elena Esposito (2015) describes this process more closely as mirroring contingency without doubling it.

References

Anders, Günter (1956), "Die Welt als Phantom und Matritze," *Die Antiquiertheit des Menschen*, Vol. 1, 97–211, Munich: Beck.

Bardini, Thierry (2000), *Bootstrapping: Douglas Engelbart, Coevolution, and the Origins of Personal Computing*, Stanford, CA: Stanford University Press.

Bolter, J. David, and Richard Grusin (1999), *Remediation: Understanding New Media*, Cambridge, MA: MIT Press.

de Certeau, Michel (1984), *The Practice of Everyday Life*, Berkeley: University of California Press.

Deleuze, Gilles (2013), *Cinema II: The Time-Image*, London: Bloomsbury Academic.

Engell, Lorenz (2011), "Ontogenetic Machinery," *Radical Philosophy* 169 (Sept./Oct.): 10–13.

Engell, Lorenz (2013), "The Tactile and the Index: From the Remote Control to the Hand-Held Computer. Some Speculative Reflections on the Bodies of the Will," *NECSUS. European Journal of Media Studies* 2: 323–36. Available Online: https://necsus-ejms.org/the-tactile-and-the-index-from-the-remote-control-to-the-hand-held-computer-some-speculative-reflections-on-the-bodies-of-the-will/.

Engell, Lorenz (2021), *The Switch Image*, London: Bloomsbury.

Esposito, Elena (2015), "Zwischen Medialisierung und Cloud. Medialität im Web," in Lorenz Engell, Frank Hartmann, and Christiane Voss (eds.), *Körper des Denkens. Neue Positionen der Medienphilosophie*, 231–54, München: Fink.

Flusser, Vilém (2014), *Gestures*, Minneapolis: University of Minnesota Press.

Gell, Alfred (1998), *Art and Agency: An Anthropological Theory*, Oxford: Clarendon.
Heidegger, Martin (1977), *The Question Concerning Technology and Other Essays*, New York: Garland.
Heidegger, Martin (2010), *Being and Time*, trans. Joan Stambaugh, New York: State University of New York Press.
Kittler, Friedrich (1999), *Gramophone Film Typewriter*, Stanford, CA: Stanford University Press.
Latour, Bruno (2013a), *An Inquiry into Modes of Existence: An Anthropology of the Moderns*, Cambridge, MA: Harvard University Press.
Latour, Bruno (2013b), "Den Kühen ihre Farbe zurückgeben. Von der ANT und der Soziologie der Übersetzung zum Projekt der Existenzweisen. Bruno Latour im Interview mit Michael Cuntz und Lorenz Engell," *Zeitschrift für Medien- und Kulturforschung* (ZMK) 4 (2): 83–100.
Latour, Bruno (2015), *We Have Never Been Modern*, Cambridge, MA: Harvard University Press.
Latour, Bruno, and Steve Woolgar (1979), *Laboratory Life: The Social Construction of Scientific Facts*, Beverly Hills: Sage.
Luhmann, Niklas (1981), "Über die Funktion der Negation in sinnkonstituierenden Systemen," *Soziologische Aufklärung, Vol. 3: Soziales System, Gesellschaft, Organisation*, 35–49, Opladen: Wetstdeutscher Verlag.
Luhmann, Niklas (1990), "Meaning as Sociology's Basic Concept," in *Essays on Self-Reference*, 21–79, New York: Columbia University Press.
Luhmann, Niklas (1995), *Social Systems*, Stanford, CA: Stanford University Press.
McLuhan, Marshall (1964), *Understanding Media: The Extensions of Man*, New York: McGraw-Hill.
Othold, Tim, and Christiane Voss (2015), "From Media Anthropology to Anthropomediality," *Anthropological Notebooks* 21 (3): 75–82.
Pascal, Blaise (1660), *Pensées*. Édition de 1897 à Paris, Léon Brunschvicg. Samizdat 2010. Online: http://www.samizdat.qc.ca/arts/lit/Pascal/Pensees_brunschvicg.pdf (accessed July 18, 2022).
Peirce, Charles Sanders (1998), "A Syllabus of Certain Topics of Logic," in *The Essential Peirce: Selected Philosophical Writings*, Vol. 2, 258–99, Bloomington: Indiana University Press.
Roch, Axel (1996), "Fire-Control and Human–Computer Interaction: Towards a History of the Computer Mouse (1940–1965)." Available Online: http://web.stanford.edu/dept/SUL/library/prod//siliconbase/wip/control.html.
Schabacher, Gabriele (2013), "Medium Infrastruktur. Trajektorien soziotechnischer Netzwerke in der ANT," *Zeitschrift für Medien- und Kulturforschung* (ZMK) 4: 129–48.
Serres, Michel (2008), *The Five Senses: A Philosophy of Mingled Bodies*, London: Continuum.

Voss, Christiane (2010), "Auf dem Weg zu einer Philosophie anthropomedialer Relationen," *Zeitschrift für Medien- und Kulturforschung* (ZMK), 2 (2): 170–84.

Voss, Christiane (2019), "Anthropomediale Perspektiven," in Philipp Stoellger (ed.), *Figurationen des Menschen. Studien zur Medienanthropologie*, 33–51, Würzburg: Königshausen und Neumann.

9

Neutral Time

Philip Gries

At first glance the concept of neutrality seems to be incompatible with the concept of entanglement. Maintaining the state of being neutral—as in the case of political neutrality—is an effort to not mix up, to not confuse. Is a neutral subject (be it an individual person, institution, or state) not also defined by its (ideal) immunity from modes, states, and processes of entanglement?

Being entangled means to be in relations, perhaps even to be by virtue of relations. These relations are brought about through operations, acts, and media of entanglement. Therefore, they are characterized by a temporal, powerful, and historic relatedness, which seems to contradict the state of being neutral and the concept of neutrality. Yet another counterintuitive thought: being neutral requires distinctions, or at least the (supposed) existence of distinguishable parts or entities. For neutrality as a concept only makes sense if there is more than one alternative. One has to have options in order to opt for neutrality. Thus, to join the neutral party requires to *draw a distinction*, to search for and determine the difference between entities, and to describe them as different from each other. From this perspective, opting for neutrality is a mode of critical thinking (in the wider sense of the word "critical"), in which distinctness and disentanglement play a crucial role.

Nothing, no one is born neutral but has to become neutral or decide for neutrality. In most cases the need for neutrality results from (potential) conflict, which makes a retreat to neutral ground—an act of disentanglement—necessary for at least one party. From this perspective each *birth of neutrality* clearly has a history since it needs to be enforced by a (individual or institutional) subject. Neutrality presupposes a decision to steer clear of potential conflicts and entanglements in the future. Thus, there is a temporal dimension—explicit or implicit—to the concept of neutrality. In this regard, akin to the emancipatory critical view, the neutral perspective draws on the past—as a time to leave behind.

There is another way to think of the neutral and its specific temporality that can be found in Roland Barthes's approach to the Neutral.[1] In what follows I will focus on Barthes's approach, which allows an understanding of the Neutral as a certain kind of suspension. Drawing on Barthes, I would like to show that rather than conceiving of the Neutral as the result of an act of neutralization or disentanglement, or the result of a decisive act (like a straightforward retreat, reset or disentanglement), it can also be understood as a suspension of a certain kind of temporality. I will call it *Neutral time*.

Retreat to Neutral

Neutral Time, might seem paradoxical, after all, isn't the neutral—the state of being neutral or the concept of neutrality—something that is independent of time? Can the neutral—or again, neutrality—not even be defined by the absence of all sorts of more or less critical movements such as conflict, decision, development, folding, and unfolding? For is not the neutral, already by definition, a form that is opposed to all temporal movements that "need time" to be realized? Isn't the neutral, at least from a time-specific perspective, even the counterpart of the irregular, the variation, the subjective, the rhythmic? Could not the neutral be defined as a sphere, which is in itself motionless, hence atemporal? Or, to put it differently, is not the neutral associated with a geometry that plots for motion or sets the stage for action instead of being mobile itself?

Atemporal, static, and calming—an *opt out*. A space for a pause, making the continuation of conversation and discourse more likely. There is space for rational dialogue, says the theory of political neutrality, in this case the philosopher Charles Larmore:

> In the face of disagreement, those who wish to continue the conversation should retreat to *neutral ground,* with the hope either of resolving the dispute or of bypassing it. (Larmore 1987: 57, emphasis in original)

One can understand the word "retreat," which Larmore uses as a verb here, in its more or less literal double meaning: it points to a place—a "hideaway"—and at the same time to the action or movement of departure. The *neutral ground* is an element in the ideal world of rational discourse—a crucial part of its solid, stable, and minimal architecture.

A retreat—as the *"re-"*implies—presupposes a condition that contains some sort of conflict, thus some sort of finite process, action, or operation that demands a resolution—or at least a pause. A pause is a *temporary* interruption, hence the call for a retreat *to neutral ground* is evidently temporal—it is, in other words, a call for *Neutral time*. The call for a Neutral time, of course, presupposes a complementary non-neutral realm, which is conflictual or even violent.

Things break apart, words are spoken, passed by, all sorts of performative acts take place. States of being, identities are altered by events, processes, and operations. Any decision needs and takes time. Notions such as crisis, evolution, revolution, and decomposition bring together the concepts of time and decision.

The *neutral ground* on the other hand does not take time to be called into being. It is just there: plain and flat, thus unfoldable: the opposite of rhythm, I am tempted to say. It does not age.

Roland Barthes's lecture course on the Neutral, which he delivered in 1977 and 1978 at the Collége de France, points out that there is a crucial connection between time—or temporality—on the one side and the Neutral on the other. Barthes starts off his lecture by giving a definition: "I define the Neutral as that which outplays the paradigm, or rather I call Neutral everything that baffles the paradigm" (Barthes 2005: 6).

The paradigm—or *paradigmatic meaning*—is understood here in a linguistic sense. Thus it is "the opposition of two virtual terms from which, in speaking, I actualize one to produce meaning" (Barthes 2005: 7). Typical examples for such an opposition are *either/or, masculine/feminine, active/passive*, and so on.

In this perspective actualizing one term in favor of the other—which implies rejecting one of the terms—produces meaning. That is why meaning relies on the existence of a conflict. The processes of the Neutral, which Barthes describes as "baffling" or "outplaying," concern the conflict, or, more precisely, the decisive process itself, the decision-making. So, what is "baffled"—or, rather, what shall be baffled—is the conflict that presupposes a necessity for a decision. Since each actualization of one term is obviously an event in time, *baffling* and *outplaying* likewise need to be understood as temporal processes. Therefore, the Neutral is realized—if it is realized—in time and as a time. This time can be called *Neutral time*.

Barthes's course on the Neutral is—as he states in the preliminaries of the first session—a course on "the Desire for Neutral" (Barthes 2005: 1). Thus, what he calls "Desire" is seen as the driving force. What is desired is a "suspension ... of orders, laws, summons, arrogances, terrorisms, puttings on notice, the will-to-possess" (Barthes 2005: 12), but what is desired at the same is the "refusal of pure discourse of opposition" (Barthes 2005: 12). So we can conclude that the humble, at times appealing, at times confusing—and most of the time overstressed—word "resistance" is simply not enough.

Desire is, however, not only the motor and the principle of the lecture course, but also a guiding idea of Barthes's conception of the Neutral. Here, desire is "the truth" (Barthes 2005: 12) of the course: its "origin and that it stages." He adds "the course exists because there is a desire for Neutral: *a pathos* (a patho-logy?)" (Barthes 2005: 12).

In his inaugural lecture, delivered at the Collège de France in January 1977 (Barthes 1979), one year before the course on the Neutral, Barthes reflects on the role of the desire as a starting point—in this specific case a "fantasy." He declares: "I sincerely believe that at the origin of teaching ... we must always locate a fantasy" (Barthes 1979: 15).[2]

What are the implications of placing the desire at such a critical position within a theoretical framework? What does it imply to start from it? What kind of strategy is employed here? Furthermore, which role is played by desire as the driving force in Barthes's thinking of the Neutral?

First of all, beginning with desire means beginning with a force. However, what is a force? There are three qualities of a force that are most important with regard to the Neutral. I will address them with reference to Christoph Menke. First, a force is an "inner principle" (Menke 2012: 194) that does not "fulfill a function" (Menke 2012: 194). Expressions of a force as an inner principle are "without direction or purpose" (Menke 2012: 194). Second, "a force acts *of itself* [Menke's emphasis]; its activity is not governed by the subject, hence the subject is not conscious of it" (Menke 2011: 14) Third, "a force is *formative*, hence *formless* [Menke's emphasis]. A force gives rise to forms, and it reshapes every form it shapes." (Menke 2011: 14) As a consequence, each new expression of a force brings about a new form. Each new form is inevitably *temporal*. In this way a formation governed by the principle of a force strictly contrasts a dialectical logic of the general and the particular, in which each instance is seen as a particular expression of the general.

So, a force as a principal continually generates forms and at the same time destroys existing forms—it does so by regenerating them. Formations rendered by forces have a destructive aspect to them. The desire for the Neutral can be described as a force in Menke's sense. It is a specific mode of desire since it is unlike other modes of desire, "nonmarketable" (Barthes 2005: 13). "Nonmarketable" means that it cannot be exchanged or be traded. Something that cannot be exchanged or traded is a thing without a relative value. Instead the desire for the Neutral is defined by its "absolute singularity" (Barthes 2005: 13).

Back to the beginning. The question of the beginning not only concerns the form of Barthes's lecture course, it is also one of the main subjects of the Neutral. The Neutral entails a sense of beginning, points to a process, which is about to start, about to emerge. This situation, in which something is about to begin, about to happen, is a "suspended-time (= a definition of the Neutral as such): like an airlock" (Barthes 2005: 37). It is a phase that Barthes also connects with a certain type of awakening: "the white, neutral awakening" (Barthes 2005: 37). The notion of beginning associated with Barthes's thinking of the Neutral is specific, since it does not refer to a distinct point in time (like a starting point[3]). Whereas a starting point can be set at discretion, the neutral beginning is an "awakening," and is therefore based in a state of passivity. The term "awakening" also outlines that it is not a "birth" (not the first time), but a process of annulling or resetting; awakening is always *re*-awakening. There is no Neutral without presupposition. Therefore, there is no Neutral without a process of neutralization. Consequently, the notion of beginning associated with the Neutral does not refer to "a primacy of the world without meaning" (Hill 2010: 118) but to operations which evoke an "exemption of sense." It is, as Leslie Hill stresses, "a release from meaning" (Hill 2010: 118). The "exemption of sense" plays a pivotal role in several of Barthes's texts. It appears prominently as the title of a chapter in his book *The Empire of Signs*, which is an exploration of ideas such as Zen Buddhism and is also one of the continuous motifs in this study. The idea of an exemption is still employed in the latter text, but the wording has undergone a tiny, yet significant variation.[4] In *Empire of Signs* (1970) (Barthes 1983) Barthes defines the "haiku's task ... to achieve exemption from meaning" (Barthes 1983: 81). The exemption takes place "within a perfectly readerly discourse ..., so that to our eyes the haiku is neither eccentric nor familiar: ... it seems to us simple, close, known" (Barthes 1983: 81). Because of these qualities "it resists us" and "enters into that suspension of meaning" by making "impossible the most ordinary exercise of our language, which is commentary" (Barthes 1983: 81). It renders the exercise (which is habitual and relies on repetition like any exercise or practice) impossible by suspending it, and it does so by interrupting the temporality of the discourse by feeding it with Neutral time. It needs to be emphasized that Barthes is not referring to "ordinary language," but to its exercise, and therefore to the processuality and the temporality of its articulation. In his book *Roland Barthes* (1975), Barthes describes such a liberating, cancelling passage:

> The point is not to return to some kind of pre-meaning [un pré-sens], an origin to the world, life, things, prior to meaning, but rather to imagine a sort of post-meaning [un après-sens]: what is needed, as in a journey of initiation, is to pass through the whole of meaning [tout le sens], in order to extenuate it, and exempt it. (Barthes 1994: 87)

At this point I would like to highlight two features of the neutral that can be associated with the processes of exemption as just addressed. First, the neutral or the suspended time is called into being through an operation, so there is no *Neutral time* without a neutralization. Something needs to be stopped; something needs to be negated. Second, the exemption connected to the phase I call *Neutral time* is an expression of forces. In *Neutral time*, an interruption arises from what Barthes calls "force of *suspension* [Barthes's emphasis]"—a force inducing "a stoppage that congeals all recognized values" and that he explicitly links to the "*neuter* [Barthes's emphasis]" (Barthes 1975: 65).

An interruption presupposes a sequence—or at least some sequential order. In this light an interruption can be regarded as a rhythmic element.

The time of the Neutral is made rhythmic through movements of "exemption, cancellation" (Barthes 2005: 130), which are set in a "revolving sequence both disturbed and disturbing" (Barthes 2005: 130). Hence, it can be thought of—Barthes puts in the manner of Gaston Bachelard—as oscillating or "vibrating time" (Barthes 2005: 84).

For Barthes, however, rhythm is, as has been said, like an airlock and thus an in-between. An airlock connects dissimilar spaces that would otherwise remain unbridged. But unlike an airlock used in technological environments, neutral rhythm does not run like clockwork. Instead it is characterized by deferral, variation, untimeliness. Drawing on a famous remark by the cellist Pablo Casals, Barthes writes: "rhythm is all in the delay" (Barthes 2005: 184).

The neutral's mode, the way in which it evolves and operates, is *intensity*. Its changes result from changes of intensity rather than alteration (Barthes 2005: 199).

The model for this intensity can be found in the effervescence of a certain drink:

> We ... call Neutral the field of nonparadigmatic intensities (those introducing a trick into the paradigm), and in consequence we ask that the Neutral not be conceived, connoted as a flattening of intensities but to the contrary as a bubbling up ... (> champagne foam). (Barthes 2005: 197)

Don't Try so Hard

The Neutral, understood as actualized, as *Neutral time*, bears a challenge to conventional approaches of critical philosophies that emphasize the role of the "human capacity for action" (Arendt 1998: 230), whereby to "act, in its most general sense, means to take an initiative, to begin" (Arendt 1998: 177). Beginning, according to this perspective, is clearly an ability, and its formation does—as is the case for all capacities—require exercise, repetition, cultivation, and discipline.[5]

The beginning as it takes place in such an oscillating, rhythmic phase, which I call *Neutral time*, cannot be understood as an action induced by a capacity. Instead, *Neutral time* neutralizes the beginning as staged by an action. It questions concepts that are centered around the powerful (human) beginner, and it undermines its underlying temporal structure, in which a beginning is identical with a distinct starting point in a linear chronological scale. To begin in (or with) a *Neutral time* implies to begin with the instability of continuous deferral, which is to say, a force. For Barthes, this force is a desire. Desire is erratic.

In his essay "Force and Signification" (1963) Jacques Derrida (1978) reflects on the question of how theory can deal with force—or the concept of force.[6] According to Derrida force is "the other of language without which language would not be what it is" (Derrida 1978: 27), and as such it is a principle of creation constantly transcending established forms, patterns, or habits embodied in language. In line with Derrida, Menke understands force as a principal that is at once creative and excessive.[7] For Derrida, focusing on the *form* of language instead of dealing with the generative principle—its *force*, that which brings about language—implies missing the decisive part of language: the moment in which it is created and which I have tried to conceptualize as *Neutral time*.

> "*Form* fascinates," he writes, "when one no longer has the force to understand force from within itself. That is, to create." (Derrida 1978: 4–5, emphasis in original)

"Don't try so hard," Derrida might have said. "Don't try so hard," Derrida might have repeated. Attempting is a part of the problem here, repeating perhaps even at its core. What can be done instead is to dream of a subtle form of resistance against the *language of form*. He writes:

> Emancipation from this language must be attempted. But not as an *attempt* at emancipation from it, for this is impossible unless we forget *our* history. Rather, as the dream of emancipation. Nor as emancipation from it, which would be meaningless and would deprive us of the light of meaning. Rather, as resistance to it, as far as is possible. (Derrida 1978: 28; emphasis in original)

However, emancipation as a retreat from the *language of form* presupposes it to be a subject of violent forces. I turn to Barthes once again:

> The desire for the Neutral continually stages a paradox: as an object, the Neutral means suspension of violence; as a desire, it means violence. (Barthes 2005: 13)

Hence, for Barthes, far from being a calming and stable *neutral ground*, to which one can intentionally retreat, the Neutral is related to violence and *pathos*, as it has to be desired and brought about. In his perspective it is not only impossible to neutrally reach a neutral state, but the desired neutral state is also strictly temporal. Fleeing, but insistent—yet again in distinction from the shiftless *neutral ground*.

Conclusion

Without force, without desire there is—in Barthes's view—no time for the Neutral. Following Barthes we do not think of the neutral as the result of decisions (as it would be the case in political neutrality), corresponding to relatively simple temporal structures, in which the conflictual past (or present) is clearly separated by critical cuts from future entanglements. Instead, the Neutral is itself strictly time-based: it is called into being as Neutral time. It provides us with an approach that suspends the possibility of a distinct separation between emancipation (or criticality) and entanglement.

Notes

1. In this text, when referring to Barthes's notion of the Neutral, I follow Rosalind E. Krauss and Denis Hollier's translation, throughout which the *Neutral* is capitalized. Since the idea of a Neutral time draws on Barthes's work, it is capitalized too.
2. In the original text Barthes uses the word "fantasme": "Je crois sincèrement qu'à l'origine d'un enseignement …, il faut … toujours placer un fantasme" (Barthes 1980: 54). Richard Howard translates "fantasme" as "fantasy" (instead of "phantasma"). By doing so the original text loses some of its subtext, especially its psychoanalytical connotation.
3. Gilles Deleuze underscores that "to begin in philosophy has always … been regarded as a very delicate problem, for beginning means eliminating all presuppositions" (Deleuze 2004: 129).
4. Jean-Luc Nancy has analyzed the different ways in which Barthes refers to the idea of an exemption (or exemption) from meaning (Nancy 2008: 121–8).

5. "Having capacities or being a subject implies being capable of making an action succeed through practice and study. Making an action succeed in turn implies being capable of repeating a general form in a new, always unique situation. Capacity is the ability to repeat the general" (Menke 2010: 9).
6. Derrida's essay is an examination of certain structuralist literary studies, particularly Jean Rousset's book *Forme et signification: Essais sur les structures littéraires de Corneille à Claudel*. Nevertheless, the tension between force and form as discussed with regard to Rousset's book evokes general questions that go beyond the field of literary criticism, and perhaps the realm of language.
7. "The effectuation of forces involves *play* [Menke's emphasis], the creation of something that they have really already surpassed" (Menke 2010: 9).

References

Arendt, Hannah (1998), *The Human Condition*, second edition, introduction by Margaret Canovan, Chicago: University of Chicago Press.

Barthes, Roland (1975), *The Pleasure of the Text*, trans. Richard Miller, New York: Hill and Wang.

Barthes, Roland (1979), "Lecture in Inauguration of the Chair of Literary Semiology, Collège de France, January 7, 1977," trans. Richard Howard, October 8: 3–16.

Barthes, Roland (1980*), Leçon/ Lektion. Französisch und Deutsch. Antrittsvorlesung im Collège de France. Gehalten am 7. Januar 1977*, trans. Helmut Scheffel. Frankfurt/M.: Suhrkamp.

Barthes, Roland (1983), *Empire of Signs*, trans. Richard Howard, New York: Hill and Wang.

Barthes, Roland (1994), *Roland Barthes*, trans. Richard Howard, Berkeley: University of California Press.

Barthes, Roland (2005), *The Neutral: Lecture Course at the Collège De France (1977–1978)*. Text established, annotated, and presented by Thomas Clerc under the direction of Eric Marty, trans. Rosalind E. Krauss and Denis Hollier, New York: Columbia University Press.

Deleuze, Gilles (2004), *Difference and Repetition*, trans. Paul Patton, London: Continuum.

Derrida, Jacques (1978), "Force and Signification," in *Writing and Difference*, trans. Alan Bass, 3–30. Chicago: University of Chicago Press.

Hill, Leslie (2010), *Radical Indecision: Barthes, Blanchot, Derrida and the Future of Criticism*. Notre Dame: University of Notre Dame Press.

Larmore, Charles E. (1987), *Patterns of Moral Complexity*, Cambridge: Cambridge University Press.

Menke, Christoph (2010), "The Force of Art. Seven Theses," *Índex. Artistic Research, Thought and Education* (0): 8–9.

Menke, Christoph (2011), *Aesthetics of Equality. Ästhetik der Gleichheit*, trans. Christopher Jenkin-Jones, Ostfildern: Hatje Cantz.

Menke, Christoph (2012), "Aesthetic Nature: Against Biology," *Yearbook of Comparative Literature* (58): 193–5.

Nancy, Jean-Luc (2008), *Dis-enclosure: The Deconstruction of Christianity*, trans. Bettina Bergo, Gabriel Mallenfant, and Michael B. Smith, New York: Fordham University Press.

Part Three

Bodies in Media

10

Unfolding Bodies: Art and Ontology of the American Northwest Coast

Bernhard Siegert

Projections, Introjections, and Re-Introjections

In a 2013 article published on the occasion of a major exhibition of Surrealist art at the Vancouver Art Gallery (2011), the anthropologist Charlotte Townsend-Gault points out the frequent nods contemporary native artists make to the surrealist affinity for Northwest Coast art by incorporating references to famous surrealist iconography—Dalí's soft clocks, for example—into their own works (Townsend-Gault 2013). For André Breton, who owned a huge Kwakwaka'wakw Peace Mask, the animist credo—that material things possess a soul, and therefore are "people"—resonated with the surrealist understanding of the object in which Freud's popularized ideas on the subconscious coalesced with the concept of animism. Whereas in Breton the power of the "found object" is rooted in a subconscious desire, which is "used" by the object to impose itself onto the mind of the artist (Breton 1987: 30), Antonin Artaud in a letter of 1935 directly equated "Surrealism, Cubism, Picasso, Chirico, Balthus" with "the old animist spirit of the Mexican totems" (Artaud 1976: 348-9). The first show of Northwest Coast art to focus solely on form was in fact organized by surrealist Max Ernst, in collaboration with Barnett Newman, at the Betty Parsons Center in New York in 1946 (Bunn-Marcuse 2013: 405). The epistemological dilemma of such a cultural identification is reflected by the artist Lawrence Paul Yuxweluptun, who in some of his works displays traditional elements of native art in a style that mimics Dalí's soft watches (thus performing an act of counter-mimesis). Thus he addresses the dilemma that the appropriation of animist features by surrealist artists cannot help reenacting the colonialist gesture of incorporating the "other."

The study of cultural techniques runs the risk of ending up in a similar dilemma as it not only describes historical and contemporary assemblages of operations that precede the concepts eventually derived from them, but at the same time investigates how artifacts can behave as media that process ontological distinctions. If I, having no training in anthropology, take an interest in animistic ontologies, it bears underscoring that my intention is not to "explain" the "meaning" of Northwest Coast artifacts; on the contrary, my intention is to arrive at a more complex model of cultural techniques as media of operative ontologies. This study aims not at the "determination of other cultural techniques" but, to borrow a term from some of the participants in the anthropological discipline's ongoing "ontological turn," the "other-determination of cultural techniques" (Holbraad, Pedersen, and Viveiros de Castro 2014).

As the concept of operative ontologies aims to replace ontological distinctions with the cultural technical operations that produce and stabilize those distinctions in the first place, it continues a philosophical line of ontic-ontological questioning opened up by Martin Heidegger, if only in a more technologically informed fashion. As Geoffrey Winthrop-Young has it, "If German media theory in the Kittlerian vein focused on the materialities of communication, the study of cultural techniques takes aim at the materialities of ontologization" (Winthrop-Young 2014: 387). One can say that the ontological distinctions deconstructed by shifting the focus of media theory from communication to materialities of ontologization are the same three ontological dualisms whose destabilization Eduardo Viveiros de Castro has identified at the core of the "ontological turn" in anthropology: the subject/object dualism, the distinction between persons and things (and as follows, humans and nonhumans), and the distinction between semantic and non-semantic layers (signs and structures)—all of which are versions of the Nature/Culture dualism (Viveiros de Castro 2015: 4).

The disturbing doubling between the fascinating manifestations of an operative ontology of cultural techniques that makes Native art look almost like corroborations of recent non-hylomorphic remodelings of objects and materials, and the devastation caused by the colonial encounter, is something that needs to be considered when we read indigenous artistic practices through the lens of media theory in general, and the theory of cultural techniques in particular. It requires the study of the way Native artists relate to the animism inherent in algorithmitized commodification of cultural techniques, which is at the center of the biopolitics of so-called new media. But that is well beyond the scope of this article.

Sure enough, those mutual mimetic processes of incorporation did not only start in 2011 with the hosting of an exhibition of surrealist art on un-ceded territory in Canada, or in the 1940s with the enthusiasm of the exiled surrealists in New York for Native American Art (Mauzé

2013: 270–5). In fact, they go back to the first phase of colonization, with the establishment of a trading post by the Hudson Bay Company at Fort Rupert. It cannot be denied that the stylistic development of the Northwest Coast is deeply connected to this phase of colonization—from 1850 to 1900—when involvement in the fur trade, the canned fishing industry, and the fabrication of art works for the collector's market allowed Indigenous artists to accumulate unprecedented riches and wealth (Maurer 1982: 81–2, 86; Wardell 1978: 25–35). I would not go so far as to claim that animism itself was an effect produced by contact with the Europeans, but there can be no doubt that the way in which the new wealth boosted competition, struggles for prestige (and power), and the intensification of hierarchies among certain tribes on Vancouver Island and on the Central Northwest Coast mainland also had significant consequences for the development of artistic styles and the size and complexity of works of art (especially of masks).[1] This interplay of projection and re-introjection, which seems to be an inevitable part of colonization and postcolonial processes, is something that contributes to a nontrivial degree to the materialities of ontologization that are at stake here.

Split Representation

The 2011 exhibition performs a kind of ghostly inversion of another famous showing at the Vancouver Art Gallery in 1967. The latter exhibition, which was called "Arts of the Raven," was curated by Wilson Duff and Bill Holm, and was the first exhibition of Northwest Coast Art that presented crests, poles, blankets, bowls, and the like in the same manner as European fine art is typically presented in museums. The intentions were made perfectly clear by the subtitle "Masterworks by the North West Coast Indian." The motivation was "to move Native art from the dusty halls of ethnography to the pedestals of the art gallery" (Bunn-Marcuse 2013: 409), and in particular to present the art of the Northwest Coast as a style that rivals or outdoes Cubism. The style of the Northwest Coast was represented as a projection technique of three-dimensional objects onto two-dimensional planes, and hence—like Cubism—as an alternative to the classical Renaissance model of linear perspective.

Bill Holm's groundbreaking *Northwest Coast Indian Art: An Analysis of Form* had appeared two years earlier, in 1965 (Figure 10.1): an analysis of the formal principles of the designs of 400 objects—Chilkat blankets, spruce root hats, treasure boxes, façades of big houses, interior wall panels, dishes, screens, canoes, and so on—in order "to elevate" Native art to the level of

Figure 10.1 Cover title of the first edition of Bill Holm's *Northwest Coast Indian Art: An Analysis of Form* (1965).

modernist fine art, thereby necessarily stripping away the cultural context of the media practices in which those objects existed.

Holm demonstrated that certain elements of the designs appeared again and again, and suggested that the Northwest Coast style consisted of a finite set of discrete "symbols"—such as "ovoids"; "primary, secondary, and tertiary Us"; "split Us"; and complexes of angular, semiangular, and soft curves—that represented in abstract form the body parts of

Figure 10.2 Painting representing bear. Haida. From Franz Boas, *Primitive Art* (Oslo: H. Aschehoug, 1927), 224.

animals—eyes, eyebrows, joints, cheeks, ears, feathers, claws, flippers, hands, and so on—contoured by black and red "formlines" (Holm 2015). What the discreteness, as well as the symbols' syntactical laws of combination, suggested was an underlying formal principle guiding their composition, one as it happens, that Franz Boas had formulated in 1927 as follows (Figures 10.2 and 10.3):

> The animal is imagined cut in two from head to tail, so that the two halves cohere only at the tip of the nose and at the tip of the tail … This shows that the head itself must not be considered a front view, but as consisting of two profiles which adjoin at mouth and nose, while they are not in contact with each on a level with the eyes and forehead … either the animals are represented as split in two so that the profiles are joined

Figure 10.3 Painting from a house front representing a bear. Tsimshian. From: Franz Boas, *Primitive Art*, 225.

in the middle, or a front view of the head is shown with two adjoining profiles of the body. (Boas 1955: 223–4)

Already in 1918 Herman Haeberlin had hinted at the principle of "unfolding":

> Attention has been called to the fact that invariably the whole of the animals represented is given in the carving or painting, no matter how disproportionate the size of the different parts of the body may be. Furthermore, it has been pointed out that in order to make such an entire representation possible the device of showing the animal "unfolded"

Figure 10.4a Configurative Design. Woven spruce hat, Haida. From Bill Holm, *Northwest Coast Indian Art: An Analysis of Form* (Seattle: University of Washington Press, 2015).

Figure 10.4b Expansive Design. Woven spruce hat. Haida. From Bill Holm, *Northwest Coast Indian Art*.

either along the front or the back has been resorted to. (Haeberlin 1918: 259–60)

In 1923 Leonhard Adam identified eight principles: (1) The principle of stylization (as opposed to realistic representation), (2) principle of schematic characterization of certain features (symbolization), (3) splitting (i.e., Haeberlin's "unfolding"), (4) dislocating split body parts, (5) representing one creature by two profiles, (6) symmetry (with exceptions!), (7) reducing, and (8) principle of illogical transformation of details (Adam 1923, 1936: 8–9).

Taking his cue from Adam, Holm lays out three principles of design: configurative, expansive, and distributive. When the silhouette of the animal remains integral, undistorted, it can be considered an example of configurative design (Figures 10.4a–c). Expansive design refers to a mode of representation by which the animal is distorted, split, and rearranged to fit within a given space, but in such a way that the identity of the body parts as well as their anatomical relationship to one another remains apparent. The arrangement is called distributive design when the parts of the animal represented completely fill out a given space, consequently disavowing

Figure 10.4c Distributive Design. Woven spruce hat, Tlingit. From Bill Holm, *Northwest Coast Indian Art*.

any iconographically recognizable silhouette and ignoring the anatomical relationships between the constituent parts. Although the design may still represent an animal, the image is so distorted by the preoccupation with filling a space that it is difficult, if not impossible, to identify the abstracted animal (Holm 2015: 12).

Holm realized that the main factor in the distortion and dismemberment of the bodily forms, which so often results in the total loss of *gestalt*, is the two-dimensionality of Northwest Coast art, typical for the Northern tribes (Tlingit, Tsimshian, Haida). You sacrifice the recognizable integral body form, so to speak, on the altar of Greenbergian flatness. In the parlance of an author at times close to the Surrealist circle, Roger Caillois, the force that drives the bodies apart is something like a "real temptation" of [two-dimensional] "space" (Caillois 1984: 28), which forces the representation to give up the imaginary integrity and wholeness of the body. The compulsion exerted by two-dimensionality dismembers and rearranges the anatomy of the animal to the effect that the latter fills in the given space "most effectively"—and all this, as Holm has it, "for purely aesthetic motives" (Holm 1967).

The most important principle to achieve the transformation from three- to two-dimensionality, already addressed by Boas and his contemporaries, is that of "unfolding" or "splitting" the animal. By "'splitting' the animal, conceptually, in various ways these parts could be flattened out so that both sides of the animal could be seen and the decoration of the given space controlled" (ibid.). Large areas within the figure "were frequently elaborated with highly conventionalized portrayals of inner organs, joints and other unseen parts" (ibid.). The principle of splitting conjoins with the principle of "showing the interior."[2]

Up to this point one might get the impression that the interpretation of Northwest Coast art from the earliest studies of Boas and George Emmons, up until and including Bill Holm's, follows the art historical premise that the decoration of objects can be isolated not only from the social context and the cultural techniques in which those objects were embedded but also from any objects that perform those principles of unfolding and splitting in

Figure 10.5 Dance apron made of deerskin trimmed with red flannel and decorated with deer hoofs attached to the fringe. Tlingit. Collected by G. T. Emmons at Cape Fox, southeastern Alaska, Washington State Museum. From Bruce Inverarity, *Art of the Northwest Coast Indians* (Berkeley: University of California Press, 1950).

the real world.[3] Franz Boas's basic assumption was that art in general and "primitive art" in particular are subject to an anthropological constant which he called "esthetic [!] pleasure" or "the enjoyment of beauty," respectively (Boas 1955: 9–10). According to Boas—as for Holm, who in this respect was a true follower of Boas—the native art of the Northwest Coast was "symbolic art" in that it was "full of meaning," and thus had to be interpreted by classic iconological methods.

Nevertheless, it did not escape Holm that his description of the operation of splitting or unfolding as a mental operation corresponded to real operations that connected certain two-dimensional surfaces to plastic objects. So-called Chilkat blankets, for instance, take on three-dimensional forms if wrapped around a human body and take on, in such circumstances, a resemblance to carved poles or spoon handles (Figure 10.6) (Holm 2015: 17). Examples of typical transitions from two- to three-dimensional art, from graphic to plastic art, had already been studied by Walter Krickeberg in 1925, who described the phenomenon as "a characteristic shading (*Hinüberspielen*) of surface art into plastic art" (Krickeberg 1925: 144). But strangely enough, neither Krickeberg nor Holm, nor anybody else, mentioned that the Central Northwest Coast, in particular the territories of the Kwakwaka'wakw, abound in a special kind of object that performs the operation of "splitting the animal" in the real.

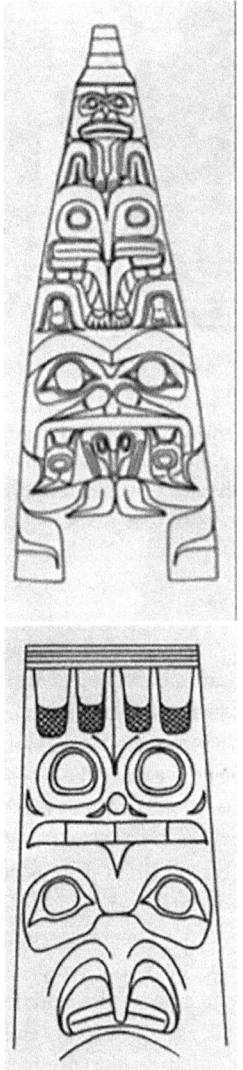

Figure 10.6a–c (continued)

Figure 10.6a–c Designs "unwrapped" from spoon handles. From Bill Holm, *Northwest Coast Indian Art*, 16.

Nobody except one. In an article first published in 1944, on "Split Representation in the Art of Asia and America"—a text so provocative that, until the end of the twentieth century, anthropologists and historians of Native art have either ignored or vehemently refuted it—Claude Lévi-Strauss sketched out a structuralist analysis that integrated the findings of Boas into a theory of social organization. Lévi-Strauss's motivation was—and this is presumably the reason his article was not even cited by Holm and has met with refusal until the 1980s at least (see, for instance, Carroll 1979)—to produce an argument that would justify comparative studies of Native art. In practice Lévi-Strauss compared the art of the Northwest Coast with the face paintings of the Caduevo in Brasil, the art of ancient China and the Maori's facial tattoos of New Zealand—all of which feature split representations of faces or animal bodies. While it is not my intention to get too wrapped up in the limits or merits of comparative anthropology, what makes this text by Lévi-Strauss so relevant for an approach that tries to contextualize the art of the Northwest Coast within a theory of cultural techniques is that his observations prompt him to conclude that "the interpretation of split representation proposed by Boas ... should be elaborated and refined" (Lévi-Strauss 1963: 259). This is a huge understatement, first because Boas had critically positioned himself against the comparative method in anthropology as early as 1896 (Boas 1896), and second, because it means nothing less than treating the "style" of the Northwest Coast not as an inner-aesthetic phenomenon but as a heteronomous phenomenon. In the final analysis what is at stake here is the relationship between the Symbolic and the Real, or more precisely the relationship between the body and the signifier in processes by which things become part of social (which is to say, symbolic) orders. What is at stake is an operative ontology of bodies and the key to it, as Lévi-Strauss shows, is given to us by "the concept of the *mask*" (Lévi-Strauss 1963: 261).

Masks are cultural techniques in the first place, not works of art, which is why they were marginalized by Holm and his predecessors. If we relate the principles of form in the Native designs to a theory of cultural techniques, the question of how art relates to ontological transformation processes—that is, to the animist ontology of the Northwest coast, and hence to the problem of changing and circulating bodily forms—becomes crucial. Therefore, before I can come back to Lévi-Strauss, I have to sketch out briefly a theory of the mask as a cultural technique in the context of animist ontology.

Operative Animist Ontology of the Mask

In spite of Marcel Mauss's, and indeed Lévi-Strauss's, classification of the tribes of the Northwest Coast as totemist, Philippe Descola has determined the ontology of the First Nations of the Northwest Coast to be animist. The characteristic feature of animist ontologies is that the distinction between humans and nonhumans does not concern the possession of a soul—as all kinds of nonhumans can be attributed with the interiority we in the West place under the exclusive purview of the human—but in terms of the forms of their bodies. By this disposition animals are anthropomorphized as a basic principle. Since they have a human soul it follows that they employ cultural techniques such as houses and masks and entertain social forms of communication with each other. And as the form of the body "is the crucial criterion of differentiation in animist ontologies" (Descola 2013: 131), it appears logical in such ontologies that those cultural techniques, which determine fundamental ontological categories, have to do with concealment and revelation of body forms, disguise, and uncovering, but also with being eaten and being vomited up again. As a consequence, masks, skins, and containers in general play a crucial role. The animal form, Descola writes, "is here an envelope (the skin) and a collection of movable attributes (the teeth, the snout, the ribs covered by their leather carapace), all of, once shed, reveal an anthropomorphic person" (ibid.: 203). This description can be applied without difficulty to the Northwest Coast style of decoration displayed on canoes, boxes, house facades, and the design of the so-called Chilkat blankets.

The masks of the Kwakwaka'wakw are *circulating body forms*, and therefore their technicality is especially pronounced. But the technicality of the masks is not restricted to the bearer of the mask's capacity to transform him or herself into the *persona* of the mask. The special feature of these masks, which are especially in use with the Kwakwaka'wakw and the Nuxalk,[4] is that they can be opened and closed by a system of strings, holes, and hinges (Figure 10.7). The unfolding of the mask can take on rather complex forms as the mask may unfold into two, three, or four parts. What appears inside the mask is by no means the face of the mask bearer. What appears is another mask, which represents an ancestor or a founding hero (i.e., a supernatural being) in the shape of an animal or an anthropo-theriomorphic hybrid (Figure 10.8). In the words of Marcel Drach and Marie Mauzé, who interpret these masks in psychoanalytic terms, the masks make manifest the idea that there is nothing else but the mask, nothing else but the Symbolic (Drach and Mauzé 2008: 40). These masks are not just about the circulation of body forms between humans and nonhumans, but about the technical operation of opening and closing by which the ontological operation of transformation between humans and nonhumans is processed. The circulation is thus technically conjoined with the dynamics of the differentiation between inside and outside.

The transformation masks are closely linked to the potlatch, that is, to the system by which the social organization between different family groups (*'na'mima*),[5] the hierarchy between different chiefs, the right to names, privileges, and political influence, is reproduced and confirmed. The third element (besides masks and names) through which the symbolic order is constituted are myths, which tell how masks and names were obtained in mythic times by the ancestor of a certain *'na'mima* or "tribe." Therefore, masks are "property" (Joseph 1998: 28). Property that is normally derived from the encounter of a first ancestor with a supernatural being, from whom the mask was in one way or another obtained. The system of names, however, does not stabilize the animist ontology, since "the permanent swapping of appearances makes it impossible to attribute stable identities to the environment's living components" (Descola 2013: 8).

Clothing oneself in a ceremonial robe of cedar bark, or dancing while donning a mask, is understood to be transformation. "Our first ancestors … could transform at will from human to bird, mammal, or other animal" (Sewid-Smith 2013: 17).[6] The traditional stories of the first ancestors quite often thematize the circulation of masks between supernatural beings and ancestors. Typically, a first ancestor steals a mask from a supernatural being, which appears in the body form of an animal, say a grizzly bear, but afterward takes off its bodily form, not *like* a mask, but *as* a mask. In the end the mask is exchanged for a name, like "Great Grisly Bear," which hereby proves to be the

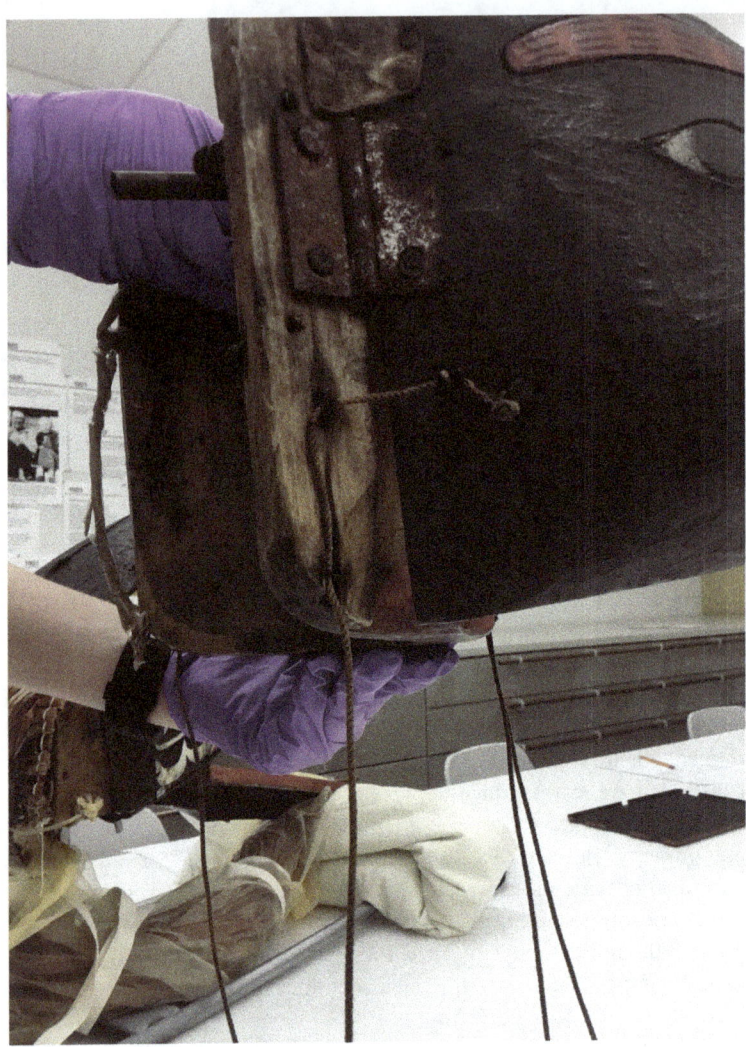

Figure 10.7 Transformation Mask (Raven/Human), Kitwancool (?), British Columbia, *ca.*1870, Museum of Anthropology, Vancouver, Object Nr. 1584/1, detail of hinges and strings. Courtesy of UBC Museum of Anthropology, Vancouver, BC. Photo: Bernhard Siegert.

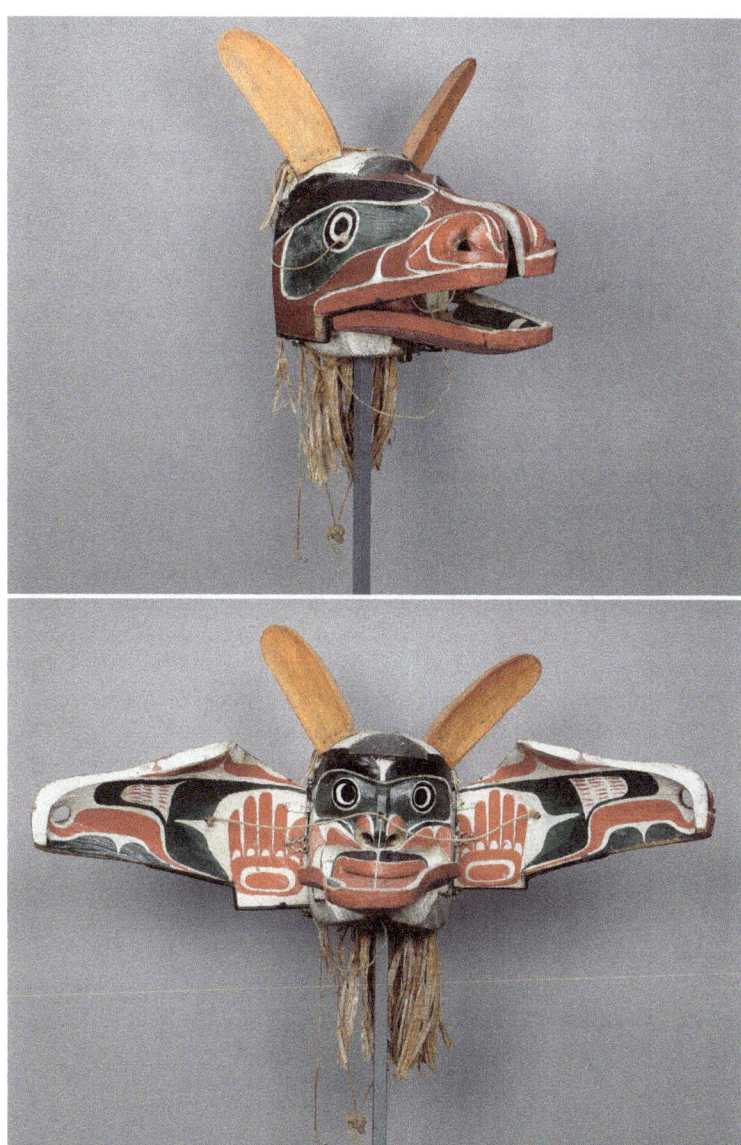

Figure 10.8 Charlie George, transformation mask, Kwakwaka'wakw Da'naxda'xw, New Vancouver, *ca.*1865. Museum of Anthropology, Vancouver, BC (A6373), (a) closed, (b) open. Courtesy of UBC Museum of Anthropology, Vancouver, BC. Photo: Jessica Bushey.

equivalent of the name (Boas and Hunt 1905: 33–6). Masks are names and names are masks (Walens 1983: 72).

Drawing on the theory of perspectivism, developed by Viveros de Castro and others, we can say that the difference between bodily forms and masks is nothing but a difference of perspectives, one that depends on whether humans see nonhumans from the perspective of humans or whether humans see nonhumans the way the nonhumans see themselves (i.e., as humans) (Descola 2013: 138–43; Viveros de Castro 1998: 469–88; 2009: 21–2). In the first case nonhumans are seen as animals, in the second case the body form is transformed into a mask. Hence it is precisely the moment of a change of perspective, which is performed by a transformation mask—a change of perspective made operational or, in other words, performed technically. Hence, it is impossible to distinguish between transformation ontology and transformation mask (or between an ontology based on switching perspectives and technology). There is also no difference between mythical time and historical time, in which the masks would have only the function of memorializing the mythical times. "For the Kwakiutl it is masks that are the agents of action, and people who are the passive channels of action" (ibid.: 71).[7] Bodily forms circulate a priori, there is no ontological difference between skin, fur, plumage, on the one hand, and mask, on the other. Thus it would be wrong to think that the mask represents the bodily form.[8] Friedrich Kittler's (in)famous statement that "only what is switchable is at all" (Kittler 2017: 5) was never more true than with regard to the mask ontology of the Northwest Coast. What we are dealing with is *an operative animist ontology*.

Switching Bodies into (Social) Existence

Lévi-Strauss's text on "split representation" allows us to relate this operative animist ontology of the mask to the formal design principles of Northwest Coast art. The "fundamental element" of Northwest Coast art, Lévi-Strauss claims, "which accounts for the … rigidity with which the technique of split representation is applied in them" is "the very special relationship which … links the plastic and graphic components" (Lévi-Strauss 1963: 260). This relationship is made operational, or in Kittler's terms "switchable" (*schaltbar*), by the transformation masks, which Lévi-Strauss calls "masks with louvers."

> These masks with louvers, which present alternatively several aspects of the … ancestor—… at one time human, at another time animal— strikingly illustrate the relationship between split representation and masquerade. (ibid.: 262)

Significant in this context is Bill Holm's observation that "in the north, among the Tlingit, Haida, and Tsimshian, surface decoration on masks is often applied with a minimum of relationship to the sculptured forms" (2015: 23). Quite in line with Lévi-Strauss's point concerning the face painting of Caduevo women, Holm goes on to relate this observation about masks to the face painting practices of the Northwest Coast:

> In concept such painting is used like the face painting of the north: flat realistic or conventionalized designs are applied with seemingly disregard for the structure of the face. In the south, particularly among the Kwakiutl, the painted forms emphasize, accent, and conform to the structure of the face. ... If a generalization could be made, it might be that mask painting in the north is independent of the structural form ..., among the Kwakiutl it coincides with the structural form. (ibid.)

What Holm omits is that the southern masks can be opened. The structural form, in these cases, is destroyed on the level of three-dimensional plasticity, whereas in the north it is destroyed on the level of the two-dimensional surface. It is astonishing that Holm forgets to incorporate this fact into his analysis, since only this fact completes the system: disregard for structure in surface designs (in the north) corresponds to disregard for structure in plastic objects (in the south).

The function of transformation masks is to offer a series of intermediate forms that insure the transition from symbol to meaning and from supernatural to social, but also, and first and foremost, from three- to two-dimensionality, from plastic to graphic (Figure 10.9), from body to graphism, from the Real to the Symbolic. This is especially stressed in the Lacanian reading given to Lévi-Strauss's text by Marcel Drach and Marie Mauzé. What Lévi-Strauss is grasping in his treatise, they contend, is that the Symbolic produces a subject only if the signifier leaves a mark on its body (Drach and Mauzé 2008: 42). The splitting of the graphism or the transformation of the mask is thus the trace left within the signifier by the function of alienation of the Symbolic: a function that consists of achieving a fundamental division between the social person and the naked human, the biological individual (ibid.: 41–2). Thanks to its distortion and its splitting "le signifiant assure sa prise sur le corps" (ibid.: 42).[9]

Although the primacy of the signifier is uncontestable in Lacanian thought, for Lévi-Strauss the relationship between "structure" and "decoration" seems rather to be some kind of mutual entanglement: "It is a relationship of opposition because the requirements of decoration are imposed upon the structure and change it, hence the splitting and dislocation; but it is also a

Figure 10.9 Beau Dick, transformation mask, Kwakwaka'wakw Dzawada'enuxw, Kincome Inlet, Gwa'yi, BC, 1983. Museum of Anthropology, Vancouver, BC (Nb3.1357), (a) closed, (b) open. Courtesy of UBC Museum of Anthropology, Vancouver, BC. Photo: Jessica Bushey. Courtesy of Fazakas Gallery, Vancouver.

functional relationship, since the object is always conceived in both its plastic and graphic aspects" (Lévi-Strauss 1963: 260). In his attempt to distinguish symbolic from material techniques, Thomas Macho admitted that both can be entwined within one another, but he adds that it makes a difference whether you whittle and adorn an arrow or whether you shoot it at an animal (Macho 2011: 45). By contrast, the lesson Lévi-Strauss taught anthropologists in 1945 should be key for all theories of art and cultural techniques:

> A vase, a box, a wall, are not independent, pre-existing objects which are subsequently decorated. They acquire their definitive existence only through the integration of the decoration with the utilitarian function. (Lévi-Strauss 1963: 260)

Thus, already in 1945 Lévi-Strauss formulated an essential insight into the non-hylomorphic "mode of existence of technical objects," which, in my opinion, lies at the center of any operative ontology. This may be extended to the very material technique applied in the fabrication of a box. This is accomplished by an ingenious folding operation. It is as if the algorithm of the decoration has invaded the very idea of the box-making technique. There are, in fact, examples of treasure boxes in which the split representation of the decoration coincides with the three-dimensional structure of the box (Figure 10.10). Lévi-Strauss goes on:

> Thus, the chests of Northwest Coast art are not merely containers embellished with a painted or carved animal. They are the animal itself. (ibid.: 260–1)

The boxes are the animal, the outer masks are the animal, because the animal itself is nothing but a body form, a container, a mask.

> Structure modifies decoration, but decoration is the final cause of structure, which must also adapt itself to the requirements of the former. The final product is a whole: utensil-ornament, object-animal, box-that-speaks. (ibid.: 261)

A box is not just a piece of furniture. It *is* the decoration that it represents: it becomes a living object. The box-that-speaks is the structure that becomes one with the decoration, and inasmuch as it becomes one with the decoration, the structure, the object, is introduced into language.

However, what is lost by the structuralist method is the historical dimension. If we include this dimension, the role of colonialism enters

Figure 10.10 Food storage box, Tlingit, Wrangell, Alaska, red cedar; the design represents a sea spirit, Kow-e-Ko-Tate. Washington State Museum. From Bruce Inverarity, *Art of the Northwest Coast Indians* (Berkeley: University of California Press, 1950), plate 22.

again into the picture. It seems that the development of the transformation masks aligns the synchronic relationship between graphic and plastic elements along a diachronic axis. Basically, one distinguishes between the Northern Style of the Haida and their neighbors and the style of the Southern Kwakwaka'wakw. According to Wilson Duff and others one can hypothesize the existence of an underlying sculptural tradition called Old Wakashan that constitutes the underlying tradition all along the coast, and has been applied to such generic Northwest Coast forms as carved posts and figures, zoomorphic bowls, masks, and bird rattles (Duff 1967). In the Northern Style, which was developed before the time of contact, the graphic or surface tradition was dominant. A painterly tradition in essence, it consists of two-dimensional designs applied to surfaces. In the Kwakwaka'wakw style, which evolved in post-contact times, the sculptural tradition of the Old Wakashan is retained, but is covered by a veneer of surface decoration that has elements drawn from the Northern Graphic tradition. At the same time, the Old Wakashan plastic technique is transformed in a significant way. Although there are some ambiguous indications that masks with movable parts predate the first European explorers' landing on the shores of the Northwest Coast in the 1770s, the evidence is inconclusive and rare.[10] In any case, the split representation of the Northern Style is much older than the sophisticated transformation masks of the central Northwestern Coast. It is probable that there is a connection: that the introduction of the Northern Graphic tradition into the southern regions where the plastic tradition was retained led to the development of a combination of both. In a more structuralist manner of speaking, it is as if the introduction of the graphic signifier forced the sculptures to unfold, or to be more precise: to operate the transition between three- and two-dimensionality, to make operable the switch from three-dimensional integrity of the body to the disintegration of the body and its distribution on a two-dimensional plane.

New Media

Of course, Lévi-Strauss does not envision anything like an operative ontology. He aims at a theory that inextricably links existence with the social: "We already foresee that split representation can be explained as a function of a sociological theory of the splitting of the personality" (1963: 259). The analysis of Lévi-Strauss is of course closely connected to the lesson of Marcel Mauss on the hierarchic duality that inheres the mask: *persona*, social person, on the one hand, and the individual person who carries the mask on the other hand (Mauss 1985). But if we take seriously the lesson the switch-ontology of the transformation masks has taught us, *persona* is not the identity guaranteed by a totem or crest or a name; rather the persona relies and depends on *mimesis* itself.

This takes us back to the mimetic entanglements between European art and the art of the Northwest Coast. In 1980 the artist Lyle Wilson created a piece called "Ode to Billy Holm" (Figure 10.11). Its upper part shows

Figure 10.11 Lyle Wilson, Ode to Billy Holm ... Lalooska ... Duane Pasco ... And Jonathon Livingston Seagull, 1980, Etching, 50.7 × 40.9 cm, UBC Museum of Anthropology. Courtesy of UBC Museum of Anthropology, Vancouver, BC, and courtesy of Lyle Wilson. Photo: Derek Tan.

a schematic silhouette of a dancer (Bill Holm?) wearing a mask in front of one of those designs Holm had analyzed with such great effort. In the lower part Wilson depicts his status card, which confirms his status as "Indian" and which he is obliged to have on him. The status card takes up the symmetry of the split representation of the design in the background of the upper field. The fact that the card is a document that is represented as if it can be unfolded like a transformation mask points to the fact that the status card is the *persona* of Lyle Wilson. Wilson thus uncovers a double failure. On the one hand is the dancer who dons a mask in front of the split representation of the background and points to Bill Holm's *persona* as non-native author of *An Analysis of Form*, which failed to address masks as the key to any understanding of split representation. This is further stressed by the title and the author's name rendered in mirror writing in the upper field: "Analysis of Form by Bill Holm." On the other hand is the native artist whose *persona* is no longer enacted by the transformation mask and its operative existential mimesis, but by the status card that inscribes his body into the symbolic order of the Canadian state. Lyle Wilson's piece makes us aware of the fact that the media that determine the native's situation in modern Canada require a new perspectivism. What would be the technical form of a mask that could operate a transition between (make switchable) these perspectives?

Notes

I would like to thank the Peter Wall Institute for Advanced Studies at UBC Vancouver, which awarded me an international scholarship in 2016, thereby enabling me to study the cultural techniques of the transformation masks; the Museum of Anthropology, Vancouver, for granting me access to their collections; T'ai Smith; Charlotte Townsend-Gault; the late Beau Dick; Geoffrey Winthrop-Young; Peter Skafish, who invited me to publish a first version of this essay with his online journal *The Otherwise*; and Matthew Harry Evans, who edited the essay.

1. Alexandra Roth has attempted to analyze the "European influences on indigenous art of the Northwest Coast," but unfortunately her "museum ethnology" approach remains too superficial, and ignores transformation masks altogether. Her result, that the introduction of steel knives enhanced and sped up the production of artifacts, is a commonplace (Roth 2002).
2. In his work on the *Art of the Northwest Coast Indians*, Robert Bruce Inverarity also wrote that "the Indians of the Northwest Coast frequently depicted the internal structure of an animal with detailed anatomical representations, as well as its external forms" (Inverarity 1950: 37). The whale depicted on a Tlingit dance apron shown in figure 10.5 is an example.
3. This discourse can be traced back to the great methodological dispute in art history in the early twentieth century between "art history as history of form" and "art history as intellectual history"; a prominent representative of the former school is Heinrich Wölfflin, a prominent representative of the latter is Max Dvorak.

4. "Larger and more elaborate masks with movable parts are typical of the Nuxalk and the Kwakiutlan- and Nootkan-speaking peoples of the central coast of British Columbia" (Carlson 2005: 50).
5. Franz Boas used the term "tribe" to distinguish the twenty village groups of the Kwakwaka'wakw, but he recognized that it is the tribal subdivisions that must be considered as the fundamental units. Instead of using terms like "gens" or "clan" he adopted the native term "'na'mima" (anglicized to the spelling of "numaym") (Boas 1920: 115; see also Joseph 1998: 35n.2). Every numaym has a distinct First Ancestor whose image was represented by the crest. It is important to highlight the fact that a numaym consists not just of living people, but of a series of noble names "that may be considered as similar to offices which must be filled" (Boas 1920: 118). Hence it may happen that the number of positions in a numaym is larger than the number of the members of the tribe.
6. See also Malin (1978: 45): "All had powers enabling them to transform themselves from one outward form to another, since external coverings were the only differences between them. They could discard their skins, feathers, or fur and assume different forms, yet they spoke a common language."
7. This object-oriented or "animistic" perspective is confirmed for instance by the late carver and hereditary chief Beau Dick, who told the story of how a block of wood found its way into his workshop in order to be given the shape of Crooked Beak of Heaven. See *Maker of Monsters: The Extraordinary Life of Beau Dick* (CND 2017, dir. Natalie Boll and LaTiesha Fazakas). The same story was told to the author by Beau Dick in his studio on October 18, 2016.
8. The same holds true for the so-called Chilkat blankets, whose origin is commonly attributed to the Tsimshian, from whom the Chilkat and other tribes learned the art later. The Tsimshian tradition links these ceremonial robes to the same animistic transformation ontology. According to the Chilkat, in mythical times animals were still men, wearing the animal skins as blankets. The coats of fur of the different species of animals were mere protective coverings to be removed at will and they often appeared in human form (see Emmons 1907: 329).
9. Drach and Mauzé quote Lacan in this context: "The body, if taken seriously, is primarily what is able to bear the mark, that which is capable of inserting it [i.e. the body] into a series of signifiers" (Lacan 2001: 409, my translation).
10. Most convincing is an antler comb that depicts a masked dancer with a bird rattle and is dated 2,000 to 1,500 years ago. Whether this mask is a transformation mask is impossible to say (see Carlson 2005: 51). In most of the other examples Carlson provides it is difficult to tell whether the image represents a mask or the animal itself, which the mask represents. Early reports of explorers describe masks with movable arms that were operated by a second person who stood behind the dancer and operated the arms with sticks, which is a kind of performance that has nothing to do with transformation.

References

Adam, L. (1923), *Nordwestamerikanische Indianerkunst*, Berlin: Wasmuth.
Adam, L. (1936), "North-West American Indian Art and Its Early Chinese Parallels," *Man* 36 (2–3): 8–11.
Artaud, A. (1976), "Draft of a Letter to the Director of the Alliance Française, December 14, 1935," in Susan Sontag (ed.), Helen Weaver (trans.), *Selected Writings*, 347–52, New York: Farrar, Straus, and Giroux.
Boas, F. (1896), "The Limitations of the Comparative Method of Anthropology," *Science*, new series 4 (103): 901–8.
Boas, F. (1920), "The Social Organization of the Kwakiutl," *American Anthropologist*, new series 22 (2): 111–26.
Boas, F. (1955), *Primitive Art*, Mineola, NY: Dover.
Boas, F., and G. Hunt (1905), *Kwakiutl Texts: The Jesup North Pacific Expedition, Memoir of the American Museum of Natural History New York*, vol. III, Leiden: E. J. Brill; New York: G. E. Stechert.
Breton, A. (1987), *Mad Love*, trans. Mary Ann Caws. Lincoln: University of Nebraska Press.
Bunn-Marcuse, K. (2013), "Form First, Function Follows: The Use of Formal Analysis in Northwest Coast Art History," in Ch. Townsend-Gault, J. Kramer, and Ki-Ke-In (eds.), *Native Art of the Northwest Coast: A History of Changing Ideas*, 404–13, Vancouver, Toronto: UBC Press.
Caillois, R. (1984), "Mimicry and Legendary Psychasthenia," trans. John Shepley, *October* 31 (Winter): 16–32.
Carlson, R. L. (2005), "Images of Precontact Masks," *American Indian Art Magazine* 30 (2): 48–57.
Carroll, M. P. (1979), "Lévi-Strauss on Art: A Reconsideration," *Anthropologica*, new series, 21 (2): 177–88.
Descola, P. (2013), *Beyond Nature and Culture*, trans. Janet Lloyd, Chicago: University of Chicago Press.
Drach, M., and Mauzé, M. (2008), "Le dédoublement de la représentation: paradoxes de la prise au corps du symbolique," in Marcel Drach and Bernard Toboul (eds.), *L'anthropologie de Lévi-Strauss et la psychanalyse*, 35–44, Paris: La Découverte.
Duff, W. (1967), "Contexts of Northwest Coast Art," in *Arts of the Raven: Masterworks by the Northwest Coast Indian* (exhibition catalogue), n.p., Vancouver: Vancouver Art Gallery.
Emmons, G. T. (1907), "The Chilkat Blanket," in *Memoirs of the American Museum of Natural History*, vol. III, 329–404, New York: Knickerbocker Press.
Haeberlin, H. K., "Principles of Esthetic Form in the Art of the North Pacific Coast: A Preliminary Sketch," *American Anthropologist*, new series 20: 258–64.

Holbraad, M., M. A. Pedersen, and E. Viveiros de Castro (2014), "The Politics of Ontology: Anthropological Positions," *Fieldsights*, January 13, 2014. Available online: https://culanth.org/fieldsights/the-politics-of-ontology-anthropological-positions (accessed November 30, 2022).

Holm, B. (1967), "The Northern Style—A Formal Analysis," in *Arts of the Raven: Masterworks by the Northwest Coast Indian* (exhibition catalogue), n.p., Vancouver: Vancouver Art Gallery.

Holm, B. (2015), *Northwest Coast Indian Art: An Analysis of Form*, 50th anniversary edn., Seattle: University of Washington Press.

Inverarity, B. (1950), *Art of the Northwest Coast Indians*, Berkeley: University of California Press.

Joseph, R. (1998), "Behind the Mask," in Peter Macnair, Robert Joseph, and Bruce Greenville (eds.), *Down from the Shimmering Sky: Masks of the Northwest Coast*, 18–35, Vancouver: University of Washington Press, Vancouver Art Gallery.

Kittler, F. (2017), "Real Time Analysis, Time Axis Manipulation," trans. Geoffrey Winthrop-Young, *Cultural Politics* 13 (1): 1–18.

Krickeberg, W. (1925), "Malereien auf ledernen Zeremonialkleidern der Nordwestamerikaner," *Jahrbuch für prähistorische & ethnographische Kunst* 1: 140–50.

Lacan, J. (2001), "Radiophonie," in *Autres écrits*, 403–47, Paris: Éditions du Seuil.

Lévi-Strauss, C. (1963), "The Split Representation in the Art of Asia and America," in Claire Jacobson and Brooke Grundfest Schoepf (trans.), *Structural Anthropology*, 245–68, New York: Basic Books.

Macho, T. (2011), *Vorbilder*, Munich: Fink.

Maker of Monsters: The Extraordinary Life of Beau Dick (2017), [Documentary], Dir. Natalie Boll and LaTiesha Fazakas, Vancouver, Canada: Athene Films.

Malin, E. (1978), *A World of Faces: Masks of the Northwest Coast Indians*, Portland, OR: Timber Press.

Maurer, E. M. (1982), "Two Northwest Coast Masks: A Study of Tradition and Style," *Bulletin of the Detroit Institute of Arts* 60 (3/4): 80–91.

Mauss, M. (1985), "A Category of the Human Mind: The Notion of Person; the Notion of Self," in Michael Carrithers, Steven Collins, Steven Lukes (eds.), *The Category of the Person: Anthropology, Philosophy, History*, 1–25, Cambridge: Cambridge University Press.

Mauzé, M. (2013), "Surrealists and the New York Avant-Garde, 1920–60," in Ch. Townsend-Gault, J. Kramer, and Ki-Ke-In (eds.), *Native Art of the Northwest Coast: A History of Changing Ideas*, 270–5, Vancouver, Toronto: UBC Press.

Roth, A. (2002), *Die Begegnung mit dem Fremden. Europäische Einflüsse auf die indigene Kunst Nordwestamerikas*. Frankfurt am Main: Goethe-Universität.

Sewid-Smith, D. (2013), "Interpreting Cultural Symbols of the People from the Shore," in Ch. Townsend-Gault, J. Kramer, and Ki-Ke-In (eds.), *Native*

Art of the Northwest Coast: A History of Changing Ideas, 15–25, Vancouver, Toronto: UBC Press.

Townsend-Gault, Ch. (2013), "'My World Is Surreal,' or 'The Northwest Coast' Is Surreal," *Journal of Surrealism and the Americas* 7 (1): 96–107.

Viveiros de Castro, E. (1998), "Cosmological Deixis and Amerindian Perspectivism," *Journal of the Royal Anthropological Institute* 4 (3): 469–88.

Viveiros de Castro, E. (2009), *Métaphysiques cannibales. Lignes d'anthropologie post-structurale*, trans. Oiara Bonilla, Paris: Presses Universitaires de France.

Viveiros de Castro, E. (2015), "Who Is Afraid of the Ontological Wolf? Some Comments on an Ongoing Anthropological Debate," *Cambridge Journal of Anthropology* 33 (1): 2–17.

Walens, S. (1983), "Analogic Causality and the Power of Masks," in N. Ross Crumrine and Marjorie Halpin (eds.), *The Power of Symbols: Masks and Masquerade in the Americas*, 70–8, Vancouver: UBC Press.

Wardell, Allen (1978), *Objects of Bright Pride: Northwest Coast Indian Art from the Museum of Natural History*, New York: Center for Inter-American Relations & the American Federation of Arts.

Winthrop-Young, G. (2014), "The *Kultur* of Cultural Techniques: Conceptual Inertia and the Parasitic Materialities of Ontologization," *Cultural Politics* 10 (3): 376–88.

11

Corporeal Literacy: Alphabetic Bodies and the Logic of the Cut

Maaike Bleeker

The notion of anthropomediality draws attention to how constellations of humans and media enable ways of knowing, thinking, and imagining. Anthropomedial configurations "open up and make possible new territories of thinking, feeling, interacting and being, along with a de- and relocation of subject-object relations" (Othold and Voss 2015: 80). From this perspective, human ways of experiencing and understanding the world, as well as human "selves," are inseparable from media and other technologies that humans interact with. They are part of what Bernard Stiegler, Katherine Halyes, Mark N. B. Hansen, and other theorists and philosophers describe as *technogenesis*: the human coevolution with their tools and technologies. This text proposes corporeal literacy as a perspective on the effects of sedimented practices of doing things (with media and other technologies, as well as otherwise) on how humans make sense of what they encounter. Literacy denotes the ability to read and write. Over the past decades, various other literacies have been proposed, expanding the notion of literacy beyond the domain of the written and printed word. The term "literacy" is used to describe the competency involved in interpreting various information, as in visual literacy, media literacy, or aural literacy. Likewise, corporeal literacy aims to expand the notion of literacy but in a slightly different way. Unlike the "media" in media literacy, "corporeal" in corporeal literacy does not denote a class of information or an aspect of objects being read but rather refers to the corporeal dimensions of making sense of what we encounter, and to how these corporeal dimensions are informed by interactions with tools and technologies including (but not limited to) writing and print.

Corporeal literacy is a strategic term meant to direct attention to how skills acquired from the interaction with writing and print "write" themselves into bodies to affect their ways of perceiving, thinking, and imagining. Corporeal literacy thus draws attention to the often overlooked corporeal dimensions of the human coevolution with writing and print, and how these dimensions manifest themselves in ways of making sense that are co-shaped by them. Corporeal literacy is also a speculative term that invites a similar perspective on other practices, including interactions with other media and technologies. How does the sedimentation of skills of various kinds co-shape ways of enacting perception and making sense? How do histories of interactions and practices of doing become part of how bodies make sense of what they encounter, and how does this affect their experience of space, time, and self? How do current media and other technologies inform new ways of being corporeally literate? And how do these developments demand the development of new ways of being corporeally literate in the sense of being consciously aware of the implications of these interactions and their effects?

The following works toward an understanding of corporeal literacy that builds on and moves beyond Walter Ong's (1988) conceptualization of literacy as a "mind-set" to draw attention to how interaction with (media) technologies affects modes of enacting perception and the organization of the human sensorium. To this end, I complement Ong's approach to literacy with Brian Rotman's (2008) notion of the alphabetic body. Whereas Ong focuses on how writing and print represent spoken language and how this makes possible new ways of doing things with language that would restructure consciousness, Rotman's new materialist and enactive approach directs attention to how writing and print come to matter for bodies engaging with them, and how this affects the ways in which bodies make sense of what they encounter. Rotman shifts attention from writing as representation toward writing as remediation to show how, as remediation, writing "engenders a clutch of interconnected discontinuities in the milieu of what preceded it; a disruption of the previous space-time consensus of its users and an altered relationship between agency and embodiment giving rise to new forms of action, communication and perception" (Rotman 2008: 6). Writing, as well as speech before it, and other media after it, intercedes in disconnections and reconnections between bodies and positions in media. Media requires users to develop the capacity to relate to such positions, and learning to do so brings about what Rotman refers to as the virtual. Virtuality, he argues, is ancient and manifests itself in how, ever since the invention of speech and writing, technologies and our interaction with them have destabilized the existing space-time continuum and have given rise to reconfigurations of agency and embodiment.

I will show how Susan Foster's (2011) observations on early dance manuals present a first step toward further fleshing out Rotman's ideas about how media, including writing and print, engenders disconnections and reconnections between bodies and media, and how this affects their modes of perceiving, thinking, and imagining, as well as their sense of self. Foster's observations confirm both Ong's and Rotman's reflections on how writing and print restructure consciousness while also drawing attention to how this restructuring involves a certain "recalibration of sensings": a reordering of the synesthetic operations of the sensorium that affects user's sense of space and of self. Foster's observations show that relating to positions given within the medium of writing and print requires developing perceptual skills that both build on and affect what Vivian Sobchak (2004), writing about film, refers to as the carnal foundations of intelligibility. These carnal foundations are given in "the cross-modal communication of our senses and the synthetic quality of the lived body that comprehends both our sensorium and our capacity for language" (2004: 72). The final part of the text brings together Rotman and Sobchack with Merleau-Ponty, Deleuze, and enactive approaches to cognition for a closer look at what Rotman describes as the corporeal axiomatic of writing and print as well as other media: how they engage with bodies of users, become part of the synesthetic operations of the sensorium, and how this contributes to what Ong describes as restructurings of consciousness. This is done in dialogue with Peter Greenaway's film *Prospero's Books* (1991), a cinematic exploration of relationships between bodies and writing and print, and how their interaction affects imagining and thinking.

Mind-Sets and Alphabetic Bodies

The technology of writing, more than providing a means to capture, store, and transmit spoken language, "restructures consciousness," as the title of chapter 4 of Ong's book *Orality and Literacy* (1988) states. The invention and widespread use of writing and print gave rise to new analytical modes of thinking and facilitated the emergence of new kinds of knowledge. Importantly, this impact of the technology of writing and print is not about the use of language per se. It is not about what words do to minds (and bodies) but about the transformations of modes of managing knowledge, thinking, and of "self," of human identity, brought about by the medium of writing and print. Ong explains these transformations from how writing and print turn language from an aural-transitory phenomenon into a visual-spatial one, and how this led to new ways of doing things with it. When written down, words remain, gain an existence independent of the situation of utterance, can circulate independently, be accumulated in libraries, be categorized and organized. Writing allows language to be taken apart in smaller pieces, be analyzed in new ways, and be accessed time and again at different places and times. Writing and print support "a sense of closure, a sense that what is found in a text has been finalized, has reached a state of completion" (Ong

1988: 129). Such closure pertains not only to the text itself but also to the possibility of the knowledge represented in it to be definitive, exhaustive, and encompassing, as well as the idea of knowledge as something that can be placed somewhere and ordered. Furthermore, writing and print partake in a "spatialization" of knowledge that manifests itself in modes of knowing in terms of determining the position of individual elements in a totality: in taxonomies, indexes, charts, and on maps. This is knowledge that places the knower in a position of overview over a spatially ordered totality, and at a distance from what is known as objectively given. All of this is constitutive of the new modes of imagining and thinking that Ong proposes calling the "mind-set" of literacy. In this context, it is worth noting the connection between Ong's approach and that of Marshall McLuhan and the Toronto School of Communication Theory. Ong's conclusion (in his two volumes *Ramus, Method, and the Decay of Dialogue: From the Art of Discourse to the Art of Reason*, and *Ramus and the Talon Inventory*, both published in 1958) that the printing press led to a shift in the way that knowledge was conceptualized, is subject of lengthy discussion in McLuhan's Gutenberg Galaxy (originally published in 1962, see also Strate 2011). Literacy, in Ong's understanding, does not merely describe the capacity to read and write but refers to ways of understanding, thinking, and imagining that are affected by the incorporation of practices of interacting with the written and printed text. Ong points out that the effects of this incorporation extend well beyond the actual doing of reading and writing. These effects come to individuals through their cultures and in different ways. An important factor in the general incorporation of written language into modes of understanding and thinking was the invention of the alphabetic letter press and the industrialization of print from about 1700. Previous to this moment, reading and writing had been the privilege of only a few, and culture had remained largely oral-aural. Print literally spread the written word and was instrumental in replacing "the lingering hearing dominance in the world of thought and expression with the sight-dominance which had its beginnings with writing but could not flourish with the support of writing alone" (Ong 1988: 119). The standardization of the letter sign and streamlined layout made texts easier to read, allowing for rapid, silent reading and supporting interiorized individual reading, thus contributing to the development of the modern subject in terms of a private interior and a public exterior. Print allows for smaller books to be produced in large quantities, for the same ideas to be shared by many, and thus for the establishment of more broadly shared worldviews. It also supported the development a sense of private ownership of words and knowledge, and gave rise to the notion of authorship, as well as of plagiarism.

Ong's theory of literacy has been criticized for how it might suggest a dichotomy, or "great divide," between oral cultures and literate ones, and invite the equation of an autonomous and monistic understanding of literacy with rationality, logic, and meaningful cultural development. Yet, as also has been pointed out, Ong's work actually shows orality and literacy to be interrelated in complex ways and not mutually exclusive (see Soukup 2007 for an overview, in particular pages 6–8 regarding the "great divide"). A closer look at the corporeal dimensions of the ways in which writing and print engage their users supports an understanding of the changes brought about by writing and print in terms of such interrelations and as part of ongoing transformations that build on the invention of spoken language, and are continued by other media technologies.

Although Ong observes the shift from the aurality of speech toward the visuality of writing and print to be key to the emergence of the "mind-set" that is literacy, he himself does not really address the corporeal implications of this shift. That is, although he points out how writing and print change the way in which language is available for perception, he does not reflect on what this change does to perception and to bodies engaged in perceiving and making sense of what they encounter. These effects are the subject of Rotman's (2008) reflections on what he terms the alphabetic body. Many have reflected on the connections between the silent and individual practice of reading written or printed language and the emergence of the modern Western subject characterized by a sense of disconnection between the private interior mind and the public exterior body. However, Rotman observes, "before disembodied agencies come embodied ones. Alphabetic writing, like all technological systems and apparatuses, operates according to what might be called a corporeal axiomatic: it engages directly and inescapably with the bodies of its users. It makes demands and has corporeal effects" (2008: 15). Like Ong, Rotman observes a relationship between the incorporation of the skills of reading and writing and the coming-into-being of new notions of time, space, and self. Unlike Ong, however, Rotman does not explain these from new kinds of representing, collecting, and organizing information made possible by writing and print, but from the modes of enacting perception afforded by writing and print.

Writing and print present users with positions or "Is" implicated in the medium and require from writers and readers the capacity to relate to these. Participating in the medium requires negotiating the relationship between a gesturo-haptic "me" and such positions or "Is" as implicated within the medium. This is already the case with spoken language. Speech too engenders a disconnection of the body speaking over here and an "I" represented in language. Rotman describes the effect as "the first consciously perceivable out-of-body phenomenon, felt as the uncanny experience of a body speaking itself" (2008: 116). In speaking, this "I" is still visibly and audibly related to the speaking body in the act of speaking and within the situation of enunciation. This relationship between the body speaking and the "I" represented in spoken language, which is still very much present in the shared situation of enunciation, is absent in writing. In writing (and not in speech), disconnected from the unique identifiable act of individual discourse, the "I" becomes an incorporeal floating agency of the text. The one to whom "I" refers is no longer given within a situation shared by speaker and listener. Instead, who this "I" is must now be deduced from the text by the reader. The same goes for the other personal pronouns as well as deictic markers like "here" and "there." As a result, writing makes possible the emergence of new agents of expression. Rotman gives the example of very early inscriptions (from the first half of the eight century BC) on objects, stating things like "I am the cup of Nestor" or "X made me." It is clear from the inscriptions that "I" and "me" refer to the objects on which these texts are written, while it is also clear that these "Is" and "MEs" are not the authors of the utterances (Rotman 2008: 129). If it strikes us as unusual to indicate ownership in this way, and not by means of a sentence like "This cup is Nestor's," this is precisely because over time writing has become invisible as a medium, as a result of which the "I" of spoken language and the "I" of writing get conflated. Actually, the ancient inscriptions demonstrate a potential opened up by writing, namely how writing allows for the emergence of agents of expression that did not exist before the advent of writing, and that are made possible precisely by the medium. The inscriptions demonstrate Jacques Derrida's (1998) point that writing cannot be understood as merely a means to represent spoken language, and that the invention of writing inaugurated ways of using language that cannot be traced back to spoken language. Rotman refers to Derrick de Kerckhove's (1980) reflections on the relationships between the spread of the use of written language in classical Greece and the birth of a theater with individual characters speaking lines written by another.

The disconnection of utterances from the embodiment of the speaker requires from the side of the reader the capacity to read for what is not there. "What writing omits from speech is the body: the feelings, the moods, emotions, attitudes, intuitions, embodied demands, declarations, expressions, and desires located in the voice, rather than consciously formulated (writable) thought. What it omits is the entire field of affect conveyed and induced by human vocality, through the voice's impulses, inflections and rhythms, its aural texture and emotional dynamics" (Rotman 2008: 27). The history of reading therefore, Rotman observes, "is largely the history of attempting to cope with what writing does not represent" (2008: 26), it is the history of "redressing what writing fails to represent" (2008: 27). In this respect too, the invention of writing, rather than marking a break with orality, continues and presents a next step in a development that already began with the invention of speech. For it seems that in listening to speech too, we listen for what is not there. Rotman refers to evolutionary neurologist Terence Deacon's observations that, actually, when listening to speech, what we are listening for is not sounds as such, nor isolatable sonic entities, but the movements of the body causing the sounds:

> Surprisingly auditory processing of speech sounds does not appear to be based on extracting basic acoustic parameters of the signal, as a scientist might design a computer to do, before mapping them onto speech sounds. Speech analysis appears designed instead to predict which oral-vocal movements produced them and ignore the rest. (Deacon quoted in Rotman 2008: 23)

We listen to speech-sounds as signs of their gestural origins. These gestural origins are doubly removed in writing as alphabetic writing eliminates the inner and outer gestures of the speaking body: the visually observable movements that accompany and punctuate speech and the movements inside speech, "the gestures which constitute the voice itself-the tone, the rhythm, the variation of emphasis, the loudness, the changes of pitch, the mode of attack, discontinuities, repetitions, gaps and elisions, and the never absent play and musicality of utterance that makes human song possible" (Rotman 2008: 3). Listening to speech and reading written language, listeners and readers "redress" what speech and writing fail to represent. They bring in their own body and bodily experiences to listen and read for what is not there.

Rotman thus helps to understand how the disconnection of expressions from the body brought about by writing does not result in disembodiment but rather places new demands on bodies, namely to interpret and fill in what is not there. These demands, and how readers negotiate relationships between their gesturo-haptic "me" over here and positions in the medium, are exemplified by Foster's observations on early dance manuals. She shows how these manuals contributed to new ways of understanding dance in ways that resonate with Ong's observations on the effects of writing and print, while her reflections also demonstrate Rotman's point that learning to use these printed manuals requires readers to relate to positions represented on the page and to use their bodily experience and knowledge to grasp what is not there, in this case literally the movements of the body. Foster shows that the incorporation of these skills brings about what she calls a "recalibration of one's sensings of one's whereabouts" (2011: 73). That is, incorporating the skills to read these manuals affects the ways in which bodies make sense of space as well as their sense of self in space.

Recalibrations of Sensings

Dance manuals are written and printed instructions for performing dances. The earliest examples date from the end of the seventeenth and the beginning of the eighteenth century, that is, from the early phase of commercialization of print culture observed by Ong. At that time, no standardized notation system for dance existed, and different authors were experimenting with different methods. In *Choreographing Empathy*, Foster discusses several examples and shows how these early attempts at representing dances on the page informed new ways of understanding what dance is and how dance can be known. Without referring to Ong, but in terms that recall his observations, Foster points out that the practice of writing dancing turned dances from transitory, constantly disappearing phenomena into objects there, "present" in their entirety. The symbolic systems developed to notate dance are based on dividing the continuity of dance movement into smaller units that can be combined and recombined in various ways, which in turn contributed to an understanding of dance in terms of a variable compendium of possibilities. The practice of notating dance as consisting of combinations of these units suggests an understanding of dance as constructed out of and analyzable in terms of a limited set of building blocks that do not participate in the specificity of the particular dance being notated.

Foster also points to connections between the transformations brought about by writing dance and the broader cultural transformations in thinking and knowing addressed by Ong. She points to similarities with systems developed to classify plants and the development of ideas about geometric laws of movement. She elaborates how dance notation systems allowed for notions of authorship and ownership to emerge; how, once turned into objects fixed on the page, dances could be circulated and traded and thus could participate in the market economy. The presumed universality of systems of notation invited an understanding of the specificities of dances from various places in the world as being mere variations on universal principles, an understanding that assisted in the project of colonialism by allowing for an assimilation of dances from everywhere into this unitary model. Like Ong, Foster observes how notation mediated in the emergence of new more abstract and unified modes of knowing. Notation systems operated to confirm the existence of an absolute set of laws to which all bodies should conform. The notation bound the dancing to the ground on which it occurred, not to its indigenous location, but rather to an abstract and unmarked ground. (Foster 2011: 26)

Foster's reflections on the manuals also illuminates something that is absent from Ong's observations on the "mind-set" of literacy, and that is how using the manuals requires specific modes of enacting perception that affect users' sense of space and of self. Instructions for using the manuals included in these early examples are compelling with regard to these new kinds of skills required to read and make sense of them. The fact that these instructions were deemed necessary suggests that these skills were not self-evident at the moment of their first appearance. They had to be learned, and Foster's reading of the instructions shows how this meant developing new modes of enacting perception that involve a renegotiation of the relationships between an embodied "me" over here and an "I" that is part of the medium. She describes how Essex (*Further Improvement of Dancing, A Treatise of Choreography*, 1710) suggested that the reader, in order to interpret the diagrams that represented the dance in the correct manner, aligns the top of the page with the top of the room (Foster 2011: 79). She refers to Feuillet's (*Choréographie*, 1700) advice to "hold the book while turning so as to maintain the correspondence between the top of the room and the top of the page" (Foster 2011: 80). And to how Tomlinson (*The Art of Dancing Explained by Reading and Figures*, 1724) "went to great lengths to instruct the dancer in how to read the notation in relation to the room in which one was dancing. He warned the dancer to calculate differences in size and shape of the rooms, some being square and others rectangular, and then to fit the floor path to that specific shape" (Foster 2011: 80). He suggested that the dancer use two books instead of one: "one placed flat and stationary on a table or the floor and the other to be carried as one marked out the steps. Alternatively, a second person, standing at the front of the room could hold up the book for the dancer to consult" (Foster 2011: 80).

The instructions demonstrate how making sense of the manuals is not merely a matter of decoding what is represented on the page but requires the capacity to relate to the position of a virtual user or "I" as indicated on the map and to negotiate the relationship between this "I" and one's own kinesthetic awareness of an embodied "me." The instructions confirm Rotman's observation that learning to use written and printed media involves learning to relate to virtual agents that are implicated within the medium and to use one's corporeal intelligence to "redress" these agents for what is not there. Like Rotman, Foster points to how skills involved in learning to read written and printed texts bring about a new sense of space and a new sense of self in relation to it. She shows how learning to use the manuals brings results in a "recalibration of sensings of one's whereabouts" (Foster 2011: 73). The manuals invite users to imaginarily take up a position (or series of positions) that mark places within a visualization of space, while at the same time inviting them to understand these positions from a view that encompasses the totality of the space visualized. The map thus intercedes in the emergence of space as a stage on which to imaginarily position oneself and to do so in relation to a point of view outside oneself from where this stage is seen. Her observations show that learning to read the manuals contributes to the awareness of a self that has made the virtual user somehow part of her sensings of her whereabouts, and also how this affects her ways of making sense of space and her position within it. Doing so, the manual mediates in what Rotman, in the title of his book, describes as "becoming besides ourselves." I will come back to this later.

The Carnal Foundations of Intelligibility

Foster's observations draw attention to what Christiane Voss, in the context of film, calls a "borrowed body": a "somatic space of meaning" in which "the action of the film can be sensuously and affectively embedded": "In their intellectual and sensory-affective response to the action of the film," the spectator complements the two-dimensional cinematic image with the "third dimension of their feeling body" (Voss 2006, 81). Key to such fleshing out of the image is what Vivian Sobchack (2004) describes as the carnal foundations of intelligibility. The basis of intelligibility, Sobchack argues, is given in how bodies are sites of synesthetic operations between the senses and between the senses and language. Sobchack refers to the phenomenological notion of the lived body actively invested in making sense and meaning in and of the world. As lived bodies "our vision is always already 'fleshed out'—and even at the movies it is 'in-formed' and given meaning by our other sensory means of access to the world: our capacity not only to hear, but also to touch, to smell, to taste, and always to proprioceptively feel our dimension and movement in the world" (2004: 60). Sobchack gives the example of how, while watching the opening scene of Jane Campion's movie *The Piano* (1993), her eyes "did not 'see' anything meaningful and experienced an almost blindness" while her "tactile sense of being in the world through my fingers grasped the image's sense" (2004: 64). Bodies make sense of what they encounter by means of synesthetic graspings that do not only involve actual perceptual input but also bring to bear their own sensory experience of and knowledge about what is shown. Sobchack brings in the concept of reversibility (also from phenomenology) to account for the body as a site of such crossings-over between senses informing each other, between the senses and language, and ultimately also between inside and outside and self and other, as perceptions of what is presented on screen mingle with the bodily experiences evoked by them.

Sobchack's elaborations on the carnal foundations of intelligibility are part of her critique of how "the easy givenness of things to see at the movies vision's overarching mastery and comprehension of objects and its historically hierarchical sway over our other senses tend to occlude our awareness of our body's other ways of taking up and making meaning of the world—and its representation" (2004: 63–4). Sobchack's point is that making sense of movies is not merely a matter of the eyes and the mind. "We see and comprehend and feel films with our entire bodily being, informed by the full history and the carnal knowledge of our acculturated sensorium" (2004: 63). Although Sobchack's subject is cinema, her observations on how a focus on vision tends to occlude awareness of the rest of our sensorium in making sense of the world and its representations also applies to other media, including writing and print. Her phenomenologically informed understanding of bodies as sites of synesthetic operations between the senses, and between the senses and language, suggests that we may understand what Rotman refers to as "redressing" written and printed utterances in terms of the body as the effect of synesthetic operations of the sensorium through which bodies comprehend writing and print. Vice versa, Rotman's understanding of writing and print, as well as other media, in terms of how they engage bodies to relate to positions implied within the medium, suggests the possibility of a further elaboration of how media bring about and affect these synesthetic operations: how media afford, contribute to, and intervene in synesthetic grasping and how the ways in which they do so in its turn affects the synesthetic operations of the sensorium. This possibility is also the subject of speculative explorations in Greenaway's film *Prospero's Books*.

Redressings and Crossings-Over

Prospero's Books is a cinematic interpretation of Shakespeare's *The Tempest* (1611), a play written at the very beginning of print culture. The film begins with a short prologue presented in writing, explaining that

> Prospero, the former Duke of Milan, now reigns over a faraway island where he lives with his only daughter Miranda. Twelve years earlier,

Prospero's brother, in league with the King of Naples, had exiled Prospero and his daughter from their home. One evening, Prospero imagines creating a storm strong enough to bring his old enemies to his island. He begins to write a play about this tempest, speaking aloud the lines of each of his characters. It is the story of Prospero's past and his revenge.

The film then cuts to an image of dripping water, and an image of a quote from *The Tempest* being written on paper, stating: "Knowing I lov'd my books, he furnished me from mine own library with volumes that I prize above my Dukedom."

Greenaway's film suggests an intimate connection between these books, writing, and the world imagined in the play. Prospero's books, so it is stated, contain all possible knowledge about everything in the world, and it seems that on his faraway island these books have become the world to him. The film shows Prospero's worldview and imagination to be shaped by the knowledge represented in the books, in line with Ong's observations on how the collection of knowledge in books, and of books in libraries, contributed to a restructuring of consciousness and a worldview informed by the knowledge represented in books. Even more, the world as imagined and inhabited by Prospero seems to be informed not only by the content represented in these books but also by how their mediological logic affords modes of enacting perception and thinking. The books give Prospero access to a great number of different realities represented on their pages, allowing him to navigate through these, to make shortcuts between different worlds, and to jump from one space-time continuum to the next. One moment we see Prospero looking like Doge Leonardo Leodan of Venice as painted by Giovanni Bellini (1501-4), the next moment he inhabits the interior depicted on the painting St Jerome in His Study by Antonella Da Messina (1474), at another moment he descends the stairs of the Laurentian Library designed by Michelangelo. Stepping through a door or turning a corner, he moves from one situation to the next, moving through time and space in a way that would be impossible in the world in which he physically finds himself. The film thus suggests that the collection of books that supposedly contain all knowledge about everything in the world does not present Prospero with a position of overview at a distance (as suggested by Ong), but rather invites one to become immersed in them, navigate through them and from one to another in ways that foreshadow the possibilities of much later technological developments like montage in film, zapping on TV, and navigating the internet. This suggestion is in line with Rotman's claim that media developments following writing and print continue the recalibrations of space-time and reconfigurations of self brought about by them. Whereas

Ong hints at the possibility of a secondary orality brought about by newer media that no longer mediate visualizations of language, Rotman directs attention to how newer media, like writing and print, engage users in what media theorist Mark Hansen (2006) describes as couplings between their bodies and what the technologies confront them with.

How media negotiate such couplings is a recurring motif in *Prospero's Books* right from the beginning. After the opening shots of dripping water and the image of the text about Prospero's books, a voice-over explains the contents of one of these books, the *Book of Water*, filled with descriptions and drawings "of every conceivable watery association," including tempests. Images of the book alternate with that of an old man—later on this man can be identified as Prospero—in a pool or bath. The man looks at the water, touches it, and is being touched by it, feels it, while the sound of dripping water is heard. The sequence invites spectators to become attentive with the man and "redress" what is presented by (mainly) visual and (to a lesser extent) auditory means in terms of their full sensorium.

The sequence of shots (alternating between the man in the pool and the man reading the book) suggests that we may understand his sensory experience and his reading of the book to mutually inform and be informed by each other in line with Sobchack's observations on the body as a site of crossings-over between the senses, between the senses and language, and between what is inside and what is outside, what is self and what is other. The film presents an image of them crossing over into one another in line with Rotman, as a moving back and forth between the position of a "me" immersed in sensorial experience and an "I" relating to information in books. From there the world of his imagination emerges as a hand is shown writing down:

Boatswain! ....
    Here, master: what cheer? ....
    Good, speak to the mariners: fall to't, yarely, or we run ourselves aground: bestir, bestir.

These are the very first lines of *The Tempest*. These lines invite readers of the text, or spectators in the theater, to imagine that they are watching a scene on a boat at sea. Unlike illusionist and naturalist types of theater that have come to dominate the Western imagination of theater after Shakespeare, his theater was of very modest means and did not attempt to recreate other worlds on stage by means of elaborate staging. In Shakespeare's theater, other worlds are evoked mainly by spoken language. It is therefore highly unlikely that spectators of this scene were seeing, or were meant to actually see, a representation of a boat in a storm at sea. Rather, they are invited to take up the position of an "I" implied within the texts written and spoken, and to imagine what they are seeing to be a scene at a boat in a storm at sea.

The beginning of Greenaway's film takes its viewers to a moment that precedes the staging of this scene, namely the moment of writing it. Cutting back and forth between images of the man in the pool sensing the water and playing with a miniature ship, the same man looking in a book, and the same man writing down the lines of Shakespeare's text, the sequence suggests an understanding of his imagination as informed by a negotiation between his experiences as a bodily "me" in the pool and the information and knowledge accessible to him via the books. After having written down the very first lines of the play quoted above, the man begins to speak them, repeating them several times in different ways, as if tasting them, like an actor probing their potential and testing out how to embody them. The sequence thus stages writing as producing a disconnection between author and text, followed by reading as a reconnection that involves a bodily "redressing" of the text. Furthermore, although it is the same old man who first writes the text and then speaks it, *Prospero's Books* does not show this "redressing" of the text to be a matter of reconnecting the text to the author, but as a fleshing out of the world that the text provides access to. And *Prospero's Books* shows such "redressing" to be facilitated by positions implied within the text.

Shortly after the man has started speaking the first lines of *The Tempest*, the film shows him looking into a book again, this time a volume called *A Book of Mirrors*. One of the mirrors shows the reflection of a group of sailors, presumably in a storm at sea. At the same time, a large mirror rises from the water in the pool showing the same image to the man in the pool. The film shows how the man in the pool responds by taking up the position of the one seeing this scene at sea and interacting with what he sees. Importantly, the man does not identify with one of the characters seen in the mirror but takes up the position from where they are seen. This position intercedes in his embodied engagement with the image.

The scene recalls Lacan's (1977) famous account of the coming into being of self and subjectivity in his essay on the Mirror Stage. However, more interesting than the similarities are the differences between Lacan's theoretical fiction and what is shown in *Prospero's Books*. Whereas Lacan's story explains the coming into being of self-identity from a child (mis)recognizing an image in the mirror for itself and taking this image as referent for its own feelings and sensations, *Prospero's Books* presents an image of becoming as resulting from the capacity of bodies to engage with positions implied by images and texts, and to use the synesthetic operations of their sensorium to make sense of these positions in terms of potential actions and feelings. The man in the pool is capable of relating to the image in the mirror not because this world reflects or resembles his world outside the mirror, or because it shows him an image in which he can (mis)recognize himself, but because the mirror reflects a potential world that his body can relate to and that can be understood in terms of potential action. This is in line with Merleau-Ponty's explanation of what happens at the moment a child develops the capacity to relate to a mirror image. Whereas Lacan assumes that the image seen in the mirror is that through which the child learns to make sense of the chaos of its corporeal sensations and to unify what is separate, Merleau-Ponty on the other hand points to the set of functions that is the body schema as that which makes it possible for the child to couple its body to the mirror image.

The body schema is "a system of sensory motor capacities that function without awareness of the necessity of perceptual monitoring." It is distinct from the body image, which is "a system of perceptions, attitudes and beliefs pertaining to one's own body" (Gallagher 2005: 24). The distinction between body image and body schema is not always made clear, not even by Merleau-Ponty himself. Nevertheless, Gallagher points out, there are good reasons to make a clear conceptual distinction between the two because they help us address different sets of questions. The concept of the body image helps us address questions about the appearance of the body in the perceptual field, whereas the concept of the body schema helps us answer questions about how the body shapes the perceptual field (Gallagher 2005: 17–18). The body schema develops out of the body's interaction with the environment. It evolves from the experience of moving, doing, touching, and in turn it shapes our perceptual field in terms of the potential for movement. This arousal of potential movement is the basis of our response to what we encounter and how we are able to relate to what we encounter, including how we are able to relate to other people. Furthermore, Merleau-Ponty observes, through this arousal of potential movement we are capable of relating not only to real situations but also to virtual and imaginary ones:

> In the case of the normal subject, the body is available not only in real situations into which it is drawn. It can turn aside from the world, apply its activity to stimuli which affect its sensory surfaces, lend itself to experimentation, and generally speaking take its place in the realm of the potential. (Merleau-Ponty 1962: 109)

This possibility for experimentation and the capacity to relate to situations that are not real is, according to Merleau-Ponty, not a matter of the body mistaking what is not real for real, but of the body's capacity to engage with what is not real by means of modes of enacting perception that build upon the possibilities, habits, and patterns that are part of our body schema.

Sensorimotor Skills and the Perceiver-Centered Character of Perception

Merleau-Ponty is an important inspiration for Sobchack's understanding of the synesthetic operations of the human sensorium and how they help to account for the ways in which bodies are engaged in making sense of cinema. This was also an important inspiration for enactive approaches to cognition as developed by Francisco Varela, Evan Thompson, and Eleanor Rosch (1991), Alain Berthoz (2000), Alva Noë (2004), and others. Enactive approaches to cognition explain how perception and cognition are fundamentally embodied and deeply intertwined with action. Perception and cognition are themselves forms of practice and informed by experience with doing things. This focus on making sense as a prereflexive activity that is informed by experience gained in doing makes enactive cognition most useful for further understanding how the use of media builds on, affects, informs, and transforms the synesthetic operations of our sensorium, and the role of positions implied within media in this.

Sensory input is multiple, manifold, ambiguous, staggered over time, it does not cover the same range of velocities, and it is often fuzzy and incomplete. From the very first moment of their lives, humans and other animals begin to develop the capacity to make sense of this multiplicity and to develop an awareness of their surroundings and, in relation to this, a sense of self. This capacity is not given, but builds up through experience with actions. Experience with the effect of perceptual variation caused by self-movement teaches us to discover patterns of contingency in sensory stimulation. Noë explains:

> To be a perceiver is to understand, implicitly, the effects of movement of sensory stimulation. Examples are ready to hand. An object looms larger in the visual field as we approach it and its profile deforms as we move about it. A sound grows louder as we move nearer to its source. Movements of the hand over a surface of an object give rise to shifting sensations. As perceivers we are masters of such patterns of sensorimotor dependence. (Noë 2004: 1)

Through doing things humans learn to distinguish patterns and synesthetic connections between various sensory input, and this forms the basis for how the world becomes available to them. Crucial to how bodies do so is the repertoire of sensorimotor schema (Berthoz) or sensorimotor skills (Noë), which act like blueprints for possible action and which organize perception even before sensory stimuli are processed. These schema are not sets of data.

Rather, they organize relationships between action, perception, and memory (Berthoz 2000: 17–19). They are part of how bodies engage with what they encounter, and the basis of how bodies do so is implicit practical knowledge of the ways movement gives rise to changes in sensory stimulation (Noë 2004: 8). An example of this kind of implicit knowledge is that movement of the eyes to the left produces movement across the visual field. Another is that, when in the dark, or with our eyes closed, if we touch different sides of a box, we not only feel a succession of surfaces but also grasp their spatial relationships as different sides of the same box. Such perceptual sense of presence results from our practical grasp of sensorimotor patterns mediating our relation to that what we are perceiving. The impression of the different sides of the box on our fingers alone cannot explain how we are capable of perceiving a box as a three-dimensional object in space that we can pick up, turn around, and open. Actually, it is the other way round: because of our experience with boxes, or more generally, with the effects of moving around as well as moving objects around, we are capable of grasping the connection between simultaneous and successive impressions. "To perceive … is to perceive structure in sensorimotor contingencies," Noë observes (2004: 105). Perceiving is not merely having sensory impressions but rather *making sense of* sensory impressions, and this happens through our sensorimotor skills. Furthermore, such understanding is not only constitutive of our experience of the world we encounter, but also the root of our ability to think about it.

Noë also helps us understand how such experiential knowledge forms the basis for relating to positions implied within media. Perceptual experience, he explains, has two dimensions: "perception is, at once, a way of keeping track of how things are, and also of our relation to the world" (2004: 168). This is what is referred to as the perceiver-centered character of perception. "To be a perceiver … you must understand, implicitly, that your perceptual content varies as things around you change, and that it varies in different ways as you move in relation to things around you" (2004: 169). Perception therefore has an intrinsically perspectival aspect. Experience with this perspectival character forms the basis for how bodies are capable of grasping contingencies in sensory impressions in relation to a point of view.

The Logic of the Cut

Rotman observes that cinema and newer media build on and continue the disconnections and reconnections brought about by writing and print. The point of connection is what might be termed the logic of the cut, referring both to how media cut the link between expression and origin, thus allowing expressions to circulate independently, and to how media allow for expressions to be cut and recombined. My use of this notion of the logic of the cut is inspired by Stamatia Portanova's (2013) theorization of the cut in relation to the digital, movement, and embodiment. I use the phrase here to address continuities between Ong's observations on writing and print and subsequent media developments. A closer look at how the logic of the cut places demands on the bodies of media users illuminates the corporeal dimensions of restructurings brought about by interaction with media, how these are the result of the ways in which media afford and intervene in modes of enacting perception, and how this in its turn affects ways of making sense, including notions of space, time, and self. The logic of the cut requires readers to read for what is not there, to negotiate relationships between their embodied "me" and positions in the medium, and to redress what is there in terms of their own sensory experience and knowledge. Learning to respond to these demands may cause a "recalibration of sensings": a reordering of the operations of the sensorium that affects how bodies perform their synesthetic graspings of what they encounter. These demands placed on bodies, and what this does to modes of enacting perception, affect how the world becomes available and mediates in new becomings of self in relation to this world. The logic of the cut intercedes in "becoming besides ourselves": in becomings that are brought about by couplings of bodies and media and result from a "reaching out" from one's bodily "me" toward positions in media and making these part of an expanded sense of self. In this respect too, the disconnections brought about by writing and print present an early stage of development toward the more radical discontinuities of distributed selves engendered by today's digital and networked technologies.

References

Berthoz, A. (2000), *The Brain's Sense of Movement*, Cambridge, MA: Harvard University Press.
Derrida, J. (1998), *Of Grammatology*, Baltimore, MD: Johns Hopkins University Press.
Foster, S. L. (2011), *Choreographing Empathy: Kinesthesia in Performance*, New York: Routledge.
Gallagher, S. (2005), *How the Body Shapes the Mind*, Oxford: Clarendon Press.
Hansen, M. B. N. (2006), *Bodies in Code: Interfaces with Digital Media*, New York: Routledge.
Lacan, J. (1977), *Ecrits: A Selection*, London: Tavistock.
Merleau-Ponty, M. (1962), *Phenomenology of Perception*, London: Routledge.

Noë, A. (2004), *Action in Perception*, Cambridge, MA: MIT Press.
Ong, W. J. (1988), *Orality and Literacy: The Technologizing of the Word*, London: Routledge.
Othold, T., and C. Voss (2015), "From Media Anthropology to Anthropomediality," *Anthropological Notebooks* 21 (3): 75–82.
Portanova, Stamatia (2013), *Moving without a Body: Digital Philosophy and Choreographic Thought*, Cambridge, MA: MIT Press.
Prospero's Books (1991), [Film] Dir. Peter Greenaway, Los Angeles, CA: Miramax.
Rotman, B. (2008), *Becoming Besides Ourselves: The Alphabet, Ghosts and Distributed Human Being*, Durham, NC: Duke University Press.
Sobchack, V. (2004), *Carnal Thoughts: Embodiment and Moving Image Culture*, Berkeley: University of California Press.
Soukup, P. A. (2007), "Orality and Literacy 25 Years Later," *Communication Research Trends* 26 (4): 1–33.
Strate, Lance (2011) "McLuhan and New Media," *Ciencias de la Comunicación*, VIII (14–15), 170–183.
Varela, F. J., E. Thompson, and E. Rosch (1991), *The Embodied Mind: Cognitive Science and Human Experience*, Cambridge, MA: MIT Press.
Voss, Christiane (2006), "Filmerfahrung und Illusionsbildung: Der Zuschauer als Leihkörper des Films," in Gertrud Koch and Christiane Voss (eds.), … *kraft der Illusion*, 71–86, Munich: Fink.

12

Torn, Crushed, Shredded: The Reconstruction of Wounded Bodies in the First World War

Johanna Seifert

For some time now, current body-technology constellations have increasingly led to theoretical approaches that think of the relationship between body and technology within the paradigms of relationality, entanglement, or symmetry. Network theories, for example, emphasize the relational interconnectedness of heterogeneous entities in network-like structures (see, for example, Latour 1993, 2005); media ecologies assume a fundamental technicity and a new significance of environments, surroundings, and atmospheres (Galloway and Thacker 2007; Hörl 2016); and the approach of relational media anthropology asserts the anthropomedial constitution of human existence and a primordial interconnectedness of humans and media (Voss 2010; Voss and Engell 2015; Voss and Othold 2015). What these positions have in common is an identity-critical and praxeological approach that shifts the focus from substantial entities and concepts to their practical performances and conditions of emergence and considers their interstices, relations, and interactions. This corresponds to a technological development that is characterized by increasing self-activity and interactivity. Thus, we speak of "intelligent" technologies that collect, evaluate, process, and connect ever larger amounts of data, or of "adaptive" technical systems that adapt to their environment and how their users behave, and of "interactive" systems, insofar as individual technologies can interconnect and form complex technical networks. In addition, current developments in technology are characterized by a trend toward miniaturization, automation, and interiorization. Technological artifacts are becoming smaller and smaller, are becoming increasingly self-active, and are permeating the human body more and more, where they actively influence physical and mental processes. In this context, prostheses play a crucial role insofar as they can be understood as a paradigmatic example of an invasive and intimate technological development that leads to increasingly seamless interfaces of body and technology. Thus, prostheses are no longer necessarily considered the epitome of an instrumental and compensatory technology, but rather are transforming into hybrid technologies that unsettle traditional concepts of body and identity and produce confounding phenomena of trans-corporalities and co-corporalities (Shildrick 2015, 2017).

Prosthesis development, however, can look back on a long history of technical developments, scientific concepts, and historical events in which the meaning of prostheses only gradually changed. In the nineteenth century, for example, prostheses were still mostly simple aids that were only able to compensate for physical deficits in a makeshift way. One might think here, for example, of the stilt-legged organ grinders that populated the streets of European capitals especially after the Franco-Prussian War of 1871 (Kienitz 2004: 337–8). Those prostheses had little in common with the spectacular models of today's high-tech prosthetics, but rather represented rudimentary compensations for a loss of bodily function. With this in mind, this essay aims to address a decisive turning point in the history of prosthetics: the prosthetic developments of the interwar period and the destruction and subsequent reconstruction of soldiers' bodies during and after the First World War. This topic is relevant to the question of the present volume in at least two ways. First, the wounded bodies of the First World War can be understood as a result of one of the first industrially waged machine wars and thus as a consequence of developments in war technology. And second, the huge number of injuries caused during the First World War prompted a comprehensive program for the technological reconstruction of wounded soldiers and their reintegration into society. The wounded bodies of the First World War are thus situated within a complex intertwining of technological destruction on the one hand and technological reconstruction on the other hand, thereby representing a prime example of an *anthropology of entanglements* or, more precisely, a fertile field for the investigation of how bodies and technologies are intertwined.

By considering the topic of war disability, this article furthermore wants to provide insight into the discourse about "repairing" bodies during the interwar period. Under the conditions of an increasingly uniform and state-regulated veteran's care program, this discourse spoke of "repairing" the numerous severely wounded bodies of the First World War by furnishing them with replacement limbs, and of "re-educating" the veterans to be "fully fledged members" of society (Biesalski 1909).[1] In contrast to previous examinations of this topic in media and cultural studies, however, I will not immediately start with the prosthetic "repairing" of these wounded soldiers' bodies and the construction of new prosthetic bodies. Instead, I will begin by taking a step back to consider the context that precedes these processes: that is, the mechanical destruction of soldiers' bodies on the battlefields of the First World War, and the subsequent measures taken for their treatment, rehabilitation, and social reintegration. My intention is to examine the period's discourse about repairing bodies, with its functionalist approach and its one-sided view of human bodies. In doing so I aim to contrast this approach against a perspective that not only looks at how defective bodies were technologically repaired but that also regards questions of loss, destruction, and injury and questions the limits of a "corporal repairability." I will be referring to examples from literature and testimonies of invalids in order to uncover a relatively overlooked perspective, namely one that seems to have played no role in the former discourse of veterans' care, and that has also been largely neglected in media studies thus far. I am talking about a perspective that links the question of how novel and collective prosthetic bodies were manufactured to the individual experience of loss and injury, by opening up a space for the negative dimension of body-prosthesis relations.

But let's begin by diving right in with the fall of 1914. Only a few weeks after the war began, the first wounded soldiers returned from the front. From then on, mutilated, disfigured, and disabled bodies populated the streets of many European cities, and provoked heated arguments about the consequences of this cruel and destructive "Great War." While some at the beginning of the war still assumed that advances in weapons technology would quickly end the conflict, and that new weapons and modern medicine meant that the coming war would be less bloody and less deadly than previous ones (see, for example, Brüning 1922; Günther 1914), they were proven wrong just a few weeks after August 1914. The first mass use of military equipment in the First World War did not lead to a more humane warfare, it led instead to wounds that posed unexpected challenges to both the civilian population at home and the medical practice of the day. Machine guns perforated, grenades shredded, flamethrowers burned, and poison gas corroded the soldiers' bodies who voluntarily or involuntarily found themselves in the trench warfare of the First World War. While in the Franco-German War of 1870–1, rifle and pistol shots still accounted for almost all wounds and deaths (Kienitz 2011: 94), the First World War brought with it an entire arsenal of new destructive techniques: artillery projectiles, grenades, mines, tanks, flamethrowers, machine guns, and—last but not least—the terrible poison gas shells that produced wounds whose severity and extent surpassed all previous war injuries (Krumeich and Hirschfeld 2013). The "whimpering and crying of the wounded," as the author and translator Hanns Günther suggested as late as 1914, did therefore not diminish in the trench warfare of the First World War (Günther 1914). Instead—to say the least—it intensified. Although in the First World War fewer soldiers died from their injuries compared to previous wars, the injuries caused by modern war technology acquired an entirely new quality. Extremely severe injuries to the head and the face, extensive tissue and bone fragmentation, complex gunshot fractures, and deeply disfiguring flesh wounds were not only difficult to look at, they also posed the question of how to deal with these severely wounded bodies. Last but not the least, what was missing here was concrete knowledge, because in the field hospitals of the First World War, the existing practices of war surgery proved no longer feasible.[2] As a consequence, at the beginning of the First World War, field hospitals still followed a conservative approach; meaning that in case of serious injuries surgery was avoided whenever possible. But this practice soon shifted to one of operating on the bodies too soon rather than too late, of cutting around inside the bodies, and cutting off parts of them. This new practice, however, turned the field hospitals at the front into horrifying "butcher's kitchens," whose infernal stench deadened the senses after just a few seconds. In his novella *Die Kriegskrüppel* (The War Cripples) the writer and staunch pacifist Leonhard Frank vividly depicts such a scene:

> The windows are closed. And three minutes later, there's the thick, warm stench of rotting, burned wounds in the butcher's kitchen, of pus, old blood, the sweat of death, the perspiration of fear, carbolic acid, and Lysol, so that when someone who is healthy and strong, and accustomed to fresh air, steps in, a minute later they see colors circling before their eyes and feel the ground swaying underneath their feet. (Frank 1919: 139)

In these places of terror the doctors sometimes treated hundreds of war-wounded with their operating, amputating, disinfecting, and bandaging; "after every half an hour" though—meaning "after one or two amputations"—the doctors had to head out "into the fresh air," "so that during the next amputation, the saw or the knife didn't fall from their hands" (ibid.: 140).[3] And yet there was a need to be quick, since "every quarter of an hour lost," as Frank writes, "could mean death" (ibid.: 139). It was here, in the field hospitals close to the trench warfare, that the soldiers, whose body parts gradually filled the mobile tubs emptied at the same time every day, experienced the most horrifying moments of this cruel war:

> The amputees who are not unconscious, who do not sleep and yet lie motionless, quite immobile and silent, with shining beads of fever in their faces, are lost; they are already floating away. The others roar, throw themselves up, bend, squirm, whimper like newborn kittens, laugh in feverish madness, or move their mutilated bodies very slowly, but incessantly. (ibid.)

In view of these countless severely wounded soldiers, whose treatment in field hospitals often did more harm than good, and who often returned home deeply traumatized and distressed, the question arose of how to best "provide care for these innumerable thousands," and how to reintegrate them into community life (Biesalski 1915a: 15). Against this backdrop, a comprehensive campaign for the instruction of the German population was launched at the end of 1914 in order to promote various measures for the "reconstruction" and reintegration of war-wounded soldiers, thereby contrasting the trauma of war, destruction, and injury with advanced medical practices and an overhauled welfare system. Through exhibitions, brochures, popular scientific writings, lectures, and guided tours through homes for the disabled (on the latter see ibid.: 13–14), this campaign sought to accustom the population to the sight of technologically repaired bodies and to extol the latest advances in medicine and technology. Above all, it was the exhibitions of the veterans' care program that played a central part in this context.[4] In addition to presenting the latest "replacement limbs and work aids" (Hartmann 1919: 19) alongside a wide-ranging entertainment program, they showcased disabled soldiers using their new prostheses. The goal of these demonstrations was for soldiers to prove the effectiveness of their prosthetic limbs and thus to convince the public that the soldiers were fit for work and everyday life. Such demonstrations, which took place among others in the *Krystallpalast* (Crystal Palace) in Leipzig in 1917 or in the Reich Institute *Ständige Ausstellung für Arbeiterwohlfahrt* in Berlin-Charlottenburg in 1916, were often accompanied by personal testimonies. As Sabine Kienitz has noted, these helped authenticate the goals of the veterans' care program, as the disabled veterans took the exhibition's propaganda declarations and presented them as their own (Kienitz 2015: 250). For example, the disabled soldier Erich Zachmann, who had lost both arms during the war, reported on the successful use of his prosthetic limbs in the column "Von den Krüppeln—Für die Krüppel" (By cripples—for cripples) in the *Zeitschrift für Krüppelfürsorge* (Magazine for Cripple Care):

> I have now made good progress in this direction too. By means of a replacement limb attached to the left arm stump .... I can eat without outside help, picking up my fork and putting my spoon down on my own. When I want to smoke a cigar, I can light my own matches. I can also dress and undress myself on my own. And I can also wash myself, without needing any help, by using a washing prosthesis. As this report, written by myself, testifies, I am now also able to write well again. (Zachmann 1917: 195)

These kinds of documents, however, are evidence that the personal testimonies and the above-mentioned demonstrations were not about the invalid as a singular subject but rather about a discourse of reassurance in which the individual with their physical injury was meant to disappear within the anonymity of a collective prosthetic body (see also Mohi-von Känel 2018: 37, 121, 130). In this sense the reports of the *Zeitschrift für Krüppelfürsorge* often emphasized the functionalist "reeducation" of the disabled soldiers and demanded "an iron will" that would allow the invalids to overcome even the most severe physical deficits. According to the orthopedist Konrad Biesalski, for example, even the most severely wounded soldiers could, with the help of suitable artificial limbs, "become able, completely independent of any outside help, to change their clothes, wash themselves, write, eat, and earn their daily bread through work of their own, even doing hard work" (Biesalski 1916: 3).

However, the question of caring for war-disabled soldiers was in the end also a technological one, since the massive number of war amputations led to a comprehensive program of "reconstructing" the damaged bodies by means of artificial "replacement limbs" and thus restoring the veteran's ability for "gainful employment." To further this effort, prize competitions were launched in the summer of 1916, often in connection with the aforementioned exhibitions (see, e.g., Bauer 1916). The purpose of these contests was to encourage established prosthetic manufacturers to collaborate with expert engineers in order to design new models of prosthetics. In addition to what were called "work arms" (*Arbeitsarme*), which were basically nothing more than rudimentary tool holders to which any number of extensions could be attached as required,[5] these competitions eventually began to drive the development and construction of "actively movable prostheses." In contrast to the passive and functionalist "work arms," the "actively movable prostheses" were machine-like devices that mimicked the body not only in functional but also in aesthetic terms, while drawing their mechanical power from the body itself.[6] The construction of "actively movable prostheses," however, had a significant prerequisite, insofar as the actively or—to quote the term used at that time—"voluntarily" movable prostheses required a renewed surgical treatment of the already treated bodies. In order to enable the residual limb muscles to control and regulate the movement of the artificial hand (and thus to allow active control of the prosthesis), the amputation stump of the invalids had to be surgically transformed and adapted to the requirements of the prosthetic limb. The surgery applied in this context was a so-called cineplastic operation (Sauerbruch 1919).

In a first step, the muscles of the amputation stump, which had often been weakened by the injury and amputation, were exposed and reformed into what was called a "power bulge" (*Kraftwulst*) (ibid.: 237–9). After having transformed the amputation stump into the so-called power bulge, an opening was drilled into the middle of the bulge, creating a channel of muscle that was subsequently lined with skin. After this intervention the amputation stump had to heal over a period of several weeks, while the muscles of the residual limb were strengthened and trained by means of muscle and traction exercises. Thus, prepared through both surgery and physical rehabilitation, the residual limb was then fitted with a prosthesis. This prosthesis represented an intimate connection to the damaged body, insofar as it was connected to the amputation stump by an ivory pin that was inserted into the muscle channel and linked to the artificial hand by an iron bracket and a link chain attached to it, enabling the force from the muscle contraction to be transmitted to the prosthetic hand. This construction created the tension and pressure sensations necessary for the movement of a prosthetic limb, which then made it possible not only to move the fingers of the artificial hand individually, but also to convey a feeling for their relative position and the way they were being held.

Such "voluntarily movable" prosthetic arms, developed above all by the surgeon Ferdinand Sauerbruch in collaboration with the engineer Aurel Stodola, were no longer passive attachments that would simply sit on the surface of the defective bodies. Instead, they were machine-like devices that obtained the necessary mechanical power from the body itself and were meant to be experienced as an integral part of one's own body.[7] The "actively movable arm prostheses" were therefore no longer external to the body, but rather were integrated into the body's own musculature and its perceptual and sensory space. In this vein, body and prosthesis were to form a "technological-organic ensemble" (Spreen 2015: 9), thus a synthesis of technology and organism in which the prosthesis was to become an integral part of the body's own structure. Compared to the passive work-oriented prostheses, the "active arm prosthesis" described here was therefore less focused on functionalist priorities, since its goal was not only the restoration of functional capability but also the reestablishment of sensitivity; nonetheless, it was still based on the idea that the body could be *repaired* and technologically *restored* by means of suitable replacement limbs.

But if we set aside the interwar discourse on prostheses and turn to the actual bodies at stake here, we encounter a phenomenon that at least partially challenges the idea of a "corporal repairability." What I am talking about is the phenomenon of phantom pain, which at that time posed a problem for those promoting the use of prosthetics, since it led to the fact that war-disabled veterans simply refused to wear their artificial replacement limbs.[8] Phantom pain, meaning the pain felt by a limb that no longer exists, was then not only a deep mystery for the staff of military hospitals, it also confronted them with a body that failed to conform to the anatomical assumptions of those promoting the rehabilitation of the war-wounded. It was a body whose injury was technically impossible to deal with and which, in a certain way, resisted its technical reparation. With phantom pain, one might say, amputees were effectively holding on to the original form of their bodies, denying the loss of their physical integrity and thus negating their injury and the resulting deficit. Seen from this perspective—and here I am thinking of the work done by the neurologist and psychoanalyst Paul Schilder—phantom pain was not only a neurological problem, but it also revealed the imaginary, phantasmatic, and ambiguous nature of bodily conditions. Phantom sensations, thus, not only questioned the assumption of an intact and integrated body but also showed that the human body was always more than a mere collection of organic functions that can be dismembered, reassembled, and ultimately repaired. But let's take a look back once again at the situation during the First World War.

The large number of severely wounded soldiers who populated the streets of many European cities shortly after the outbreak of the First World War made the phenomenon of phantom pain a central object of scientific study. In the field hospitals and the orthopedic workshops established during the war, the neurologists and psychologists entrusted with the prosthetic care of the wounded soldiers were confronted with a peculiar form of perceptual disorder. Many of the wounded soldiers complained of pain in their already amputated limbs. What appeared here was the hardly explicable phenomenon of a body sensation without a corresponding material substance, that is, a "perception without object" (Zürcher 2005: 80). The fact that "something hurts where there is nothing left" (ibid.) was especially worrying to a psychology that explained the formation of a sensory impression by the model of a receiver, transmitter, and "a perceiver" (Conrad 1933: 353).[9] In this context, phantom sensations appeared as a problem, insofar as the instance of the receiver had disappeared. A solution to this problem was then found with the introduction of the concept of the body schema by Henry Head and Gordon Holmes at the beginning of the twentieth century. Whereas up to then phantom sensations had been explained as hallucinations (Abbatucci 1894) or illusions (Katz 1921), a concept was now available that understood the phantasmic sensation of a body limb that was no longer present as a disorder of spatial orientation. According to Head and Holmes, the body schema described a postural model "against which all subsequent changes of posture are measured before they enter consciousness" (Head and Holmes 1911: 187). The body schema thus meant a figure of reference or a kind of standard, which "measures" the changes in position or movement of a limb and places them in relation to the body as a whole (Conrad 1933: 348). According to Klaus Conrad, the body schema can thus be understood as a preconscious act of "relating" or rather as a relational structure (ibid.). A relationality, more precisely, that precedes the constitution of the body as a unified and holistic entity.

In addition to Henry Head and Gordon Holmes, it is above all Paul Schilder who, with his study *Das Körperschema. Ein Beitrag zur Lehre vom Bewusstsein des eigenen Körpers*, investigates the problem of phantom sensations and significantly expands the concept of the body schema (Schilder 1923).[10] In contrast to Head and Holmes, Schilder no longer defines the body schema as a purely neurological deficit, but as a phenomenon of imaginary and psychical significance. In doing so, Schilder replaces the concept of the schema with the concept of image (the body schema becomes the body image) and draws on Freudian theory and its concepts of repression, regression, narcissism, and libido. Against this backdrop, Schilder explains phantom pain as a psychophysical strategy for restoring a disintegrated corporeality. Phantom pain, according to Schilder, is "the expression of love of one's own body" and the "inability to renounce the integrity of the body" (ibid.: 31);[11] it is a "narcissistic duplication" or "imaginary restitution," through which a phantasmatic, since not real, wholeness of the body is produced. In this sense, Schilder's understanding of phantom pain is in some ways similar to Freudian interpretations of psychopathological disorders such as, for instance, hysteria or delusion. For just as delusion can be understood as the restoration of a psychic disintegration (Widmer 2006: 142), phantom pain represents, according to Schilder, the restitution of a lost bodily wholeness. And just as hysteria can be understood as an expression of unfulfilled and sometimes corporally converted desires, phantom pain is understood in Schilder's work as the "nostalgia for the unity and wholeness of the body" and as "a kind of libidinal memorial to the lost limb" (Grosz 1994: 73, 41).[12] In this way, Schilder on the one hand shifts the focus to the phantasmatic dimension of phantom sensations; on the other hand, he generalizes, if not anthropologizes, phantom sensations, insofar as they are placed in relation to a general condition of corporeality. While Head and Holmes still understand phantom sensations in a strictly empirical manner as a physiologically determined phenomenon, Schilder leaves the clearly delineated realm of the empirical and emphasizes the phantasmatic and imaginary dimension of phantom sensations and corporeality itself. Against this background, bodies then no longer represent clearly delimited and self-contained entities, but rather complex formations, whose boundaries are ambivalent, imaginary, and provisional and thus always under the threat of displacement or dissolution.

But if this is the case, and bodies are far less stable entities than they are dynamic formations in the field of conflicting forces, then it is not just the construction of a "new prosthetic body" after the First World War that is worth studying with regard to an *anthropology of entanglements*. Perhaps it is then the body itself, whether broken or unbroken, whether sick or healthy, that is equally deserving of such an analysis. After all, the body thus proves to be a hybrid entity that is characterized—to use Jean-Luc Nancy's terminology—by a fundamental intermediality. Neither mere substance nor phenomenon, neither mere flesh nor meaning, bodies exist as liminalities on the borderlands, thereby inhabiting an intermediate position that is difficult to nail down and is always in motion (Nancy 1992). From this perspective, however, the idea of the body's repairability ultimately loses its credibility, by making room for the idea of the phantasmatic dimension of corporeality and the fundamental entanglement of bodily existence.

Notes

1. The following quotations are all translations of the original German documents. I thank Michael Taylor for his assistance with the translation.
2. This was, among other things, due to the fact that the state of knowledge of war medicine in 1914 was still based on a textbook from 1877 (von Esmarch 1877). The knowledge of war medicine at that time thus dated to a war in which artillery had already gained in importance, but did not yet have such a strategic military role as it did in 1914–18 (Hartmann 2014).
3. On the perspective of physicians in the First World War, see, among others, the autobiographies by Dearden (1928) and Kiegelmann (2012).
4. On the veterans' care program, see in particular the numerous writings of the orthopedist Konrad Biesalski (Biesalski 1915a, b, and 1916).
5. Konrad Biesalski thus describes the "work arms" as "simple cuffs with an attachment into which a wide variety of tools can be inserted" (Biesalski 1915b: 12).
6. Since 1915, it was especially the engineer and physicist Aurel Stodola and the surgeon and later head of the Department of Surgery of the Charité in Berlin, Ferdinand Sauerbruch, who worked on the construction of such prostheses (see Sauerbruch 1916).
7. On the designation of these prostheses as "machines," see: "Further, it is necessary to design this power source in such a way that it can be easily connected to the machine of the artificial hand" (Sauerbruch 1916: 9). See here also the psychologist Narziß Ach. According to Ach, the invalids were not only passive receivers of artificial replacement limbs but played an active role in this process as they were supposed to "live into" (*hineinleben*) their prostheses (Ach 1920: 27).
8. See Narziß Ach (1920: 22) who refers here to a statistic from 1916, according to which 310 of 356 arm amputees stopped wearing their prostheses after only a short time.

9. Klaus Conrad is referring here especially to the field of Associationism popular at that time.
10. For the English version, see Schilder (1935).
11. For a similar interpretation, see Grosz (1994: 72).
12. Vivian Sobchack, herself a prosthesis wearer, disagrees with such an interpretation. With regard to the incorporation of her prosthetic leg, she remarks: "Its existence is not a focalization on the past, on what was once there but is now missing. Rather, its lengthening (not longing) is a mobilization of my motor capacities to fulfil a present intention" (Sobchack 2010: 62).

References

Abbatucci, J.-P.-L.-S. (1894), *Etude psychologique sur les hallucinations des amputés*, Bordeaux: P. Cassignol.
Ach, N. (1920), *Zur Psychologie der Amputierten. Ein Beitrag zur praktischen Psychologie*, Leipzig: Verlag von Wilhelm Engelmann.
Bauer, K. (1916), *Wie können für unsere Kriegsverstümmelten die besten Ersatzglieder und Arbeitshilfen geschaffen werden?* Stuttgart: Strecker & Schröder.
Biesalski, K. (1909), *Umfang und Art des jugendlichen Krüppeltums und der Krüppelfürsorge in Deutschland nach der durch die Bundesregierung erhobenen amtlichen Zählung*, Hamburg: Verlag von Leopold Voss.
Biesalski, K. (1915a), *Die ethische und wirtschaftliche Bedeutung der Kriegskrüppelfürsorge und ihre Organisation im Zusammenhang mit der gesamten Kriegshilfe*, Hamburg: Verlag von Leopold Voss.
Biesalski, K. (1915b), *Kriegskrüppelfürsorge. Ein Aufklärungswort zum Troste und zur Mahnung*, Leipzig: Verlag von Leopold Voss.
Biesalski, K. (1916), "Ein Aufklärungswort zum Troste und zur Mahnung," in *Unseren Kriegsbeschädigten*, 3–5, Potsdam: Vereinsdruckerei G.m.b.H.
Brüning, F. (1922), "Die Kampfmittel im Weltkriege und ihre Wirkung auf den Körper," in E. Payr and C. Franz (eds.), *Handbuch der Ärztlichen Erfahrungen im Weltkriege 1914/1918*, Vol. 1: Chirurgie, 3–26, Leipzig: Verlag von Johann Ambrosius Barth.
Conrad, K. (1933), "Das Körperschema. Eine kritische Studie und der Versuch einer Revision," *Zeitschrift der gesamten Neurologie und Psychiatrie*, 147: 346–69.
Dearden, H. (1928), *Medicine & Duty: A War Diary*, London: William Heinemann.
Frank, L. (1919), "Die Kriegskrüppel," in L. Frank (ed.), *Der Mensch ist gut*, 138–95, Zürich: Max Rascher Verlag.
Galloway, A., and E. Thacker (2007), *The Exploit: A Theory of Networks*, Minneapolis: University of Minnesota Press.

Grosz, E. (1994), *Volatile Bodies: Toward a Corporeal Feminism*, Bloomington: Indiana University Press.
Günther, H. (1914), "Sind die Kriege gefährlicher geworden?" *Die Umschau* 18: 808–13.
Hartmann, K. (1919), "Die Prüfstelle für Ersatzglieder," in M. Borchardt, K. Hartmann, H. Leymann, R. Radike, G. Schlesinger, and H. Schwiening (eds.), *Ersatzglieder und Arbeitshilfen: Für Kriegsbeschädigte und Unfallverletzte*, 18–57, Berlin: Springer.
Hartmann, V. (2014), "Kriegsverletzungen und ihre Behandlung im Ersten Weltkrieg anhand von Präparaten der wehrpathologischen Lehrsammlung der Bundeswehr," *Wehrmedizin und Wehrpharmazie* 58 (12): 427–34. Available online: https://wehrmed.de/geschichte/kriegsverletzun gen-und-ihre-behandlung-im-ersten-weltkrieg-anhand-von-praepara ten-der-wehrpathologischen-lehrsammlung-der-bundeswehr.html (accessed June 2, 2021).
Head, H., and G. Holmes (1911), "Sensory Disturbances from Cerebral Lesions," *Brain* 34: 102–254.
Hörl, E. (2016), "Die Ökologisierung des Denkens," *Zeitschrift für Medienwissenschaft* 8 (14): 33–45.
Katz, D. (1921), *Zur Psychologie des Amputierten und seiner Prothese*, Leipzig: Verlag von Johann Ambrosius Barth.
Kiegelmann, F.-J. (2012), *Der Krieg 1914-1918. Wie ich ihn erlebte. Tagebuchaufzeichnungen des Sanitätsunteroffiziers Clemens Bedbur*, Frankfurt am Main: Vindobona Verlag.
Kienitz, S. (2004), "Der verwundete Körper als Emblem der Niederlage? Kriegsinvaliden in der Weimarer Republik," in H. Carl, H.-H. Kortüm, D. Langewiesche, and F. Lenger (eds.), *Kriegsniederlagen. Erfahrungen und Erinnerungen*, 329–42, Berlin: Akademie Verlag.
Kienitz, S. (2011), "Re-Konstruktionen. Der Erste Weltkrieg und die 'Krise des Körpers,'" in J. Fleischhack and K. Rottmann (eds.), *Störungen. Medien, Prozesse, Körper*, 90–108, Berlin: Reimer.
Kienitz, S. (2015), "Schöner gehen? Zur technischen Optimierung des kriegsinvaliden Körpers im frühen 20. Jahrhundert," *Body Politics* 3 (6): 235–59.
Krumeich, G., and G. Hirschfeld (2013), "Die Industrialisierung des Krieges," in G. Krumeich and G. Hirschfeld (eds.), *Deutschland im Ersten Weltkrieg*, 189–218, Frankfurt am Main: S. Fischer.
Latour, B. (1993), *We Have Never Been Modern*, trans. Catherine Porter, Cambridge, MA: Harvard University Press.
Latour, B. (2005), *Reassembling the Social: An Introduction to Actor-Network-Theory*, Oxford: Oxford University Press.
Mohi-von Känel, S. (2018), *Kriegsheimkehrer. Politik und Poetik 1914-1939*, Göttingen: Wallstein.
Nancy, J.-L. (1992), *Corpus*, Paris: Métailié.

Sauerbruch, F. (1916), *Die willkürlich bewegbare künstliche Hand. Eine Anleitung für Chirurgen und Techniker*, Berlin: Springer.
Sauerbruch, F. (1919), "Die plastische Umwandlung der Amputationsstümpfe für willkürlich bewegbare Ersatzglieder," in M. Borchardt, K. Hartmann, H. Leymann, R. Radike, G. Schlesinger, and H. Schwiening (eds.), *Ersatzglieder und Arbeitshilfen: Für Kriegsbeschädigte und Unfallverletzte*, 234–52, Berlin: Springer.
Schilder, P. (1923), *Das Körperschema. Ein Beitrag zur Lehre vom Bewusstsein des eigenen Körpers*, Berlin: Springer.
Schilder, P. (1935), *The Image and the Appearance of the Human Body: Studies in Constructive Energies of the Psyche*, London: Paul Kegan.
Shildrick, M. (2015), "Why Should Our Bodies End at the Skin? Embodiment, Boundaries and Somatechnics," *Hypathia* 30 (1): 13–29.
Shildrick, M. (2017), "Individuality, Identity and Supplementarity in Transcorporeal Embodiment," in K. M. Cahill, M. Gustafsson, and T. S. Wentzer (eds.), *Finite but Unbounded: New Approaches in Philosophical Anthropology*, 153–72, Berlin: De Gruyter.
Sobchack, V. (2010), "Living a 'Phantom Limb': On the Phenomenology of Bodily Integrity," *Body & Society* 16 (3): 51–67.
Spreen, D., *Upgradekultur. Der Körper in der Enhancement-Gesellschaft*, Bielefeld: Transcript.
von Esmarch, F. (1877), *Handbuch der Kriegschirurgischen Technik*, Hannover: Carl Rümpler.
Voss, C. (2010), "Auf dem Weg zu einer Medienphilosophie anthropomedialer Relationen," *ZMK – Zeitschrift für Medien- und Kulturforschung* 2: 170–84.
Voss, C., and L. Engell (eds.) (2015), *Mediale Anthropologie*, Paderborn: Fink.
Voss, C., and T. Othold (2015), "From Media Anthropology to Anthropomediality," in *Anthropological Notebooks* 21 (3): 75–82.
Widmer, P. (2006), *Metamorphosen des Signifikanten. Zur Bedeutung des Körperbilds für die Realität des Subjekts*, Bielefeld: Transcript.
Zachmann, E. (1917), "Von den Krüppeln—für die Krüppel. 2. Erich Zachmann. Mit 9 Figuren," *Zeitschrift für Krüppelfürsorge* 10: 191–5.
Zürcher, U. (2005), "Wenn es schmerzt, wo nichts mehr ist. Aspekte einer Körper-Geschichte der Phantomschmerzen," in *Historische Anthropologie* 13 (1): 61–90.

13

Material Dialectics of the Hard Body

Ivo Ritzer

The body is spirited—let us leave the soul out of play.
—Friedrich Nietzsche

Once a privileged subject in anthropology, the body has also become a key concern in Cultural Studies and Critical Theory in more recent times. Not to mention ethical discussions about reproductive biotechnology or everyday life with beauty and sports studios, neo-Marxism in Theodor W. Adorno and Max Horkheimer, poststructuralist vitalism in Gilles Deleuze and Félix Guattari, discourse analysis in Michel Foucault, gender and queer philosophy in Judith Butler, theater and performance theory in Erika Fischer-Lichte, visual studies in Hans Belting, or phenomenological film theory in Vivian Sobchak, they have all "discovered" the body anew and made it the center of their attention. They are concerned, for all their different conceptions in detail, with reflections on nature and culture, presence and absence, identity and alterity, whereby the body becomes the point of crystallization for polemical speculation and argumentative reasoning alike.

In this chapter, I will first give a short overview about media-anthropological thinking of the body, focusing on the body and mediality, also mapping out the body's relationship to representation. Second, I will recapitulate the cultural history of the body in modern society, or rather, provide introductions to the major philosophical approaches to the body of society, thereby placing special emphasis on the notions of discipline and control. This will, third, be supplemented by a close look at the relationship between materiality and immateriality, as well as the role of age which is of key importance to understanding the body in the society of control, the latter in turn itself an economic formation that is very much characterized by mediated bodies, in a field of tension between digitization and flesh, a vanishing and a returning body. As part of this, the return of the body will be reflected by drawing on material dialectics and its ontology of body, event and subject, as well as the peculiar place of the cinematic body in this constellation.

Keeping in mind aesthetics' lesson that philosophy has no access to truth but can only try to preserve truths and the insights produced by art, the material dialectics of the body will finally be discussed by focusing on the work of its most consistent and important cinematic practitioner: Director Walter Hill.

It is clear that the body is no longer conceived as an evidential, "natural" quantity, but rather in its historical-social dimension. It is always representation, even if it is not yet represented by second-order representations. The body is itself an image even before it is reproduced in images, and the image is not what it claims to be, namely reproduction of the body, rather it is in truth production of an image of the body that is already predetermined in the self-representation of the body (Belting 2011). Therefore, the body is not to be understood biologistically, but as a cultural construct, even if this construct is to be linked back to bodily experience. Experience is understood as the connection between body and representation, material body, and symbolic presence, which is linked to perception. It is about (mental) realizations of conceptions as well as (material) representations of ideas, which stand in a psychological-physical relation to the body. In fact, it possesses a double skill: the body is first used to create endogenous, that is, internal representations, and second to receive objective, that is, external, representations. Endogenous representations are produced imaginatively by the body itself, objective representations depend on a media body through which they become perceptible as cultural practices.

Where representation as a complex process of symbolization is thus to be assigned to the mental, the medium is positioned on the side of materiality. By acting as a mediator between body and representation, however, it amalgamates mental and material qualities into a unified effect constituted in sensual perception. It makes it possible to distinguish represented bodies from present bodies in that, to take up a famous idea of Niklas Luhmann's, its form creates perceptible consolidations by selecting from possibilities between possible combinations.

Media representations imply a twofold recourse to the body. On the one hand, they allow the medium to be understood as a current carrier or virtual body, that is, a container of the manifest material body, from which the representation gets its shape. Because a representation does not have a body, it requires a medium to embody it. Or, we might even say that no representation can do without a body. Representation is embodied, or there is no representation. Media make bodies present, while the representation refers to something absent, which it represents vicariously. The carrier medium, which the representation requires in order to be received, is the medium of representation. The carrier medium functions as a basic guarantor of symbolic techniques that make representations appear.

On the other hand, media access the recipient's anatomical body, whose self-perception and perception by others is determined and modified by the structures prefiguring that perception. The receiving body, in turn, first disembodies the objective representation until it then reembodies it as an "organic" medium itself. This secondary animation imaginatively separates medium and representation to produce a virtual second-order body. The medium thus functions neither as a mere mediator between representation and perceiving subject nor, in Marshall McLuhan's sense, as a substitutive prosthetic extension of its human body (McLuhan 1964), while representation by no means appears as the producer of that auratic "here and now" that Walter Benjamin (1969) speaks about with reference to art. The carrier medium and the receptive body rather exchange their roles in the act of perception, whereby the representation oscillates between medium and body. It is subject to a process that works in both directions, it is connected with the medium that embodies it and with the bodies that detach or absorb it. Thus, it is possible not only to conceptualize the mediality of representation as a product of embodied experience, but also to mediate productively between a cultural history of the body and a media history of representation. We might even think about a further abstraction of this idea toward all representation, yet suffice it to say for the sake of this chapter that there can certainly be no valid theory of medium and representation without acknowledging the historical role of the body in it.

The digitalization of culture as the previous endpoint of a technicization of bodily representations does not dispense with this process. Although the analogical connection between medium and representation is dissolved, the medium as a carrier of representation does not lose its symbolic body at all. Once again, it becomes apparent that the relation between medium and representation is not exhausted in a technical context. Neither do technical innovations necessarily provide alternative modes of representation, nor do new perceptive mechanisms necessarily develop. In the case of digital media, there is merely a shift in emphasis that manifests itself in the relation between the receiving body and the representation. Just as the body and the brain continue to figure as an inescapable condition of all human perception, media channels also maintain their familiar functional surfaces. The representation of the image remains bound to the screen (Belting 2011). Even if digital representations today only provide a virtual visualization of binary data and no longer a reproductive "ontology of the model" (Bazin 2004), the question of the specific practice of representation remains just as relevant as the specific medium in which the body is specifically represented. While the body operates as a biological "hardware," it is above all the representative practices, in addition to the media systems, that form themselves as historical variables.

Bodies do not exist in a vacuum. The study of their media representations only appears to be productive if the potential for the dialectics between a general concept of representation and specific conventions of a particular quality is reflected on. In other words, the analysis only becomes meaningful if the overall perspective can be derived from its individual sub-identities. The challenge then, of course, still remains to not fall back into empiricism, but combine theoretical insight with concrete intuition.

Disappearance of the Body

The body is expendable. This is what postmodern media theory has told us for a long time, mostly within the school of "French Theory" as practiced by philosophers such as Paul Virilio, Jean Baudrillard, or Jean-François Lyotard. Here, we are basically told that the body is disappearing, perhaps it has already completed its dispersion. The audiovisuality of modern mass media is held responsible for this, not least the images and sounds of film freed from celluloid by electronic and digital technology. Its gravitational force seems to cause a loss of space that liquidates the human body with every form of primary experience. Perhaps Paul Virilio, more than anyone else, has never tired of emphasizing how the electromagnetic functioning of video has implemented a radical change of paradigm. The relative speed of mechanical processes becomes an absolute speed. In addition to potential and kinetic energy, a third energy is introduced: the energy of information. This kinematic energy results from the abstract sum of all technical accelerations that run through an image. It is this energy that results from the effect of movement and its more or less great rapidity on the ocular, optical and optoelectronic perceptions. According to Virilio (1991), electronic images are characterized by the fact that they no longer define information by content, but by speed of transmission. The geographical space of human experience thus becomes a deterritorialized network of virtual fields, possessing no longer any center, or "roots." The movement of a body from one place to another is replaced by perception as dispersive vision, that is, as communication between machines of seeing. In this process, what is near and far collides, the acceleration of kinematic energy destroys the awareness of distances. Therefore, for Virilio, modern media communication always means the loss of spatial context at the same time. He has repeatedly emphasized that this is about adapting the human body to the age of the absolute speed of electromagnetic waves. The qualitative paradigm shift from the primacy of the body to the dominance of media technology ensures a liquidation of traditional subject–object dichotomies as they have been valid since antiquity. For Virilio (2005), the emphasis is no longer on measuring the greatest possible distance as rapidly as possible in the shortest possible time; instead, the endpoint of modern media communication is the loss of any experience of space. Appearance takes precedence over being. Digitalization only radicalizes the electromagnetic potential of this: distances are no longer defined topographically. Contrary to the walk-in, haptically accessible archive, where information was located on material carriers, digital worlds make it possible through associative connections to use telepresent direct access without mechanical transport routes. Simulations and hyperrealities emerge, and bodies as final reference points of perception and reflection dissolve into fractal images; the fate of the subject follows this process. Corporal interaction with the environment becomes a function of immaterial data streams. As a result, the end of relative speed dissolves individual bodies, making them disappear like a face drawn in sand at the edge of the sea (Foucault 2002). Inside and outside merge into an amorphous continuum whose global virtuality replaces the body with its media reduplication.

If one accepts this diagnosis by postmodern media theory in Virilio, or Baudrillard's *Simulations* (1983) and Lyotard's *Les Immatériaux* (1985) for this matter, the established result inevitably entails problems for the body image in cinema, whose basic constant is a positioning of bodies in and through space. Especially the action image with its absolute identity of image and movement must find itself in a dilemma if it does not want to give up the body as the central carrier of mobility. If film images are understood as discursive embodiments of social practice, then the question arises as to how they react to the putative loss of meaning of the body in the object world. In other words, is there a feedback process between the virtualized and the virtual body, does the loss of the body in media culture symptomatically radiate onto the media image? In fact, a relation of equivalence seems to emerge between cinematic and social body discourses. Where the body must ultimately become an annoying obstacle to a utopian cyberspace due to its physiochemical limitations, cinema visibly constructs simulative spaces by working on the generation of a real without origin or reality, bringing the so-called reality in its entirety into congruence with its simulation models (Baudrillard 1994). It is striking that the recent simulation models precisely do not target the human body due to their amazing "photorealism." The digital cinema of special effects likes to bring fantastic worlds to life—instead of duplicating physical "reality" it wants to create "real" imaginary spaces, for which the human body is only a disturbing accessory of a post-biological future, or an unwelcome reminder of the nature we carry within us (Belting 2011). Their utopia seems to be a leap out of the fetters of the flesh into the pure world of the matrix, of boundless streams of information.

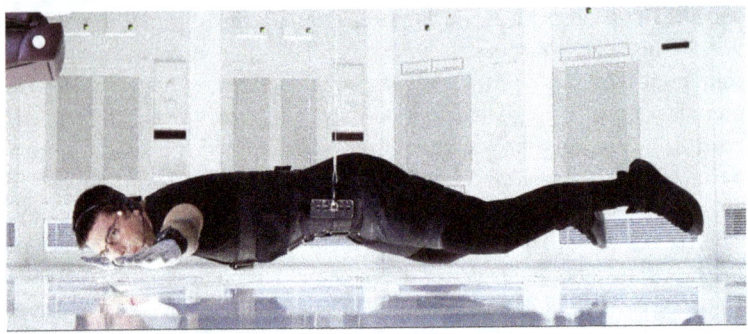

Figure 13.1 *Mission: Impossible* (1996, Paramount Pictures).

A, no actually *the* film that reflects on this development with analogous methods and thereby provides a sophisticated commentary on the precarious status of body images in digital cinema is Brian De Palma's masterpiece *Mission: Impossible* (1996). In a sequence that has become famous, De Palma shows his team of agents breaking into the CIA's highly secured computer headquarters. Using a ventilation shaft, Ethan Hunt (Tom Cruise) rappels down into the room of the central computer. He can only manage to move with the utmost caution and extreme slowness. He must try to act disembodied, because every acoustic signal, every haptic contact, even his mere body heat is enough to activate the threatening alarm. De Palma fully exploits the tense dramaturgical potential of the situation when a single drop of sweat almost causes the operation to fail (Figure 13.1). In addition to the virtuosity of his mise-en-scène, he thus succeeds in a congenial reflection of media-historical processes through the figurative arrangement: it is his body that Hunt/Cruise must make disappear in order to complete the impossible mission. Now, of course, it could be argued that, most importantly, the body has to remain unnoticed, and it is the drop of sweat, caught by hand, which designates the perfect body managing to remain unnoticed.[1] Yet, at the same time, it is obvious that even the perfect body has its limits and a very hard time to make the impossible mission a possibility.

Return of the Body

With protagonists like Ethan Hunt, embodied by Tom Cruise, an entire generation of earlier heroic figures has become obsolete, but especially the hard bodies shaped by Sylvester Stallone with proletarian figures like Rocky Balboa and John Rambo, for whom the sometimes hyperbolically muscular body becomes the last possible guarantor of subject constitution in a thoroughly technologized era—both for individual and collective, that is, national identity.[2] These hard bodies have not played a role in popular cinema for a good fifteen years, starting with the early 1990s. After Cruise and with actors like Keanu Reeves, George Clooney, Brad Pitt, Will Smith, and Nicolas Cage, a new form of masculinity dominated cinema. However, by 2006, we have seen *Rocky Balboa* in theaters with great commercial success, followed by *John Rambo* (2008) and, most recently, *Rambo: Last Blood* (2019). In all these films, the title characters and Sylvester Stallone have undergone a significant aging process, and Stallone does not allow the physical effects of the appearance of aging to be hidden. Rather, they are clearly signified by externally visual features on Stallone's body: by his thin hair, by his furrowed skin, by his age pigments, by his wrinkled varicose veins, even by his slowed movements. While the Rambo movies have the protagonist return primarily as an iconic phantom, especially in *Rocky Balboa* these physical signs of aging find an explicit discursivation. They are directly made an issue because Balboa has to compete here against a significantly younger boxer who could be his son. Stallone's film operates through a binary model that is built between the protagonists. While the young African-American boxer is associated with virtuality and digital appearance—a computer-simulated boxing match—Balboa still stands for the "authentic body" of an analogue nature. Age here does not signify illness or death, as it has usually been the case in Hollywood cinema. Rather, the old age can teach the youth a lesson in qualities such as strength, endurance, and determination. "There ain't nothin' over till it's over," is Balboa's motto, and to his young opponent's question, "Where's that from, the '80s?," he answers laconically, "That's probably the '70s." Balboa's laconism is resolutely connected to his ability to suffer. The maltreated body of the protagonist is emphasized even more than in all the other films of the franchise. In the final boxing match, Balboa's only priority is not to go down. What his bleeding body can take in terms of blows and pain is what makes him the true martyr of a nostalgic longing for "authenticity," the body as the zero point of experience, as it is supposed to guarantee subjectivity with integrity and the ability to act decisively. At the end of the film, Balboa may lose the fight, but he remains the moral victor. By defying his opponent, he also opposes time and his deteriorating physique.

The discourse around body nostalgia and aging hard bodies is once again intensified by Stallone with his programmatically titled film *The Expendables* (2010), referring to John Ford's eponymous war movie from 1945, starring John Wayne, the forefather of all hard bodies. Without a doubt, Stallone knows his Ford, since *Rocky Balboa* already lovingly quoted *She Wore a Yellow Ribbon* (1949), with the husband at the grave of the deceased wife. But where

Ford's film about the patrol boats of the US Army in the Second World War still shows a young John Wayne, Stallone emphasizes the desolate situation of his protagonists also through their advanced age. It could be argued, however, that Stallone does not historicize the aged body at all, but rather adapts it to the present—in a hysterically violent and, in its unabashed embracing of neoliberal capitalism and its "post-continuity" (Shaviro 2016), aesthetically very dubious film. It seems reasonable to say that *The Expendables* wants to prepare us for a future in which the young body will no longer be dominant, but rather the old one. It is a future that is about this type of body being used productively. Far from being merely a defiant response to increasing processes of body distancing, the hysteria and violence of *The Expendables* sensitize us to new forms of aging. The enormous success of Stallone's film, with sixty million dollars in box office takings in just ten days—not to speak of its accompanying productions in films like Harrison Ford's *Indiana Jones and the Kingdom of the Crystal Skull* (2008), Bruce Willis's *A Good Day to Die Hard* (2013), or even Clint Eastwood's *Gran Torino* (2008), *The Mule* (2018), and *Cry Macho* (2021)—would prove it right: as a seismograph of a sociodemographic development that is looking for ways to shape even more and increasingly older bodies.

In his influential analysis of social structures, Michel Foucault (1978) spoke of two different configurations of power that operate on different axes but interpenetrate each other orthogonally. One is centered on the anatomical body as a machine, while the other takes aim at the generic or collective body. Where the first axis focuses on the individual and directs it along multiple practices of surveillance and control, the telos of the second axis is designed to regulate the population as a whole. On the one hand, power shapes the individual body in order to make it usable according to its needs; on the other hand, power focuses on the collective in order to organize the compound body of individuals according to ruling standards. For Foucault, this creates a new principle of power without a clear center (Foucault 1978). It no longer gains strength through the potential imposition of a violent death, but rather pursues the promotion of life. One could say that the old right to make die or let live has been replaced by a power to make live or to push into death. This explains the disqualification of death, expressed today in the demise of the rituals that accompany it. Now the power directs its accesses to life and its whole course; the moment of death is its limit and withdraws from it; it becomes the most secret, the most private point of existence. The threat of death is replaced by a responsibility for life that subordinates the body to power. Modern societies are based on the fundamental power of a generic bio-power, as in the field of political practices and economic observations, the problems of birth rate, life span, public health, migration, and settlement arise. The most diverse techniques for subjugating the body and for controlling the population appear from the ground and inaugurate the era of a bio-power. According to Foucault (2004), this new bio-power or life-power is based on completely different mechanisms of functioning. Its purpose is to bring forth, to grow, and to order forces rather than to inhibit, bend, or destroy them.

Now, in any case, the right over death shifts or relies on the requirements of a power that administers and manages life and subordinates itself to these requirements. Bio-power does not destroy, it secures; it does not restrain, it incites; it does not annihilate, it develops. Foucault sees the constitution of a normed society as a logical consequence of its functioning, that is, one defined by constants circulating between subjects. Since it manages life, bio-power is concerned with arranging individuals according to dominant directives. It permeates the entire social complex and extends to production as well as reproduction rather than destruction. Such power must qualify, measure, assess, rank, rather than manifest itself in an outburst. Instead of drawing the boundary line that separates the obedient subjects from the enemies of the sovereign, it aligns the subjects with the norm by arranging them around it. A normalizing society is the historical effect of a power technology directed at life. Now when power is directed at the life of the body, its goal is to mobilize potential, it works to maximize life, and this maximization, according to Foucault, is what gives power access to the body. Foucault shows that individuals are not only governed but also modulated by bio-power's access to their bodies. By shaping the body of the subject and endowing it with a transcendental "authenticity," power not only creates controlled configurations of subjectivity, but at the same time constitutes the individual as an entity that imagines itself autonomous and independently submits to power and its control. The subject orients its action to invisible imperatives of the bio-power, and is thus freed from the hegemony of an identifiable sovereign, but without being able to live in sovereign freedom. Out of its own responsibility with its "own" perspectives it regulates itself, but these perspectives are never really at the choice of the individual.

Thus, it is no longer necessary to discipline the subject by force, omnipresent impulses of standardization allow it to provide for self-control out of its own volition. Gilles Deleuze (1992), following Foucault, speaks of the transition from a disciplinary society to a society of control, where sanctioning measures are replaced by control mechanisms that take on a life of their own. Modulations of the post-disciplinary control society do not function exclusively, but inclusively; they provide for an infinite dynamization of life. In the control society, fixed institutions of disciplining are replaced by permanent instructions to the body that operate discretely but by no means aimlessly. Precisely because of this, domination is intensified and abstracted at the same time, extending to all areas of existence. What used to be the factory is now called the company. There, motivation as well as identification are demanded, whereby the only constant is paradoxically called flexibility. An ostensible "democratization" makes work seem like leisure, and leisure seem like work. The factory assembled individuals into a body, to the dual advantage of the patronage that supervised each element of the masses, and of the unions that mobilized a mass of resistance. The company, however, constantly spreads an inescapable rivalry as a salutary competition and excellent motivation that sets individuals in opposition to each other, runs through each of them, and divides them within themselves. The modulatory principle of wages according to merit even seduces the state educational institutions. For as the enterprise replaces the factory, permanent training tends to replace the school, and continuous control replaces the exam. This is the safest way to surrender the school to the company. In disciplinary societies, one never stopped starting (from school to barracks, from barracks to factory), while in the control societies, one never finishes with anything. Enterprise and further education service are metastable and coexisting states of one and the same modulation that resembles a universal distorter. The process of control, therefore, cannot find an end, it must always remain unfinished. It produces a life in permanent postponement. The subject is constantly required to adapt to its environment, to think and act situationally. Up to death, the consciousness as well as the body of the subjects are penetrated by the complex accesses of bio-power. Or, to put it differently: they cannot finish being productive—even into old age. The bio-power of the control society wants to optimize the body of the subject, to make it useful for as long as possible. If it is less vulnerable, its value increases, that is, its usability for power. The formation of a hard body and its maintenance into old age can be considered strategies for producing reliable bodies that are characterized by maximum functionality.

In contrast to the disciplinary society, the control society is no longer concerned with punishing and confining deviant subjects; rather, it attempts to regulate individual and collective bodies through multiple incentives. The traditional corset of standardizing impulses of power gives way to a pluralization of life designs and social forms, which entail new demands on the body. Contrary to industrial society, which constantly trained the body in everyday processes of work and exploitation, it must reconstitute itself as a body in the post-Fordist communication society, in which the distribution of the means of production is no longer an expression of social domination, but the monopoly over signs and codes (Baudrillard 1994). For, in this media society, it no longer has to endure an overstraining of the physical but precisely its under-straining. The exponential increase in the mechanization of work as well as, in the last two decades, the pervasive digitalization of both productive and bureaucratic, cognitive and economic, communicative and social operations has led to the fact that the highest performance that bodies have to provide is at the level of concentration and attention. It is a lack of movement that demands compensation in postindustrial society. Thus, work on the body is accomplished in the gym instead of the factory. There, medicine, the leisure, and sports industry earn money by offering a leisure program for physical training. The hard body is regarded as the activated competence of a corporal virtuality, which becomes the confirmation of a "successful" life design. The matrix of a "successful" evening of life is formed by fitness and performance, on which basis the body can remain productive even in old age. Here, techniques of self-care take care of the body, as an instrument of the self to be developed, strengthened, and cultivated. This corporeal self-modulation is always about embracing resources, expanding resources, and utilizing resources. The subject becomes an entrepreneur of herself (Foucault 2004), regarding the body as an investment. Investments are carried out in the practice of life.

In this context, the body functions as a reference point for processes constituting identity and, at the same time, as a medium of distinction for social positioning. It appears as an entity that can be modulated both collectively and individually. It offers a bodily capital that, in its biosocial relevance beyond Pierre Bourdieu (1986), could not only be described as a subcategory of cultural capital, but evolves into an independent form of capital through accumulated work. The incorporation of body labor by means of self-care leads to the formation of corporal capital, which in turn can be transferred into other types of capital: through sale of labor into economic capital, through acquisition of prestige into social, symbolic and cultural capital, whereby the habitus of the body in its function as a communication space and sign carrier decides on the potentials for participation in social space. Therefore, considerable time and effort are invested in the body. No effort seems too great, no body ever too old, for the potentiation or conservation of corporeal capital. Aging is thus to be evaluated as a specific social practice that demands a continuous process of public body presentation. Age becomes a socially negotiated construct that can be shaped performatively. It is about presenting and staging the body, exhibiting it on the basis of cultural techniques and practices of signification, through which something is brought to appearance. The subject is thus not as old as it feels, it is as old as it acts. Through the distinctive execution of actions, social status is defined by parameters such as inclusion and exclusion.

In this context, active aging is positively valued, which aggressively wants to rejuvenate the aging body. Today's bio-power demands a concealment of that process of deterioration and decay to which the body is inevitably subjected. If with advancing age successive corporeal capital fades away, the subject is all the more obliged to modulate the aging process, to influence it by compensatory bodily techniques. The realization that death nevertheless stands at the end of every life span is lost out of sight through the "invisible" age and instead allows competencies formerly connoted with youth, such as mobility, spontaneity, and expressivity, to diffuse into later phases of life. The horizon for this is formed by a postulated utilization of resources of corporeal capital, which, under the sign of the demographic development of occidental societies of control, is to be made available increasingly to old people. Therefore, the aging body is by no means "expendable," does not appear as a biological fate to be accepted, it is rather apostrophized in its plasticity, it is presented as a body to be worked on.

This body work appears as concern for health and life enhancement, but behind the putative self-optimization there is always a utilitarian imperative of post-*operaist* social structures, that is, the focus of contemporary capitalism on exploiting leisure time and creative work. Here, the young glossy body annihilates all other ages, with the fun effects that it promises and rarely delivers, it anesthetizes any compassion for those who are not *in* but *out*, as well as any co-responsibility for the division of the world not on the basis of cultural differences, but into the old universal division of the rich and the poor. The icon of the beautiful body, once a gift, has become the seal of success. Therefore, in a very concrete sense, we can observe a return of the body as material fact in capitalism, well this side of representation and mediality. Yet, the material body certainly is no ultimate reference, nor a stable referent, for sure. Rather, its modulation implies an irreducible phantasmatic quality, leading us back to basic embodiment of the body itself. Through the commitment to work out and fitness, through the belief in its efficiency and beauty, the hard body is adapted to the requirements of the control society's forms of organization. Individual well-being through self-modulation practices is prescribed and takes place in the service of a productive life. The body as a medium for experiencing pleasure is not an end in itself but a function. It optimizes performance. While work, at least for the middle classes, today may be largely disembodied and occur as the immaterial production of goods such as culture, services, knowledge, or communication, a "fit" body provides optimal predispositions for this affective work as well. It functions as a basal guarantor of concentration, creativity, and fine motor skills. Labor power is therefore reproduced today by leisure activities for the individual body. The goal of continuous vitality is therefore the permanent accumulation of corporeal capital, no longer confined to a limited phase of life. Behind its putative nostalgia, a film like *The Expendables*, which is as popular as it is dubious, propagates exactly that: a productive body well into its senior years. It is the body that the biopower of the control society dictates to be shaped and created today.

Bodies and Truths

While most of poststructuralist media theory has—through its fixation on semiotics, discourse, and language—not been able to come up with a concept of the body as "subject matter," the most sophisticated attempt to think a dialectics of the body is currently to be found in Alain Badiou's neo-ontology of multiplicity. Badiou (2005) preserves on the one hand the anti-idealistic postulate of difference, which marks the distance of two terms by a third one. At the same time, on the other hand, the sovereignty of thesis and antithesis is supplemented by a supplemental quantity. This is the quantity of truth: an exceptional process that creates new facts in the world. "There are only bodies and languages, except that there are truths" (Badiou 2009: 4), and these truths are disembodied bodies, senseless languages, generic infinities, unconditional supplements. In addition to the individual singularity of bodies and the cultural constructs of language, there are truths that are materially constituted by bodies and language but are neither traceable nor reducible to them. Truth here means, on the one hand, a universally valid statement about being. On the other hand, the being of truth is thought to be immanent to being per se: "a subject is nothing other than an active fidelity to the event of truth," and that "a truth does not retain anything expressible from that situation" (Badiou 2005: xii–xiii). Therein, for Badiou, lies its materialist evidence. Badiou's dialectics thus paradoxically no longer operates dialectically but rather disjunctively. Truth is not an effect of the revelation of the bodies grasped by language; it lies outside of bodies like language but is nevertheless in the world. In Badiou's thought, the tension between being and event is constituted by this principle of truth. In Badiou's constellation, truth, event, and being refer to each other in a circular way. Where a truth communicates itself to the being subject in an eventful way, the event in its non-intentional truth is dependent on the witnessing of the being subjects. In the event, an idea of truth emerges, which is never finite, but always works processually. It subjectivizes the individuals and commits them in fidelity to the eternal universality of metahistorical truth. Thus, a subject is constituted that appears as the site of a universal singularity of presuppositionless truth. With the eventful subjectivation the given order is thwarted, and a rupture in existing is articulated. In this rupture, the truth of that being is revealed, which constitutes the existence of the subject.

For Badiou, the medium of film has a special place in the dialectics of bodies and truths (Badiou 2013). It is opposed to the traditional understanding of the arts in that its democratic potential does not represent the sensually perceptible form of an idea. Instead of implementing an idea in the act of aesthesis, film reveals how idea and body are separated from each other. In Badiou, ideas are always only realized as a visitation or procedure: a "rule of passage" (2005: 151–5). They always only come to view temporarily and disappear again from the container of the medium after an ephemeral presence. The art of cinema is therefore not primarily, as with Deleuze (1989), an ordering of images, but an organization of ruptures. Its passages create discontinuities that allow the spectator-subject to be seized by truth-events as part of its experience of the film. Film demonstrates this evocation precisely by the fact that it behaves subtractively to the other arts by its "false movements" (Badiou 2013: 88–93). Film itself cannot be, but can always only act. Because it possesses no essential idea, it works on a continuous subtraction of other arts. Film, then, takes the specifics from these other arts in order to have them appropriated by a broad audience.

No film accomplishes a Badiouan passage of the body more appropriately than Walter Hill's late masterpiece, neo-noir *Bullet to the Head* (2013). Hill tells the story of the hitman Bobo, embodied by Sylvester Stallone, who until now has operated in the service of the masters against the servants. Bobo is a modern-day St. Paul who commits himself to an event, and thereby disavows his former principles in the name of "doing what's right." This commitment to the event constitutes the basis for heroic action. The potential of generic conventions, especially appreciated by Badiou, is rooted in their constitution of such heroic acts. He acknowledges genres as heirs to ancient tragedy, their "capacity for heroism, amazing in the way that Greek tragedy could be" (Badiou 2013: 211). Heroic acts create gratifications on the side of reception, as "presenting typical characters of the great conflicts of human life to an enormous audience." Film is thus concerned with ethics and affects, an affective ethics: "Cinema deals with courage, with justice, with passion, with betrayal. The major genres of cinema … are in fact ethical genres, genres that are addressed to humanity so as to offer it a moral mythology" (Badiou 2013: 211). For Badiou, the ethics of genres is realized in the design of heroic protagonists.

Bobo in *Bullet to the Head* is a protagonist precisely in this sense. The hero's subjectivity here is based on his fidelity to the event. The murder of his partner triggers a procedure of truth in this deeply disillusioned and cynical contract killer. He now tells himself and us that "sometimes you have to abandon your principles and do what's right." This might well mean to punish the guilty without earning a dime, and even "to save a cop." The very saving of the most detested is already shown right at the beginning of the story, before the plot opens a long flashback, thus retroactively prefiguring the event. The event articulates a call to embrace the truth of the event and to realize its being in the world. While the hero does not intentionally seek the event, he must nevertheless choose the revealed truth. By remaining faithful to it, a truth process is set in motion whose movement allows the truth to become. Badiou sees the moment of fidelity as absolutely crucial, as it is exactly truth that produces fidelity in a situation. If the subject is faithful to the event of truth, it can make itself immortal. By this Badiou does not mean the bodily existence of man. As a somebody, every human being inevitably dies. As a subject, however, it can defy the transience of existing in being: The "someone" who is conceived as a witness to the fact that he belongs as a fulcrum to the process of a truth is at the same time himself, nothing other than himself, a multiple singularity that can be spotted among all, and is in relation to himself in excess, because the accidental trace of fidelity passes through him, freezes his singular body, and inscribes him, from the interior itself of time, in a moment of eternity (Badiou 2009). The "true" human being in Badiou is thus a disinterested being that places itself at the service of truth. This selfless interest is realized by the fact that the human being abstains.

Bobo in *Bullet to the Head* acts very much in this spirit: he sacrifices all material goods to remain faithful to the event, whether it is his car or his residence. Like so many protagonists in Walter Hill's films, in *Hard Times* (1975), *Streets of Fire* (1984), *Extreme Prejudice* (1987), *Johnny Handsome* (1990), *Last Man Standing* (1996), or *Undisputed* (2002), this Bobo is a lonely man who seeks to assert himself in a corrupt capitalist world by almost stoically defying it. In *Bullet to the Head*, it is neoliberal real estate speculators led by nouveau-riche Nigerian Robert Nkomo Morel (Adewale Akinnuoye-Agbaje) who, together with criminal politicians and police officers, want to gentrify the damaged city of New Orleans in order to enrich themselves from the demolition of social housing projects. Bobo faces them and eventually puts an end to their actions. That is, he successively seeks out all those responsible and kills them one by one. His path is one of violence. Just as Alain Badiou, like Friedrich Nietzsche, understands revolutionary violence as a reevaluation of all values, Bobo also situates himself beyond any morality:

> The theme of total emancipation, practiced in the present, in the enthusiasm of the absolute present, is always situated beyond good and evil. This is because in the circumstances of action, the only known

good is the one that the status quo turns into the precious name for its own subsistence. Extreme violence is therefore the corollary of extreme enthusiasm, because it is in effect a question of the transvaluation of all values. (Badiou 2007: 63)

Values such as compassion or consideration are regarded by Bobo as the resentment of the weak, which he overcomes through his fidelity to the event of truth.

Only when all the guilty are finally punished does Bobo return to the ranks of "mortals" at the end. Significantly, *Bullet to the Head* then closes with a look forward. While the entire film is staged as one big analepsis structured by Bobo's noir voice-over, at the end the retrospective turns to the future. "Nothing much changed," Bobo sums up, "except some people got killed that nobody's ever gonna miss. And I ended up needing a new car, so I went out and bought myself a special ride. Why not? You don't live forever." As the film closes with these words, the "do what's right" spoken as a voice-over at the very beginning is taken up again and almost proleptically turned around. What *Bullet to the Head* thus provides is a reference to future events that will generate new subjectivities and initiate new processes of fidelity. While corporeal beings may not live forever, truths in *Bullet to the Head* outlast the decay of body and language.

Walter Hill explicitly historicizes the ageing hard body of Stallone through a series of stills from Stallone's younger years—in its hyper masculine physique, *Bullet to the Head* not only refers to the precarious situation of the proletarian, which is increasingly threatened by advanced technology, the film thus also establishes a connection between the yesterday and today of generically structured star images (Figures 13.2–13.3). Even if Stallone's body is difficult to integrate into the world in which it lives, Hill refuses to withhold the body's performative acts. Furthermore, Hill achieves a synthesis such as that defined by Alain Badiou with his materialist dialectics. Hill does not simply "erase" the history of cinema, but rather reconfigures an aesthetic system that has increasingly been moving into the field of fantasy and virtuality since the 1990s. Badiou speaks of a post-cinema of "special effects of any kind," of "a sort of Late Roman Empire consummation" as "the obvious ingredients of current cinema" (Badiou 2013: 141). This post-continuity cinema operates as an event and has largely disavowed the tradition of reflective storytelling. For Badiou (2013: 141), recent film still refers to traditional narrative cinema, but replaces it with a primacy of images that are largely organized arbitrarily:

They are inscribed in a proven tradition, but there is no longer much of an attempt to embed them in a consistent fable with a moral, indeed

Figures 13.2–13.5 *Bullet to the Head* (2013, Warner Bros.).

Figure 13.3

religious, vocation. They derive from a technique of shock and one-upmanship, which is related to the end of an epoch in which images were relatively rare and it was difficult to obtain them. The endless discussions about the "virtual" and the image of synthesis refer to nothing other than the overabundance and facility of the image, including the spectacularly catastrophic or terrorizing image.

Fantasy and virtuality thus generate a cinema of spectacle that indulges in a self-purposeful and thus ultimately aleatory sequence of images.

Bullet to the Head now breaks with both tendencies, that of fantasy and that of virtuality, though decidedly not in a reactionary mode. The film eschews any media nostalgia, making use of digital effects and the potentials of nonlinear editing, reaching back to the age when Walter Hill first revolutionized montage in such work as *The Warriors* (1979) and *Streets of Fire* (1984) for postclassical cinema (Ritzer 2009). *Bullet to the Head* also relies on a mode of production for B-movies, at least compared to the expensive special effects A-movies of the post-continuity era, highlighting the historical nature of production possibilities that are temporary. Yes, says Hill himself, the niche of lower budgets and expectations with little producer interference no longer exists: "The middle ground has fallen out of the studio system" (Hill 2006: 120). Instead of fantasy and virtuality, Hill takes postclassical blockbuster cinema back into the tradition of crime and noir fiction on the one hand, and on the other hand centers a physique of corporeal confrontation that is particularly characteristic of the genre cinema of the 1970s and 1980s. Thus, his mise-en-scène is defined by an emphasis on somatic effects, which materialize especially in moments of corporeal confrontations, yet without any of the hysteria and the aleatory aesthetics found in Stallone's own *The Expendables*. Rather, Hill stages fistfights and firefights with a focus on the power as well as the vulnerability of bodies and objects. In doing so, he not only works toward a splatter aesthetic by relying on fake blood, but also intensifies the profilmic arrangement through the use of cinematographic means. Here Hill achieves a true dialectical synthesis of classical sequences of shots and postclassical clip aesthetics. On the one hand, establishing and reaction shots based on the principle of shot and counter-shot create a permanent orientation in the diegetic space; on the other hand, Hill employs zoom effects, handheld camera, as well as a rapid editing frequency, which additionally immensely dynamize all profilmic action by the actors. The telos of the mise-en-scène, however, is not a signifier of mere hectic, as in *The Expendables*; rather, camera, editing, and not least depth-heavy sound design apostrophize the destructive consequences of bullets, blows, and kicks. The result is a truly "materialistic" aesthetic of intensity (Figures 13.4–13.5).

In cinéphile film criticism, this very mise-en-scène of the "best American movie in years" is particularly appreciated then:

> Walter Hill, the director, hadn't made a movie in 10 years prior to *Bullet to the Head*. But he made *Bullet to the Head* like no one's made a movie since 1943, like film was still young and undefined—and during *Bullet to the*

Figure 13.4

Figure 13.5

> *Head*, man, it seems like it. Hill shot the kind of scenes we've seen a million times in a million films like he was discovering them for the first time: snap zooms and tilts where you'd expect a stationary low-angle, stuff like that. Only it's in the editing, too, which is so alive it seems polyrhythmic, like your body's systems running together. Some of the shots literally burn into the others. The whole movie's pulsing and alive and on fire. (Benton 2013)

Bullet to the Head thus inscribes itself in the tradition of the classical, but always creates nuances of a difference that uses the existing for the unknown.

Hill focuses the spectator and her own body on the affective dimension of what is being portrayed, without, however, becoming absorbed in the decorative worlds of digital special effects. No one brings this dialectics into images as well as into concept more brilliantly than Walter Hill himself (quoted in Vallan 2013: 56–9):

> I don't want to sound like one of these old fuckers who's always saying everything was better before, because I don't believe that at all. ... When I was a young guy in Hollywood in the late Sixties and early Seventies, there was a lot of debate about a shifting paradigm in storytelling. Were the genres dead? Did we have to find an entirely new model of storytelling based simply on character, everyday incident, and interior logic? Or could the genres be reworked in a way that made sense to audiences and to the whole process of telling stories through film? ... I came down very hard on the idea of sticking with the traditional concerns—but there was certainly no question that you had to do things in a different way. You couldn't simply do what had already been done in the past and, many times, done very successfully. You had to find new ways to be traditional.

The "new traditional" might very well be the most sophisticated configuration in a material dialectics of the hard body. The latter, by turn, continues to be of interest for any philosophical investigation from an anthropological perspective. It provides the second of the "two bodies" of representation, reminding us that the former renders it possible to understand mediality as embodiment, for representations are dependent on media's bodies. The medium of representation is the body, which in turn, (re) appears both as representation's object and the reception's subject. In other words, subjectivity and objectivity come together when representations make themselves present. That this presence is not only a question of mediating an absence, but also the temporality of both a cultural history of the body and a media history of representation, can be observed in Walter Hill. Hill's aesthetics of the cinematic body, its embodied representation as well as the actors' hard bodies, produce the new in the traditional, and might therefore be a privileged sight of any anthropology of entanglement.

Notes

1. My thanks for this observation to Lorenz Engell—the great theorist of agency and the agent.

2. Yvonne Tasker has shown that this does not necessarily involve reactionary ideology: "The all-American nationalism so much discussed in relation to the RAMBO films—Rambo as a 'pin-up for the president'—is also strangely oppositional and absent, articulating a love of nation which is based on a complex relationship to America. ... Indeed the articulation of masculinity and national identity through the figure of the muscular anti-hero offers a more complex set of signifiers than left/liberal discourses can seem to allow" (1993: 99/108). Tasker convincingly elaborates on the ambivalence of the hard body of Stallone's Rambo, who as a Vietnam veteran is in an overdetermined love-hate relationship with the United States.

References

Badiou, Alain (2005), *Being and Event*, New York: Continuum.
Badiou, Alain (2007), *The Century*, Cambridge: Polity Press.
Badiou, Alain (2009), *Logics of Worlds*, London: Bloomsbury.
Badiou, Alain (2013), *Cinema*, Cambridge: Polity.
Baudrillard, Jean (1983), *Simulations*, New York: Semiotext(e).
Baudrillard, Jean (1994), *Simulacra and Simulation*, Ann Arbor: University of Michigan Press.
Bazin, André (2004), "The Ontology of the Photographic Image" (1945), in *What Is Cinema?*, Berkeley: University of California Press.
Belting, Hans (2011), *An Anthropology of Images: Picture, Medium, Body*, Princeton, NJ: Princeton University Press.
Benjamin, Walter (1969), "The Work of Art in the Age of Mechanical Reproduction," in Harry Zohn (trans.), Hannah Arendt (ed.), *Illuminations*, New York: Schocken.
Benton, Tom "Bullet to the Head, a Straight Shot into the Classics." http://www.basementmedicine.org/arts-entertainment/2013/02/07/bullet-to-the-head-a-straight-shot-into-the-classics.
Bourdieu Pierre (1986), "Forms of Capital," in John Richardson (ed.), *Handbook of Theory and Research for the Sociology of Education*, 241–58, Westport: Greenwood.
Bullet to the Head (2013), Dir. Walter Hill, Los Angeles, CA: Warner Bros.
Deleuze, Gilles (1989), *Cinema 2: The Time-Image*, Minneapolis: University of Minnesota Press.
Deleuze, Gilles (1992), "Postscript on the Societies of Control," *October* 59 (Winter): 3–7.
Foucault, Michel (1978), *The History of Sexuality*, New York: Vintage Books.
Foucault, Michel (2002), *The Order of Things*, London: Routledge.
Foucault, Michel (2004), *The Birth of Biopolitics: Lectures at the Collége de France, 1978–1979*, New York: Palgrave MacMillan.

Hill, Walter (2006), "Walter Hill: Last Man Standing. Interviewed by Patrick McGilligan," in *Backstory 4: Interviews with Screenwriters of the 1970s and 1980s*, 102–30, Berkeley: University of California Press.

John Rambo (2008), Dir. Sylvester Stallone, Los Angeles, CA: Nu Image.

McLuhan, Marshall (1964), *Understanding Media: The Extensions of Man*, New York: McGraw Hill.

Rambo: Last Blood (2019), Dir. Adrian Grünberg, Los Angeles, CA: Millennium Media.

Ritzer, Ivo (2009), *Walter Hill*, Berlin: Bertz+Fischer.

Shaviro, Steven (2016), "Post-Continuity: An Introduction," in Shane Denson and Julia Leyda (ed.), *Post-Cinema: Theorizing 21st-Century Film*, 51–64, Falmer, UK: REFRAME Books.

She Wore a Yellow Ribbon (1949), Dir. John Ford, Culver City, CA: Argosy Pictures.

Tasker, Yvonne (1993), *Spectacular Bodies: Gender, Genre and the Action Cinema*, London: Routledge.

The Expendables (2010), Dir. Sylvester Stallone, Los Angeles, CA: Nu Image.

Vallan, Giulia D'Agnolo (2013), "Last Neo-Traditionalist Standing," *Film Comment* 49 (1): 54–60.

Virilio, Paul (1991), *The Aesthetics of Disappearance*, New York: Semiotext(e).

Virilio, Paul (2005), *Negative Horizon: An Essay in Dromoscopy*, London: Continuum.

14

She Is Inseminating: On the Secret of Life in Claire Denis's Science Fiction Film *High Life* (2018)

Astrid Deuber-Mankowsky

First there's a slowly changing, haunting electronic sound. A humid green garden appears from the black screen. The camera moves slowly across the green plants, over dark green moss, ripe pumpkins, and through the damp fog, while we are still hearing the sound. The setting is reminiscent of paradise, fertility, perhaps even evokes the origin of life. At the same time it recalls the beginning of Andrei Tarkovsky's classic 1972 science fiction movie *Solaris*. But suddenly the camera passes over a dirty men's shoe sticking out from the ground. There is no time to pursue the riddle. The next scene is introduced by the image of a transparent door separating the garden from an outside. The plaintive crying of a small child replaces the fading electronic sound. A male voice calms the child down while the camera, having unlocked its gaze from a metal ladder leading downward, moves into a point-of-view shot, like in a horror movie, through an ill-illuminated corridor, to finally find the one-year-old child sitting alone in an improvised playpen, now chattering quietly. The playpen is like an image for the narrowness of the environment, which resembles a prison. We see white texts running on black screens and colorful lights. We are obviously in a spaceship.

    The toddler is playing and chattering, the male voice answers gently: "Dadada." Where does the voice come from? It comes from another outside, from outer space, which, in the course of the film, will turn out to be another inside. We see a young man in a space suit and glass helmet, played by Robert Patterson, talking to the toddler via telecommunication. His voice, coming from the black outer space, fills the whole small room in which the child is playing and chattering in his playpen in front of the screens with the running white texts. The man—his name is, as we will learn later, Monte—holds a spanner in his hand and tightens a screw. He is moving slowly because of the lack of gravity, like in a dream.

What kind of science fiction movie is *High Life*, being composed so carefully and operating in such an elaborate fashion with the difference between the seeable and the sayable, with sound and moving pictures? How does it manage to create meaning and at the same time to destroy it? How does it cause and dissolve affections? How can it, with such virtuosity, play with the power to anticipate, postpone, and contradict an effect?

As I will show in the following, *High Life* can be read as a complex philosophical commentary on the entanglement of sexuality, gender, reproduction, and the historicity of life under the current conditions of science and technology. *High Life* exposes the gendered and racially differentiated violence of thanatopolitics inherent in biopolitics, and shows the ways in which the death drive can become a resistant moment that opposes the current conflation of reproductive technology and thanatopolitics. Following Gilles Deleuze, I will show that, in *High Life*, the secret of life is not revealed from the perspective of "individual life" but from the perspective of the "between moments" of "*a* life that is impersonal and yet singular" (Deleuze 1997: 5). Indeed, despite the omnipresence of death, the question that *High Life* poses concerns not death itself, but the in-between of death and individual survival.

The movie is able to do this because Claire Denis uses film and its digital-aesthetic components—such as sound, the use of light, camera technology, the possibilities of condensing and stretching time, the visualization of film history—as a medium itself, creating new forms of anthropomedial entanglements. By using fictitious settings such as spaceships, for example, and genre-elements from science fiction, the movie not only shows and tells us but also enacts and mediates what it means, to be and to deal with an anthropomedial formation. (Voss 2018) Hence this essay can be understood as a media-philosophical contribution to a media anthropology, which renders modes of entanglements of heterogeneous factors to be prevalent.

No Space Odyssey

Two thin, long tubes connect Monte to the shuttle—like umbilical cords. While working, he continues speaking to the child. In countershots, we see Monte in his space suit in medium and close-up shots repairing the shuttle outside and speaking to the toddler without seeing her. We also see the little child in a close-up shot looking around, searching for the source of the voice.

Suddenly a scene from a historical 16-mm black-and-white ethnological film playing on an LED screen catches the toddler's eye. A Native American

Figure 14.1 *High Life* (2018, Alcatraz Pictures).

sitting on a horse seen in worm's-eye view and another running around a fire, smoke billowing (Figure 14.1).

Images are being sent from Earth to the spaceship. The child gets scared and screams out loud. We see Monte lose his nerve, hearing the penetrating screams. The tool drops from his hand and disappears into black space. While falling, the spanner turns around itself.

And all of a sudden there is the memory of the iconic scene of the bone hurled up into the air in Kubrick's 1968 film *2001: A Space Odyssey*: The spanner resembles the bone triumphantly thrown up toward the sky by the prehuman ancestor, upon having discovered that a bone can be used as a tool and/or a weapon (Figure 14.2).

In Kubrick's movie the bone, flying toward the sky, indicates the evolutionary step from ape to man, from nature to culture, the beginning of an evolution that ends in the conquest of space.

It is completely different in Claire Denis's *High Life*. Here the spanner revolving around itself raises the traumatic memory of the bloody hand and the stone, thrown into a deep well, with which Monte had killed a human being long ago, while he was still a boy. It is Monte's own hand that let the stone fall, but it seems strange and disembodied, as if it were someone else's hand. The victim was a young girl, who, as we later learn, had slain Monte's dog. These images were also recorded on 16-mm film, like all other scenes on Earth, while the scenes in the spaceship were captured with a high-resolution digital camera, which not only changes and affects the optics, but also the

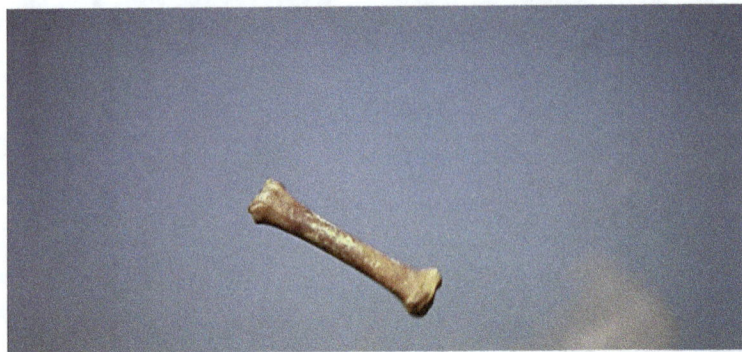

Figure 14.2 *2001: A Space Odyssey* (1968, Stanley Kubrick Productions).

Figure 14.3 *High Life* (2018, Alcatraz Pictures).

acoustics and the interplay between them. The film subtly plays with the aesthetic differences between analog and digital (Figure 14.3).

The tool disappearing into space does not introduce a step into a progressive future but leads into the past. It evokes the memory of a traumatic and violent event.

The temporality in Denis's film, thus, neither adheres to the conception of the empty homogenous time of progress (Benjamin 1939: 195), and hence does not refer to the progress-oriented rationality of evolution. The rhythm of time is structured by repetition and by difference, not by continuity and progress. The well-considered use of technical-aesthetic means of expression sings the temporal rhythm in which the past is the actual engine. This goes hand in hand with the very different function of the figure of the child and the child's origin in both movies.

Human Life in Space

In *High Life* as well as in *2001: Space Odyssey*, the figure of the child is associated with the question of the possibility of human life in space. The figure of the child represents and guarantees, in other words, the existence of a future in space. Conversely, this means that the future depends on there being human reproduction (Deutscher 2017). The film *2001: Space Odyssey* ends with the magical transformation of the old astronaut Bowman into a fetus enclosed in a transparent orb of light. In the famous last scene this angelic "Star Child" floats in space beside Earth, gazing at it, suggesting a further evolution of mankind (Figure 14.4).

There is no woman involved in this act of procreation. It's a white man's fantasy of a spiritual self-creation in the name of humanity, in correspondence with the ideology and self-understanding of the space science of the 1960s. The perspective of women and their contribution to procreation have no place in this science-fictional overcoming of mortality. This exclusion of women must in turn be understood as part of heteronormative biopolitics.

Figure 14.4 *2001: A Space Odyssey* (1968, Stanley Kubrick Productions).

In contrast, women are very present in *High Life*. However, not in the role of loving mothers. None of the female figures submits to the biopolitical task associated with women in human reproduction—with the consequence that the question of reproduction arises all the more urgently. By insisting in bodily and material conditions of reproduction, the film brings to light thanatopolitics as the flip side of biopolitics, whose goal, after all, as Michel Foucault showed, is to multiply life. Yet, as the theorists of thanatopolitics has argued following and critically engaging with Foucault, the death of some groups of the population is by this present form of power systematically accepted and provided for in order to optimize life as such.[1]

The child in Denis's film is the product of very body-focused experiments performed by a female physician, Dr. Dibs, obsessed with the idea of breeding a child who would be resistant to radioactive rays in space. And the product of Dibs's experiments, the baby girl Willow (Scarlett Lindsay) (whose performance, alongside Monte's, begins the film) is very real, in the sense of being tangible—as is the relation and interaction between Monte and Willow. One has in fact rarely seen such physical intimacy between a man and a baby in a movie. Monte is cooking for the baby, feeding her, making her sleep and pee, watching over her sleep; he practices her first steps with her and teaches her what culture is and what a taboo is. At the same time, the baby is full of trust, even when she is crying. She is in contact with Monte at all times. The baby's reactions and gestures move time forward and keep Monte alive. Those scenes between him and the toddler are impressive, fascinating, and disturbing, and in some moments even uncanny. For example when he says to her, while she is sleeping, that he could have killed her as easily as a kitten. Or when the closeness between the two, lying together in bed, becomes too intimate and physical, almost sexual.

According to Denis, the idea that in order to explore space outside the solar system, children have to be born on the trip and be protected from radiation comes from the physicist Stephan Hawking ("Claire Denis on Sex as an Escape" 2019). One lifetime is not enough to leave the solar system, and that is why babies have to be born in space: a rather "down-to-earth" consideration, which resonates with current scientific speculation (ibid.). Science fiction, as Denis laconically comments, forces you to "really think about time" (ibid.). Yet, since Dibs, the physician played by Juliette Binoche, is also haunted by her past, one presumes that her strong desire for a space-born child results more from her traumatic experiences than from rational reasoning. But as Freud showed, and long before Freud Kant, what we think is rational very often turns out to be the rationalization of speculation (Deuber-Mankowsky 2007: 11).

Reproduction

As becomes clear over the course of the film, Dibs murdered her own children in their beds, stabbed her husband to death and tried unsuccessfully to kill herself by stabbing herself in the uterus with a knife. This is not shown by means of a flashback, as is the case with Monte's memories, but is told in conversation in a very confidential and almost tender moment shared by Dibs and Boyse. Boyse, played by Mia Goth, is one of the women on whom Dibs conducts her experiments (Figure 14.5).

Sentenced to death, as are the other altogether ten members of the crew (five female and five male), Dibs agreed to serve science and to be part of a search mission in space looking to extract energy from a black hole. Dibs inseminates the female members of the crew against their will with the sperm of the male crew. None of the women want to get pregnant. They explicitly and violently refuse to serve as a medium of reproduction. They know for a fact that their bodies are exposed to death in these experiments (as is still the case with every birth). Moreover, they have neither the desire for a child nor for reproducing at all. They have no hope and no future. At some point, Boyse says to Dibs, full of anger and contempt: "It is our willpower that kills the fetuses." Only Dibs, who has destroyed her reproductive organs, is obsessed with the idea of creating a child through artificial procreation that will be "perfect" and strong enough to survive in space.

Figure 14.5 *High Life* (2018, Alcatraz Pictures).

The long-haired Dibs is strong, manipulative, and potent herself. She is not only a scientist obsessed with the idea of breeding the perfect baby, but also the only sexually active woman. One of the most impressive and unsettling scenes shows Dibs skillfully masturbating in the so called fuck room, accompanied by the dramatic electronic sound created by Stuart Staples. With the waist-long hair wrapping itself around her body, the wild and yet concentrated movements, the camera so close and the music so intense, the scene is reminiscent of a witch's dance (36:00). Actually, as Dibs states in a short exchange with Monte while leaving the "fuck room": "I know I look like a witch." And Monte answers: "You are foxy and you know it." Asked why she still holds onto the scientific mission of their expedition, while everybody else has recognized that it is just a suicide mission, she answers: "I am totally devoted to reproduction" (40:40). Dibs is totally devoted to a reproduction that does not happen through her own body. To her, reproduction means scientifically supported reproductive medicine that enables her to reproduce without pregnancy and giving birth, detached from her sex and the expectations of her gender affiliation. The elaborate masturbating machine is not a studio creation, but stems from "real life." It was, as Claire Denis reports, offered and bought on the internet. ("Claire Denis, Mia Goth and the High Life Cast. BFI in Conversation." Filmed May 9, 2019, 11:52–12:52).

By daringly mixing reality and the surreal in this way, the film contradicts our expectations, makes us wonder, and forces us to think (Deuber-Mankowsky 2017: 73). In doing so, *High Life* also reveals, as the following example makes clear, the gender- and race-differentiated violence inherent in thanatopolitics: While Dibs, the strong and sexy woman with hair down to her waist, who even succeeds in raping the sedated Monte, who decided to abstain from sexuality altogether, thus obtaining his sperm against his will, is white, Elektra, played by Gloria Obianyo, the first woman who dies because of her experiments, is black. This is no coincidence. And that it is no coincidence is stated explicitly by Tcherny, the other black crew member, played by André Benjamin: "Even up here, black ones are the first who have to go" (52:30).

A Prison without an Outside

The film *2001: Space Odyssey* and Andrej Tarkovsky's 1972 *Solaris* have obviously influenced *High Life*. All three films use the genre of science fiction to raise the big questions of the technoscientific present in the medium and with the means of film. As in *2001: Space Odyssey* and in *Solaris*, the

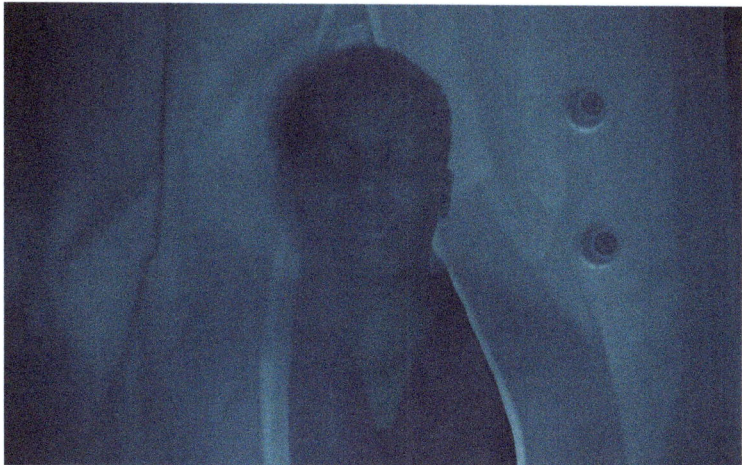

Figure 14.6 *High Life* (2018, Alcatraz Pictures).

soundtrack in *High Life* is an active and important part of the film. It is composed and performed by Stuart Staples, the English musician and lead singer of the indie band Tindersticks, with whom Denis has worked for more than twenty years, since her 1996 *Nénette et Boni*. The music was made before *High Life* was shot. The first piece completed, "The Yellow Light," was composed for the 2014 short film *Contact* by Denis and Olafur Eliasson (Staples 2019b). Staples's description of the work process gives a vivid impression of the central importance of the music for the creating of the "bloc of sensations" (Deleuze and Guattari 1994: 163)[2] that *High Life* is:

> For this, each instrument/part was played into silence with arbitrary start points creating random movements and relationships when brought together. This theme/way of working runs through the entire making of the score for *High Life*. Musicians generally worked "in the darkness." (Staples 2019b)

The sound contributes in an impressive way to the creation of this atmospheric environment, in which human beings are not anymore at the center of attention but rather perceived as being part of the becoming of the cosmos. This is also hinted at in Stuart Staples's lullaby for Willow, which plays with the literal meaning of the name Willow, that is, the willow tree. Willow is playing hide and seek, deep in the trees, while spiders and centipedes crawl across her hands and feet. She is walking across the sand, playing with the waves, she is "listening to the city wheezing," she is everywhere and beyond space and time. The musical theme of the Willow Song runs through the film and at the end is sung by Robert Pattison for the now sixteen-year-old Willow.

And as in Tarkovsky's *Solaris*, memory and the past play a central role in *High Life* as well. In all three of the films, the narrative form is elliptic. The cutting and the coupling of images, sound, and perceptions follow a surreal dream logic rather than a logic of the plot. Atmosphere, sensation, and aesthetic expression are more important than the storyline. The aim is not to tell a story, but, to quote Kubrick's famous statement about the meaning of *2001: A Space Odyssee* in an interview with Playboy Magazine (1968) "gripping the audience on a deep level" (SciHi Blog 2021). This also applies to *High Life*. All three films use the genre of science fiction as a film experimental arrangement in order to learn more about the state of the present and the human psyche in its relation to technology, nature and culture, sexuality, and temporality.

And yet, as mentioned before, *High Life* differs fundamentally from the other science fiction movies. This has to do with the fact that *High Life* is not a literary adaption like *Solaris* and *2001: Space Odyssey*, but was written by Claire Denis herself and Jean-Paul Fargeau (also a frequent collaborator of Denis's).

Apart from the fact that *High Life* is sensitive to the gender and race-differentiated violence of techno-scientific biopolitics and thanatopolitics, the film sets itself apart in that it treats death as omnipresent in a striking, unusual, concrete, and material way. Fetuses are dying, newborns are dying, all ten members of the crew die, except for Monte and Willow, the latter of whom was born in space. They die from violence, from different acts of suicide, from pregnancy, or due to radiation. The captain, played by Lars Eidinger, develops leukemia, suffers a stroke, and is then tenderly euthanized by Dibs. Boyse, who was forced to give birth to Willow, climbs, after having killed the pilot (Agata Buzek) with a shovel, aboard the shuttle, flies into the first black hole on the mission's way and dies by so-called spaghettification. That is, being fatally stretched by the immense gravitational forces, when entering the event horizon, shown impressively and in great detail. Even Dibs, after having successfully fulfilled her mission, leaves the ship seriously injured and disappears slowly into the blackness of space. Instead of being, as promised, an escape from the death penalty, the mission turns out to be just another form of it. The spaceship is not equipped with the latest technical gadgets, but is gloomy and cramped like a prison, with the difference that there is no outside of prison in space. *High Life* in fact refers as much to the prison film as to the genre of science fiction.

There is the impression of narrowness created by the poor lighting and the gloomy colors. There is no direct light and no luster in the whole film—except in the very last scene, which culminates in the yellow light installation by the artist Olafur Eliasson. But I will deal with this last scene and the bright white light later on. The sense of a prison environment is reinforced by many point-of-view shots in which one can hear the breath of the character whose point of view it suggests. The camera work condenses an atmosphere of eeriness, threat, and vulnerability that is intensified by the soundtrack. The crew members have no private space, they sleep in bunk beds, women separated from men. They get sedatives from Dibs, who is in total control of their bodies. For the delivery of their sperm, the men receive an extra dose of sleeping pills. Again reminiscent of prison films, there is physical exercise that everyone has to participate in. Outbreaks of violence and aggression are as present as increased sexual attraction, while at the same time sexual intercourse is not permitted.

Claire Denis and cinematographer Yorick Le Saux worked closely with the actors, close to their bodies in the studio. There seem to be no strangeness and no shame between the camera and the bodies, between the organic and technology. The camera moves as smoothly from one part of the body to the next as it did across the plants in the garden in the first scene of the film. Sometimes the actors' bodies appear like sculptures through the illumination, the intimacy, and the unusual and strange beauty of their movements, gestures, and facial expressions. We know this cinematic work with and on the bodies of actors and the resulting tension between sexual attraction, tenderness, care, and brutal violence, which extends all the way to cannibalism and incest, from other films by Claire Denis.[3]

The Secret of Life

The reference to the connection between the prison film and science fiction actually allows Denis to continue her cinematic exploration of the secret of life and even to intensify it under the very different temporal and spatial conditions brought about by space travel. And indeed, the collapse of space and time to a moment of eternity in a black hole plays a central role for the experience of temporality and sexuality explored in the film as well as the cumulative elimination of any notion of an outside.

Following Gilles Deleuze and his last short text "Immanence: A life …," (1997) we could say that in *High Life* the secret of life is not revealed from the perspective of the "individual life" but of the "meantimes (*des entre-temps*), between moments" (5) of "a life that is impersonal but singular nevertheless"

(4). Indeed, the question that *High Life* poses, despite the omnipresence of death in the film, does not concern death itself, but the in-between of death and individual survival. Deleuze quotes the following impressive example from Charles Dickens's novel *Our Mutual Friend* to outline more precisely what "a life that is impersonal but singular nevertheless" means. This example will also clarify the relation to the way in which the secret of life is approached in *High Life*:

> A good-for-nothing, universally scorned rogue is brought in dying, only for those caring for him to show a sort of ardent devotion and respect, an affection for the slightest sign of life in the dying man. Everyone is so anxious to save him that in the depths of his coma even the wretch himself feels something benign passing into him. But as he comes back to life his carers grow cold and all his coarseness and malevolence return. Between his life and death there is a moment which is now only that of *a* life playing with death. The life of the individual has given way to a life that is impersonal but singular nevertheless. (Deleuze 1997: 4)

In the scenes in which the protagonists in *High Life* die in so many different ways, exactly this moment seems to arrive, which is no longer about the death of an individual life but only that of *a* life playing with death. In this moment alone the chance appears that everything could change and the past would no longer determine the future. This is especially evident in the scene at the end where Willow and Monte decide to fly together into/through a black hole.

Deleuze gives another example of the appearance of the singularities constitutive of *A Life*, in order to demonstrate that *A Life* is "everywhere, in all the moments a certain living subject passes through and that certain lived objects regulate," and that it is not "contained in the simple moment when individual life confronts universal death" (5). This second example leads us back to the beginning of *High Life* and the first scenes with Monte and the baby-girl Willow. At the same time it provides a possible explanation for the impressive effect of Denis's cinematic work with the bodies of the actors: for the meaning of their gestures and facial expressions that are at the same time singular, yet not individual, affective, and not conscious. In order to distinguish singularities and events that constitute *a* life and the "accidents of *the* corresponding life," or the life of an individual, Deleuze refers to very young children and their specific gestures:

> Very young children, for example, all resemble each other and have barely any individuality; but they have singularities, a smile, a gesture,

a grimace—events which are not subjective characteristics. They are traversed by an immanent life that is pure power and even beatitude through the sufferings and weaknesses. (Deleuze 1997: 5)

This matches exactly the scenes in which Monte interacts with little Willow and explains why the effect of those scenes is so intense. It is as if the gestures, the smile, the screams of the little child were reflected in the gestures of Monte, involving him in a process of transformation. He becomes able to remember his past and have it define him less, even if he is haunted by his memories. This is explicitly expressed by Monte himself. In a central scene, Monte explains to the toddler, who listens to him without understanding a word, what a taboo is. A taboo forbids you, according to Monte, "to drink your own piss" and "to eat your own shit," even if, as he adds "it is recycled. Even if it doesn't look like piss or shit anymore" (07:45). After having underscored that this taboo is not valid for Willow, the "sweet little girl" that was born in space, Monte all of a sudden mentions his father, "If my old man could see me now," and quotes him: "Break the laws of nature and you'll pay for it, little son of a bitch!"

On the one hand, this statement must be placed in relation to that other statement, according to which Monte was not raised by parents but by his dog (and, on the other hand, to the fact that all of the members of the crew were treated like trash, "refuse, that didn't fit in to persist" (28:50), until, to quote Monte again, "somebody had the bright idea of recycling us" (28:58). This explanation by Monte comes as a voice-over during a flashback to the time on Earth before Monte and Boyse were arrested. This reminiscence was preceded by the daily report Monte had to give to the spaceship's information system in order to keep the life system, which is actually a recycling system, running. The perversion of the death penalty, as we learn in this subtle lesson, is the reduction of life to a recycling system. It is obvious that this insight is also valid once it is reversed: that life becomes a death penalty where it is reduced to a recycling system.

If we follow Deleuze's two examples for the appearances of the singularities of *A Life*, it no longer seems to be a coincidence that the film begins with the scenes showing the interaction between Monte and the little child. In these scenes we get a glimpse of the power of *A Life* that is "impersonal but singular nevertheless," and that is not "contained in the simple moment when individual life confronts universal death." In this way, the film begins with a moment of affirmation in which the power of change is felt. It not only allows Monte to remember, but also allows the film to tell the story in flashbacks, showing what led to all the other crew members' deaths.

The Intervention of the Death Drives in the Perception and Rhythm of Time

In her study on Deleuze and psychoanalysis, Monique David-Ménard (2005) points out that death for Deleuze has to do with the impersonal and that Deleuze borrows Freud's concept of the death drive to describe the ability of the "I" to free itself from its own contents (58). In his central work *Difference and Repetition* Deleuze distinguishes two different aspects of death:

> The first signifies the personal disappearance of the person, the annihilation of *this* difference represented by the I or the ego. This is a difference which existed only in order to die, and the disappearance of which can be objectively represented by a return to inanimate matter, as though calculated by a kind of entropy. Despite appearances, this death always comes from without, even at the moment when it constitutes the most personal possibility, and from the past, even at the moment when it is most present. The other death, however, the other face or aspect of death, refers to the state of free differences when they are no longer subject to the form imposed upon them by an I or an ego, when they assume a shape which excludes *my* own coherence no less than that of any identity whatsoever. (Deleuze 1994: 113; see also David-Ménard 2005: 58)

This distinction corresponds to the description Deleuze gives in his "Immanence: A Life ...," when he states that between the life of an individual and his death "there is a moment that is only that of *a* life playing with death." (Deleuze 1997: 4) Yet here Deleuze uses the impersonal not for death, but to mark *a* life beyond any distinction between a particular individual life and a particular individual death. There is obviously a certain indistinguishability between life and death in *A life*.

This leads me back to the question of reproduction and temporality and to Freud, who taught us that the sexual life unfolds in complex relations to both life and death. Sexuality does not—as Freud made thoroughly clear in his speculative text *Beyond the Pleasure Principle* (1921)—merge into reproduction. If one assumes, as Freud suggests, that the compulsion to repeat is more original than the pleasure principle and that the death drives are in constant tension to the life drives then the secret of life is in fact hidden in the question of how, under those conditions, reproductive sexuality should even be possible. Equally mysterious is the survival of organisms and the existence of a continuous future.

As Freud (1955: 40-1) says about the contrast between death drives and life drives, "It is as though the life of the organism moved with a vacillating rhythm. One group of instincts rushes forward so as to reach the final aim of life as swiftly as possible; but when a particular stage in the advance has been reached, the other group jerks back to a certain point to make a fresh start and so prolong the journey." Only if we consider that the goal of life in Freud's speculative consideration is death, does it become clear how complex this rhythm is, in which the future (and with it also survival) depends on the detour and the "'jerking back." This is made even more complicated by the fact that this speculation is written from the perspective of a thinking bound to a living being, for whom the inorganic lies just as far beyond the horizon of experience as death. Freud, to put it in a nutshell, is well aware that the origin of life can only be thought of retrospectively. Thus, even if he, on the one hand, as Deleuze points out and criticizes, identifies death with the return to inanimate matter, Freud knows, on the other hand, that this is just part of a necessary speculation (David-Ménard 2005: 46; Freud 1955: 37-9).

Given the fact that, not only for Deleuze but also for Freud, death is "the source of problems and questions, the sign of their persistence over and above every response" (Deleuze 1994: 112), we have good reason to ask why Freud sticks to the death drive and the primacy of the repetition compulsion over the pleasure principle. Even if, as he admits at the end of *Beyond the Pleasure Principle*, "the life instincts have so much more contact with our internal perception—emerging as breakers of the peace and constantly producing tensions whose release is felt as pleasure—while the death instincts seem to do their work unobtrusively" (Freud 1955: 63). As a result, the death drives are much harder to prove.

The reason Freud holds on to the death drives and to the primacy of the repetition compulsion is simple and yet surprising: it is the discovery that the psychoanalytic cure—"die Kur"—depends on the repetition compulsion and makes it useful to itself (18). As Freud underscores, psychoanalysis is not only an art of interpretation. The possibility of changing the vicissitudes of the instinct (*Triebschicksal*) depends on the transference, and this means that the repressed must be repeated as a present experience and not only as a conscious memory. Hence, psychoanalytically, the possibility of a change in compulsive behavior depends on an obsessive repetition. To sum up: the death drive is intertwined with the concept of time as a reluctant, vacillating rhythm ("*Zauderrhythmus*") in the life of organisms and hence responsible for the fact that the present is defined by the past. Yet on the other hand, the possibility of a change in the vicissitudes of the instinct (Triebschicksal) and of a disruption of the empty repetition also depends on the death drive. Deleuze recognized this very well and therefore considered the "impersonal" death as a "pure and empty form of time." Taking up Nietzsche's concept of eternal repetition, Deleuze concludes: "The form of time is there only for the revelation of the formless in the eternal return" (1994: 91).[4] Thus, to return to *High Life*: Death in this impersonal aspect would at the same time show a way out of the perversion of the death penalty, that is, of reducing life to a recycling system. In this way, the death drive becomes, as the film shows, a resistive moment turning against the current conjunction of reproductive technology and thanatopolitics. This is evident not only in the women's refusal to submit to the compulsion to reproduce, which after all is nothing more than an extension of the death penalty they sought to escape by traveling into space, but also in the in-between-life-and-death moments of Monte and baby Willow's encounter and the later decision of the two to voluntarily travel into the black hole.

High Life as Intensification of Life; or, the Point at Which the Difference between Time and Space Vanishes

Freud also asks himself how sexual reproduction is to be explained. For if one assumes the primacy of the repetition compulsion and the death drive, then "conjugation," to quote Freud (1955: 57), "works counter to life and makes the task of ceasing to live more difficult." Freud then briefly considers the theory of Aristophanes, which Plato presents in the *Symposium*. According to this theory of spherical beings, there were originally not two, but three sexes: the feminine, the masculine, and the androgynes. Everything about these beings was double: they had four arms, four legs, and two faces. But then Zeus decided to cut them in two. After this division the two parts, desiring each his other half, "threw their arms," as Freud writes, quoting thereby Platon's *Symposium*, "came together, and threw their arms about one another eager to grow into one" (1955: 58) This theory would explain the existence of life or sex drives with the longing of the two halves to be joined together and unite the sphere.

Even if Freud (1955: 59) admits that he himself neither believes in this theory nor promotes it, and even if he leaves the question open, with Freud we can investigate the question of the relationship between reproduction and sexuality more concretely than with Deleuze, who shows little interest in the question of sexual reproduction. For in *High Life*, sexual reproduction is viewed from the thanatopolitical perspective of women forced to give birth and men trading their sperm for sedatives. From this perspective, human reproduction appears like a kind of recycling system. The film thus raises the question of how life is experienced under the technical, temporal, and spatial conditions of a prison in outer space without outside or beyond. Violence, death, and sexuality all become strategies to avoid being recycled.

In fact, only Dibs and Monte choose other ways to escape this perversion of a death penalty. Monte opts for sexual abstinence and an ascetic, monastic life and Dibs approaches reproduction from a scientific perspective with the aim of perfecting human life. For her, reproduction is associated with a scientific passion and the idea of living on in her scientific creation. Both ways would be led, according to Freud, by the death drives and the ego drives, respectively, which serve the self-preservation of the individual. That is why it is so important that Dibs renders Monte unconscious with the help of sedatives before she seduces him against his will and introduces his sperm into Boyse's uterus against her will. There is no heterosexual love involved and no desire for a child or for a family.

High Life artistically brings to light, in a perfect way, the "unobtrusive work" (Freud 1955: 63) of the death drive. In doing that, the film also shows that death, in its impersonal face, as "pure and empty form of time," undoes the circle of eternal return, which, to quote Deleuze (1994: 91) "has as its content the passing present and as its shape the past of reminiscence" and thus points beyond pure repetition. We cannot see Willow growing up and getting bigger. In one scene Monte wakes up because his hands caress soft female hair. It is Willow's hair, she has entered puberty and had been lying in Monte's bed (01.13:20–01.14:20). As soon as he is awake, Monte throws her out of bed. That is the point at which she experiences her first menstruation. After all the crew members have died but him, and after Dibs had told him shortly before she disappeared into space that he was Willow's father, we see Monte accepting the infant, in spite of his initial resistance. In the next scene there is the garden—the recycling system still works—and the sixteen-year-old Willow. Monte still "feeds the dog," as he calls the odious task of keeping the system from shutting down with his daily reports. Their vessel approaches a spaceship inhabited only by dogs. Willow wants a puppy, but Monte refuses because the risk of infection is too high. Finally they approach a black hole that is big enough to try to cross it. Willow wishes to approach the black hole, she says she can feel that the density is very low and that they will make it through. Monte agrees. While preparing, Willow asks whether she looks like her mother. Monte denies this, and only when they are already on their way to the event horizon of the black hole, and Willow answers Monte's question "Shall we?" with "Yes," does Willow all of a sudden resemble Dibs in an uncanny way. Together with them, we emerge into the shots of Olafur Eliasson's yellow light installation from the 2014 short film *Contact*, ending in a radiant white pouring all over the screen.

Denis deliberately leaves open whether this entry into the event horizon of a black hole means death for the two or an intensification of life. Yet she makes clear that, even if they do not die, what they experience in the event horizon is different from surviving: "The word surviving does not exist any more. Shall we stay in eternity? Me, I am surviving every day when I get up from my bed. They have reached a point, which is called singularity, where space and time are zero. They are somewhere else. They get what they want" ("Claire Denis, Mia Goth and the High Life Cast" 2019: 12:52). This quote from Denis shows that she refers to the current astrophysical theories about black holes, singularities, event horizons, and the corresponding theories about the merging of space and time.[5] She could also have referred to Deleuze, who in turn refers to Freud's concept of the death drive and the tension between form and the dissolution of form and to Hölderlin's concept of the "Unförmliche": "The extreme formality is there only for an excessive formlessness (Hölderin's *Unförmliche*). In this manner, the ground has been superseded by a groundlessness, a universal ungrounding which turns upon itself and causes only the yet-to-come to return" (1994: 91). Denis shows this "secret of life" in her film by using digital techniques and aesthetics, the latest astrophysical theories, experimenting with them and combining them from a feminist perspective with a sharp critique of current thanatopolitical regimes of reproduction. By insisting on the bodily and material conditions of reproduction, she proves the science fiction film to be a privileged medium of (epistemic) access to urgent media-anthropological questions.

Notes

1. Cf. in detail the fourth chapter "Immunity, Bare Life, and the Thanatapolitics of Reproduction: Foucault, Esposito, Agamben," in Penelope Deutscher's book *Foucault's Futures. A Critique of Reproductive Reason* (Deutscher 2017: 105–42).
2. Contrary to an aesthetics that conceives of works of art—images, sounds, texts, films—as representations, reflections, or symbols, Deleuze interprets works of art as *preserved* sensations, as "bloc of sensations," or as they also terms them, as "the being of the sensible" (*êtres de sensations*) (ibid.: 155).
3. I'm thinking of her first movie, *Chocolat* (1988), about a French family that lives in colonial Cameroon in the 1950s and the forbidden sexual tension between the young white mother and the Black "houseboy." This film, like all of her subsequent films except *L'intrus*, was also written with Jean Paul Fargeau. *Nénette et Boni* (1996), the first collaboration with Tindersticks, about Boni, the elder brother of Nénette, who fights for his newborn nephew, born against his mother's will. Her perhaps best-known movie *Beau travail*

(1999), set in Djibouti in the French Foreign Legion, in which she explores male bodies in the desert; *Trouble Every Day* (2001), which explicitly refers to the horror genre, in which sexual desire interferes with cannibalism, the soundtrack again by Tindersticks; or *L'intrus* (2004) based on Jean-Luc Nancy's essay about his having received a heart transplant, a film, again, with a soundtrack by Stuart A. Staples. *White Material* (2009) is about a young white French woman and struggling coffee producer in a French-speaking African country facing an imminent civil war, and finally *Les salauds* (2013), dealing with incest and the abuse of a daughter at the hands of her father, cowritten with Fargeau as well. The soundtrack of both of these last two films is also by Tindersticks.

4. Deleuze again follows a hint from Freud, who points this out in *Beyond the Pleasure Principle*: "As a result of certain psycho-analytic discoveries, we are to-day in a position to embark on a discussion of the Kantian theorem that time and space are 'necessary forms of thought.' We have learnt that unconscious mental processes are in themselves 'timeless'" (Freud 1955: 28).
5. Denis was advised by the French astrophysicist Aurélien Barrau, who had also coauthored a book with Jean-Luc Nancy (2014).

References

Barrau, Aurélien, and Jean-Luc Nancy (2014), *What's These Worlds Coming To?*, trans. Travis Holloway and Flor Méchain. Preface by David Pettigrew. New York: Fordham University Press.
Benjamin, Walter (2003), *Selected Writings, Volume 4: 1938–1940*, ed. Howard Eiland, Michael Jennings, Cambridge, MA: Harvard University Press, 2003
"Claire Denis, Mia Goth and the High Life Cast. BFI in Conversation." Filmed May 9, 2019, at the British Film Institute (BFI), London. YouTube video, 19:22. Available online: https://www2.bfi.org.uk/video-high-life-claire-denis (accessed January 17, 2022).
"Claire Denis on Sex as an Escape—in Space! High Life. TIFF 2019." Toronto International Film Festival (TIFF). YouTube video, 2:23. Available online: https://www.youtube.com/watch?v=1pM0wXy77O4 (accessed January 17, 2022).
David-Ménard, Monique (2005), *Deleuze et la psychanalyse*, Paris: Presses universitaires de France.
Deleuze, Gilles (1994), *Difference and Repetition*, trans. Paul Patton, New York: Columbia University Press.
Deleuze, Gilles (1997), "Immanence: A Life …," trans. Nick Millett, *Theory, Culture & Society* 14 (2): 3–7.
Deleuze, Gilles, and Felix Guattari (1994), *What Is Philosophy?*, trans. Hugh Tomlinson and Graham Burchell, New York: Columbia University Press.

Deuber-Mankowsky, Astrid (2007), *Praktiken der Illusion. Kant, Nietzsche, Cohen, Benjamin bis Donna J. Haraway*, Berlin: Vorwerk 8.
Deuber-Mankowsky, Astrid (2017), *Queeres Post-Cinema: Yael Bartana, Su Friedrich, Todd Haynes, Sharon Hayes*, Berlin: August Verlag.
Deutscher, Penelope (2017), *Foucault's Futures: A Critique of Reproductive Reason*, New York: Columbia University Press.
Freud, Sigmund ([1953–74] 1955), *Beyond the Pleasure Principle*. In *The Standard Edition of the Complete Psychological Works of Sigmund Freud*, in James Strachey (ed. and trans.), *Beyond the Pleasure Principle, Group Psychology, and Other Works (1920–22)*, 24 vols, vol. 13, 1–64, London: Hogarth.
SciHi Blog (2021), "2001: A Space Odyssey." Available online: http://scihi.org/2001-a-space-odyssey-kubrick/ (accessed January 17, 2022).
Staples, Stuart A. (2019b), "Music for Claire Denis' High Life." Available online: https://cityslang.com/releases/stuart-a-staples-music-for-claire-denis-high-life (accessed January 17, 2022).
Voss, Christiane (2018), *"Anthropomedialität. Zur Einführung,"* in Andreas Ziemann (ed.), *Grundlagentexte der Medienkultur. Ein Reader*, 39–44, Wiesbaden: Springer VS.

List of referenced films

2001: A Space Odyssey (1968), Directed by Stanley Kubrick. Stanley Kubrick Productions.
Beau travail (1999), Directed by Claire Denis. La Sept/Arte.
High Life (2018), Directed by Claire Denis. Alcatraz Films.
L'intrus (2004), Directed by Claire Denis. Ognon Pictures.
Nénette et Boni (1996), Directed by Claire Denis. Dacia Films.
Les salauds (2013), Directed by Claire Denis. Alcatraz Films.
Solaris (1972), Directed by Andrei Tarkovsky. Mosfilm.
Trouble Every Day (2001), Directed by Claire Denis. Rezo Productions.
White Material (2009), Directed by Claire Denis. Why Not Productions.

Contributors

Julia Bee is Professor for Media Aesthetics at the University of Siegen. Her work is situated at the intersection of media philosophy and praxeology. At the moment she works on gender and media, ethnographic filmmaking and forms of sustainable mobility, such as cycling. In June 2022 she published a book that she coauthored with Ulrike Bergermann, Linda Keck, Herbert Schwaab, Marcus Stauff, and Franzi Wagner: *Fahrradutopien. Medien, Ästhetiken und Aktivismus*, 2022 (Cycling Utopia. Media, Aesthetics, and Activism).

Jane Bennett is Andrew W. Mellon Professor of the Humanities at Johns Hopkins University. Her recent essays have appeared in *Grain/Vapor/Ray* ("Odradek and the End of the World"), *Evental Aesthetics* (Vital Materialism), *MLN* ("Mimesis: Paradox or encounter"), *LA+: Interdisciplinary Journal of Landscape Architecture*, and *Zeitschrift für Medien- und Kulturforschung* ("Out for a Walk"). She is the author of *Influx & Efflux: Writing up with Walt Whitman* (2020), *Vibrant Matter: A Political Ecology of Things* (2010), *The Enchantment of Modern Life* (2001), *Thoreau's Nature* (1994), and *Unthinking Faith and Enlightenment* (1987). She is currently working on notions of a creative cosmos, in Lucretius and Taoist philosophies.

Maaike Bleeker is a Professor of theatre, dance, and performance in the Department of Media & Culture Studies at Utrecht University. Her work engages with questions of perception, cognition, and agency from an interdisciplinary perspective, with a special interest in performance, embodiment, movement, and technology. In her research, she combines approaches from the arts and performance with insights from philosophy, media theory and cognitive science. Publications include her forthcoming monograph *Doing Dramaturgy: Thinking through Practice* (forthcoming), the coedited volume *Thinking through Theatre and Performance* (2019), and the edited volume *Transmission in Motion. The Technologizing of Dance* (2016). She is currently leading the research project "Acting Like a Robot: Theatre as Testbed for the Robot Revolution."

Christoph Carsten is a doctoral student and journalist living in Magdeburg. He was a scholar at the Media-Anthropology Centre of Excellence (KOMA) at Bauhaus-University Weimar, Germany, and holds a master's degree in

Media and Cultural Studies from Heinrich-Heine-University Düsseldorf. In his thesis he is working on a "Micropolitics of Everyday Life." Other research interests are affect theory, the politics of perception, and process philosophy.

Astrid Deuber-Mankowsky is Professor of Media Studies at the Ruhr-University Bochum. She has published extensively on topics in gender media studies, media theory, epistemology, and philosophy. She was a visiting scholar at UC Berkeley (2007), visiting professor at the Centre d'études du vivant, Université Paris VII—Diderot (2010), Max Kade Professor at Columbia University (2012 and 2017), and Senior Fellow at the IKKM Weimar (2013). She is also an associate member of the Institute for Cultural Inquiry, Berlin (ICI Berlin), external affiliate of the Centre for Philosophy and Critical Thought (Goldsmiths University of London), and spokesperson of the Scientific Advisory Board of the Deutsches Historisches Museum, Berlin.

Lorenz Engell is Professor of Media Philosophy at Bauhaus-Universität Weimar, Germany, where he was the founding dean of the Faculty of Media from 1996 to 2000 and codirector of the International Research Center for Cultural Techniques and Media Philosophy (IKKM) from 2008 to 2020. His research interests include philosophy of film and of television, media anthropology, aesthetics of the diorama, philosophy of the comedy, and studies on seriality and causality. Recent publications include *The Switch Image. Television Philosophy* (2021), *Relevanz der Irrelevanz* (2021, with Christiane Voss), *Thinking through Television* (2019), *Medienanthropologische Szenen* (coed., 2019), *Mediale Anthropologie* (coed., 2015), *Film Denken. Essays zur Philosophie des Films* (coauthor, 2015). *Fernsehtheorie zur Einführung* (2012), *Playtime* (2010), and *Körper des Denkens* (coed., 2013). He is also coeditor of the *Kursbuch Medienkultur* (1998), of the *Zeitschrift für Medien- und Kulturforschung (ZMK)*, and the *Film Denken* book series.

Philipp Gries (Bauhaus University Weimar) is currently writing his PhD thesis, in which, drawing on F. Nietzsche, R. Barthes, and C. Malabou, he deals with the relationship between the concepts of force and critique. He also runs the record label Corinne de Berne, and lives in Berlin.

Mark B. N. Hansen is the James B. Duke Professor of Literature and Computational Media Arts & Cultures and Chair of the Program in Literature at Duke University. Hansen is the author of *Embodying Technesis: Technology beyond Writing* (2000), *New Philosophy for New Media* (2004), *Bodies in Code* (2006), and most recently, *Feed-Forward: On the*

Future of Twenty-First-Century Media (2015). Focused on the hermeneutics of information, Hansen's current research stages a dialogue between A N. Whitehead and Gilbert Simondon, with the aim of theorizing information generically as a process of individuation or environmental receptivity across biotic-abiotic divides and multiple scales.

Tim Othold is a research associate and coordinator at the DFG post-graduate program for "Media-Anthropology" at the Bauhaus-University Weimar. His work has been funded by the State of Thuringia and the German Academic Scholarship Foundation, and he is currently finishing his PhD thesis on the narratives of collectivity in digital networks, masses, and swarms. He has also published on media philosophical approaches to digital culture, the internet of things, games, and the concept of remnants and remainders.

Jason Pine writes, makes installations, and gives performance lectures on alternative economies and ecologies in the United States, Italy, and Iceland. His publications include *The Art of Making Do in Naples* (2012) and *The Alchemy of Meth: A Decomposition* (2029), both published by University of Minnesota Press.

Ivo Ritzer holds the Chair of Comparative Media Studies at the University of Bayreuth. He has given invited talks all over the world for many years, while his publications include multiple essays as well as several monographs and edited volumes, with topics such as media aesthetics, media philosophy, and media archaeology. His most recent book publications among more than twenty titles are *Media and Genre* (2021), *Key Works in Media Studies* (2020), *Politics of the Popular: Media—Culture—Theory* (2019), *Media Theory of Globalization* (2018), *Media Dispositives* (2018), and *Mediality of Mise en scène* (2017).

Gabriele Schabacher is Professor of Media and Culture Studies (Medienkulturwissenschaft) at Johannes Gutenberg University Mainz, Germany. Her research areas include media and cultural theory; the media history of traffic, mobility, and infrastructures; the cultural techniques of repair; the media history of seriality; and the theory of autobiography. Among her recent publications is a monograph on infrastructure work (2022), coedited volumes on the cultures of repair (2018, together with Stefan Krebs and Heike Weber) and on the practices of workarounds (2017, together with Holger Brohm, Sebastian Gießmann, and Sandra Schramke), as well as the articles "Time and Technology. The Temporalities of Care"

(2021), and "Staged Wrecks. The Railroad Crash between Infrastructural Lesson and Amusement" (2019).

Johanna Seifert studied philosophy and German literature at Humboldt Universität zu Berlin, Freie Universität Berlin, and Università degli Studi di Palermo. From 2015 to 2019, she was a PhD student at the Media Anthropology Centre of Excellence at the Bauhaus-University Weimar. Since 2019, Seifert is a research associate in the Emmy Noether Research Group, "The Phenomenon of Interaction in Human-Machine Interaction," at the Institute of Philosophy, Fern Universität in Hagen. Her research interests include Philosophy of Technology, Media Theory, Human-Technology Relations, and Theory and History of the Body.

Bernhard Siegert is Gerd Bucerius Professor for History and Theory of Cultural Techniques at the Media Faculty at the Bauhaus University Weimar. From 2008 to 2020 he was codirector of the International Research Center for Cultural Techniques and Media Philosophy at Weimar (IKKM). Since 2021 he leads the project "The New Real—Past, Present, and Future of Computation and the Ecologization of Cultural Techniques" funded by the NOMIS Foundation.

Siegert was Max Kade Professor at the University of California at Santa Barbara (2008 and 2011), Phyllis and Gerald LeBoff Visiting Scholar at the Department for Media, Culture, and Communication at New York University (2015), International Visiting Research Scholar at the Peter Wall Institute for Advanced Studies, University of British Columbia, Canada (2016), Eberhard Berent Visiting Professor and Distinguished Writer in Residence at the Department of German, New York University (2017), DAAD Visiting Scholar at the Faculty of English, University of Cambridge, UK (2017), Fellow at the Center for Advanced Studies "Evidence of Images: History and Aesthetics" at the Freie Universität Berlin (2018), Guest Lecturer at the Department of Culture and Aesthetics, Stockholm University, Sweden (2018), and Visiting Professor at the Department of Visual and Environmental Studies at Harvard University (2019).

Christiane Voss is Professor of Philosophy and Aesthetics at the Bauhaus-University Weimar (since 2010). Her main research areas are media anthropology, aesthetics, philosophy of media and film, philosophy of feelings, theories of democracy, on which she has given many talks in Germany and abroad. She received her doctorate in philosophy at the Free University of Berlin (*Narrative Emotions*, 2003); and a habilitation in philosophy at the Goethe University Frankfurt am Main (*Der Leihkörper. Erkenntnis* *und Ästhetik der Illusion*, 2013). She is director of the DFG post-graduate program on Media Anthropology (GRAMA, since 2020), and was director of the earlier Media Anthropology Centre of Excellence (KOMA, 2014–2020), funded by the State of Thuringia. She recently published *Die Relevanz der Irrelevanz* (2021), together with Lorenz Engell. Imporant editorships include *Körper des Denkens* (2013), *Mediale Anthropologie* (2015), *Black Box Leben* (2017), and *Medienanthropologische Szenen* (2018).

Index

Note: Figures are indicated by page number followed by "f". Endnotes are indicated by the page number followed by "n" and the endnote number e.g., 20 n.1 refers to endnote 1 on page 20.

Abbatucci, J. -P. -L. -S. 252
Ach, Narziß 254 n.7, n.8
active voice 43
actor-network theory 179
Adam, L. 203
Adorno, Theodor W. 135, 259
aesthetics 15, 20, 23–4, 29 n.4, 276, 298 n.2
   everyday escapes 82–8
   in everyday life 81
   thinking from middle 89–90
affect, concept of 2, 3, 6, 21, 28, 43, 81, 91–2, 242
Ah Humanity! (film) 53, 57–61, 58f, 59f, 60f, 74
Allan, G. 99–100, 125 n.1, 126 n.5, n.6
Almeida, Tatiana 68
alphabetic bodies 227–232
American Northwest Coast
   art and ontology of 197
   introjections 197–9
   new media 217–19
   operative animist ontology of mask 208–212
   projections 197–9
   re-introjections 197–9
   split representation 199–208
   switching bodies into (social) existence 212–17
Amoore, L. 111
Anders, Günter 22, 172
Andrejevic, M. 153
anthropocene 2, 15
anthropocentrism 18, 32
   of surrealism 40

anthropomediality 8–10, 18–19, 22, 44, 45f, 53, 72, 93 n.1, 123, 170, 225
   entanglement 106–112
   humane exit from anthropocentrism 23–8
   see also media anthropology
Antonio das mortes (film) 66
Arendt, Hannah 190
Artaud, A. 197
Aufderheide, P. 67
aural literacy 225

Bacon, Roger 146 n.3
Badiou, Alain 271–4
Baker, M. B. 63, 72
Barad, Karen 53, 62, 73
Barclay, B. 74 n.2
Bardini, Thierry 173
Barrau, Aurélien 299 n.5
Barry, Elizabeth 49 n.23
Barthes, Roland 18, 43, 186–192, 192 n.2, n.4
Bartleby, the Scrivener (short story) 57, 87
Baudrillard, Jean 262, 263, 268
Bauer, K. 250
Baum, L. Frank 138, 140, 142f
Bazin, André 261
Beat It (song) 67
Beau travail (film) 298–9 n.3
Beckett, Samuel 49 n.23
Bee, J. 54, 74 n.1
behavioral recognition systems 159–162

Bellini, Giovanni 236
Belting, Hans 154, 259, 260, 261, 263
Benjamin, Walter 261, 288, 284
Bennett, Jane 10 n.2, 127 n.10
Bennke, Johannes 93 n.1
Bensaud-Vincent, Bernadette 147 n.14
Bense, Max 24, 25, 27
Benton, Tom 277
Benveniste, Émile 43
Bergson, Henri 48 n.19, 49 n.20, 66, 119
Berlin Südkreuz project for intelligent video analysis 153–4, 163 n.1
Berthoz, Alain 240, 241
Bessire, L. 73
Bicicletas de Nhanderú (film) 67
Biesalski, Konrad 246, 249, 250, 254 n.4, n.5
Black God, White Devil (film) 66
Black, M. J. 165 n.19
Blanchot, Maurice 82–90
BlnBDI (Berliner Beauftrage für Datenschutz und Informationsfreiheit) 164 n.7
blogs 16
Blunden, M. 164 n.10
BMI (Bundesministerium des Inneren, für Bau und Heimat) 164 n.12
Boas, F. 201f, 202f, 204–5, 207, 212, 220 n.5
Bolger, Ray 143f
Bolter, J. David 174
A Book of Mirrors (book) 238
bots 23
Bourdieu, Pierre 269
Box, Steve 134f, 135
Brault, Michel 65
Breton, A. 197
broadcasts 16
Broeckmann, Andreas 10 n.1
Brüning, F. 247

de Bruyn, Eric C. H. 48 n.14
Bullet to the Head (film) 272–6, 277f
Bundespolizei 152–9, 161, 162, 164 n.7, n.8
Bunn-Marcuse, K. 197, 199
Butler, Judith 18, 259

Cage, Nicolas 265
Caillois, R. 204
Canada 65, 72, 198, 219
capitalism 55, 128 n.16, 133, 135, 136, 140, 181, 270
Capitalist Sorcery (book) 135
Carelli, Vincent 68
Carlson, R. L. 220 n.4, n.10
carnal foundations of intelligibility 227, 234–5
Carroll, M. P. 207
de Carvalho, Ernesto 68
Casid, Jill H. 145
Castaing-Taylor, Lucien 53, 54, 56f, 57, 60f, 62, 74
CCC (Chaos Computer Club) 156, 158
Ceddo (film) 66
de Certeau, Michel 181
Chalmers, D. 114
Chase, Jefferson 164 n.8
Chen, Mel Y. 144
China 47 n.8, 151, 158, 162–3, 207
Chocolat (film) 298 n.3
Choi, Ji-Hye 29 n.5
Chóliz, M. 29 n.5
Choy, Timothy 144, 147 n.16
Christopher, Wright 54
Chronicle of a Summer (film) 65
cinema 7–8, 21, 23, 53, 64, 66–7, 72–4, 265, 272, 276
and media 241–2
Clark, A. 114
Clarke, R. 153
climate catastrophe 16
Clooney, George 265
"cognitive nonconscious" 113

collaborative filmmaking 54, 67, 73–4
  and shared anthropology 62–4
communications theory 17, 21
Connolly, Bill 49 n.20
Conrad, Klaus 252–3, 255 n.9
contingency and virtuality 176–7
control of algorithms 151
  behavioral recognition systems 159–161
  facial recognition systems 154–9
  intelligent video analysis at Berlin Südkreuz 153
  situation recognition systems 159–161
  train stations and security issues 152–3
"corporal repairability" 247, 251
corporeal literacy 225–6
  carnal foundations of intelligibility 234–5
  logic of cut 241–2
  mind-sets and alphabetic bodies 227–232
  recalibrations of sensings 232–4
  redressings and crossings-over 235–9
  sensorimotor skills and perceiver-centered character of perception 240–1
Corrêa, Mari 67, 68, 71
cosmic causality 97
"Creative Confession" 35–6, 36f
Crocker, S. 63, 73
Cruise, Tom 264–5, 265
Cry Macho (film) 266
Cubitt, S. 60
"cultural activism" 67, 72
Culver, Stuart 140

David-Ménard, Monique 294, 295
Deacon, Terence 231
Dearden, H. 254 n.3
Debaise, D. 107, 109, 129 n.19
"deconstruction" 18

Deleuze, Gilles 8, 36, 37, 42, 44, 47 n.9, n.12, 48 n.19, 57, 88, 89, 90, 92, 112, 147 n.16, 175, 177, 192 n.3, 227, 259, 267, 272, 282, 289f, 291, 292, 293, 294, 296, 298 n.4
Denis, Claire 281, 282, 284, 288, 291, 299 n.5
Derrida, Jacques 18, 147 n.7, 191, 193 n.6, 230
Descola, P. 208, 209, 212
Deuber-Mankowsky, Astrid 286, 288
Deutsche Bahn 152–3, 164 n.12
Deutscher Bundestag 156, 158, 159
Deutscher, Penelope 285, 298 n.1
Dewey, John 127 n.13
Dickens, Charles 292
Difference and Repetition (book) 36, 88, 294
digital cinema 263–4
digital media 7, 261
"digital natives" 7
Digitalcourage 164 n.8
digitialzation 263
"discourse analysis" 18
doodles 32, 35–40, 48 n.15
double click 170–9
Drach, M. 209, 213, 220 n.9
Druick, Z. 63
Dudley, Kathryn Marie 147 n.10
Duff, W. 199, 216, 217
Duller, Y. 164 n.9
Dumit, Joseph 144

economics 17
Eerland, Anita 42
Egbert, S. 160
Egert, G. 54
Eleven in Delwara (film) 63
Eliasson, Olafur 289, 291, 297
Elsaesser, Thomas 54
Emmons, G. T. 204, 220 n.8
Empire of Signs (book) 189
Engell, Lorenz 61, 93 n.1, 106, 115, 127 n.12, 173, 177, 178, 245

Entranced Earth (film) 66
Ericson, R. V. 151, 158
Esposito, Elena 182 n.3
essay 31–2
Essays in Radical Empiricism (book) 84
"excentric positionality" 18–19
"excentricity" 18–19
The Expendables (film) 265, 255, 271, 276
Extreme Prejudice (film) 273

fabulation 64–6, 72, 74
facial recognition systems 154–9
Fargeau, Jean Paul 298 n.3
feeling 112–18
Ferguson, A. G. 164 n.14
Ferguson, Kathy E. 32
Ferreira, Patrícia 67
fictionalization of catastrophe 59–60
Fierrez, Julian 157
filmmaking 72
  anticolonial 66
  collaborative 54, 67, 73–4
  documentary 62, 64
  ethnographic 54, 64, 74 n.5
  indigenous 74 n.5
  participatory 63
  and shared anthropology 62–4
first World War
  reconstruction of wounded bodies in 245
Fischer-Lichte, Erika 259
Flusser, Vilém 178–9
Ford, Harrison 266
Ford, John 265
Fortun, Kim 131
Foster, Susan 226, 233, 234
Foucault, Michel 18, 42, 48 n.18, 54, 153, 259, 263, 266, 267, 269, 286
Franco-German War of 1870–1 247
Frank, L. 248
"French Theory" 262
Freud, Sigmund 29 n.3, 294–5, 296, 297, 299 n.4

Fricke, John 143
Frohne, U. 153

Gallagher, S. 239
Galloway, A. 245
Ganchrow, Raviv 46 n.7
Gates, K. A. 155
Gehlen, Arnold 17
Gell, Alfred 179–180
A gente luta mas come fruta (We Struggle But We Eat Fruit) (film) 69–71f, 72
Germany
  media philosophy 20, 29 n.2, n.4
Getino, O. 74 n.3
GIFs 16
Gille, Bertrand 128 n.15
Ginsburg, F. 65, 68
Gómez-Barris, Macarena 57
A Good Day to Die Hard (film) 266
Graham, Z. 67, 68, 72
Gran Torino (film) 266
Great Britain 151, 162–3
Greek 43, 49 n.23
Grimshaw, A. 54
Grosz, E. 253, 255 n.11
Grusin, Richard 174
Gu, Xinyu 29 n.5
Guajajara, Edivan dos Santos 68
Guajajara, Erisvan Bone 68
Guajajara, Flay 68
Guattari, Félix 8, 57, 89, 90, 92, 112, 147 n.16, 259, 289f
Gumbrecht, Hans Ulrich 35
Günther, H. 247

habits 6–7
  media-based 7
Haeberlin, H. K. 202
Hagener, Malte 54
Haggerty, K. D. 151, 158
Hahn, Changtae 29 n.5
Halyes, Katherine 225

Index

Hansen, Mark B. N. 10 n.2, 122, 126 n.3, 127 n.8, n.9, n.13, 225, 237
Haraway, Donna J. 48 n.17, 61, 73, 144–5
Hard Times (book) 273
Harreveld, Fren kvan 42
Hartmann, K. 249
Hartmann, V. 254 n.2
Hayles, N. Katherine 10 n.2, 106, 112, 113, 114–15, 128 n.16
Head, Henry 252–3
Heat (film) 68
Heidegger, Martin 172, 174, 177
  concept of "being-in-the-world" 18
Heider, K. 53–4
Hewish, Andrew 46 n.4, n.5, 48 n.16
High Life (film) 281, 283f, 284f, 287f, 289f
  as intensification of life 296–8
Hill, Leslie 189
Hill, Walter 272, 273, 276
Hinton, David 34, 42, 47 n.8
Hirschfeld, G. 247
Hoffer, Lee D. 144
Hoffmann, D. T. 165 n.19
Hohenberger, E. 64
Holbraad, M. 198
Hollier, Denis 192 n.1
Hollywood, John S. 164 n.14
Holm, B. 199, 200f, 201, 203f, 204f, 213, 218–19
Holmes, Gordon 252–3
Horkheimer, Max 135, 259
Hörl, E. 245
Hui, Yuk 10 n.1
humans 4
  life in space 285
  and media 1, 8, 225
Hunt, G. 212

ideograms 47 n.8
From the Ikpeng Children to the World (film) 67
Ikpeng, Karané 71

immanent relation 90, 93 n.1
indexicality 179–180
Indiana Jones and the Kingdom of the Crystal Skull (film) 266
indigenous collaborative filmmaking 67–9, 74 n.2, n.5
"influencers" 7
Ingold, Tim 46 n.6
"intelligent video analysis" 151
  behavioral and situation recognition systems 159–162
  at Berlin Südkreuz 153–4
  facial recognition systems 154–9
  testing 153
introjections 197–9
Inverarity, B. 219 n.2

Jackson, Michael 67
James, William 84
Jany, S. 152
Jenkins, Janice H. 144
Johnny Handsome (film) 273
Jones, J. 99, 126 n.5
Joseph, R. 209, 220 n.5
Jung, Carl 39

Ka'a Zar, Ukyze Wà (Forest Owners in Danger) (film) 68
Kahn, H. 162
Kaplan, A. E. 54
Kara, S. 56
Karel, Ernst 56
Katz, D. 252
Kaufmann, M. 160
de Kerckhove, Derrick 230
Kiegelmann, F.-J. 254 n.3
Kienitz, Sabine 246, 247, 249
Kim, Dai-Jin 29 n.5
Kirkland, Anna 146 n.1
Kittler, Friedrich 5, 6, 22, 174, 212
Klee, Paul 32, 35, 37, 44, 46 n.4, 48 n.13
Klein, Bonnie Sherr 63
Kloppenburg, S. 156

knowledge and being 62
Koch, L. 163 n.2
Krämer, Sybille 6
Krauss, Rosalind E. 192 n.1
Krickeberg, W. 205–6
Kristeva, Julia 18
Krtilova, Katerina 93 n.1
Krumeich, G. 247
Krupar, Shiloh R. 144
Kubrick, Stanley 283, 290
Kwon, Min 29 n.5

L'intrus (film) 299 n.3
Lacan, J. 213, 220 n.9, 238, 239
Lacerda, R. 68
languages 15, 21, 31, 43, 47 n.8, 49 n.21, n.23, 66, 271
Larmore, Charles E. 186
Last Man Standing (film) 273
Latour, Bruno 8, 9, 10 n.2, 25, 54, 112, 127 n.10, 135, 147 n.8, 151, 169, 170, 172, 174, 245
Lea, Tess 147 n.6
Lee, Joon-Yeop 29 n.5
Leese, M. 160
Lefebvre, Henri 82, 85
Les Immatériaux (film) 262, 263
Les salauds (film) 299 n.3
Les Sauteurs (Those Who Jump) (film) 63
Leviathan (film) 54–7, 55–6f
Levin, T. Y. 153
Lévi-Strauss, C. 207, 208, 212, 213, 215, 217
linguistic order 85, 187
  external diathesis 43
  internal diathesis 43
"literacy" 225
Littlefield, Henry M. 138
Locke, John 126 n.4
logic of cut 241–2
Luhmann, Niklas 175, 176, 177, 181, 260
Luxton, A. 163 n.2

Lyon, D. 153
Lyotard, Jean-Francois 262, 263

MacDougall, D. 62, 63
Macho, T. 215
MacKenzie, J. M. 163 n.3
Maclagan, David 37
magazines 16
Malin, E. 220 n.6
Manning, Erin 49 n.25, 91
Marin, M. 163 n.2
Martin, Emily 144
Martin, Randy 133, 146 n.5
Martírio (film) 68
Marx, G. T. 157
mass media 3, 4, 17, 20, 21, 154, 262
Massumi, Brian 82, 83, 89, 90, 91–2
material dialectics of hard body 259
  bodies and truths 271–8
  disappearance of body 262–4
  return of body 264–271
Maurer, E. M. 199
Mauss, M. 208, 217
Mauzé, M. 198–9, 209, 213, 220 n.9
McInnis, Brian 164 n.14
McLean, Stuart 144
McLuhan, Marshall 173, 178, 228, 261
media 16, 103, 105, 226, 237, 241–2, 260
  anthropology: *see* media anthropology
  algorithmic 121
  computational 118, 119
  culture 263
  digital 261
  German studies 3–6
  historical evolution of 5
  and humans 4, 8
  literacy 225
  materiality of 5, 20, 21
  philosophy: *see* media philosophy
  posthumanist theories 17
  practices and habits 6
  research 8

studies and theory 1, 18
technical 105-6, 120
technologies 4, 6, 111, 160, 162, 262
theory 198, 271
transhumanist theories 17
media anthropology 2, 3, 8, 9, 15, 17, 19, 24, 29 n.1, 53, 73-4, 85, 92, 93 n.1, 170, 181, 245
of mouse click 173-4
posthumanist theories 17
transhumanist theories 17
see also anthropomediality
media philosophy 1, 15, 19-22, 44-5, 169
components of 20-1
in Germany 20, 29 n.2, n.4
subject-object relationship 22
mediality 3, 5, 6, 21, 57, 259, 270
of human existence 8
mediatization 1
medical technologies
and prosthetics 16
Melville, Herman, 57
memes 16, 23
Menke, Christoph 188, 193 n.3
Merleau-Ponty, M. 35, 227, 239, 240
Meth = Sorcery (book) 134f, 135
methamphetamine 135
Metzl, Jonathan M. 146 n.1
micropolitics
of affect 90-2
middle-voiced verbs 31, 43-5
military technology 16
Min, Jung-Ah 29 n.5
mind-sets and alphabetic bodies 227-232
Mission: Impossible (film) 264
Mitchum, R. 157
mobile devices 7
mode double click 170-3
anthropology of 169
behind screen 174-5
contingency and virtuality 176-7
in front of screen 178-9

indexicality 179-180
on screen 175-6
upload and double
contingency 180-1
modern Hungarian 49 n.23
Modes of Thought (book) 101-2, 104
Mohi-von Känel, S. 250
Moi, un noir (film) 64
Morales, Aythami 157
Morin, Edgar 65
Morise, Max 39
Mühlhoff, R. 164 n.15
The Mule (film) 266
Murphie, Andrew 61
Murphy, Michelle 144
My First Contact/Pïrinop (film) 71-2

Nancy, Jean-Luc 192 n.4, 254, 299 n.5
Nanz, T. 163 n.2
nature 1, 2, 20
writing 32
Nénette et Boni (film) 298 n.3
Netzpolitik 164 n.5
neutral time 185
retreat to neutral 186-190
new media 217-19
Nietzsche, Friedrich 31, 273
Noë, Alva 240
Noeri, Gunzelin Schmid 135
nomophobia 26
nonalgorithmic theory of algorithms 122-5
nonlinguistic media 21
Nowak, A. 60, 61

Obianyo, Gloria 288
object-oriented ontology 1
"occasional philosophy" 22
Ong, Walter 226, 227-8, 229, 232
operative animist ontology of mask 208-212
Orality and Literacy (book) 227
Ortega, Ariel Duarte 67
Ortega-Garcia, Javier 157

Othold, Tim 10 n.3, 44, 115, 170, 178, 182 n.3, 225, 245
Our Mutual Friend (book) 292

Papadopoulos, Dimitris 133
Paravel, Véréna 53, 54, 56f, 57, 60f
Parikka, Jussi 10 n.2, 60
Park, Jae-Woo 29 n.5
Parkinson, Gavin 43
Pascal, Blaise 181
passive voice 43
pattern recognition technologies 160
Patterson, Robert 281
Pause, J. 163 n.2
Pedersen, M. A. 198
Peirce, Charles Sanders 178, 179
Perez, G. 62
'perpetual perishing' 126 n.4
Perrault, Pierre 53
Perry, W. L. 164 n.14
Peters, John Durham 10 n.2
Phaedrus 32
phenomenotechnics 127 n.8
philosophical anthropology 15
"photorealism" 263
photos 16
The Piano (film) 234
pictures 16
Pignarre, Philippe 135, 136
Pinhanta, Isaac 69
Pink, S. 54
Pitt, Brad 265
Piyăko, Wewito 69
Plato 32
Plessner, Helmut 17, 18–19
van der Pligt, Joop 42
van der Ploeg, I. 156
plurality 8, 19
Portanova, Stamatia 242
Potthast, J. 152
Pour la suite du monde (film) 65, 72, 74
Povinelli, Elizabeth 137, 144, 147 n.9
Price, Carter C. 164 n.14

Process and Reality (book) 101, 103, 111, 127 n.13
projections 197–9
Prospero's Books (film) 227, 235, 237, 238
prosthesis for feeling 97
   anthropomedial entanglement 106–112
   feeling before thought 112–18
   nonalgorithmic theory of algorithms 122–5
   superjects and societies 99–102
   technical feeling 119–122
   technical media 102–6
"protogeometry" 38
psychology 17

Rambo, David 127 n.12, 128 n.15
Rambo, John 264–5
Rambo: Last Blood (film) 265
Rammert, Werner 25
"rationalism" 107–8
Ravetz, A. 54
recalibrations of sensings 232–4
redressings and crossings-over 235–9
Reeves, Keanu 265
re-introjections 197–9
"Rekognition" software 156
re-mediatization 1
reproduction 287–8
Rhythm of Time 294–6
Richards, J. 163 n.3
Ritzer, Ivo 276
Roch, Axel 173
Rocha, Glauber 66
Rocky Balboa (film) 264–5
Roland Barthes (book) 189
Rosch, Eleanor 240
Rose, Nikolas 144
Roth, A. 219
Rotman, Brian 226, 227, 229, 230, 231, 233
Rotteveel, Mark 42
Rouch, J. 53, 64

Rousset, Jean 193 n.6
ryegrass 35

Sanskrit 43, 49 n.23
Sauerbruch, Ferdinand 254 n.6, n.7, 250
Schabacher, Gabriele 152, 163 n.1, 164 n.11, 169
Scheppler, G. 66
Schilder, Paul 252, 253, 255 n.10
Schiwy, Freya 67, 68, 71, 74 n.2
Schlosser, Allison V. 144
Schneider, A. 54
Schneider, Iris K. 42
Science and the Modern World (book) 103
Scott, Charles 49 n.21
secret of life 291–3
Seibel, S. 63
Seifert, Johanna 93 n.1
selfies 16
self-tracking data 16
Sellars, W. 107
Sembène, Ousmane 66
sensorimotor skills and perceiver-centered character of perception 240–1
sensory ethnography 54–61
Serres, Michel 178, 180
Sewid-Smith, D. 209
Shakespeare, William 237
Shapiro, Nicholas 147 n.15
shared anthropology 53
    collaborative filmmaking and 62–4
Shaviro, Steven 266
She Wore a Yellow Ribbon (film) 265
Shildrick, M. 246
Shirshekan, Jonathan 143
short messages 16
Sidibé, Abou Bakar 63
Siebert, Moritz 63
Siegert, Bernhard 93 n.1
Siegler, Martin 93 n.1
Simondon, Gilbert 8, 53, 54, 90, 107

Simulations (book) 262, 263
situation recognition systems 159–162
Smith, Susan 164 n.14
Smith, Will 265
Snow, J. 156
Sobchak, Vivian 227, 234, 235, 240, 255 n.12, 259
social media 7, 16, 26
social networks 23
Socrates 32
Solanas, F. 74 n.3
Solaris (film) 288–290
Soukup, P. A. 229
Souriau, Etienne 8, 54
Spinoza, Baruch de 8, 91
split representation 199–208
"spontaneous images" 39
Spreen, D. 251
Stallone, Sylvester 264, 265
Stanley, J. 153
Staples, Stuart A. 289f
Stengers, Isabelle 8, 73, 135, 136, 147 n.7, n.14
Stephenson, Niahm 133
Steyerl, H. 157
Stiegler, Bernard 114, 225
Stodola, Aurel 254 n.6
van der Stoep, Nathan 42
Strate, Lance 228
Streets of Fire (film) 273, 276
strolling lines 35–40
superjects and societies 99–102
"surfing" 27
suspect 86
switching bodies into (social) existence 212–17
"symmetrical anthropology" 25

Tang, S. 165 n.19
Tarkovsky, Andrei 281, 288
Tasker, Yvonne 279
Taussig, Michael 135, 136
technical feeling 119–122
technical media 102–6

"technical nonconscious" 113
technodeterminism 1
technology
  entanglements of 16
television series 16
The Tempest (play) 235–6, 238
Terberl, Christina 93 n.1
Thacker, E. 245
Thain, A. 56, 57
Third cinema 66, 72, 74 n.2, n.3
Thompson, Evan 240
Thoreau, Henry David 32, 33, 34, 41, 46 n.7, n.11, 47 n.9, n.11
  writing up 40–2
Thrift, Nigel 10 n.2
Time and Space 296–8
Tin Woodman 139f
Tolosana, R. 157
Tomlinson 233
Toub, Jim 39
Townsend-Gault, Ch. 197
train stations and security
  issues 152–3
Trouble Every Day (film) 299 n.3
Tsianos, Vassilis 133
Turner, T. 68–9
tweets 16
2001: A Space Odyssey 1968 (film)
  283, 284f, 285f
Txicão, Karané 67
Txicão, Kumaré 67
Txicão, Natuyu Yuwipo 67
Tzionas, D. 165 n.19

U.S. Department of Justice, Office of
  Public Affairs 146 n.2
Uexkuell, Jakob von 7, 20
Undisputed (film) 273
United States 162–3
upload and double contingency
  180–1
urban settings
  surveillance technologies in 151
"users" 7

Vallan, Giulia D'Agnolo 278
The Vanishing Lady (film) 142f
Varela, Francisco 240
Vera-Rodriguez, Ruben 157
video analytics
  and human–machine relations at
  train station 151
video game 7
Video nas Aldeías 67, 72
Virilio, Paul 262–3
visual anthropology
  to media anthropologies 53,
  73–4
visual literacy 225
Viveiros de Castro, E. 198, 212
von Esmarch, F. 254 n.2
Voss, Christiane 8, 10 n.3, 44, 49 n.24,
  53, 73, 93 n.1, 115, 170, 174, 178,
  234, 245, 282
VTR St-Jacques (film) 63

Wagner, Estephan 63
Walens, S. 212
walking 32–5
Wardell, Allen 199
The Warriors (film) 276
Watson, Benjamin 48 n.15
Waugh, T. 63, 72
Weibel, P. 153
Weigel, S. 154
Weisheit, Ralph 146 n.4
Wendehorst, C. 164 n.9
Weston, Kath 147 n.15
Where Did the Swallows Go (film)
  68
White Material (film) 299 n.3
White, Hayden 43
White, S. A. 63, 69, 73
Whitehead, Alfred North 40, 83, 89,
  97, 98, 99pp, 125 n.1, 126 n.3,
  n.4, n.5, n.7, 127 n.12, n.13, 128
  n.17, 129 n.19, n.21, n.22
Whitman, Walt 37, 42, 43, 44
Wichum, R. 164 n.6

Widmer, P. 253
Wiener, Norbert 4
Wilson, Lyle 217, 218f, 219
Winthrop-Young, G. 198
Winton, E. 63, 72
The Wizard of Oz (film) 138, 140, 141f, 142f
Won, Wang-Youn 29 n.5
Woolgar, Steve 174

Young, Kimberly S. 29 n.5

Zachmann, Erich 249
Zee, Jerry 144, 147 n.16
Zeus 31, 296
Zoettl, P. A. 63, 73
"zone of indeterminacy" 90
Zürcher, U. 252
Zwaan, Rolf A. 42